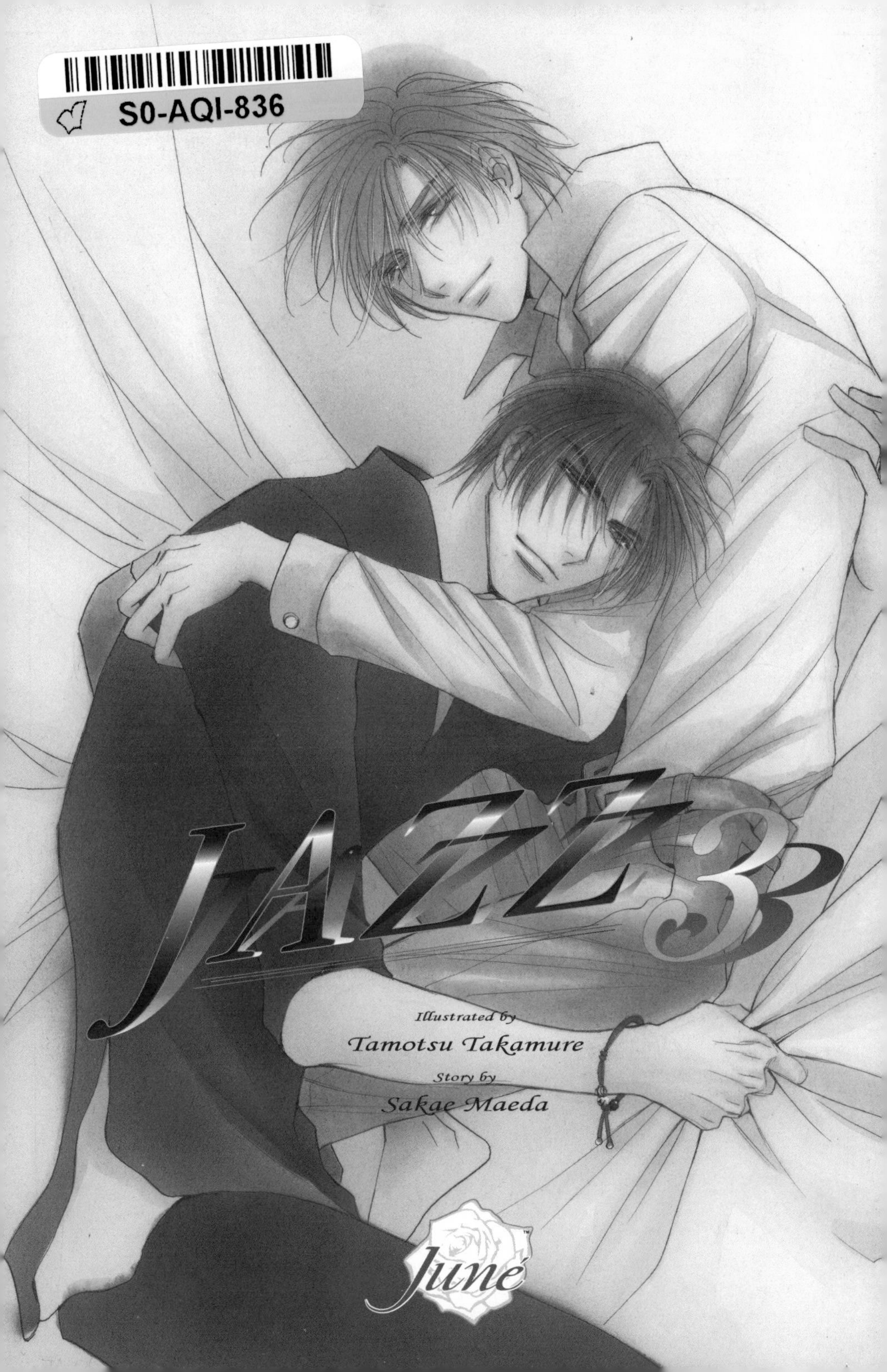
JAZZ 3
Illustrated by
Tamotsu Takamure
Story by
Sakae Maeda
Juné

JAZZ 3

Translation	Sachiko Sato
Lettering	Eva Han
Graphic Design	Fred Lui
Editing	Stephanie Donnelly
Editor in Chief	Fred Lui
Publisher	Hikaru Sasahara

JAZZ volume 3 © TAMOTSU TAKAMURE / SAKAE MAEDA / SHINSHOKAN 2005. Originally published in Japan in 2005 by SHINSHOKAN Co., LTD. English translation rights arranged through TOHAN CORPORATION, TOKYO. English translation copyright © 2006 by DIGITAL MANGA, Inc. All other material © 2006 by DIGITAL MANGA, Inc. All rights reserved. No portion of this publication may be reproduced or transmitted in any form or by any means without written permission from the copyright holders. Any likeness of characters, places, and situations featured in this publication to actual persons (living or deceased), events, places, and situations is purely coincidental. All characters depicted in sexually explicit scenes in this publication are at least the age of consent or older. The JUNÉ logo is ™ of DIGITAL MANGA, Inc.

English Edition Published by
DIGITAL MANGA PUBLISHING
A division of DIGITAL MANGA, Inc.
1487 W 178th Street, Suite 300
Gardena, CA 90248

www.dmpbooks.com

First Edition: October 2006
ISBN-10: 1-56970-888-6
ISBN-13: 978-1-56970-888-0

1 3 5 7 9 10 8 6 4 2

Printed in China

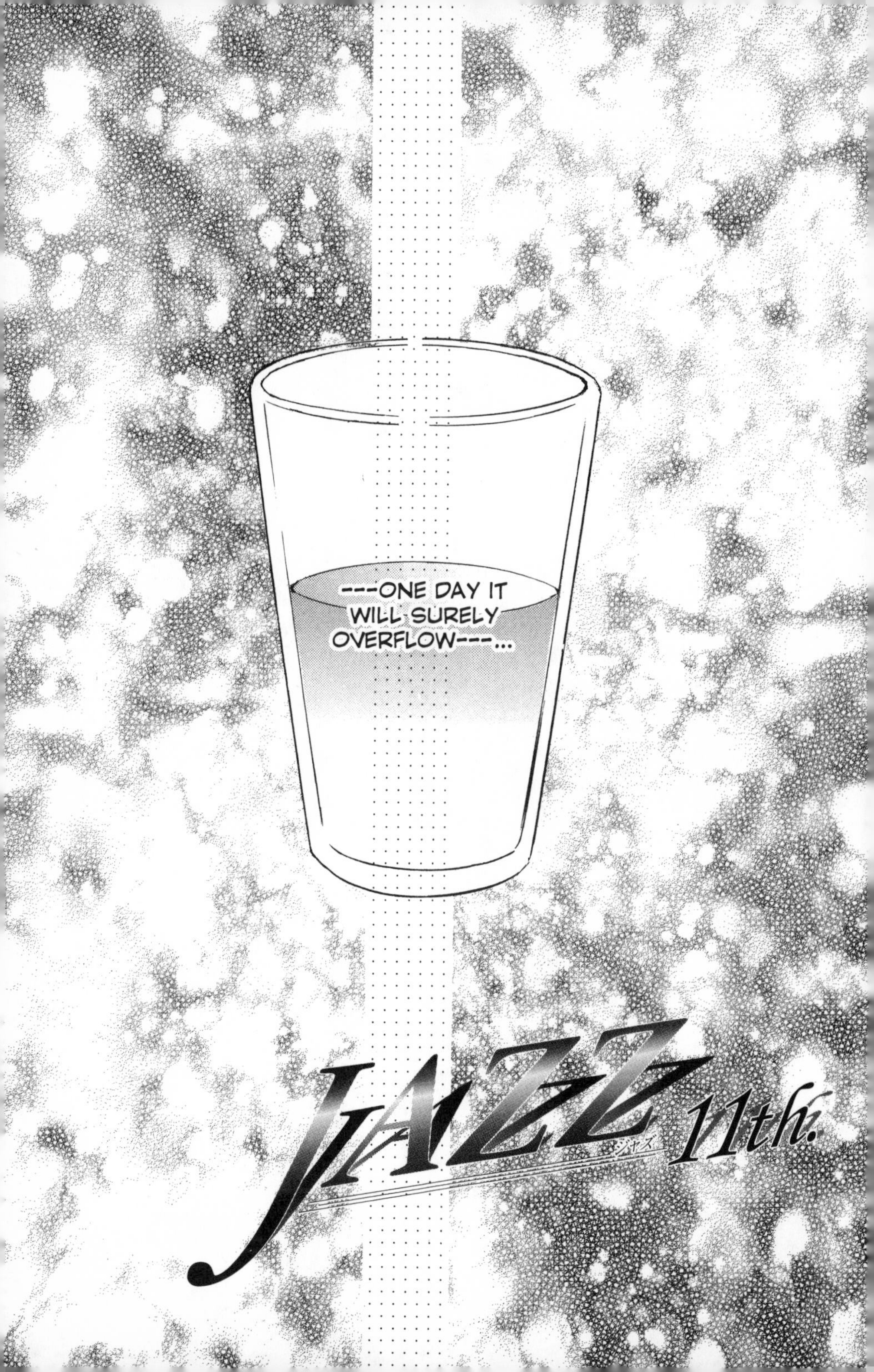
---ONE DAY IT WILL SURELY OVERFLOW---...
JAZZ
ジャズ
11th.

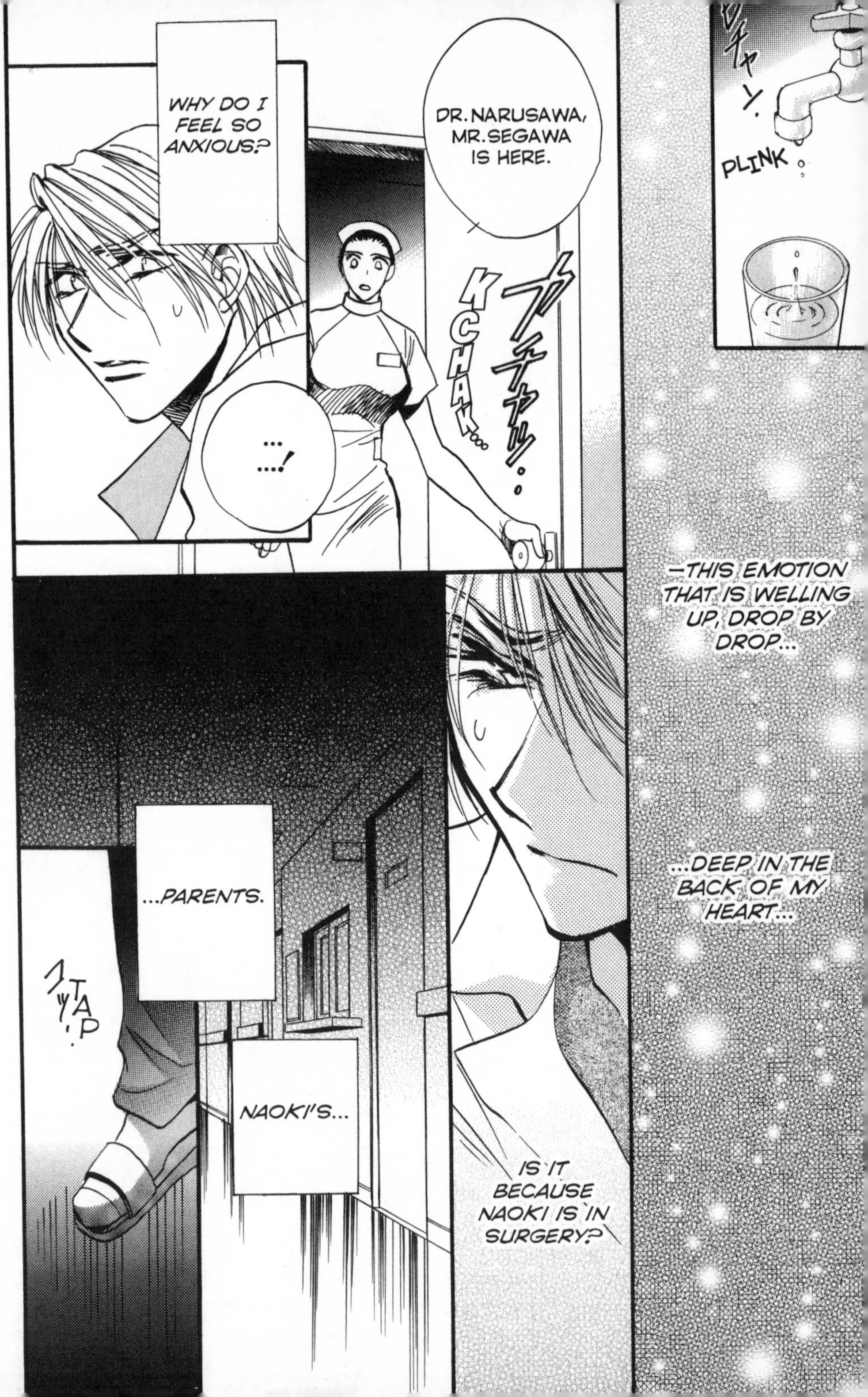
PLINK
—THIS EMOTION THAT IS WELLING UP, DROP BY DROP...
...DEEP IN THE BACK OF MY HEART...
DR. NARUSAWA, MR. SEGAWA IS HERE.
KCHAK...
WHY DO I FEEL SO ANXIOUS?
...
...!
IS IT BECAUSE NAOKI IS IN SURGERY?
NAOKI'S...
...PARENTS.
TAP

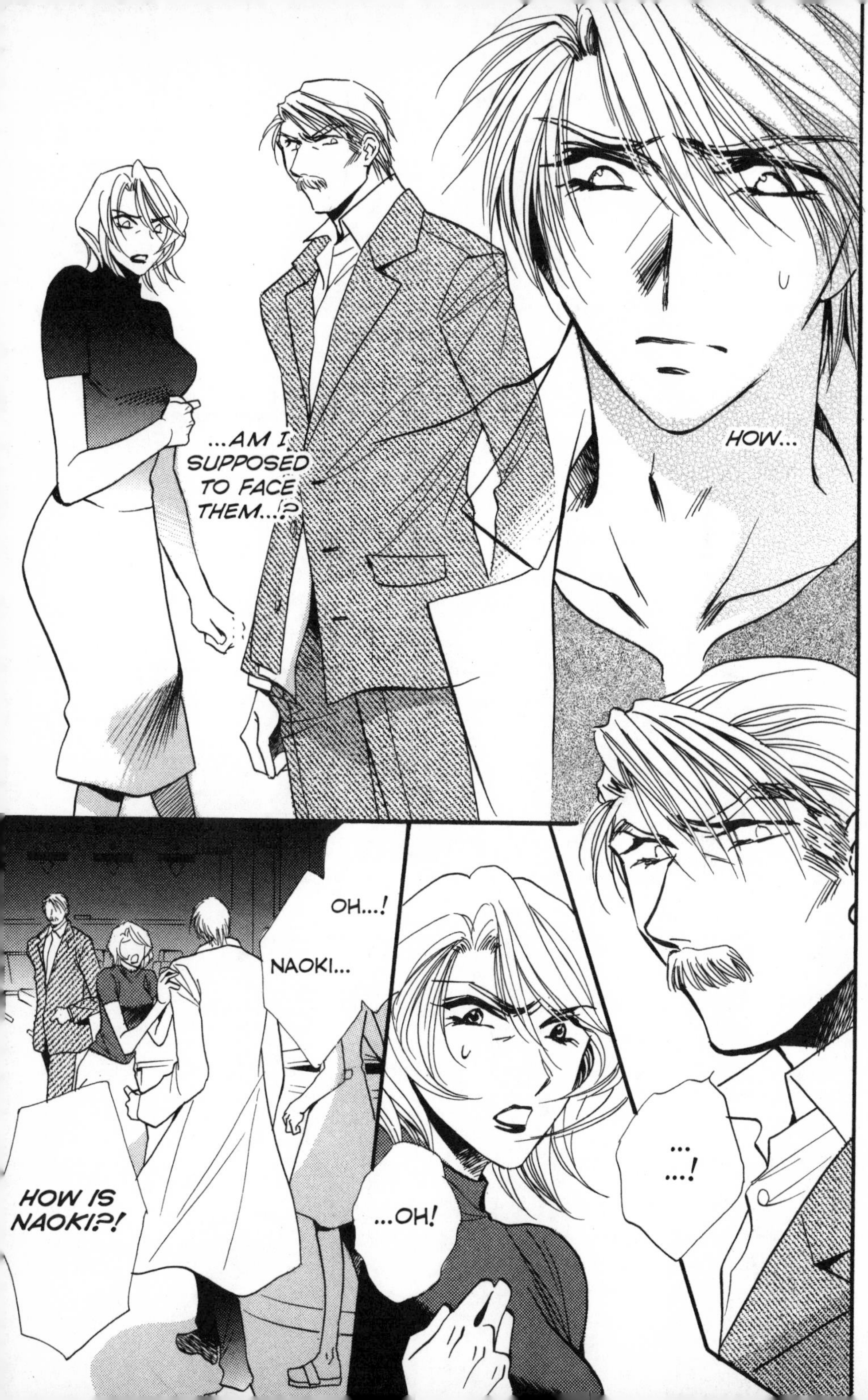
HOW...
...AM I SUPPOSED TO FACE THEM...!?
...
...!
...OH!
OH...!
NAOKI...
HOW IS NAOKI?!

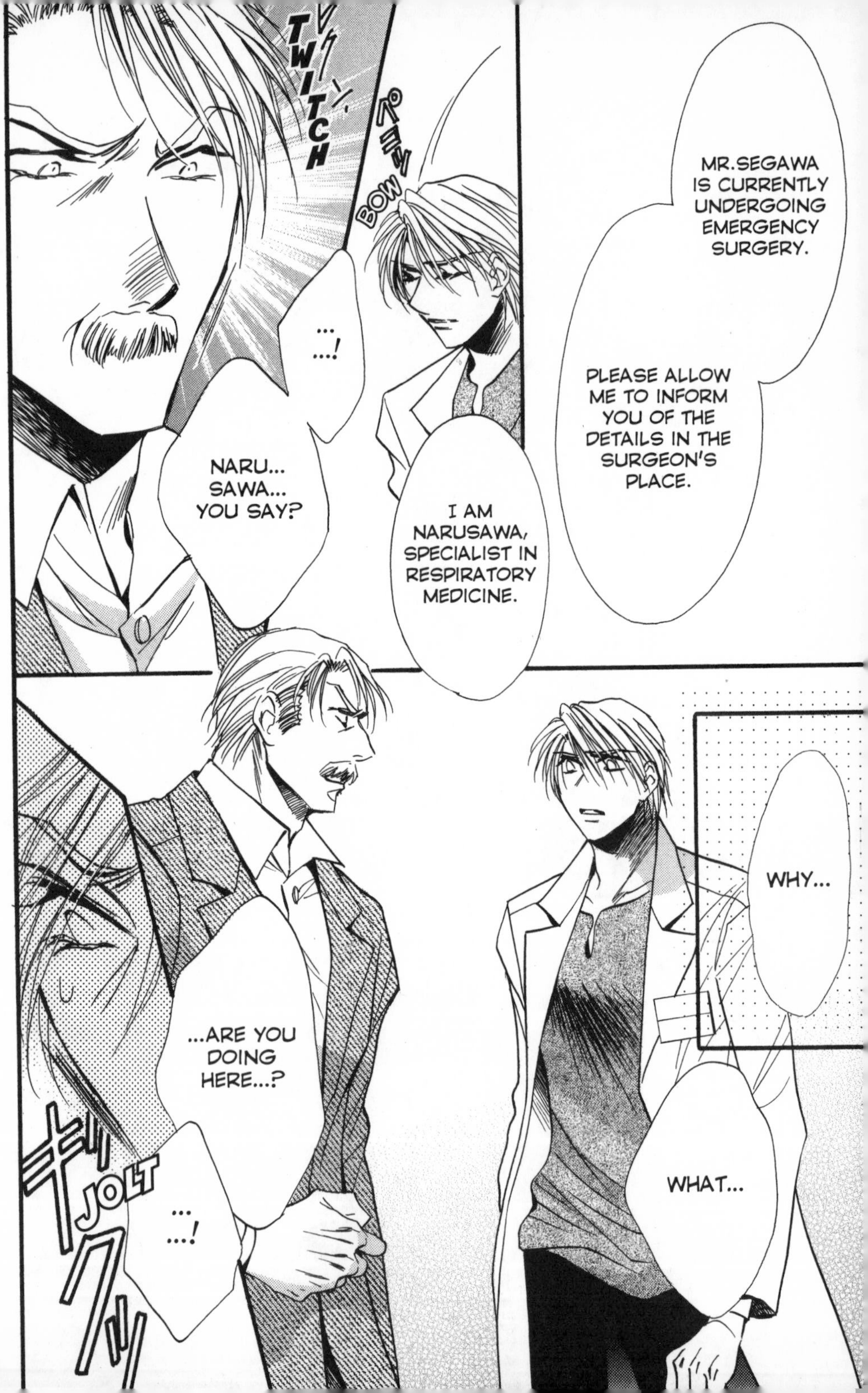
MR.SEGAWA IS CURRENTLY UNDERGOING EMERGENCY SURGERY.
PLEASE ALLOW ME TO INFORM YOU OF THE DETAILS IN THE SURGEON'S PLACE.
BOW
I AM NARUSAWA, SPECIALIST IN RESPIRATORY MEDICINE.
TWITCH
... ...!
NARU... SAWA... YOU SAY?
WHY...
WHAT...
...ARE YOU DOING HERE...?
JOLT
... ...!

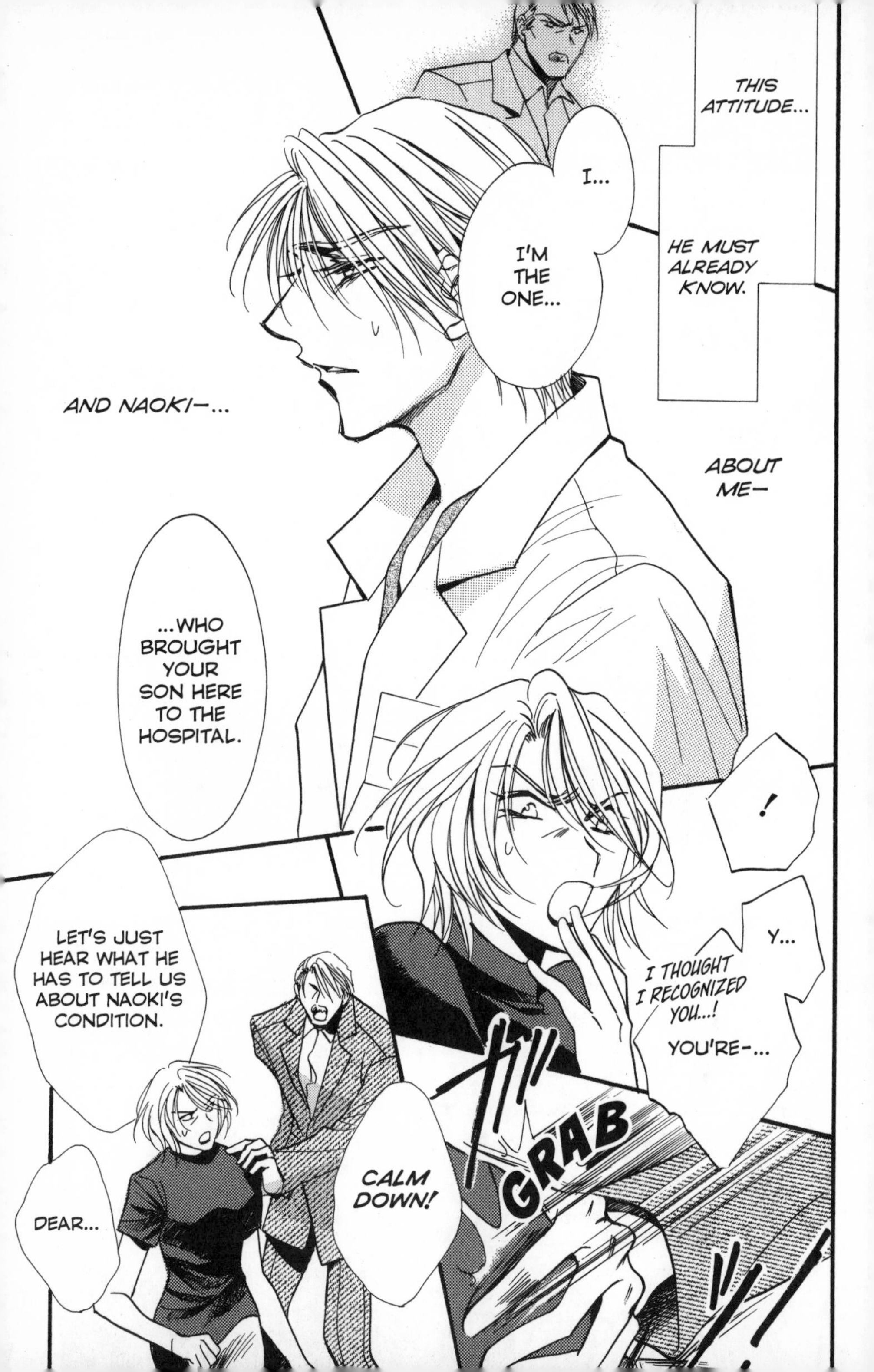
THIS ATTITUDE...
HE MUST ALREADY KNOW.
ABOUT ME—
I...
I'M THE ONE...
AND NAOKI—...
...WHO BROUGHT YOUR SON HERE TO THE HOSPITAL.
!
Y...
I THOUGHT I RECOGNIZED YOU...!
YOU'RE-...
GRAB
CALM DOWN!
LET'S JUST HEAR WHAT HE HAS TO TELL US ABOUT NAOKI'S CONDITION.
DEAR...

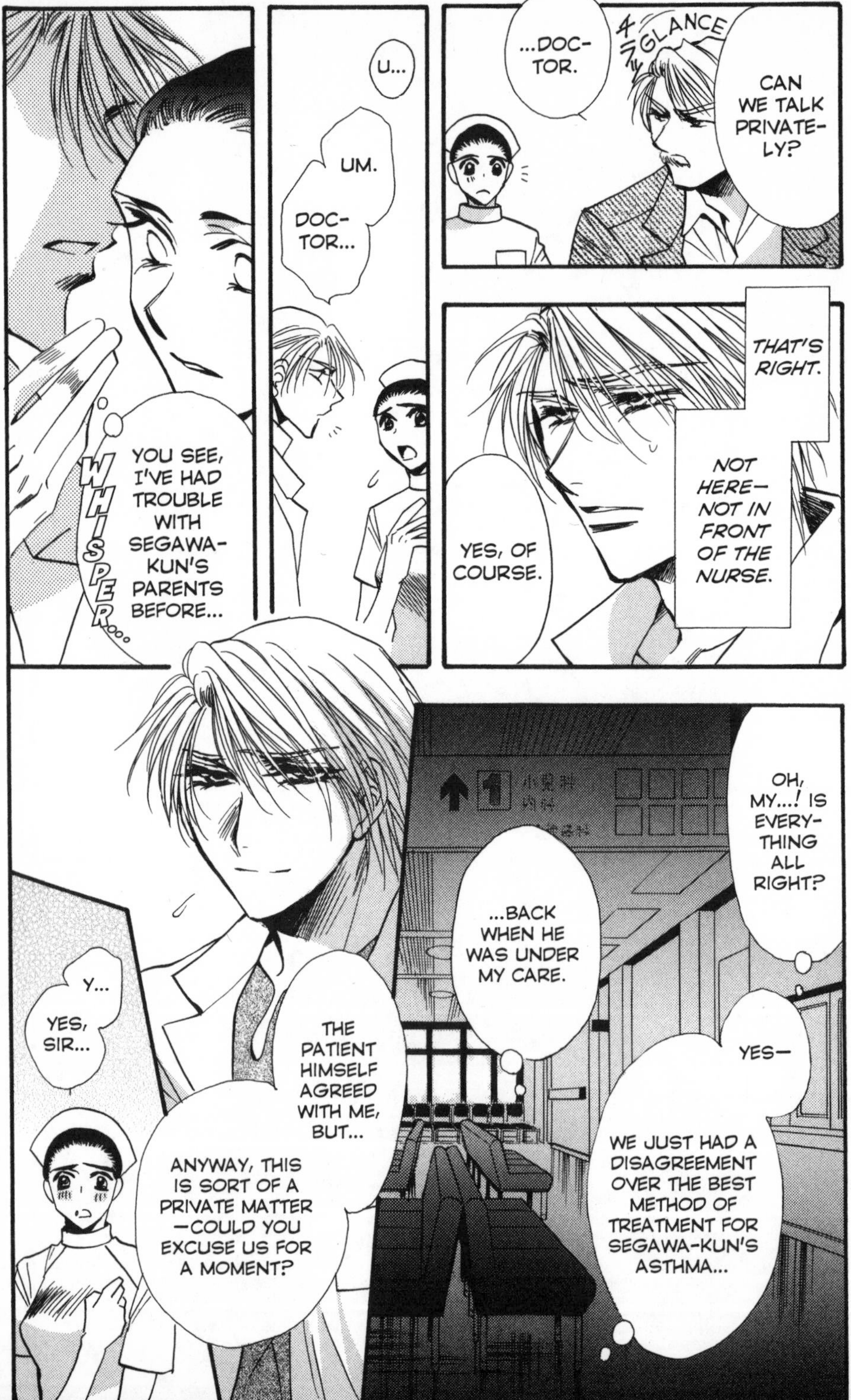
CAN WE TALK PRIVATELY?
GLANCE
...DOCTOR.
THAT'S RIGHT.
NOT HERE—NOT IN FRONT OF THE NURSE.
YES, OF COURSE.
U...
UM.
DOCTOR...
WHISPER...
YOU SEE, I'VE HAD TROUBLE WITH SEGAWA-KUN'S PARENTS BEFORE...
OH, MY...! IS EVERYTHING ALL RIGHT?
YES—
WE JUST HAD A DISAGREEMENT OVER THE BEST METHOD OF TREATMENT FOR SEGAWA-KUN'S ASTHMA...
...BACK WHEN HE WAS UNDER MY CARE.
THE PATIENT HIMSELF AGREED WITH ME, BUT...
ANYWAY, THIS IS SORT OF A PRIVATE MATTER—COULD YOU EXCUSE US FOR A MOMENT?
Y...
YES, SIR...

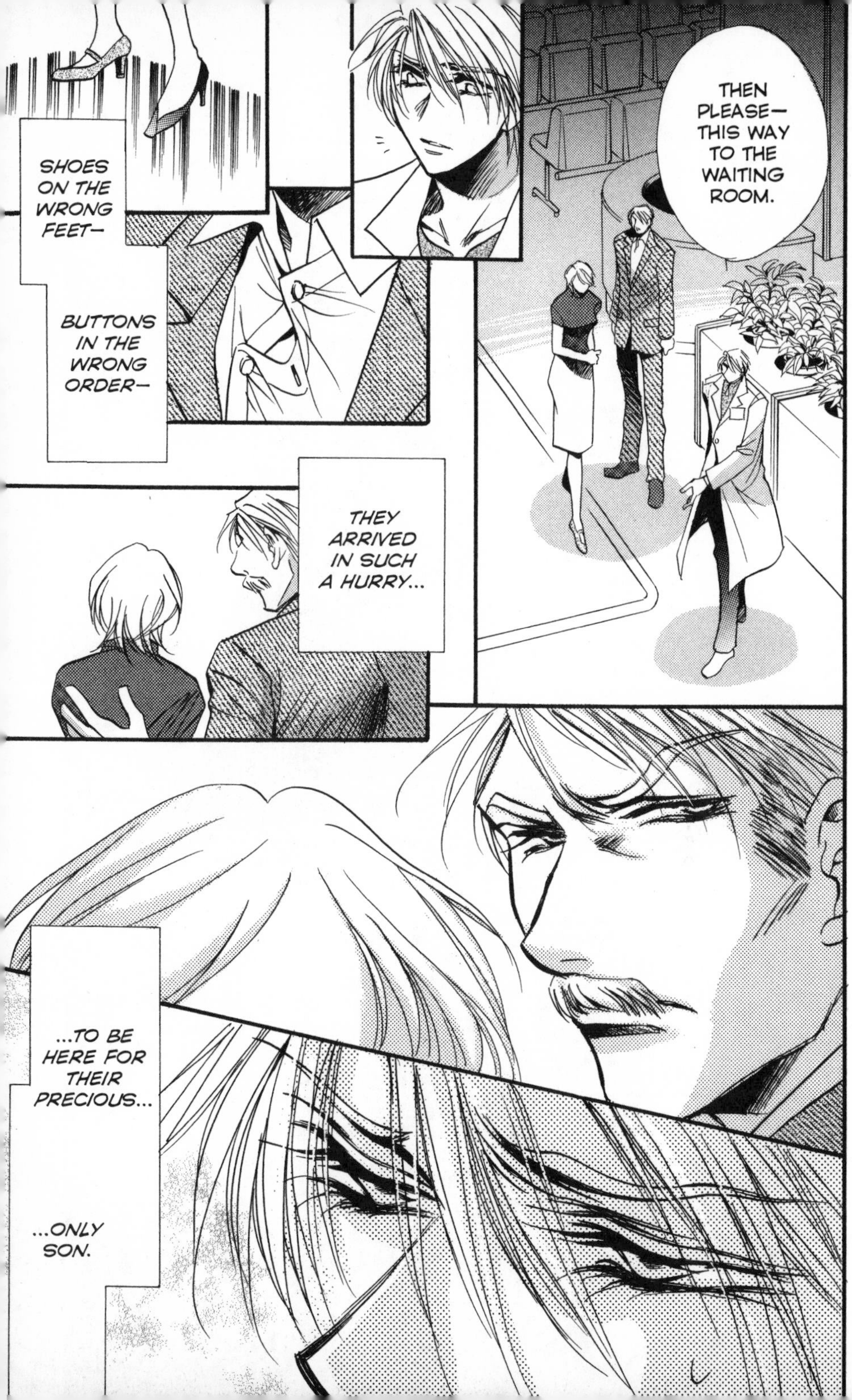
THEN PLEASE— THIS WAY TO THE WAITING ROOM.
SHOES ON THE WRONG FEET—
BUTTONS IN THE WRONG ORDER—
THEY ARRIVED IN SUCH A HURRY...
...TO BE HERE FOR THEIR PRECIOUS...
...ONLY SON.

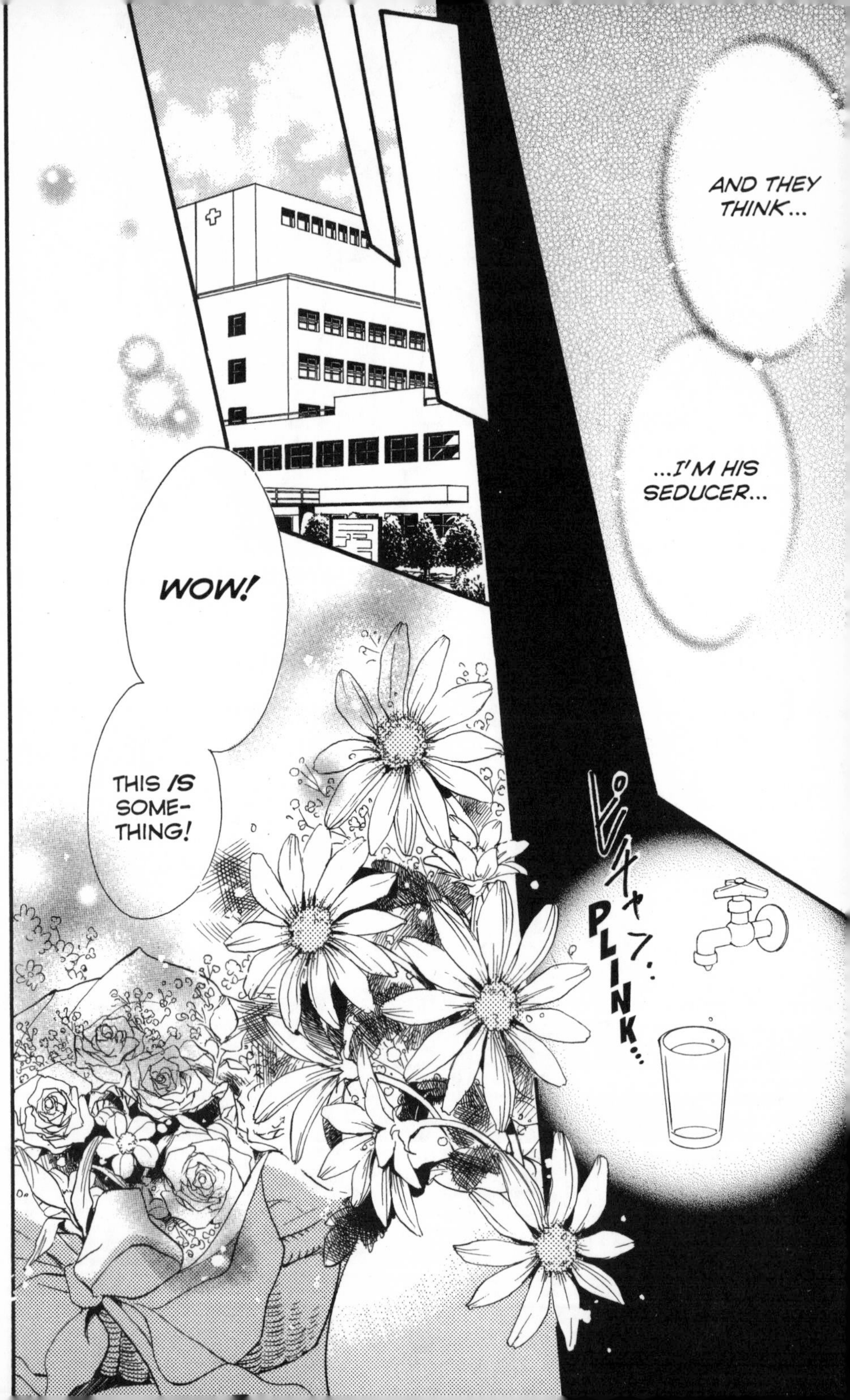
AND THEY THINK...
...I'M HIS SEDUCER...
ピチャン..
PLINK...
WOW!
THIS IS SOME-THING!

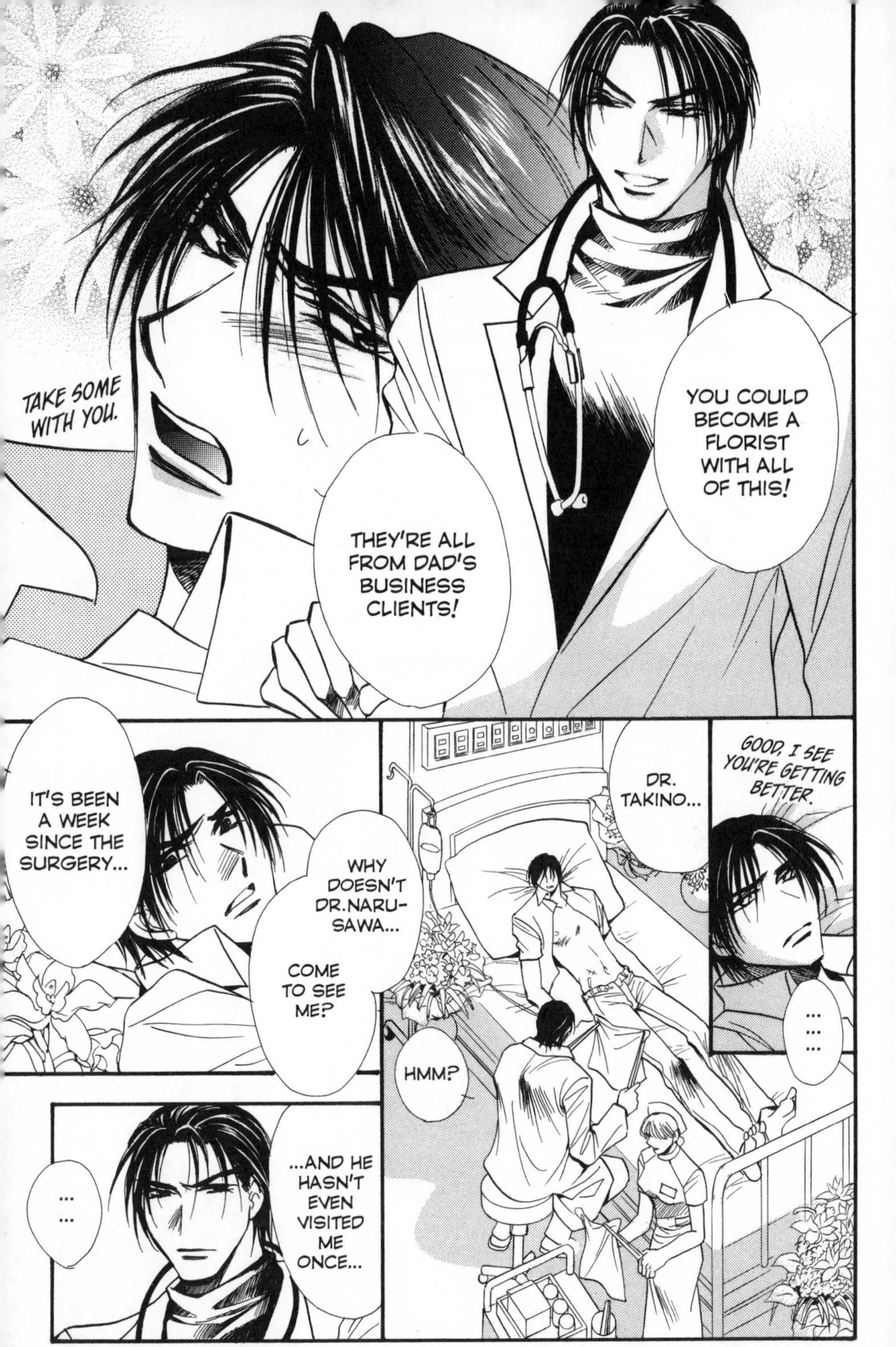
YOU COULD BECOME A FLORIST WITH ALL OF THIS!
THEY'RE ALL FROM DAD'S BUSINESS CLIENTS!
TAKE SOME WITH YOU.
GOOD, I SEE YOU'RE GETTING BETTER.
... ...
DR. TAKINO...
HMM?
IT'S BEEN A WEEK SINCE THE SURGERY...
WHY DOESN'T DR.NARU-SAWA...
COME TO SEE ME?
...AND HE HASN'T EVEN VISITED ME ONCE...
... ...

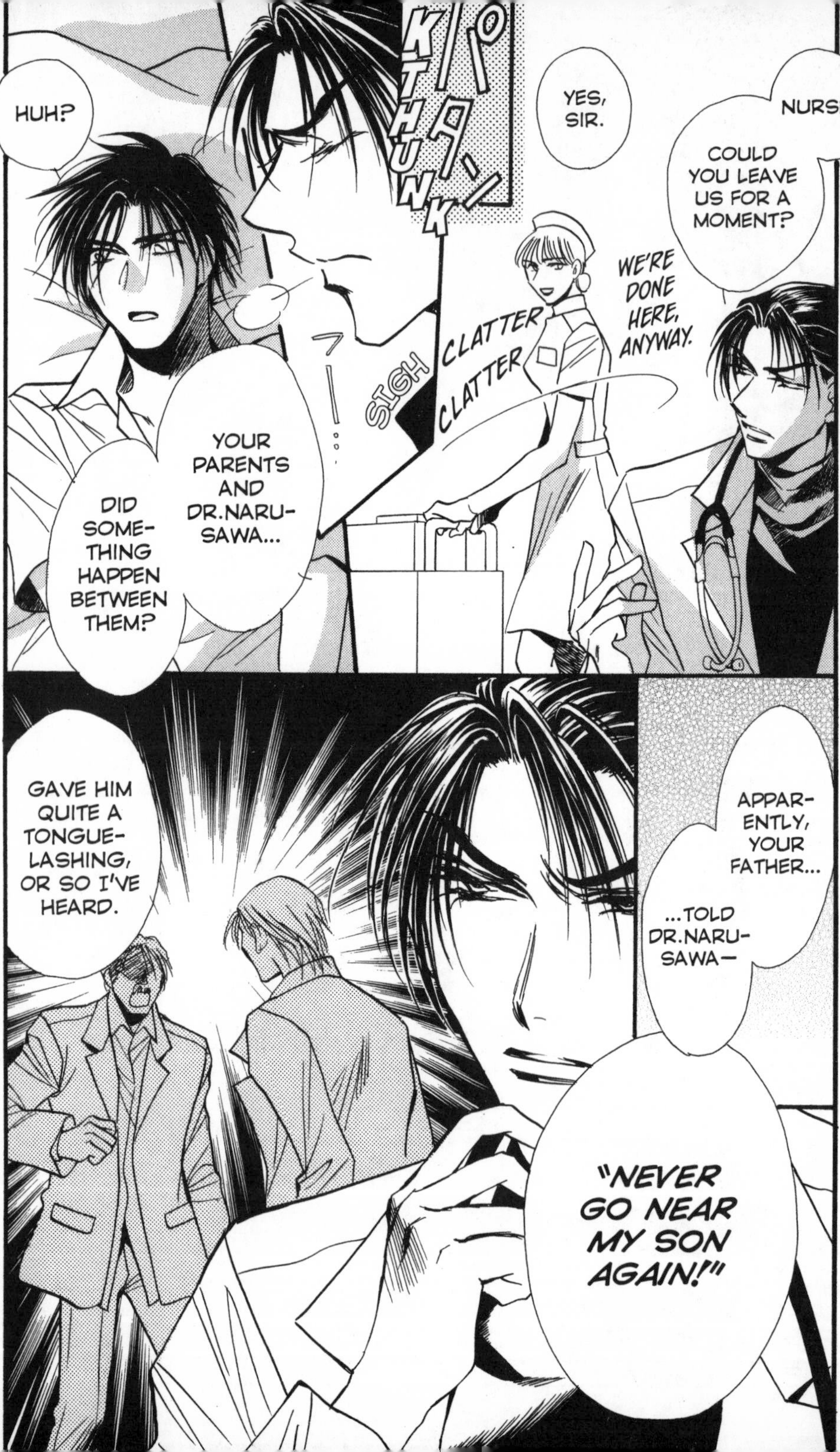
NURSE?
COULD YOU LEAVE US FOR A MOMENT?
YES, SIR.
WE'RE DONE HERE, ANYWAY.
CLATTER
CLATTER
KTHUNK
HUH?
SIGH
YOUR PARENTS AND DR.NARU-SAWA...
DID SOME-THING HAPPEN BETWEEN THEM?
APPAR-ENTLY, YOUR FATHER...
...TOLD DR.NARU-SAWA—
"NEVER GO NEAR MY SON AGAIN!"
GAVE HIM QUITE A TONGUE-LASHING, OR SO I'VE HEARD.

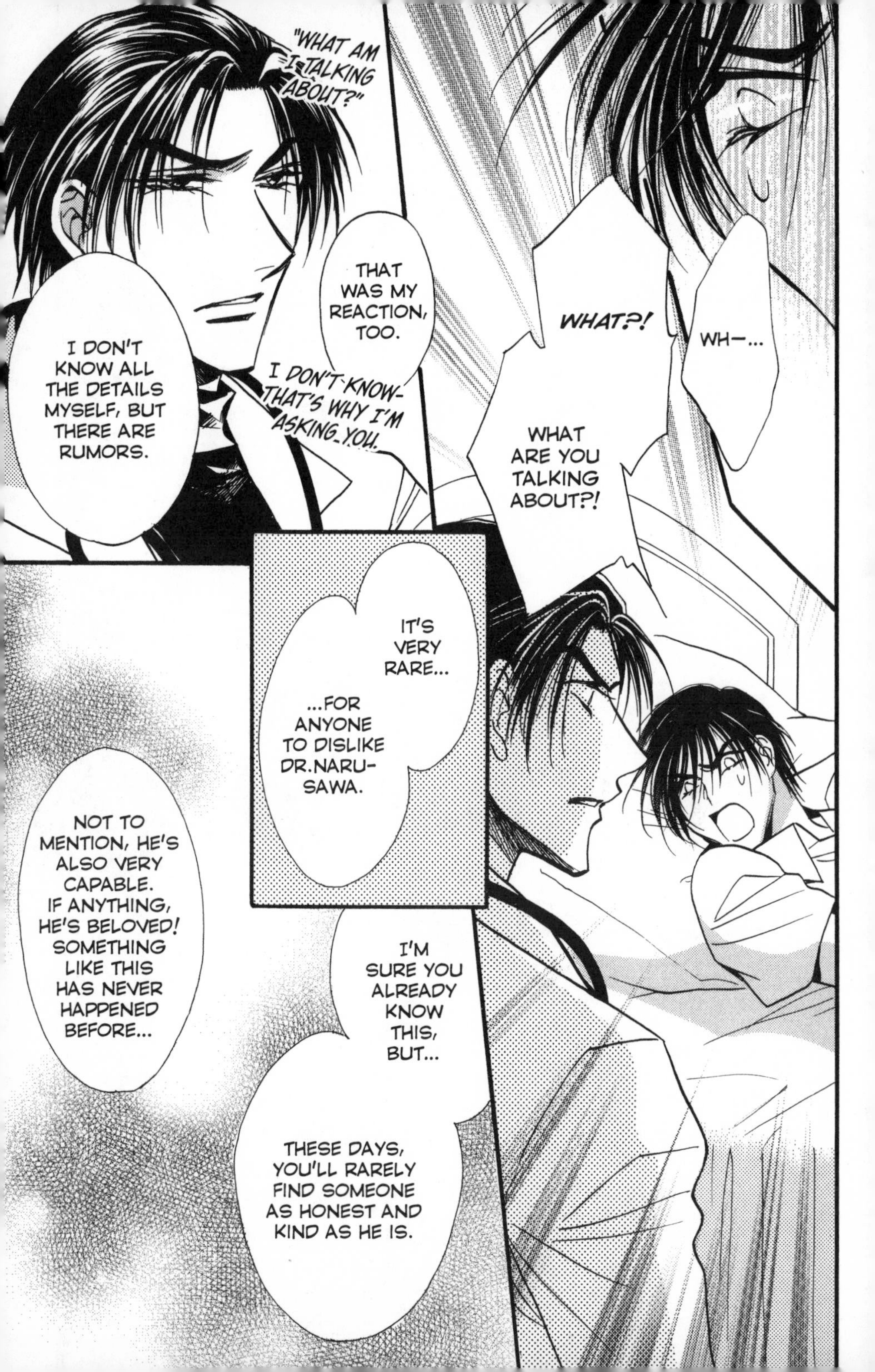
WH—...
WHAT?!
WHAT ARE YOU TALKING ABOUT?!
"WHAT AM I TALKING ABOUT?"
THAT WAS MY REACTION, TOO.
I DON'T KNOW-THAT'S WHY I'M ASKING YOU.
I DON'T KNOW ALL THE DETAILS MYSELF, BUT THERE ARE RUMORS.
IT'S VERY RARE...
...FOR ANYONE TO DISLIKE DR.NARU-SAWA.
I'M SURE YOU ALREADY KNOW THIS, BUT...
THESE DAYS, YOU'LL RARELY FIND SOMEONE AS HONEST AND KIND AS HE IS.
NOT TO MENTION, HE'S ALSO VERY CAPABLE. IF ANYTHING, HE'S BELOVED! SOMETHING LIKE THIS HAS NEVER HAPPENED BEFORE...

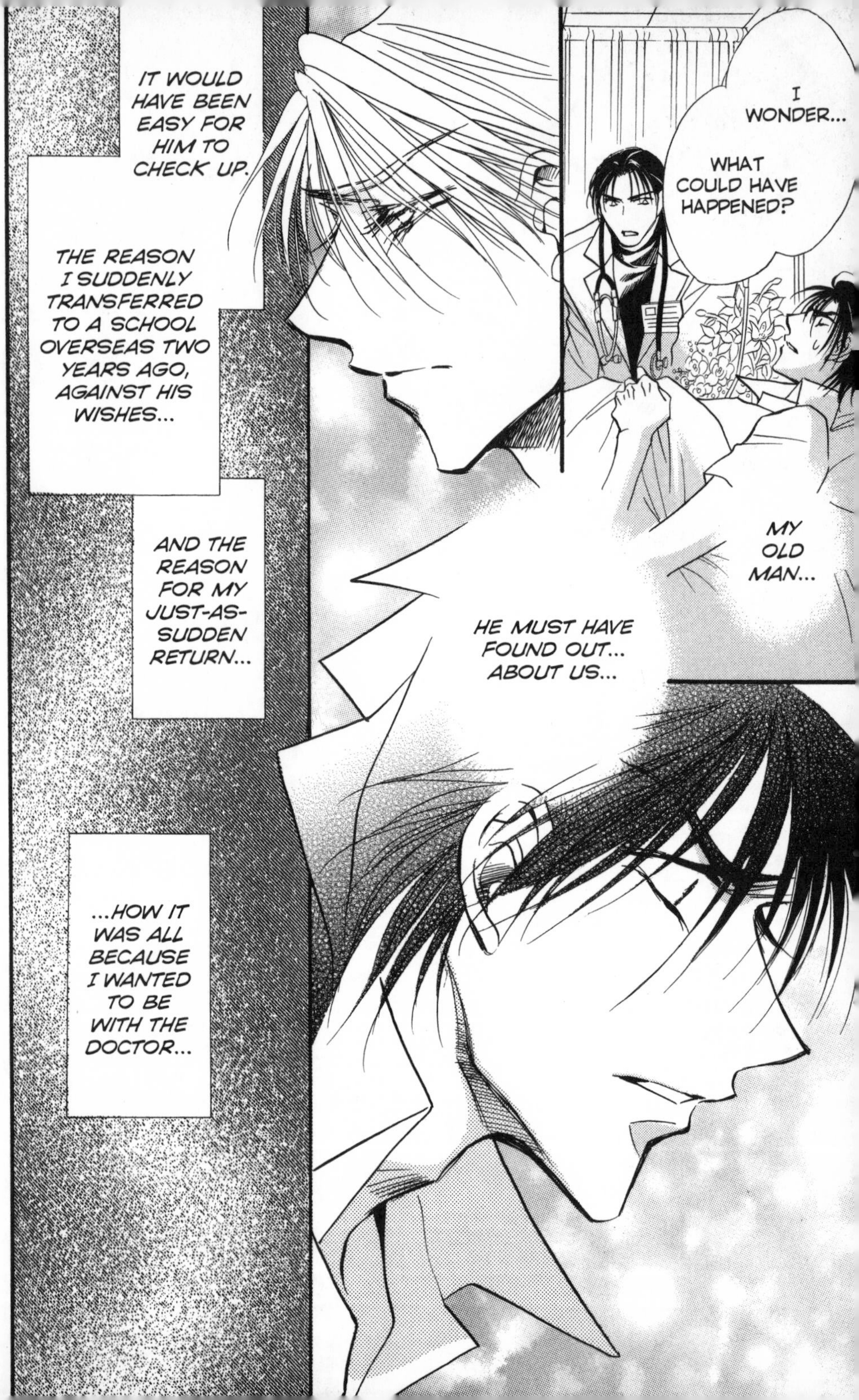
I WONDER...
WHAT COULD HAVE HAPPENED?
MY OLD MAN...
HE MUST HAVE FOUND OUT... ABOUT US...
IT WOULD HAVE BEEN EASY FOR HIM TO CHECK UP.
THE REASON I SUDDENLY TRANSFERRED TO A SCHOOL OVERSEAS TWO YEARS AGO, AGAINST HIS WISHES...
AND THE REASON FOR MY JUST-AS-SUDDEN RETURN...
...HOW IT WAS ALL BECAUSE I WANTED TO BE WITH THE DOCTOR...

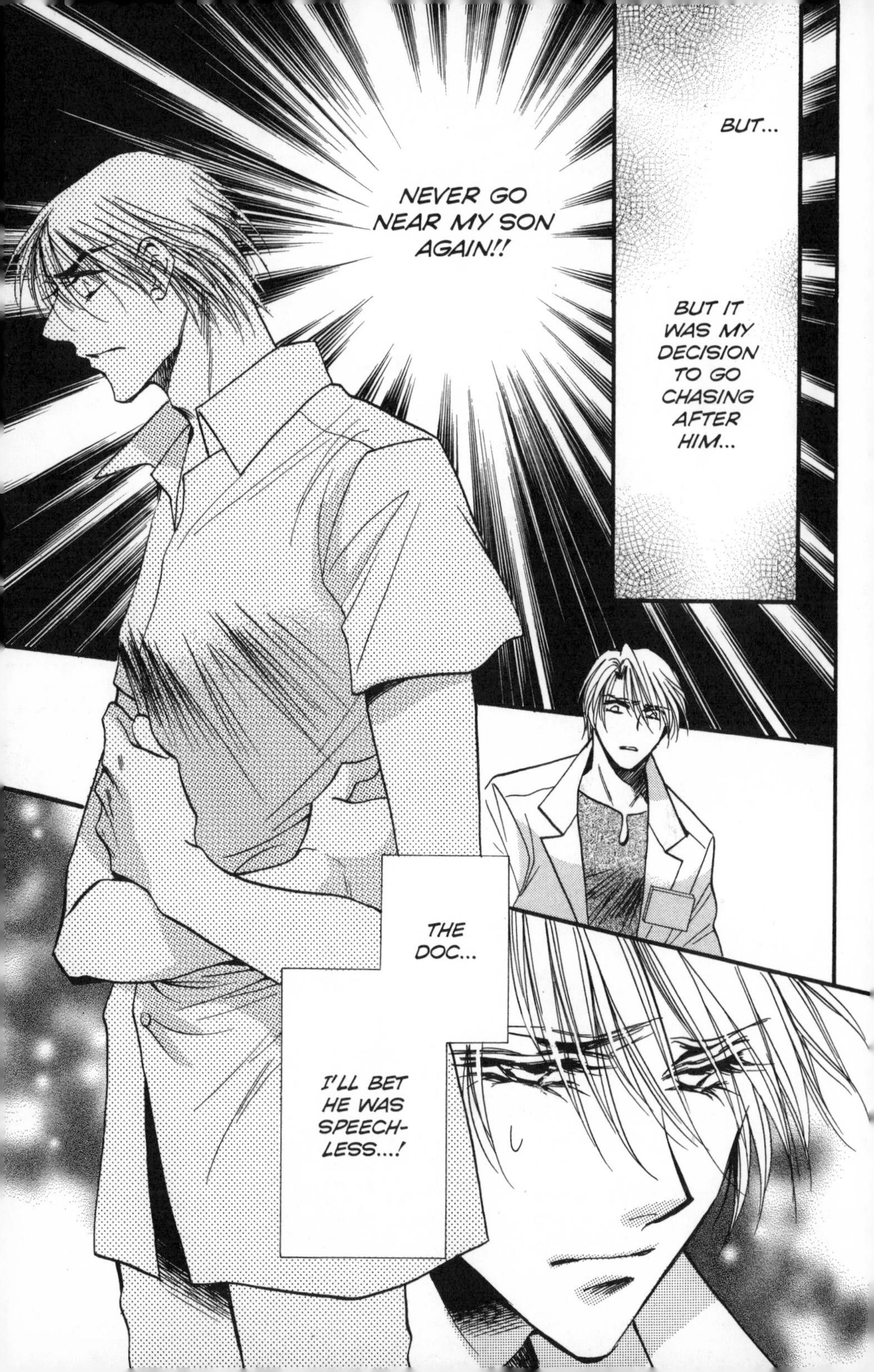
BUT...
BUT IT WAS MY DECISION TO GO CHASING AFTER HIM...
NEVER GO NEAR MY SON AGAIN!!
THE DOC...
I'LL BET HE WAS SPEECH-LESS...!

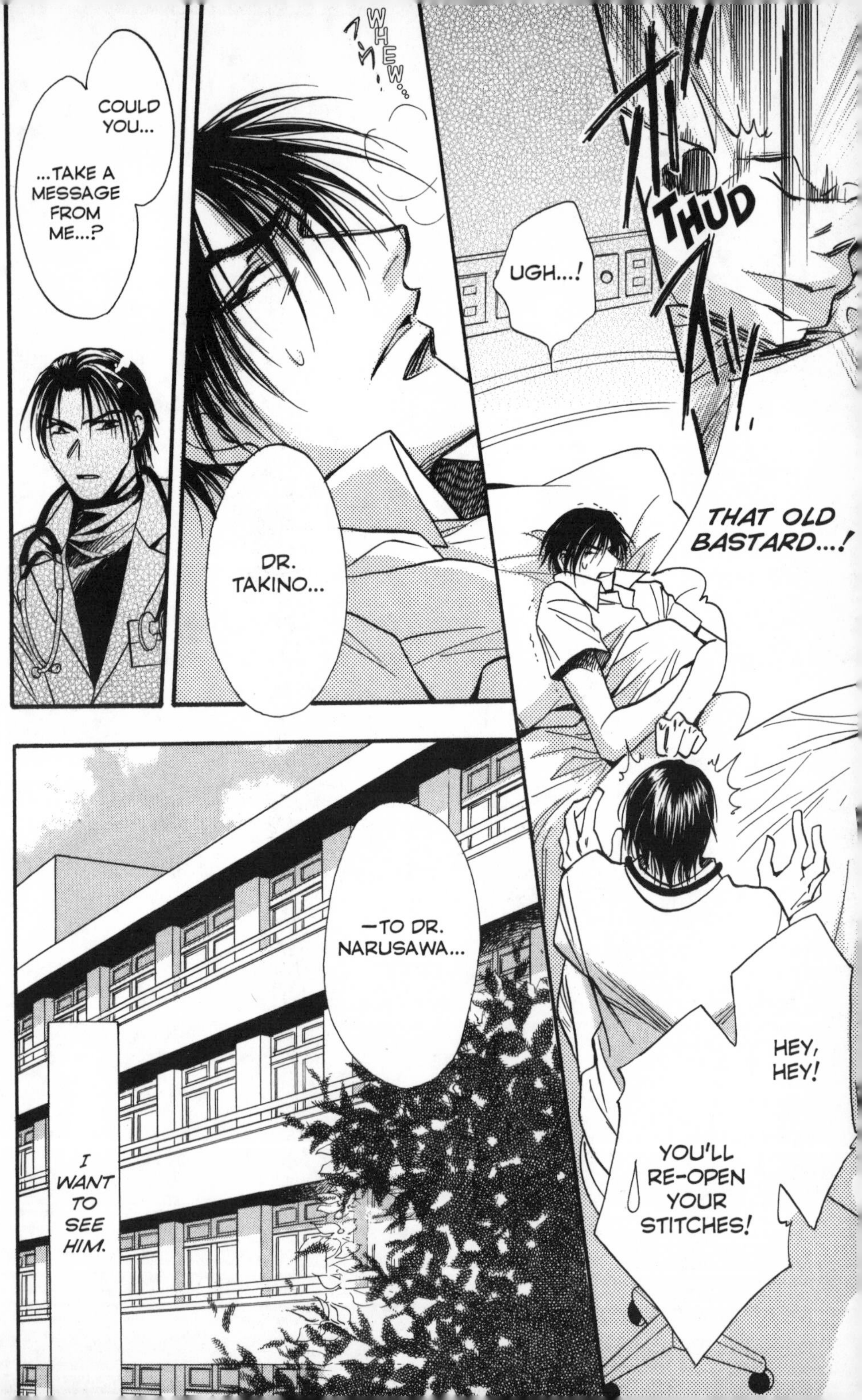
THUD
UGH...!
THAT OLD BASTARD...!
HEY, HEY!
YOU'LL RE-OPEN YOUR STITCHES!
WHEW...
DR. TAKINO...
COULD YOU...
...TAKE A MESSAGE FROM ME...?
—TO DR. NARUSAWA...
I WANT TO SEE HIM.

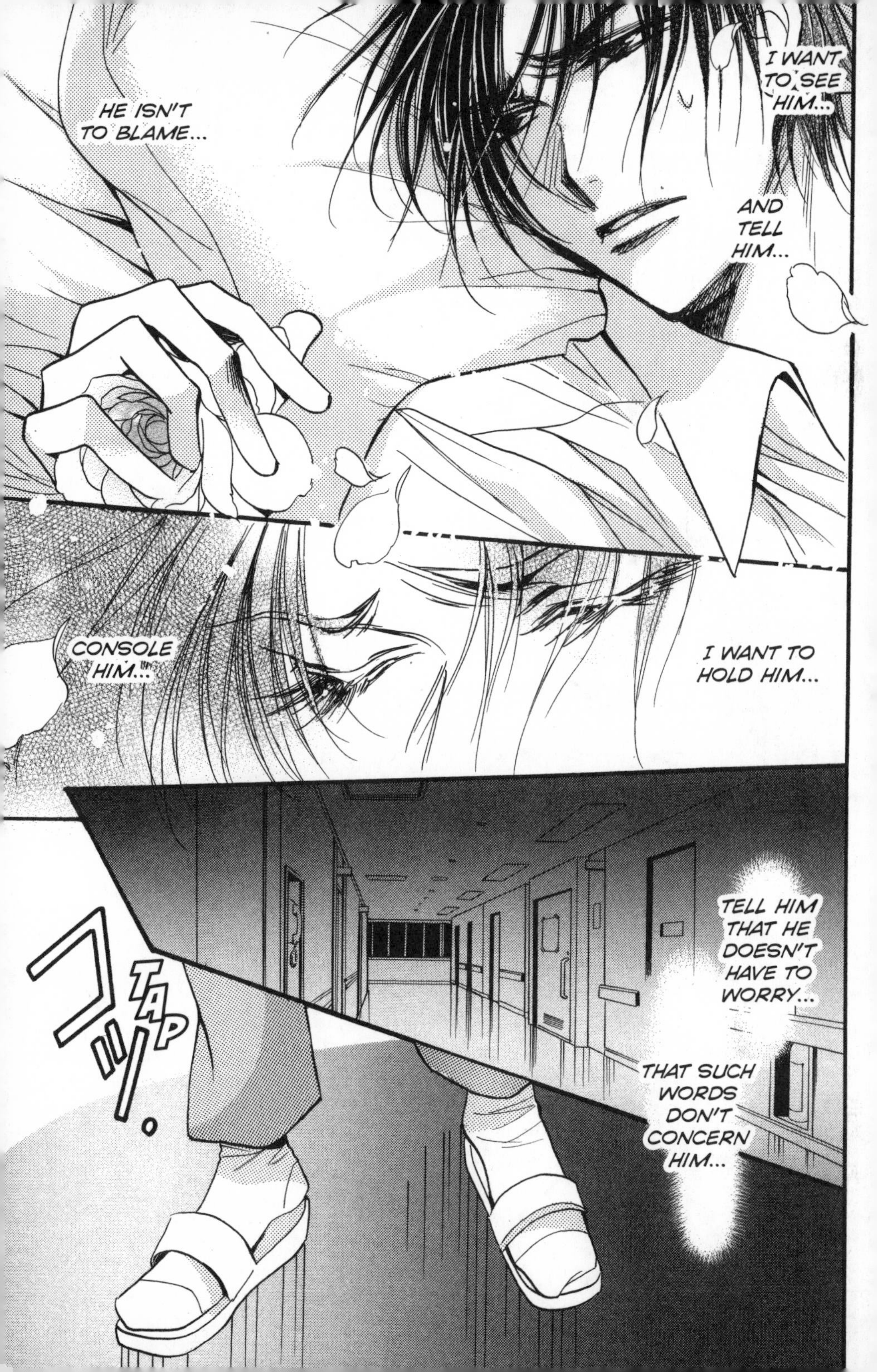
I WANT TO SEE HIM...
AND TELL HIM...
HE ISN'T TO BLAME...
I WANT TO HOLD HIM...
CONSOLE HIM...
TELL HIM THAT HE DOESN'T HAVE TO WORRY...
THAT SUCH WORDS DON'T CONCERN HIM...
TAP

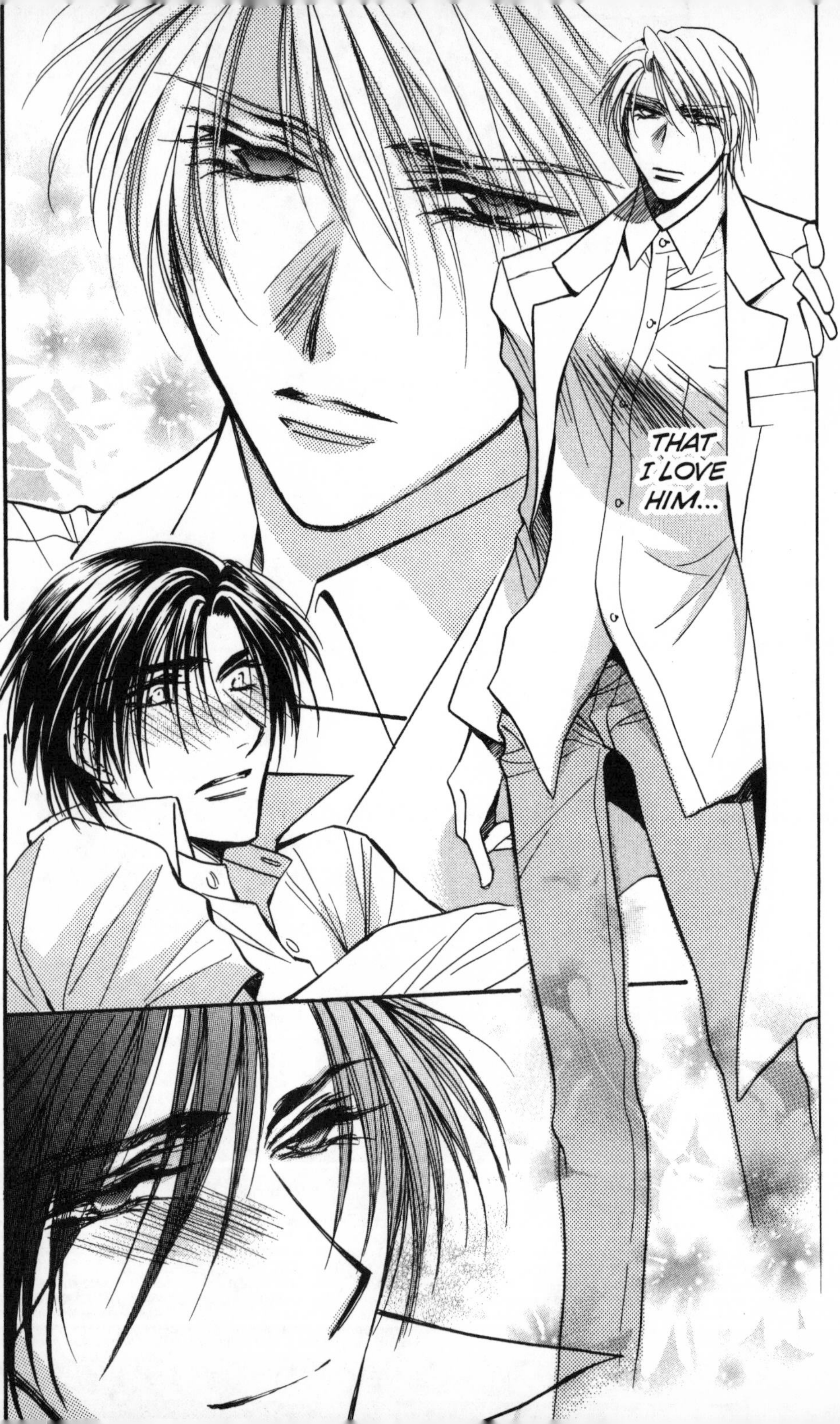
THAT I LOVE HIM...

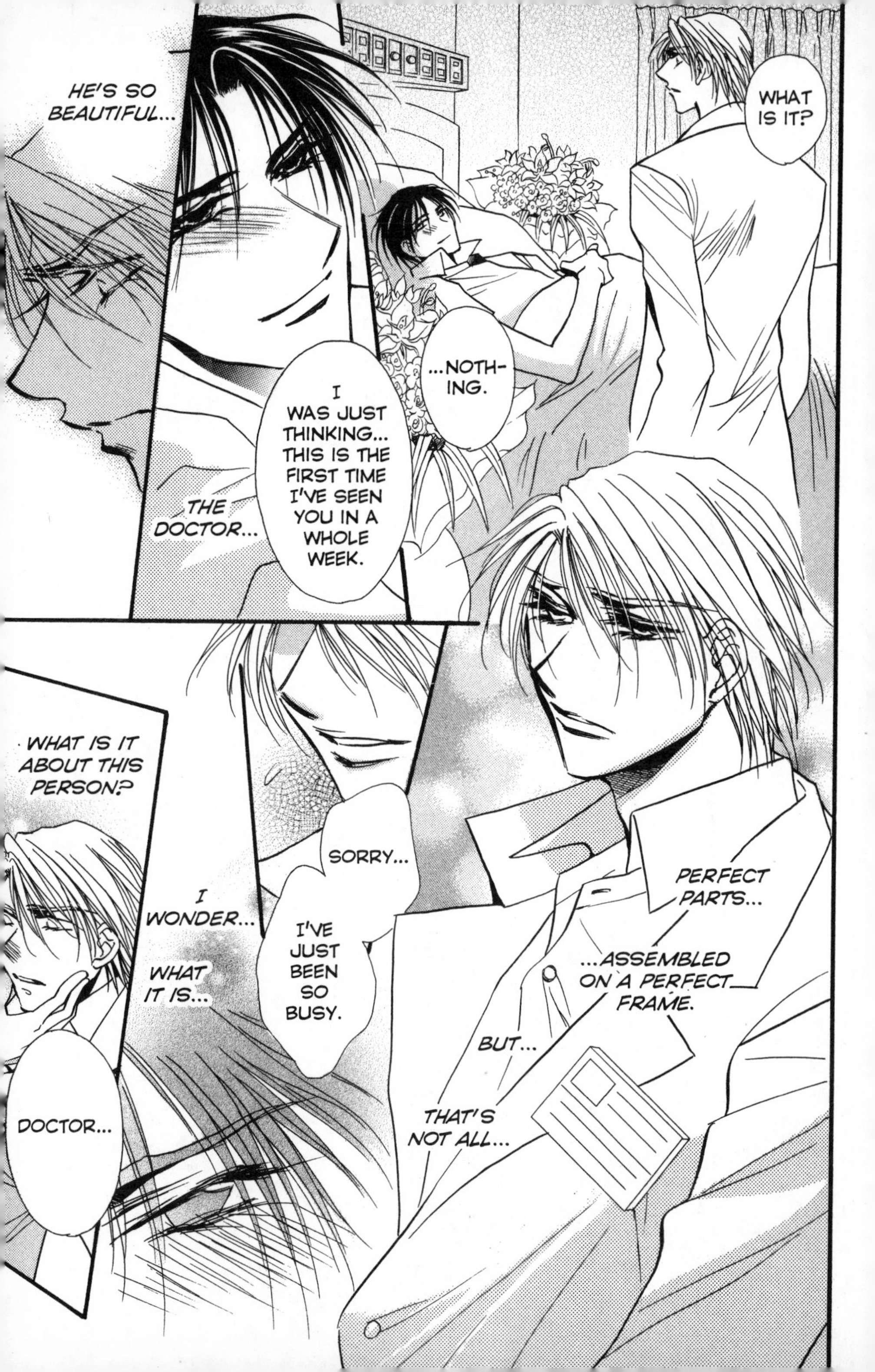
WHAT IS IT?
...NOTHING.
I WAS JUST THINKING... THIS IS THE FIRST TIME I'VE SEEN YOU IN A WHOLE WEEK.
THE DOCTOR...
HE'S SO BEAUTIFUL...
SORRY...
I'VE JUST BEEN SO BUSY.
PERFECT PARTS...
...ASSEMBLED ON A PERFECT FRAME.
BUT...
THAT'S NOT ALL...
I WONDER...
WHAT IT IS...
WHAT IS IT ABOUT THIS PERSON?
DOCTOR...

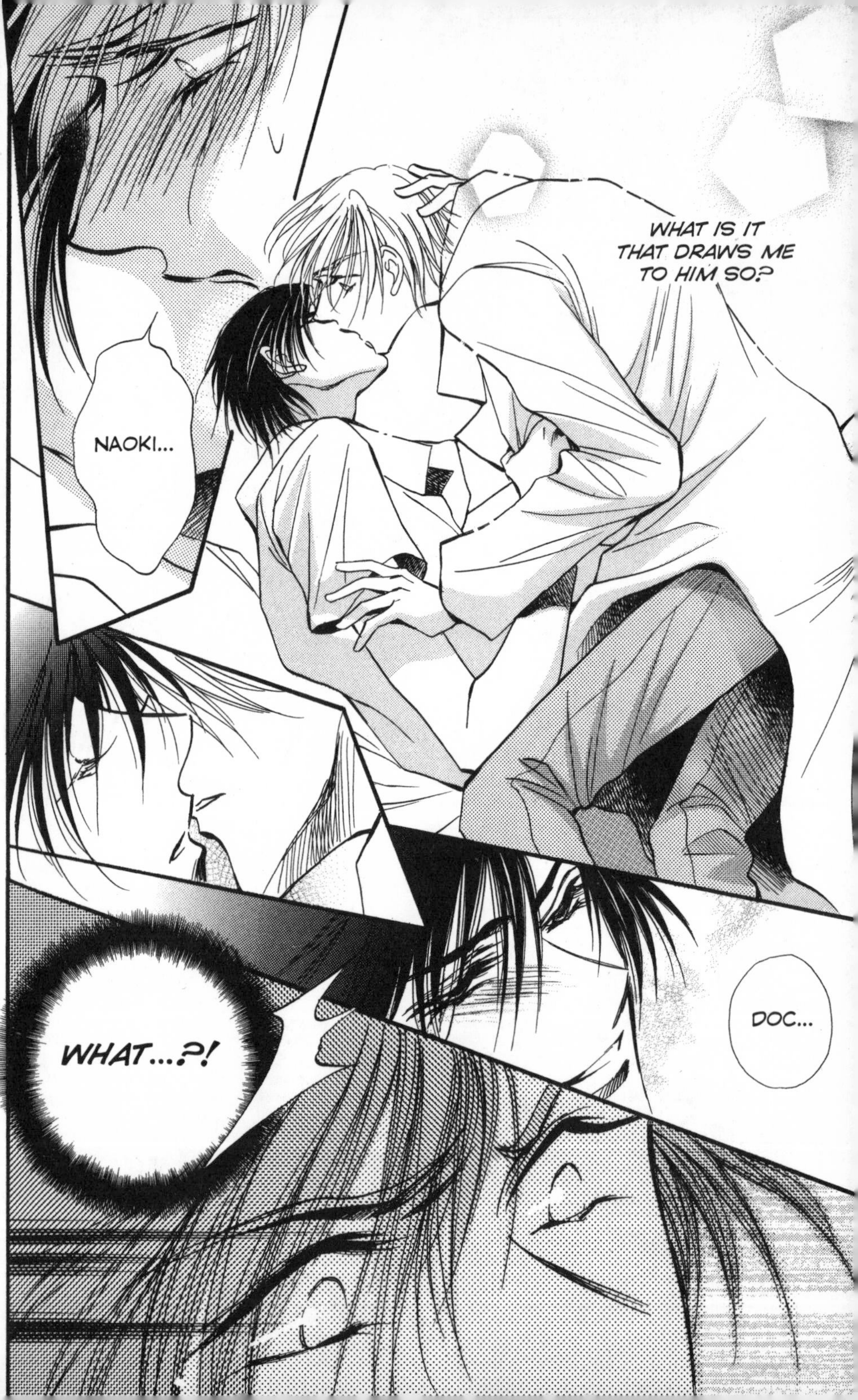
WHAT IS IT THAT DRAWS ME TO HIM SO?
NAOKI...
DOC...
WHAT...?!

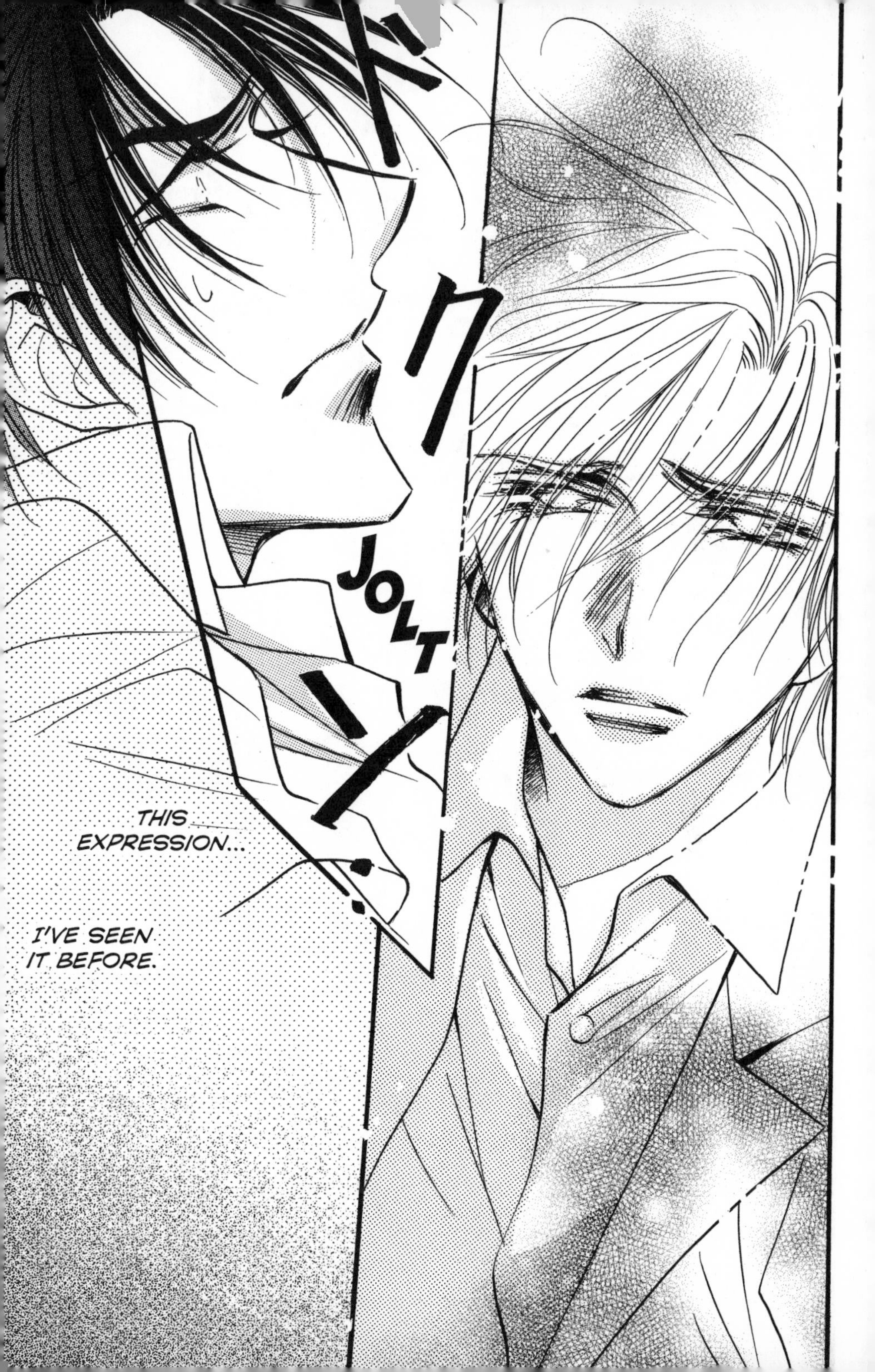
JOLT
THIS EXPRESSION...
I'VE SEEN IT BEFORE.

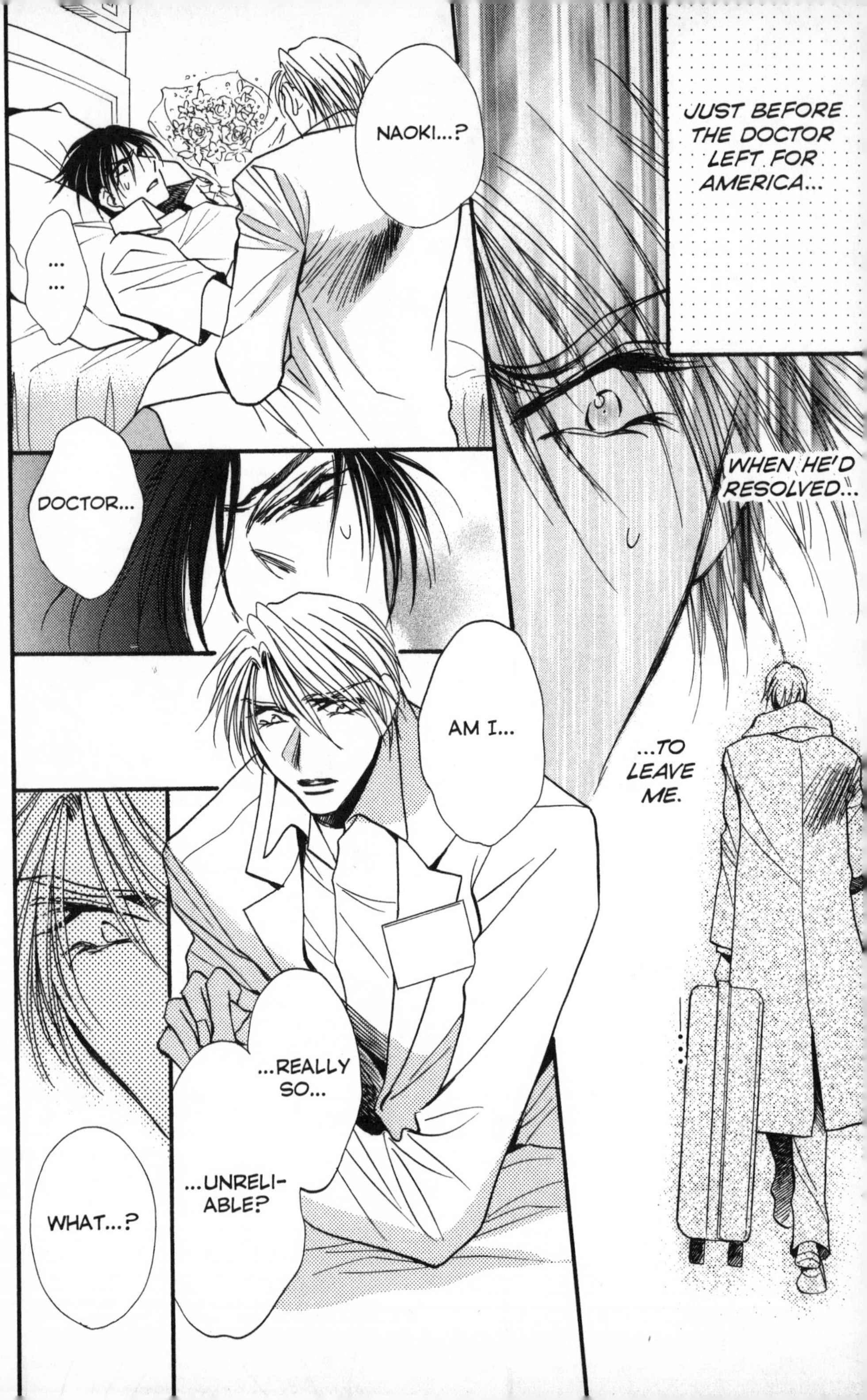
JUST BEFORE THE DOCTOR LEFT FOR AMERICA...
WHEN HE'D RESOLVED...
...TO LEAVE ME.
...
NAOKI...?
... ...
DOCTOR...
AM I...
...REALLY SO...
...UNRELI-ABLE?
WHAT...?

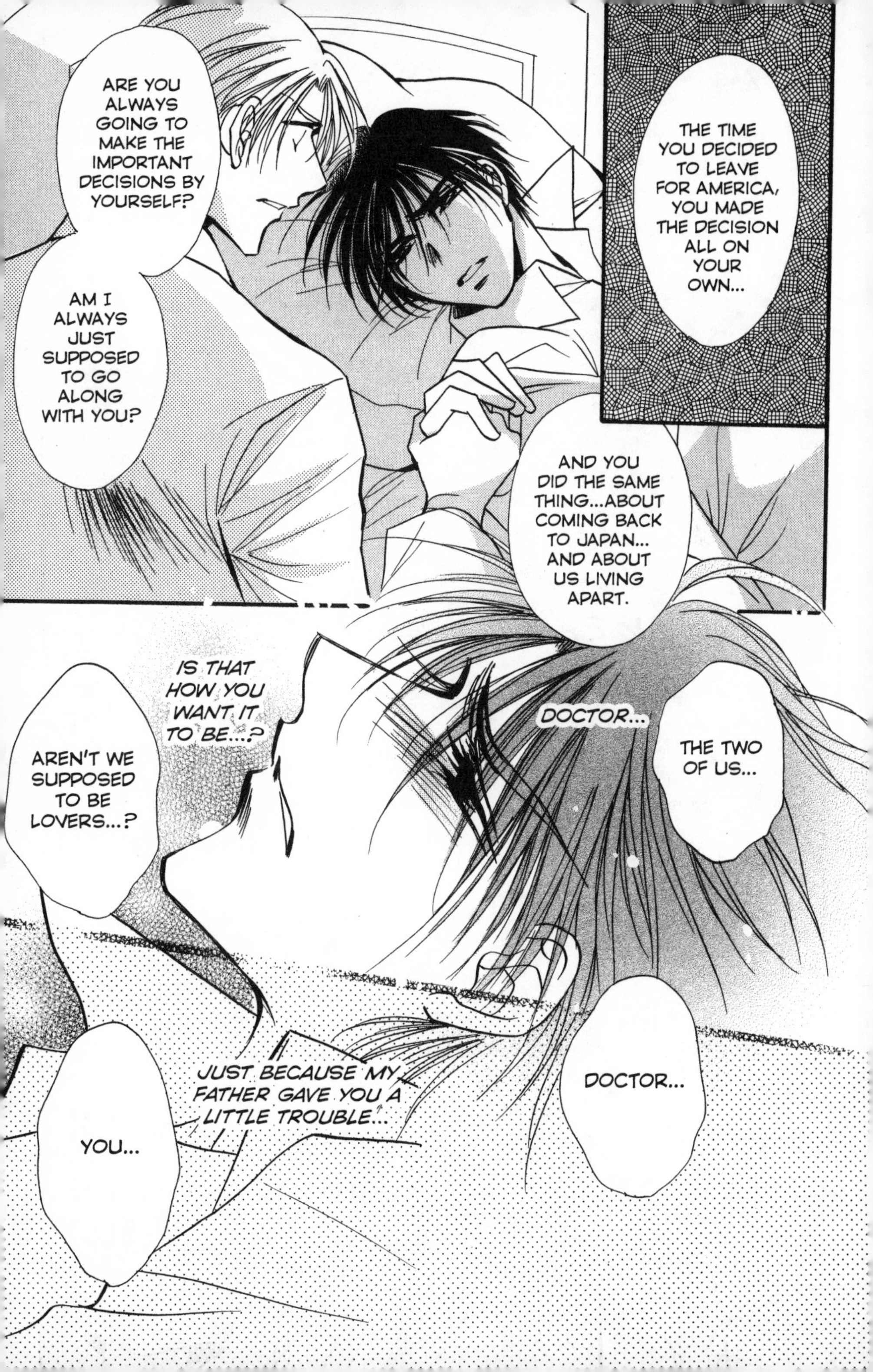
THE TIME YOU DECIDED TO LEAVE FOR AMERICA, YOU MADE THE DECISION ALL ON YOUR OWN...
AND YOU DID THE SAME THING...ABOUT COMING BACK TO JAPAN... AND ABOUT US LIVING APART.
ARE YOU ALWAYS GOING TO MAKE THE IMPORTANT DECISIONS BY YOURSELF?
AM I ALWAYS JUST SUPPOSED TO GO ALONG WITH YOU?
DOCTOR...
THE TWO OF US...
IS THAT HOW YOU WANT IT TO BE...?
AREN'T WE SUPPOSED TO BE LOVERS...?
DOCTOR...
JUST BECAUSE MY FATHER GAVE YOU A LITTLE TROUBLE...
YOU...

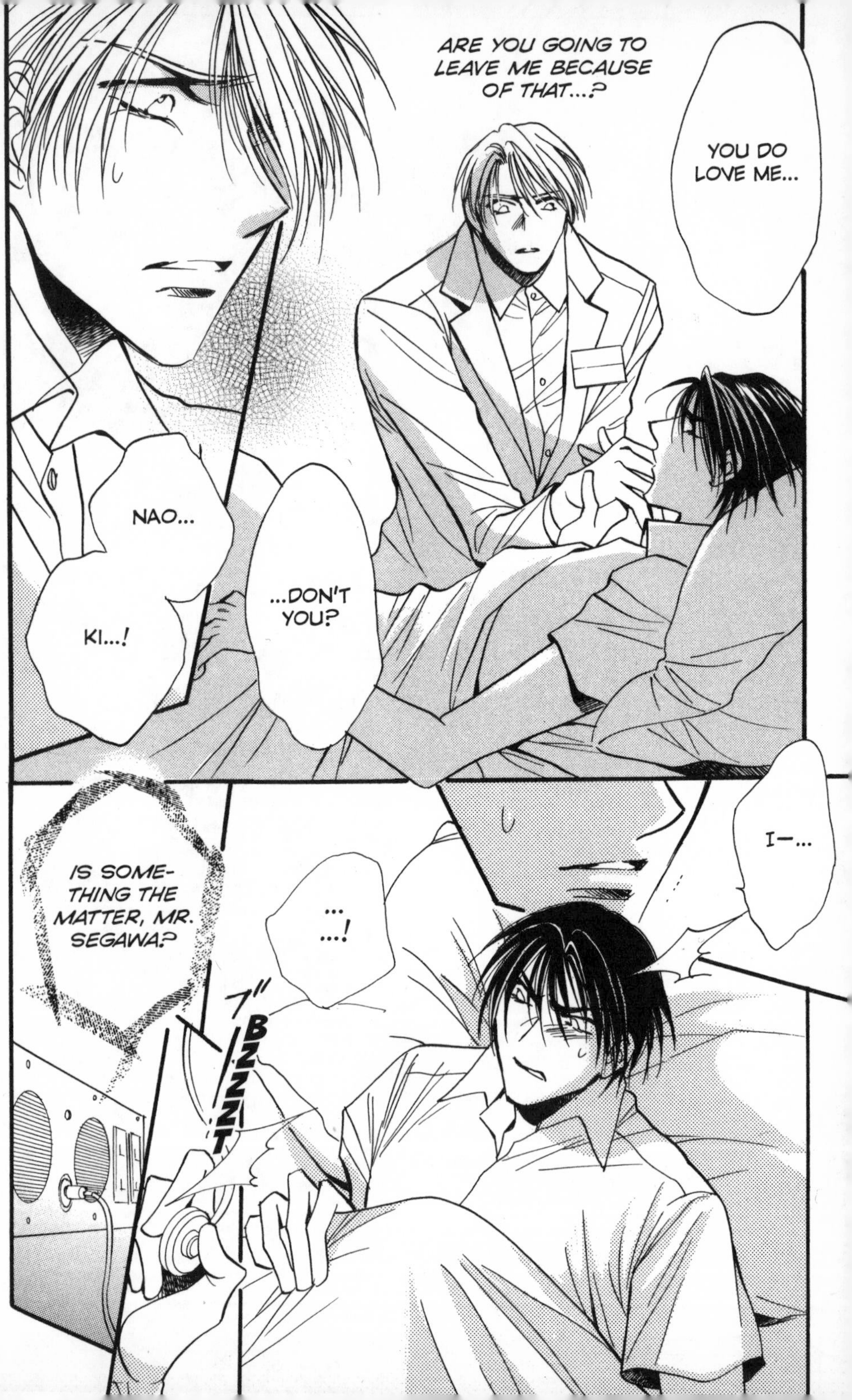
ARE YOU GOING TO LEAVE ME BECAUSE OF THAT...?
YOU DO LOVE ME...
...DON'T YOU?
NAO...
KI...!
I—...
... ...!
IS SOME-THING THE MATTER, MR. SEGAWA?
ブ
BZZZZT

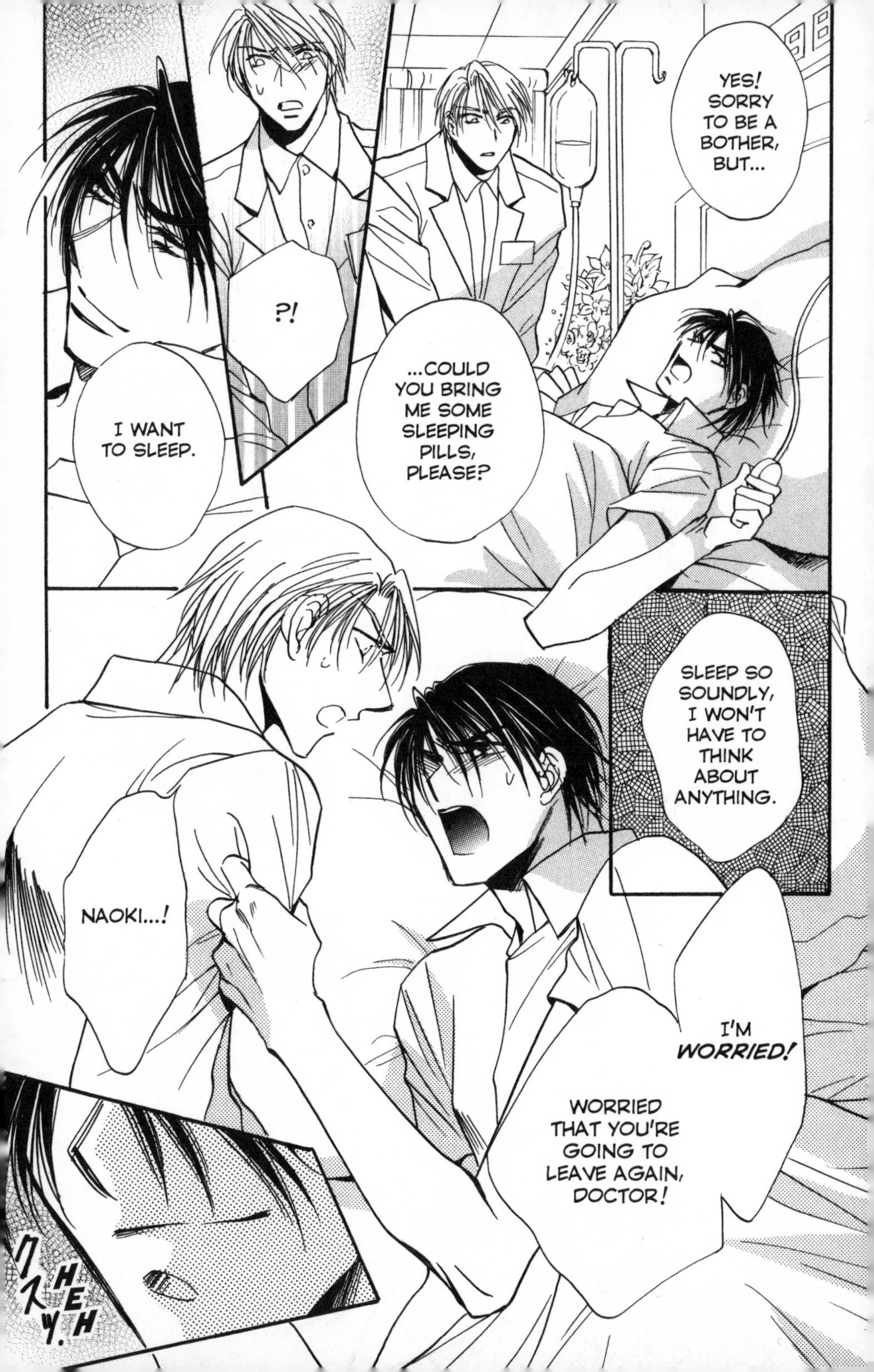
YES! SORRY TO BE A BOTHER, BUT...
...COULD YOU BRING ME SOME SLEEPING PILLS, PLEASE?
?!
I WANT TO SLEEP.
SLEEP SO SOUNDLY, I WON'T HAVE TO THINK ABOUT ANYTHING.
I'M **WORRIED!**
WORRIED THAT YOU'RE GOING TO LEAVE AGAIN, DOCTOR!
NAOKI...!
クスッ
HEH HEH

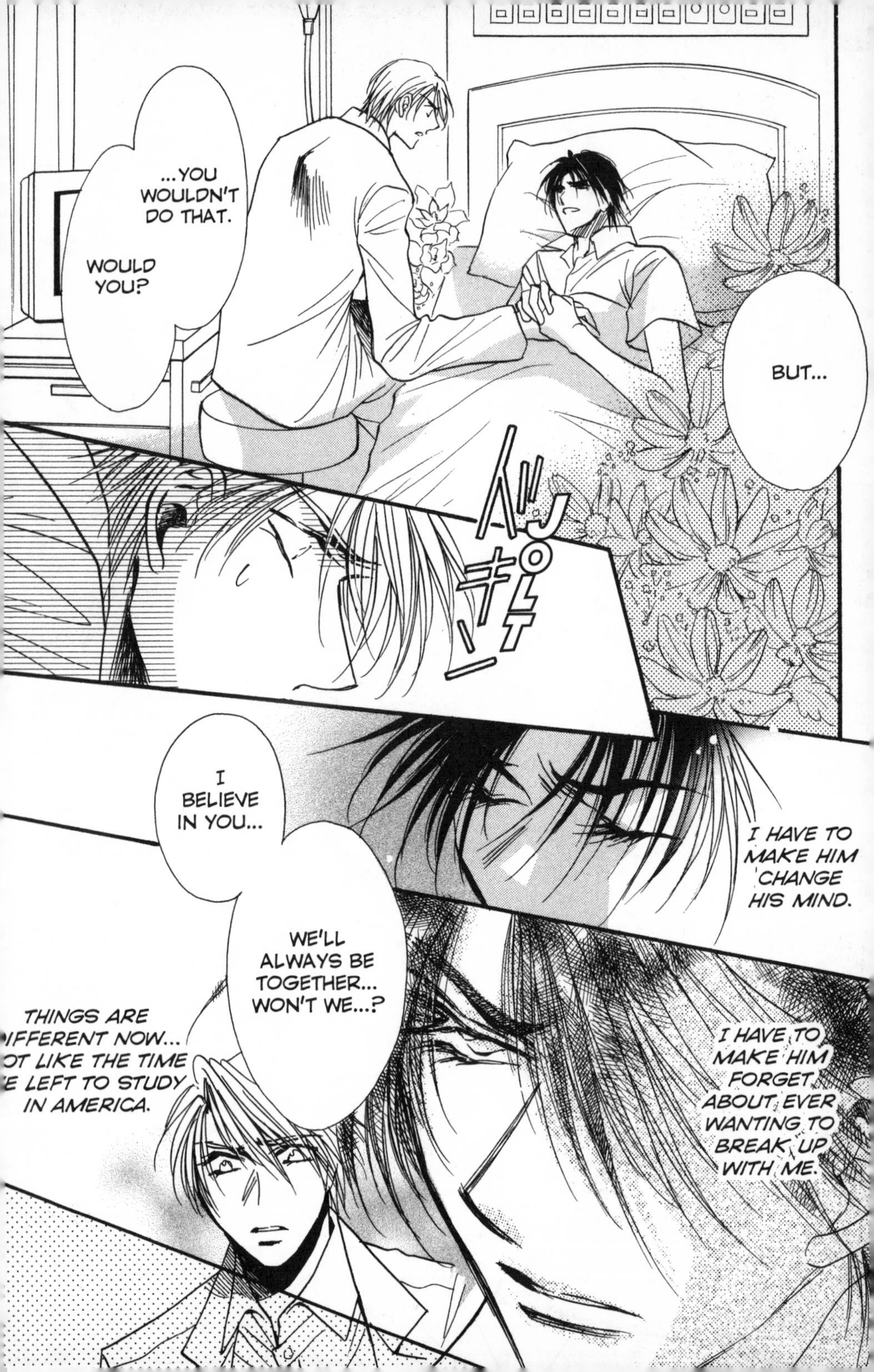
BUT...
...YOU WOULDN'T DO THAT.
WOULD YOU?
JOLT
I BELIEVE IN YOU...
I HAVE TO MAKE HIM CHANGE HIS MIND.
WE'LL ALWAYS BE TOGETHER... WON'T WE...?
I HAVE TO MAKE HIM FORGET ABOUT EVER WANTING TO BREAK UP WITH ME.
THINGS ARE IFFERENT NOW... OT LIKE THE TIME E LEFT TO STUDY IN AMERICA.

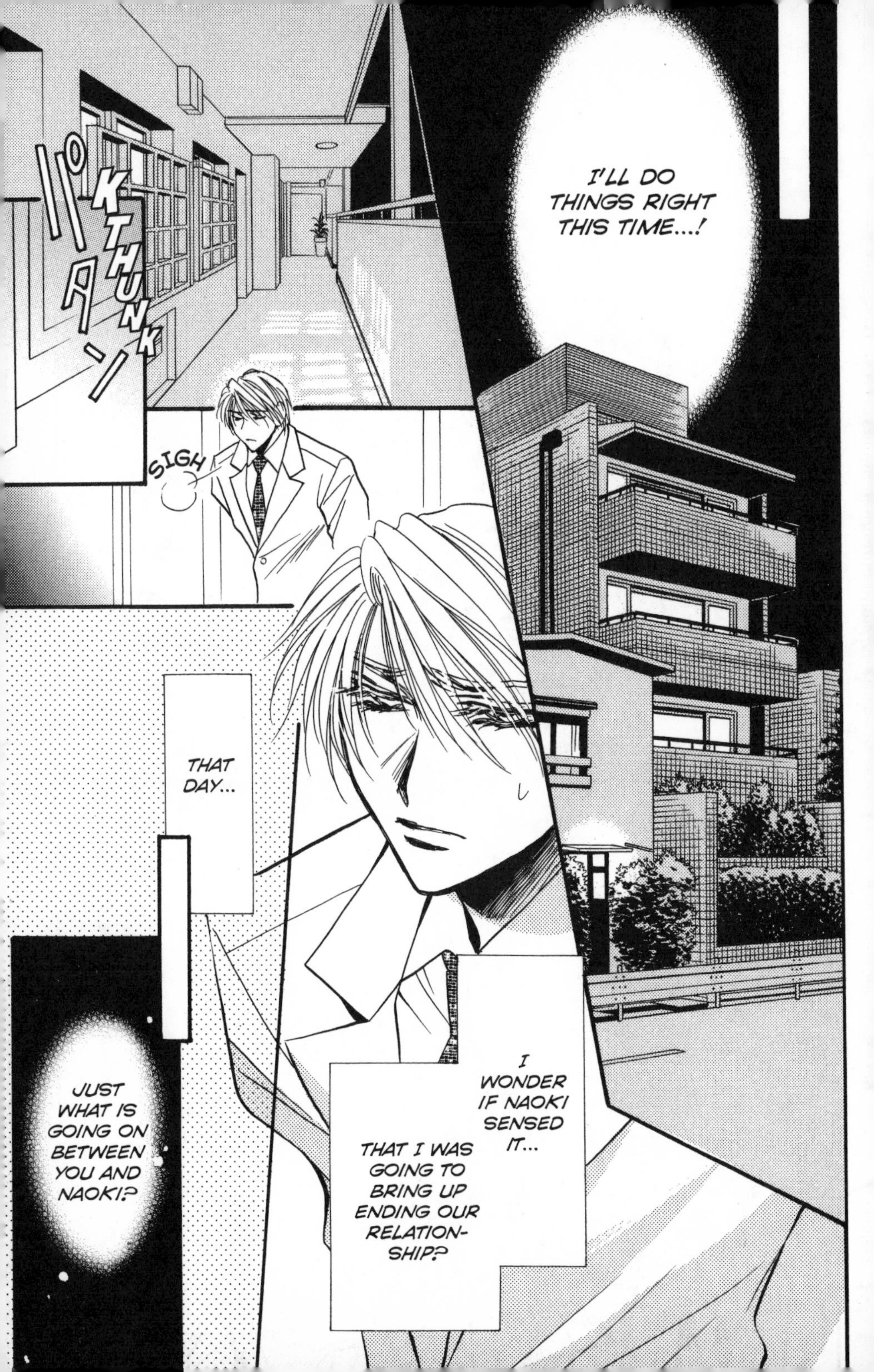
I'LL DO THINGS RIGHT THIS TIME...!
パターン
KTHUNK
SIGH
THAT DAY...
JUST WHAT IS GOING ON BETWEEN YOU AND NAOKI?
I WONDER IF NAOKI SENSED IT...
THAT I WAS GOING TO BRING UP ENDING OUR RELATION-SHIP?

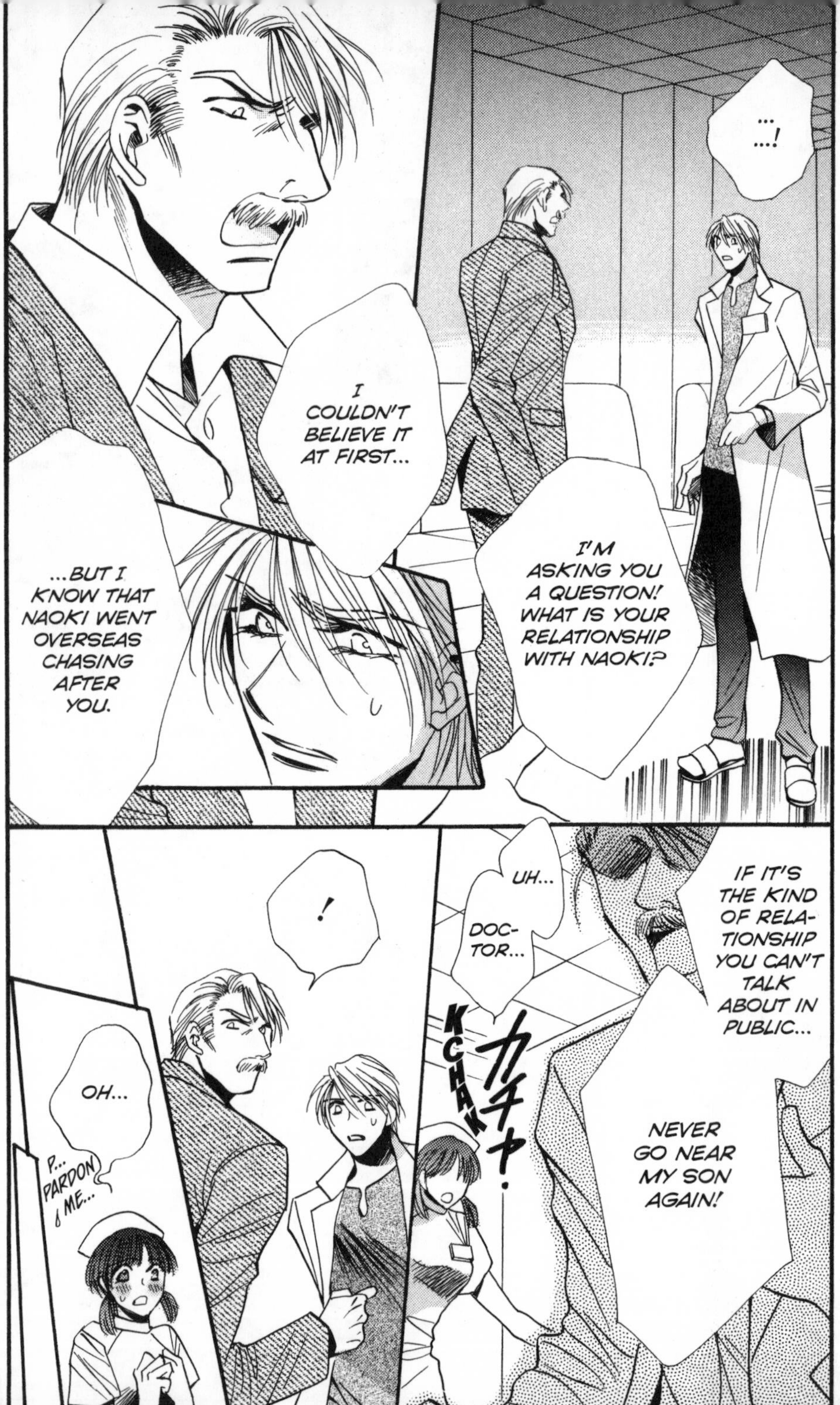
...
...!
I'M ASKING YOU A QUESTION! WHAT IS YOUR RELATIONSHIP WITH NAOKI!?
I COULDN'T BELIEVE IT AT FIRST...
...BUT I KNOW THAT NAOKI WENT OVERSEAS CHASING AFTER YOU.
IF IT'S THE KIND OF RELA-TIONSHIP YOU CAN'T TALK ABOUT IN PUBLIC...
NEVER GO NEAR MY SON AGAIN!
UH...
DOC-TOR...
KCHAK
!
OH...
P... PARDON ME...

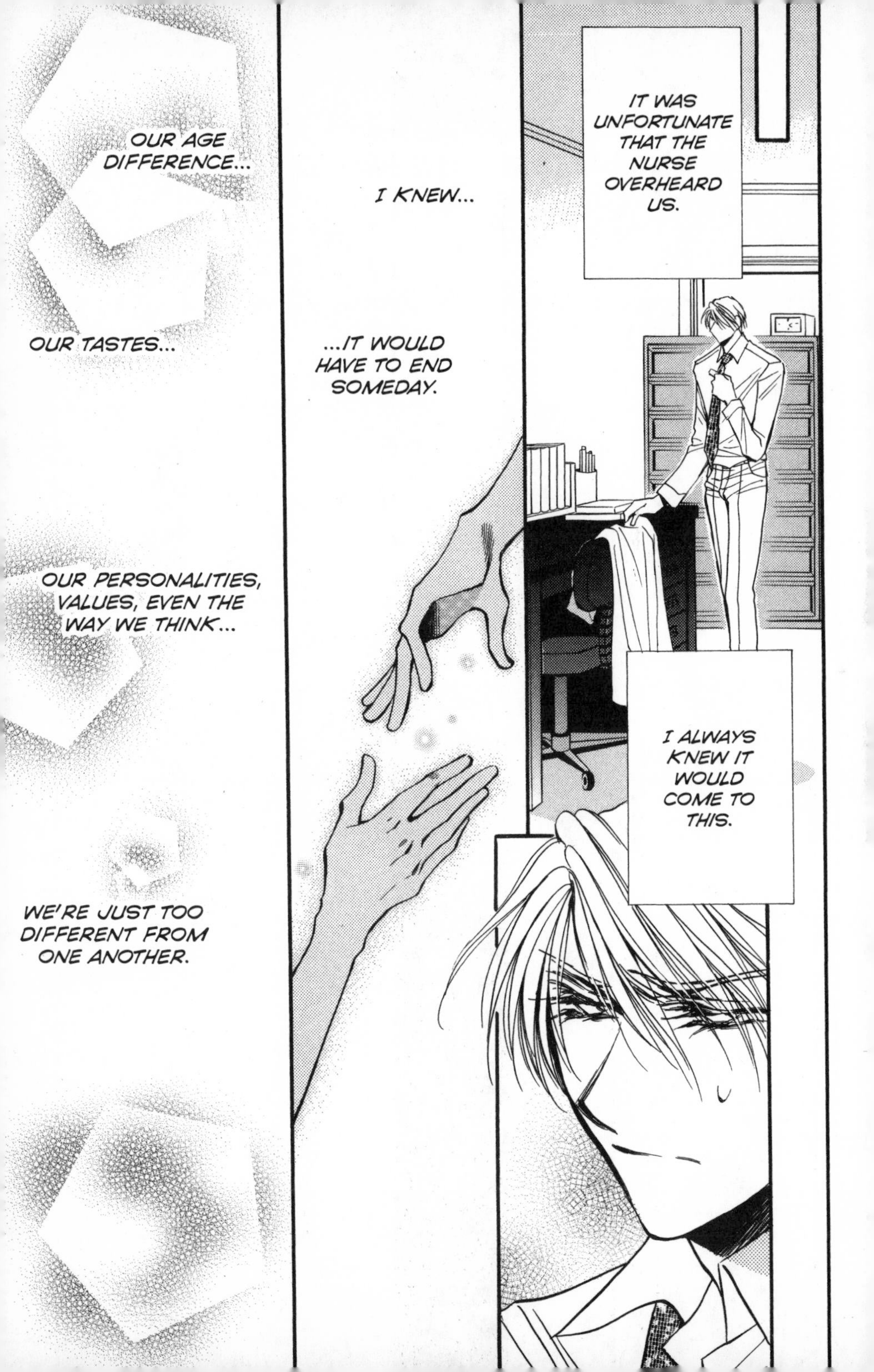
IT WAS UNFORTUNATE THAT THE NURSE OVERHEARD US.
I ALWAYS KNEW IT WOULD COME TO THIS.
I KNEW...
...IT WOULD HAVE TO END SOMEDAY.
OUR AGE DIFFERENCE...
OUR TASTES...
OUR PERSONALITIES, VALUES, EVEN THE WAY WE THINK...
WE'RE JUST TOO DIFFERENT FROM ONE ANOTHER.

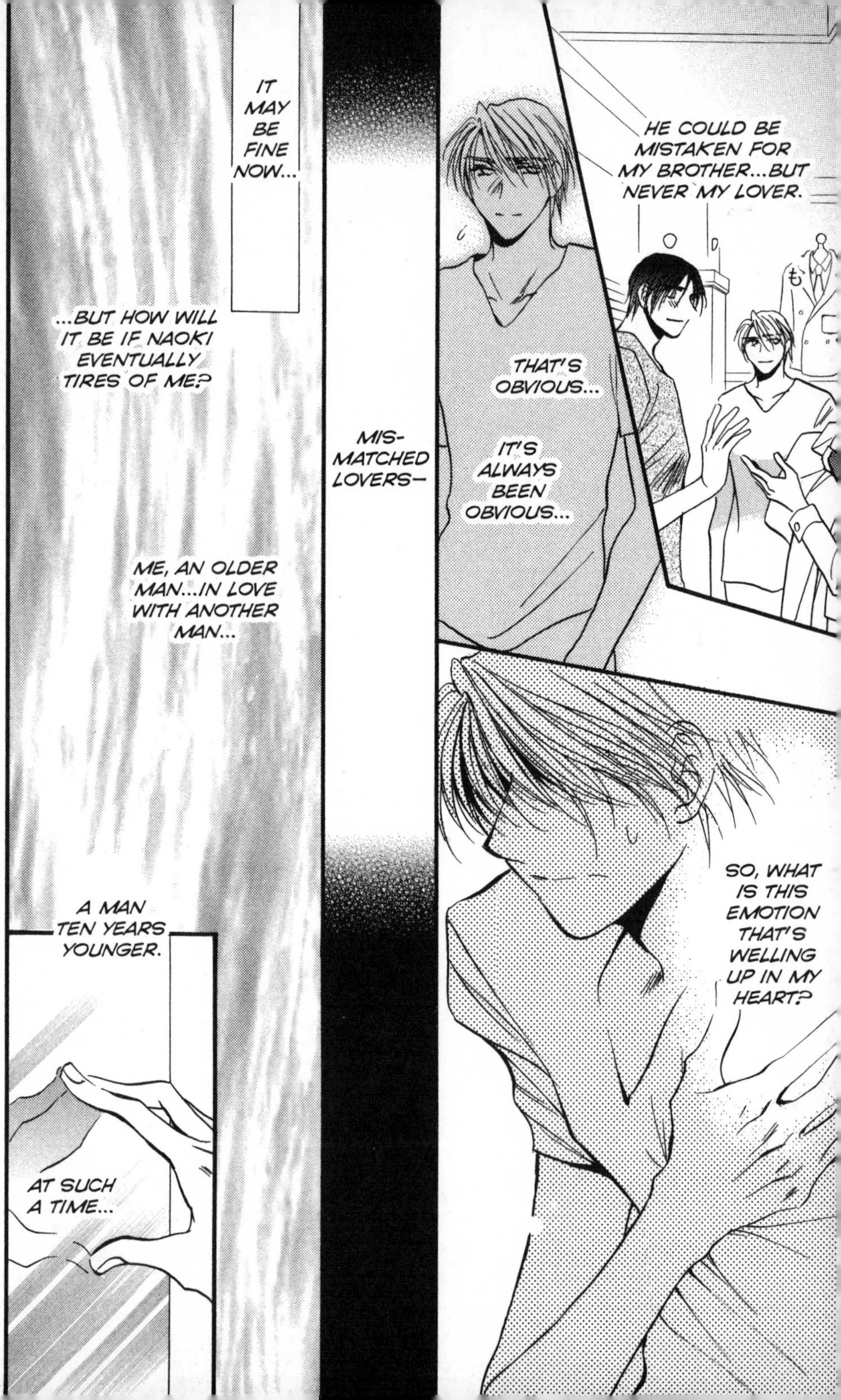
HE COULD BE MISTAKEN FOR MY BROTHER...BUT NEVER MY LOVER.
THAT'S OBVIOUS...
IT'S ALWAYS BEEN OBVIOUS...
MIS-MATCHED LOVERS—
SO, WHAT IS THIS EMOTION THAT'S WELLING UP IN MY HEART?
IT MAY BE FINE NOW...
...BUT HOW WILL IT BE IF NAOKI EVENTUALLY TIRES OF ME?
ME, AN OLDER MAN...IN LOVE WITH ANOTHER MAN...
A MAN TEN YEARS YOUNGER.
AT SUCH A TIME...

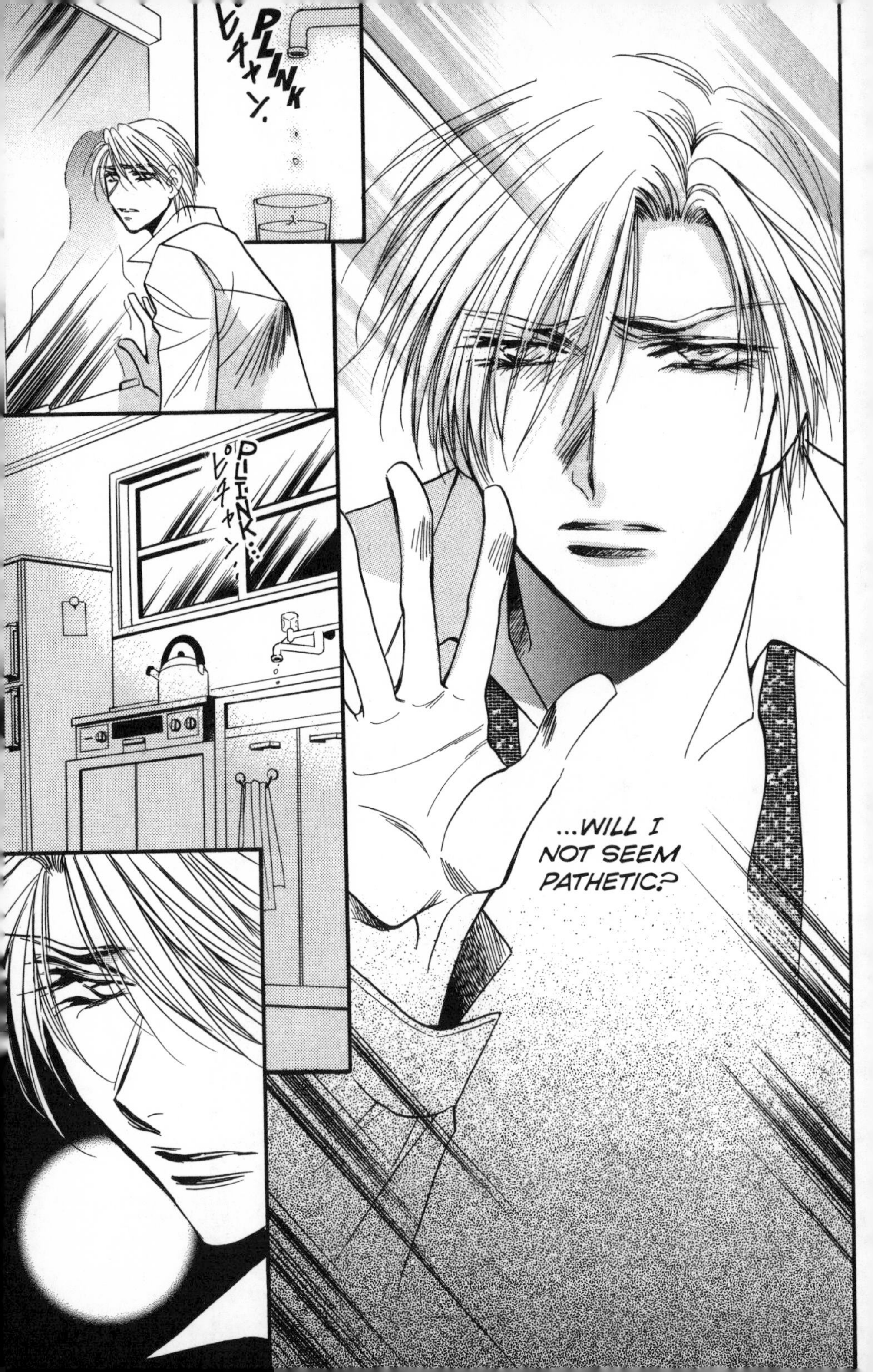
...WILL I NOT SEEM PATHETIC?
PLINK
ピチャン.
PLINK...
ピチャン...

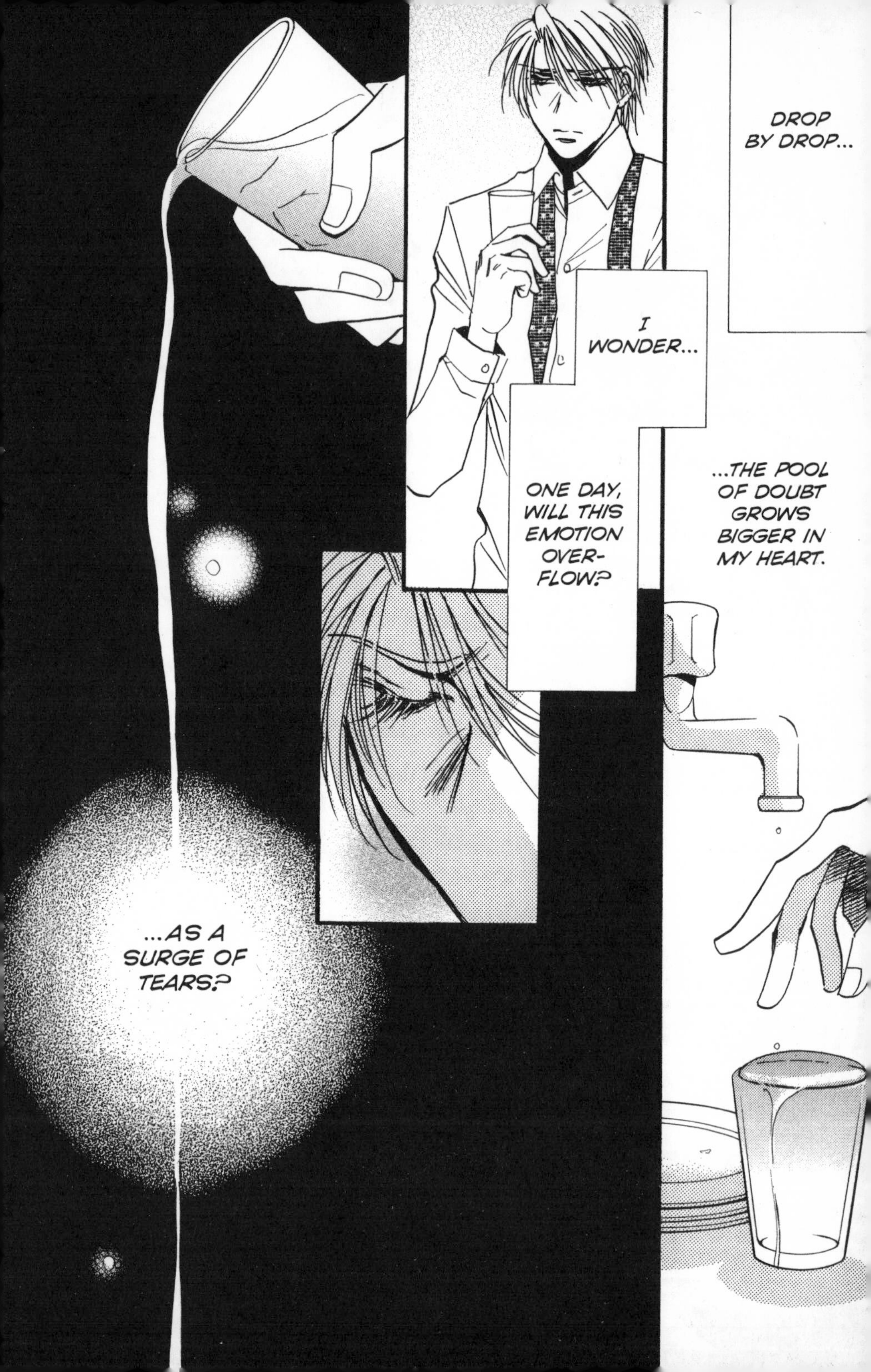
DROP BY DROP...
...THE POOL OF DOUBT GROWS BIGGER IN MY HEART.
I WONDER...
ONE DAY, WILL THIS EMOTION OVER-FLOW?
...AS A SURGE OF TEARS?

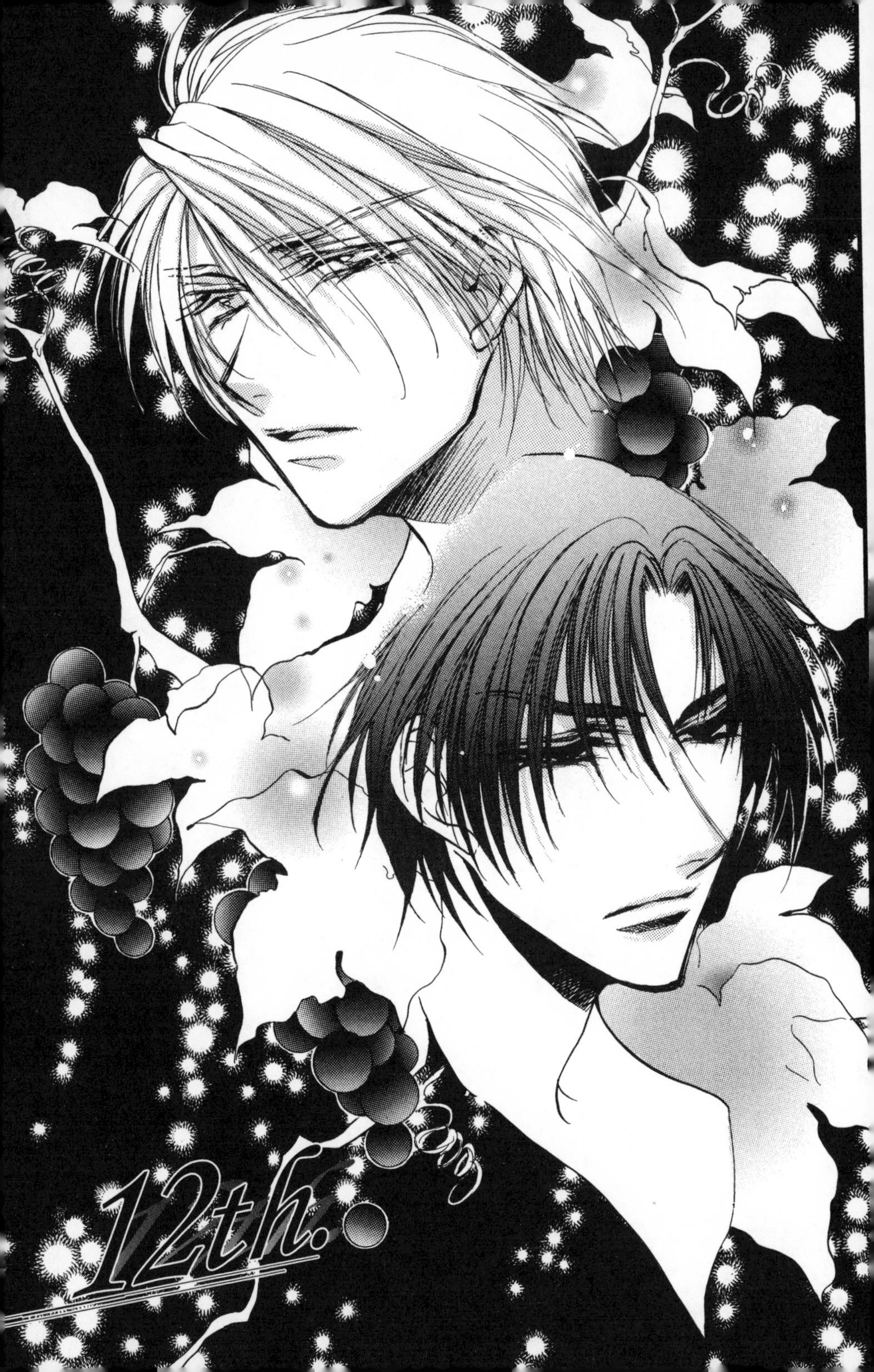
12th.

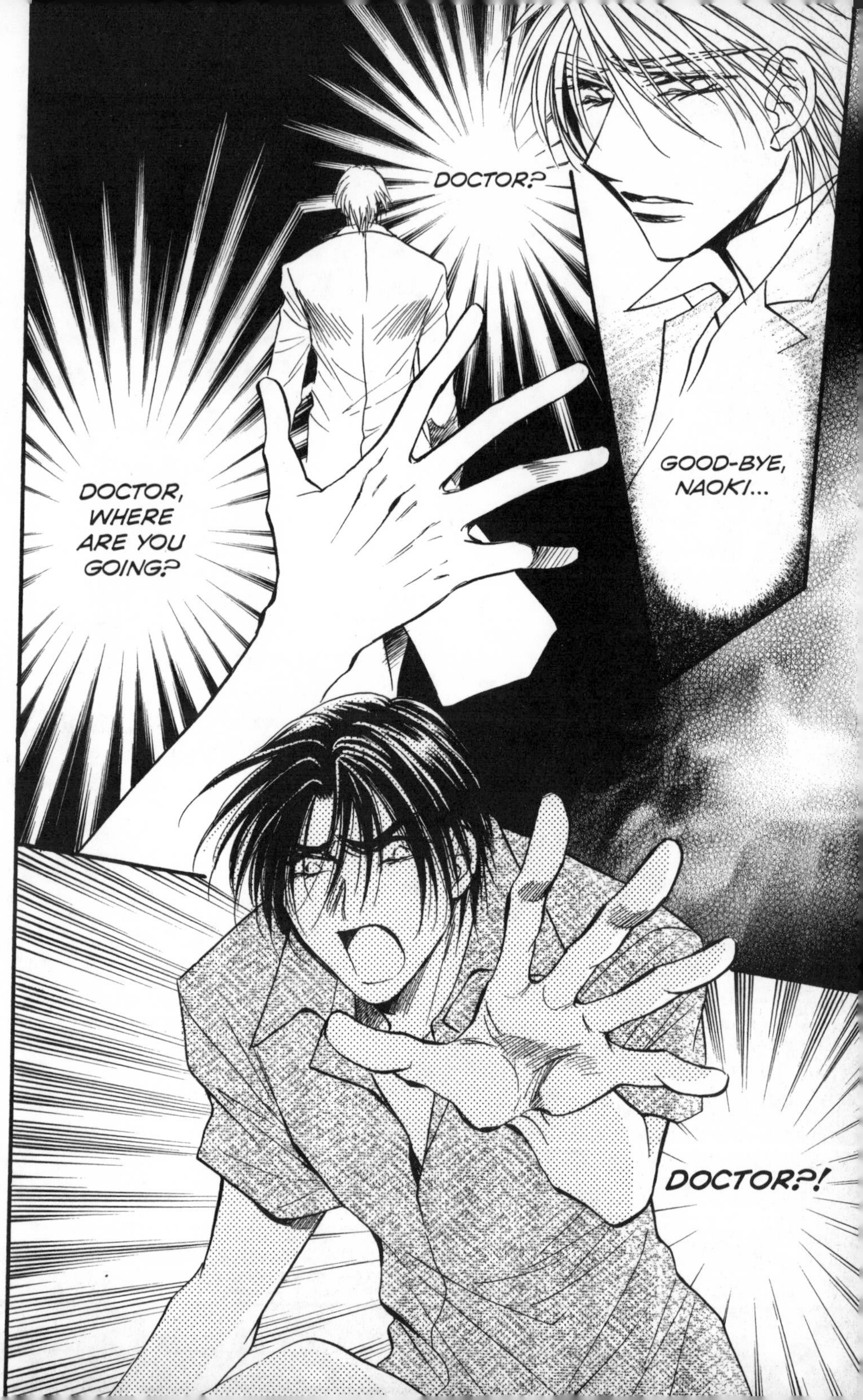
DOCTOR?
GOOD-BYE, NAOKI...
DOCTOR, WHERE ARE YOU GOING?
DOCTOR?!

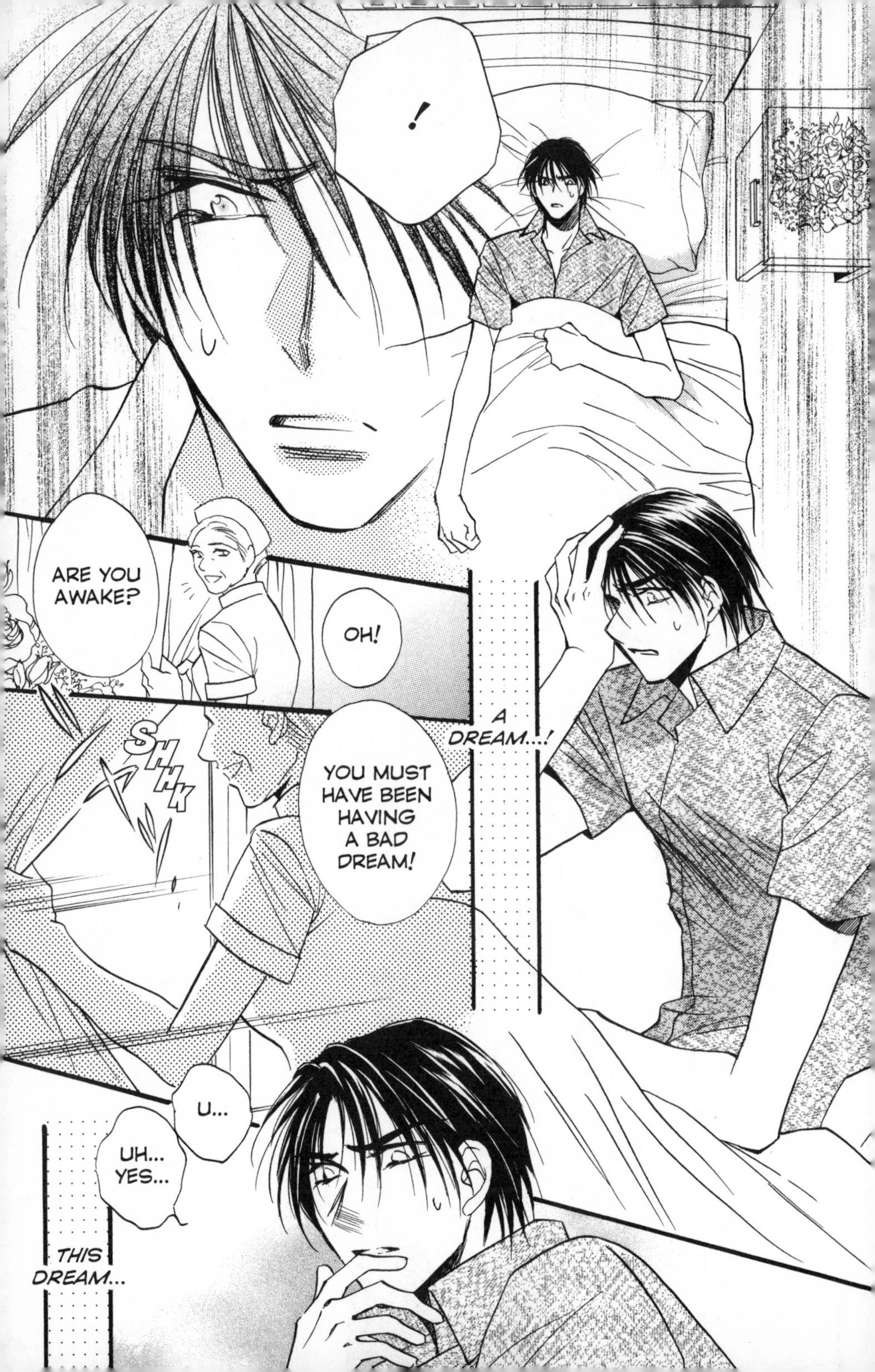
!
A DREAM...!
ARE YOU AWAKE?
OH!
SHHK
YOU MUST HAVE BEEN HAVING A BAD DREAM!
U...
UH... YES...
THIS DREAM...

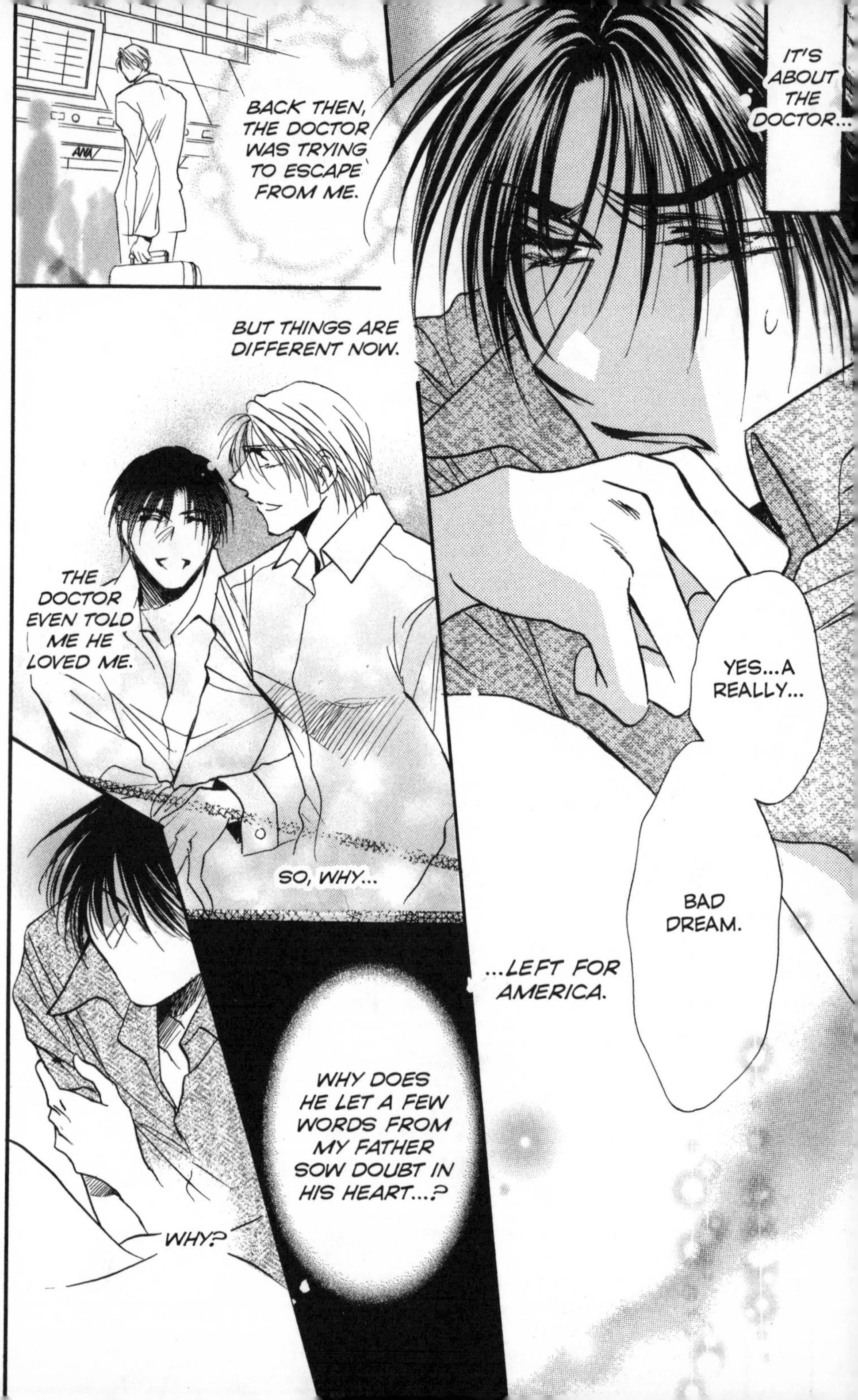
IT'S ABOUT THE DOCTOR...
YES...A REALLY...
BAD DREAM.
BACK THEN, THE DOCTOR WAS TRYING TO ESCAPE FROM ME.
ANA
BUT THINGS ARE DIFFERENT NOW.
THE DOCTOR EVEN TOLD ME HE LOVED ME.
SO, WHY...
...LEFT FOR AMERICA.
WHY DOES HE LET A FEW WORDS FROM MY FATHER SOW DOUBT IN HIS HEART...?
WHY?

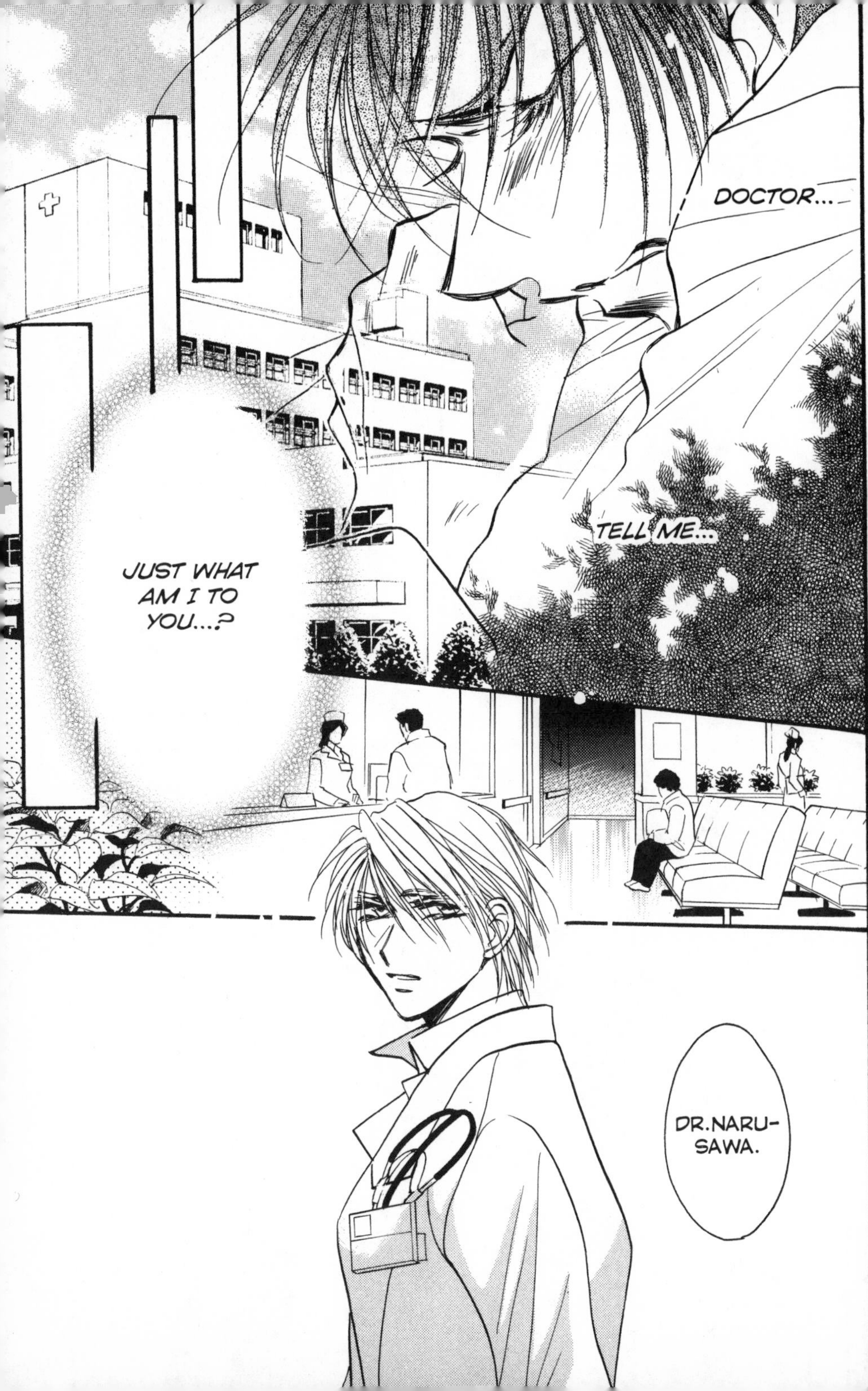
DOCTOR...
TELL ME...
JUST WHAT AM I TO YOU...?
DR.NARU-SAWA.

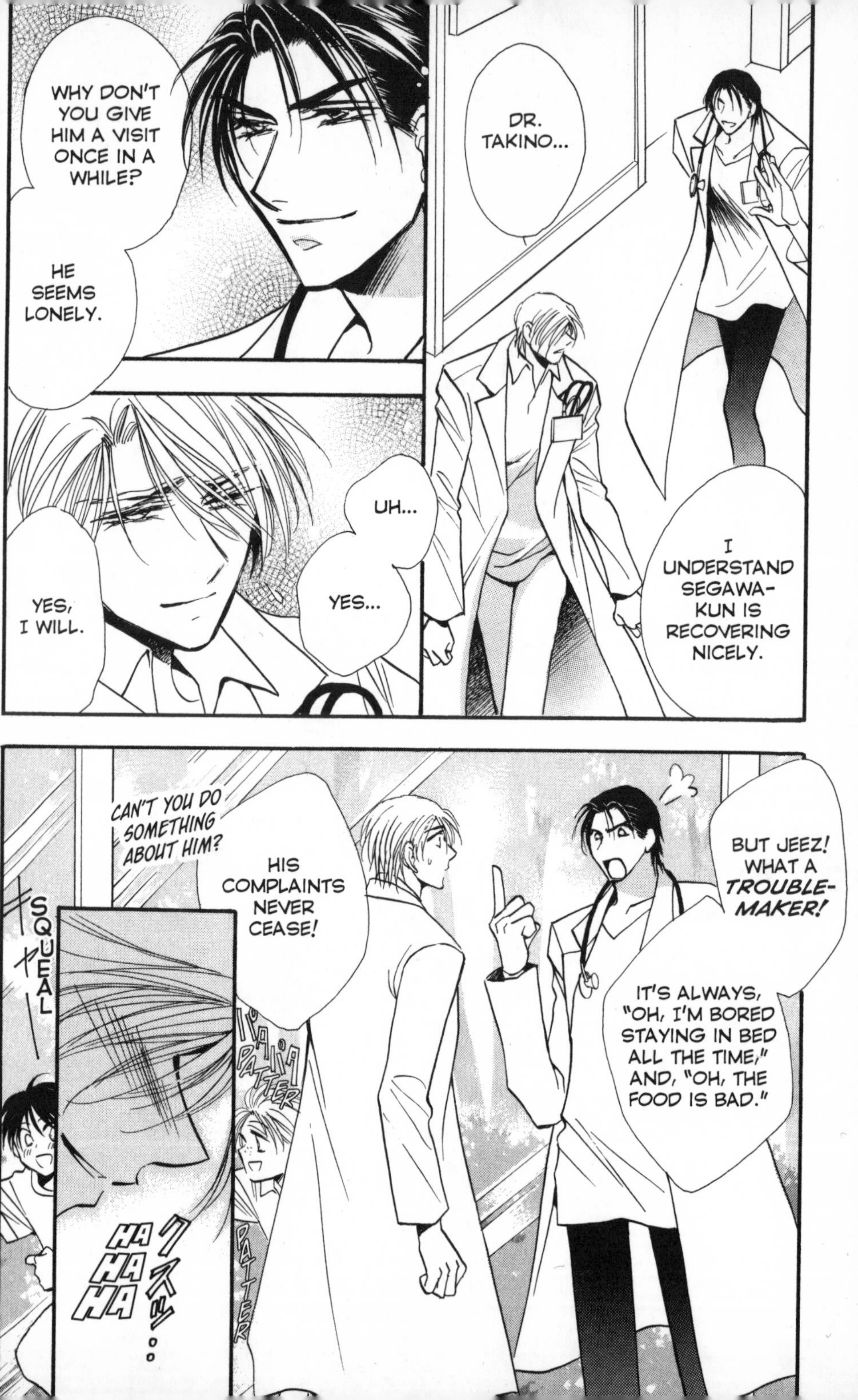
DR. TAKINO...
I UNDERSTAND SEGAWA-KUN IS RECOVERING NICELY.
WHY DON'T YOU GIVE HIM A VISIT ONCE IN A WHILE?
HE SEEMS LONELY.
UH...
YES...
YES, I WILL.
BUT JEEZ! WHAT A TROUBLE-MAKER!
IT'S ALWAYS, "OH, I'M BORED STAYING IN BED ALL THE TIME," AND, "OH, THE FOOD IS BAD."
HIS COMPLAINTS NEVER CEASE!
CAN'T YOU DO SOMETHING ABOUT HIM?
PATTER
PATTER
SQUEAL
HA HA HA

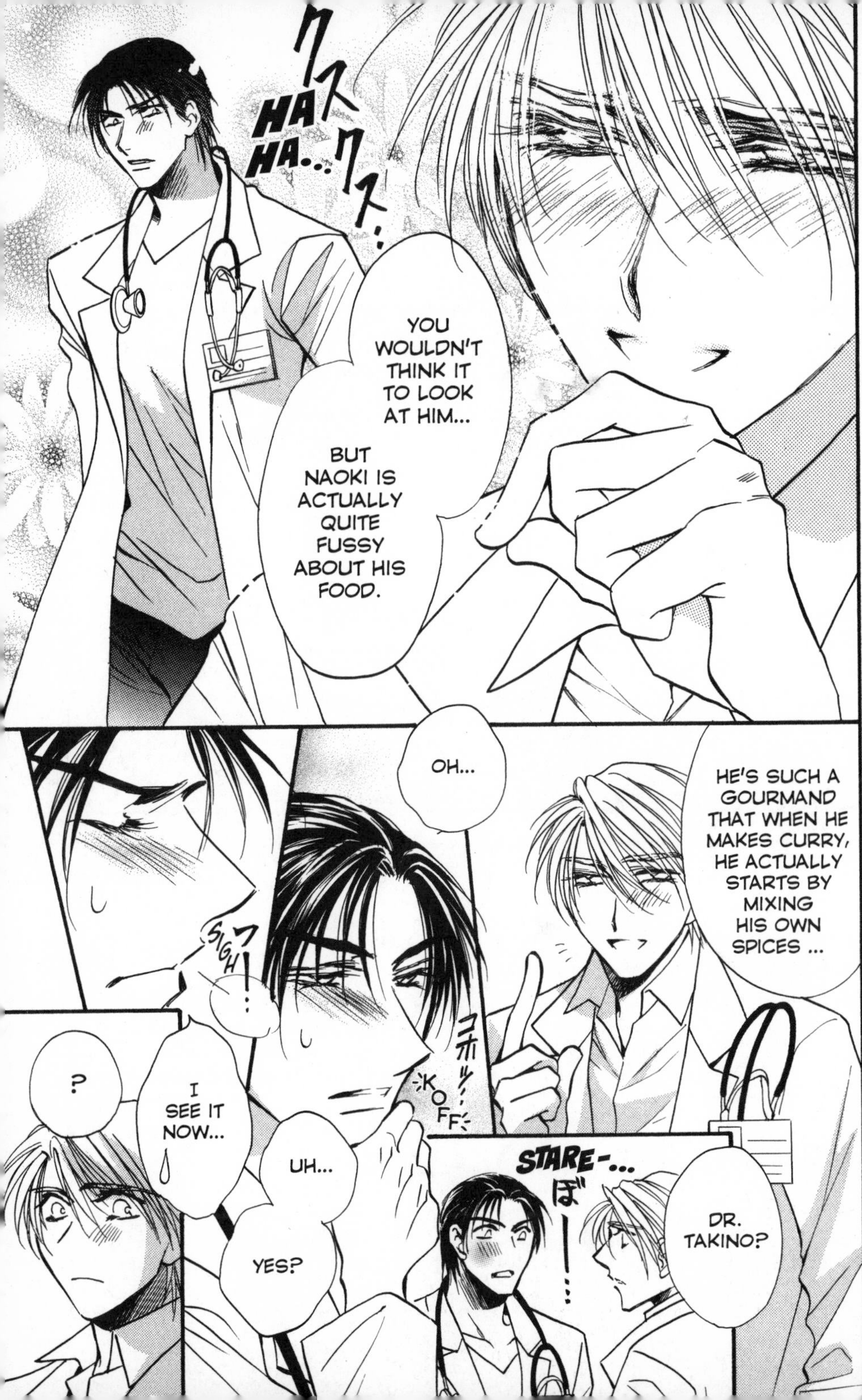
HA HA...
クスクス...
YOU WOULDN'T THINK IT TO LOOK AT HIM...
BUT NAOKI IS ACTUALLY QUITE FUSSY ABOUT HIS FOOD.
HE'S SUCH A GOURMAND THAT WHEN HE MAKES CURRY, HE ACTUALLY STARTS BY MIXING HIS OWN SPICES ...
OH...
SIGH
コホッ
KOFF
STARE-...
ぼー
DR. TAKINO?
UH...
YES?
I SEE IT NOW...
?

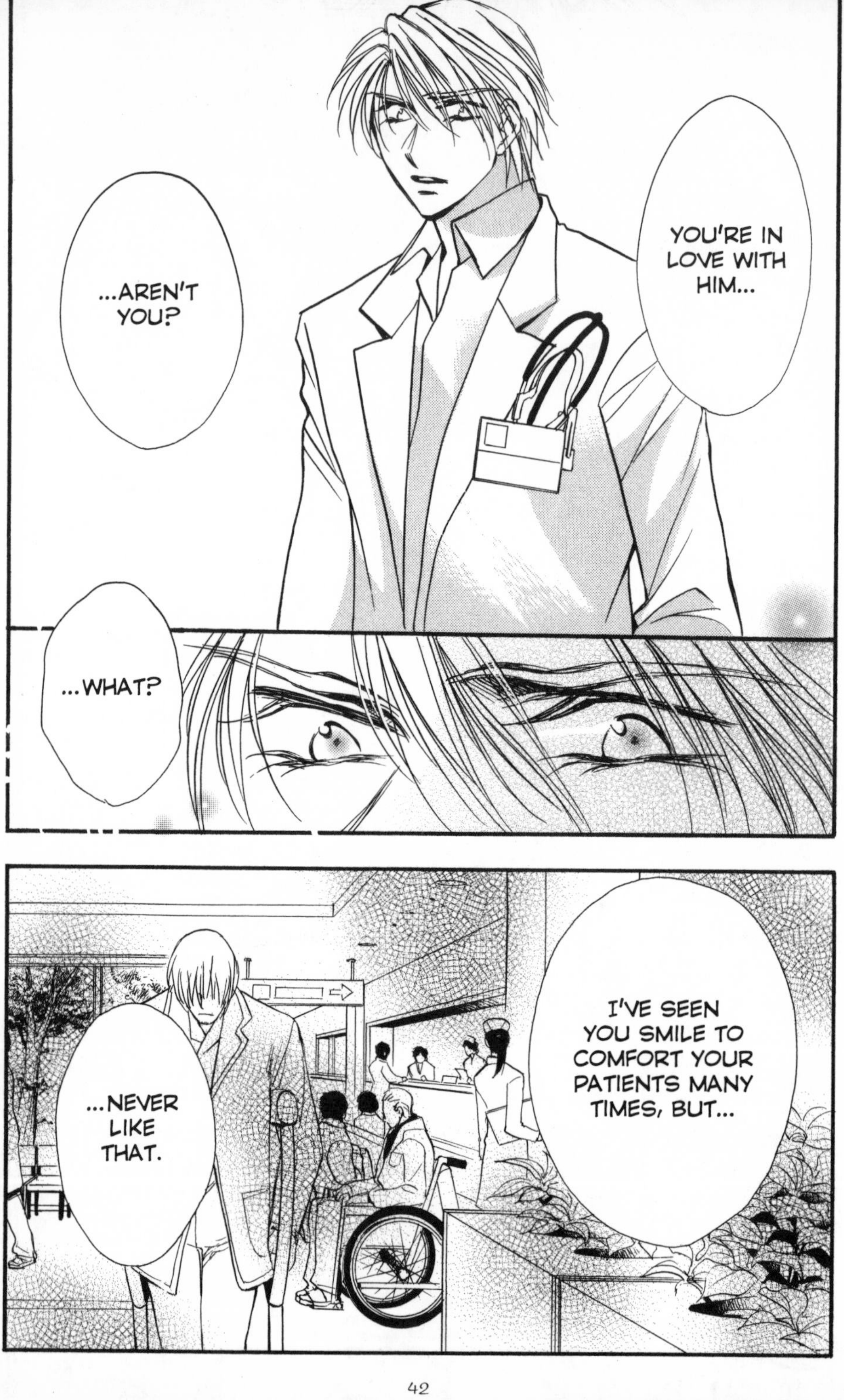
YOU'RE IN LOVE WITH HIM...
...AREN'T YOU?
...WHAT?
I'VE SEEN YOU SMILE TO COMFORT YOUR PATIENTS MANY TIMES, BUT...
...NEVER LIKE THAT.

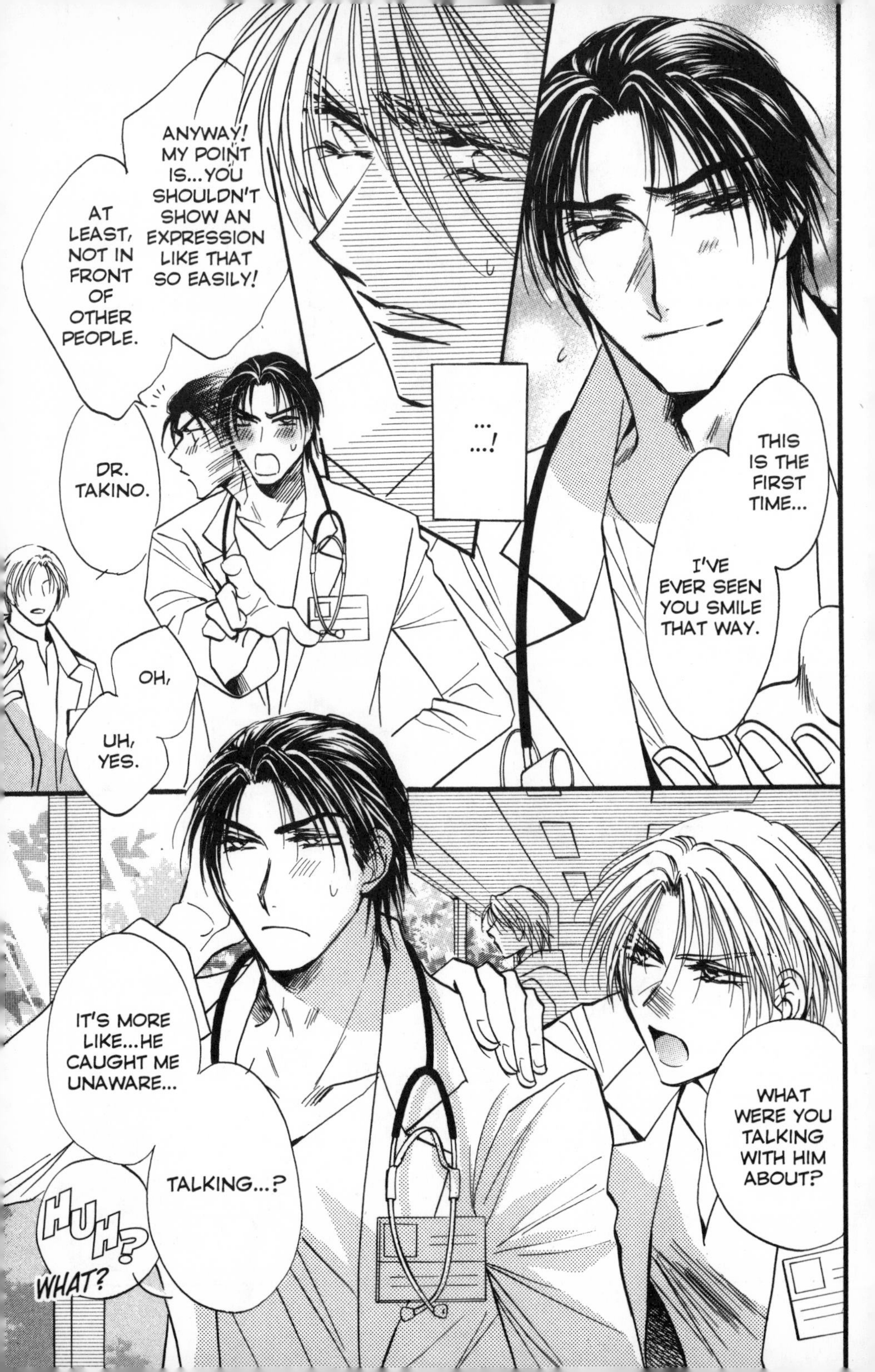
THIS IS THE FIRST TIME...
I'VE EVER SEEN YOU SMILE THAT WAY.
... ...!
ANYWAY! MY POINT IS...YOU SHOULDN'T SHOW AN EXPRESSION LIKE THAT SO EASILY!
AT LEAST, NOT IN FRONT OF OTHER PEOPLE.
DR. TAKINO.
OH,
UH, YES.
WHAT WERE YOU TALKING WITH HIM ABOUT?
IT'S MORE LIKE...HE CAUGHT ME UNAWARE...
TALKING...?
HUH?
WHAT?

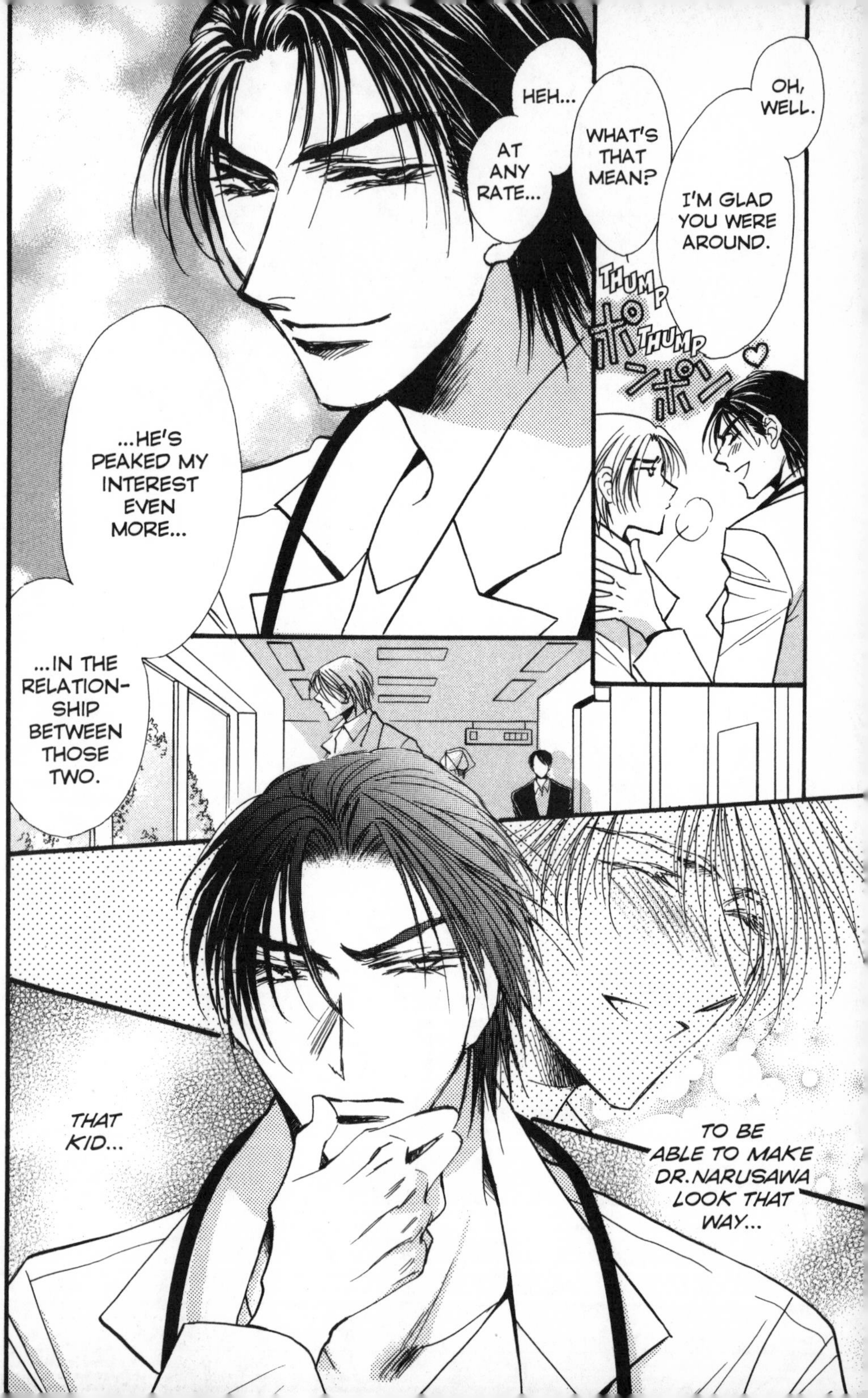
OH, WELL.
I'M GLAD YOU WERE AROUND.
WHAT'S THAT MEAN?
THUMP THUMP
HEH...
AT ANY RATE...
...HE'S PEAKED MY INTEREST EVEN MORE...
...IN THE RELATION-SHIP BETWEEN THOSE TWO.
TO BE ABLE TO MAKE DR.NARUSAWA LOOK THAT WAY...
THAT KID...

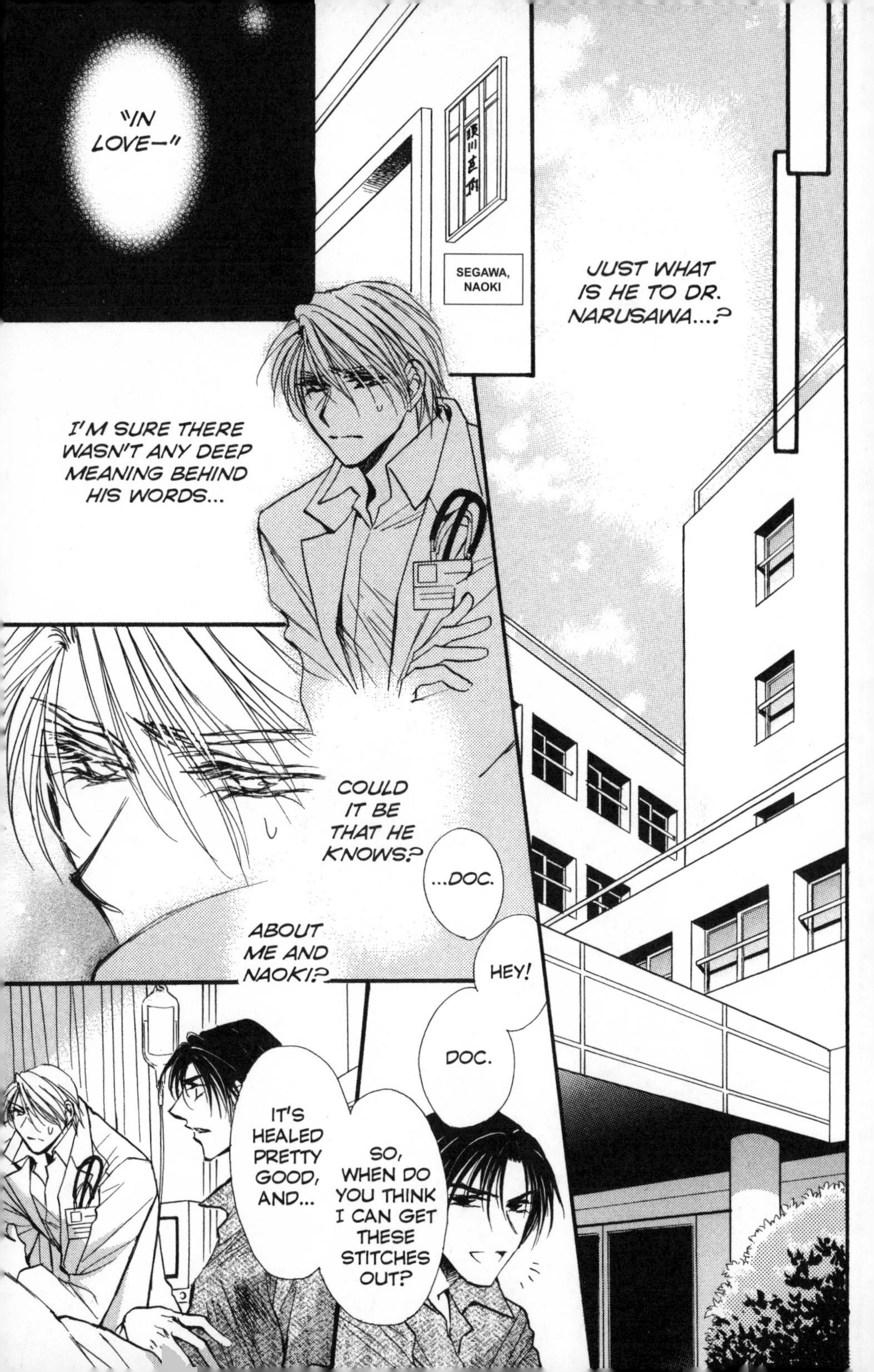
SEGAWA, NAOKI
JUST WHAT IS HE TO DR. NARUSAWA...?
"IN LOVE—"
I'M SURE THERE WASN'T ANY DEEP MEANING BEHIND HIS WORDS...
COULD IT BE THAT HE KNOWS?
ABOUT ME AND NAOKI?
...DOC.
HEY!
DOC.
IT'S HEALED PRETTY GOOD, AND...
SO, WHEN DO YOU THINK I CAN GET THESE STITCHES OUT?

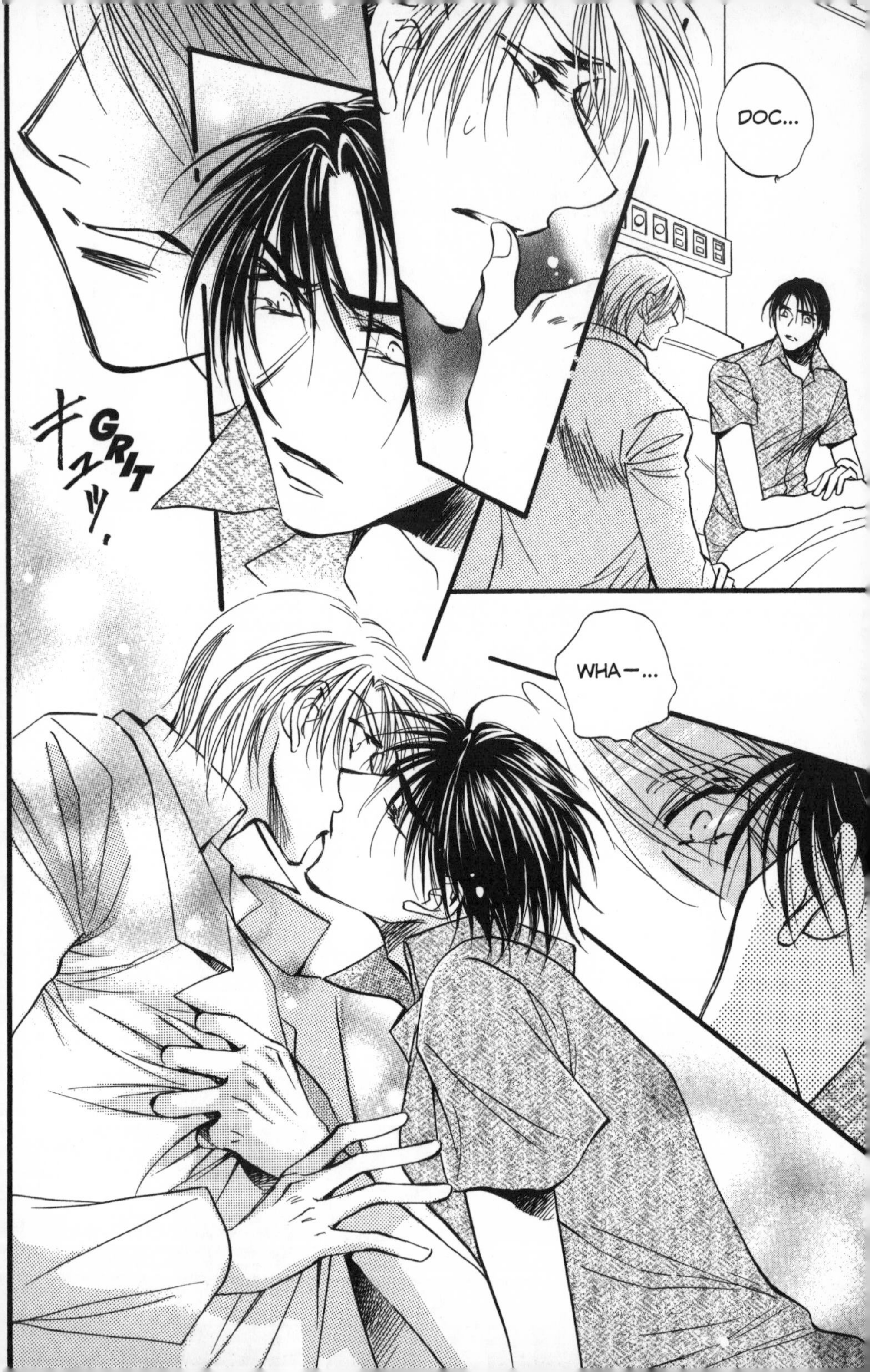
DOC...
キュッ
GRIT
WHA—...

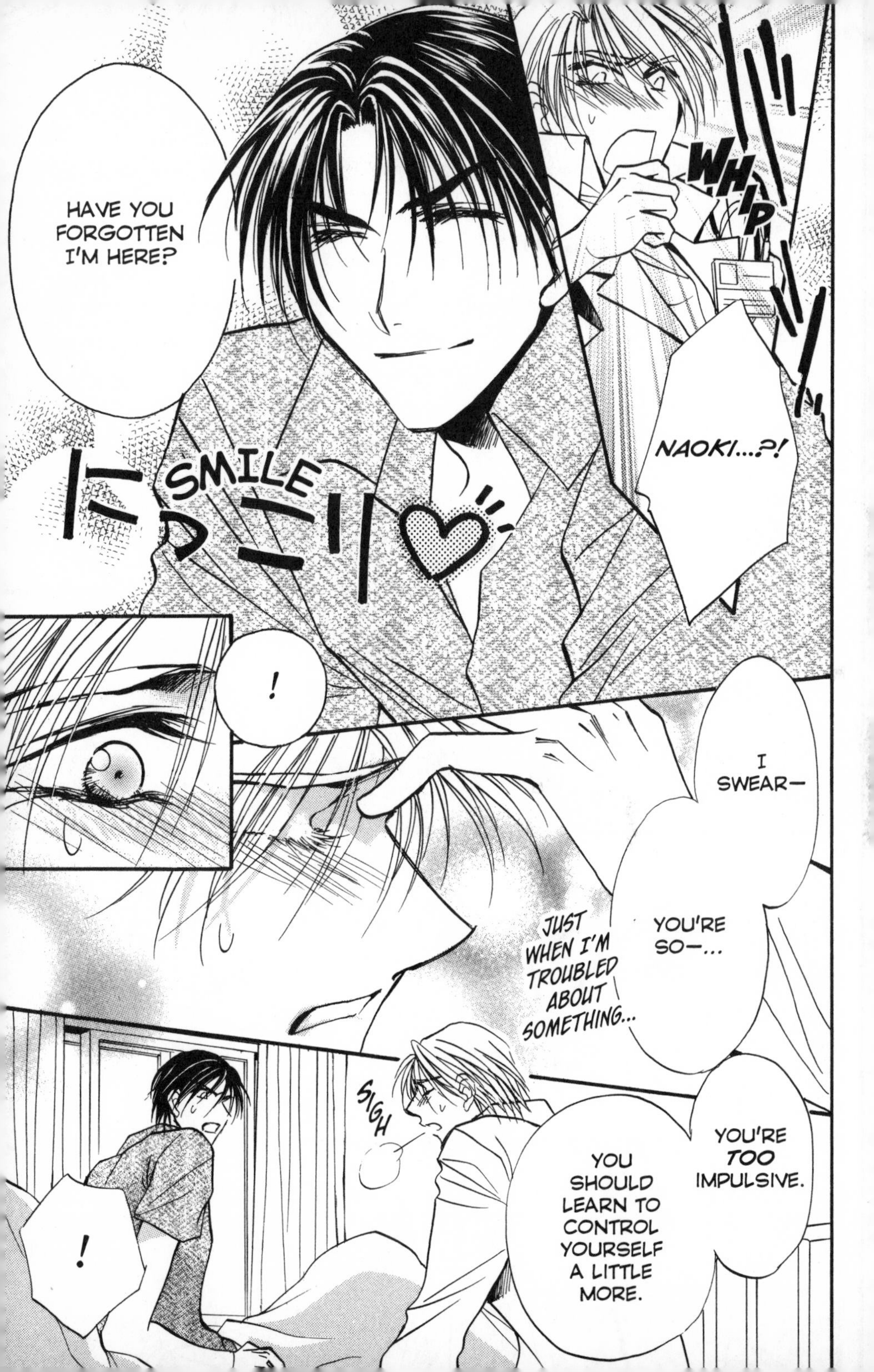
WHIP
NAOKI...?!
HAVE YOU FORGOTTEN I'M HERE?
SMILE
I SWEAR—
YOU'RE SO—...
JUST WHEN I'M TROUBLED ABOUT SOMETHING...
!
YOU'RE *TOO* IMPULSIVE.
YOU SHOULD LEARN TO CONTROL YOURSELF A LITTLE MORE.
SIGH
!

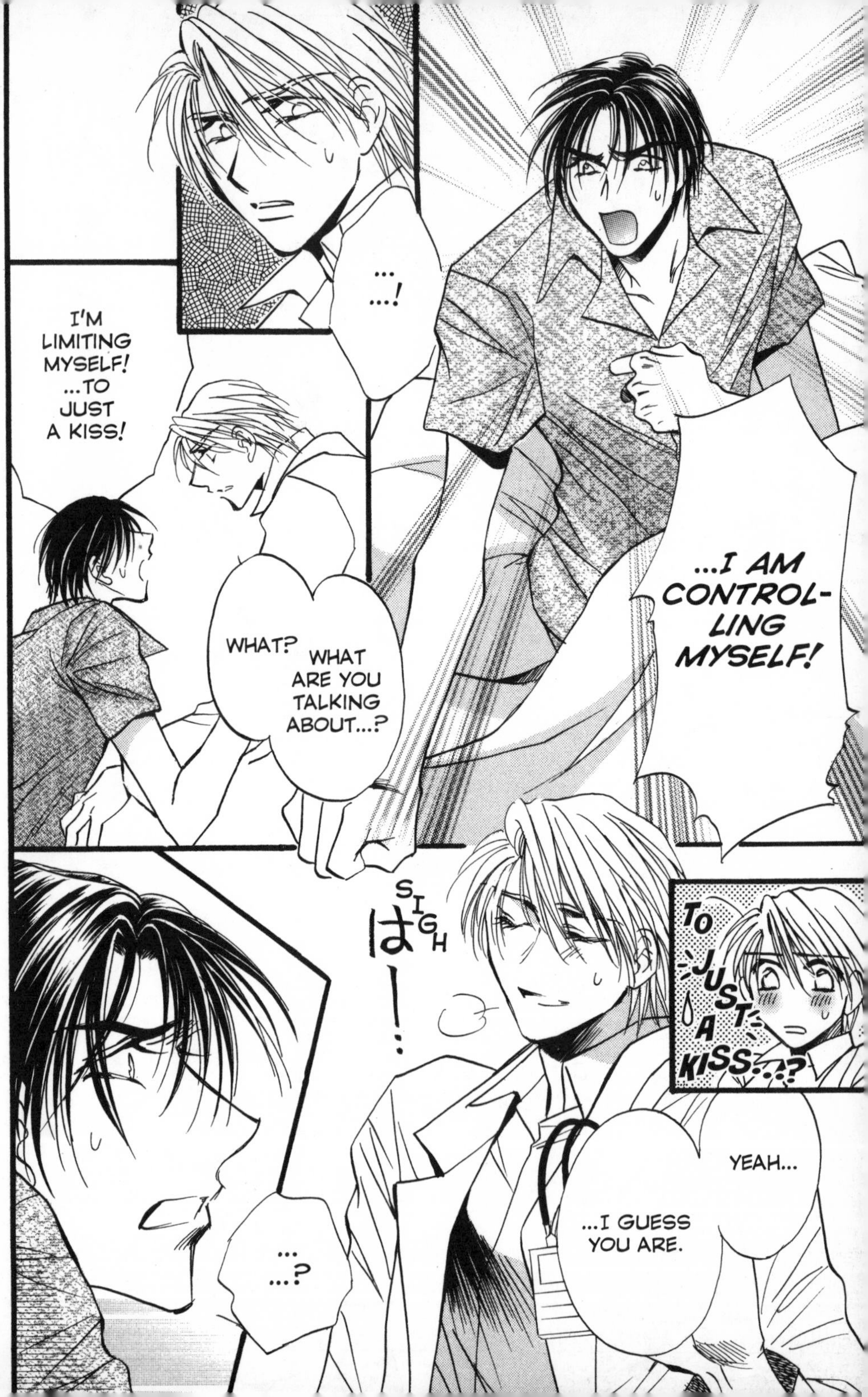
...I AM CONTROL-LING MYSELF!
... ...!
I'M LIMITING MYSELF! ...TO JUST A KISS!
WHAT? WHAT ARE YOU TALKING ABOUT...?
TO JUST A KISS...?
は SIGH
YEAH...
...I GUESS YOU ARE.
... ...?

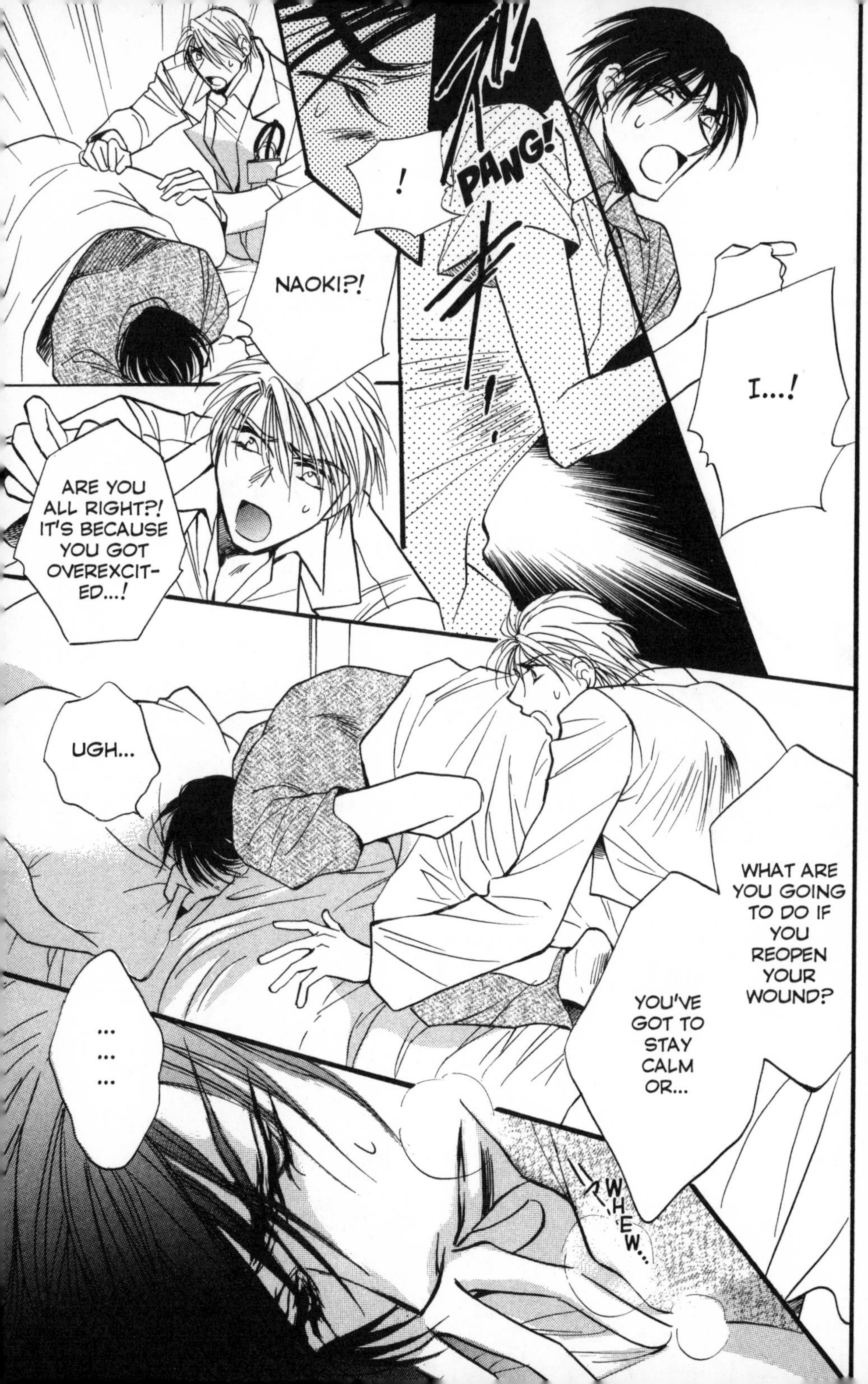
PANG!
I...!
!
NAOKI?!
ARE YOU ALL RIGHT?! IT'S BECAUSE YOU GOT OVEREXCIT-ED...!
WHAT ARE YOU GOING TO DO IF YOU REOPEN YOUR WOUND?
YOU'VE GOT TO STAY CALM OR...
UGH...
WHEW...
... ...

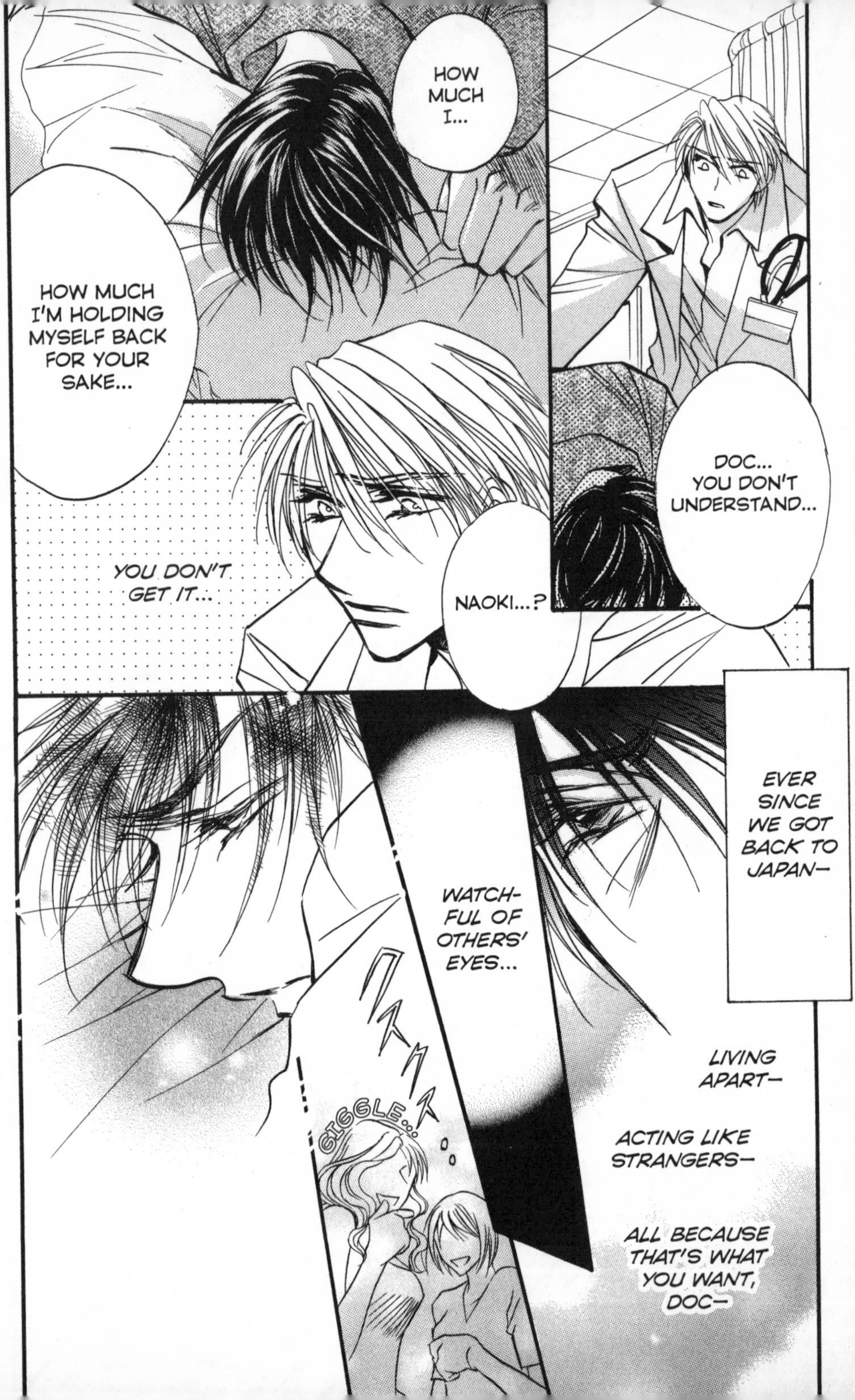
DOC... YOU DON'T UNDERSTAND...
HOW MUCH I...
HOW MUCH I'M HOLDING MYSELF BACK FOR YOUR SAKE...
NAOKI...?
YOU DON'T GET IT...
EVER SINCE WE GOT BACK TO JAPAN—
WATCHFUL OF OTHERS' EYES...
GIGGLE...
LIVING APART—
ACTING LIKE STRANGERS—
ALL BECAUSE THAT'S WHAT YOU WANT, DOC—

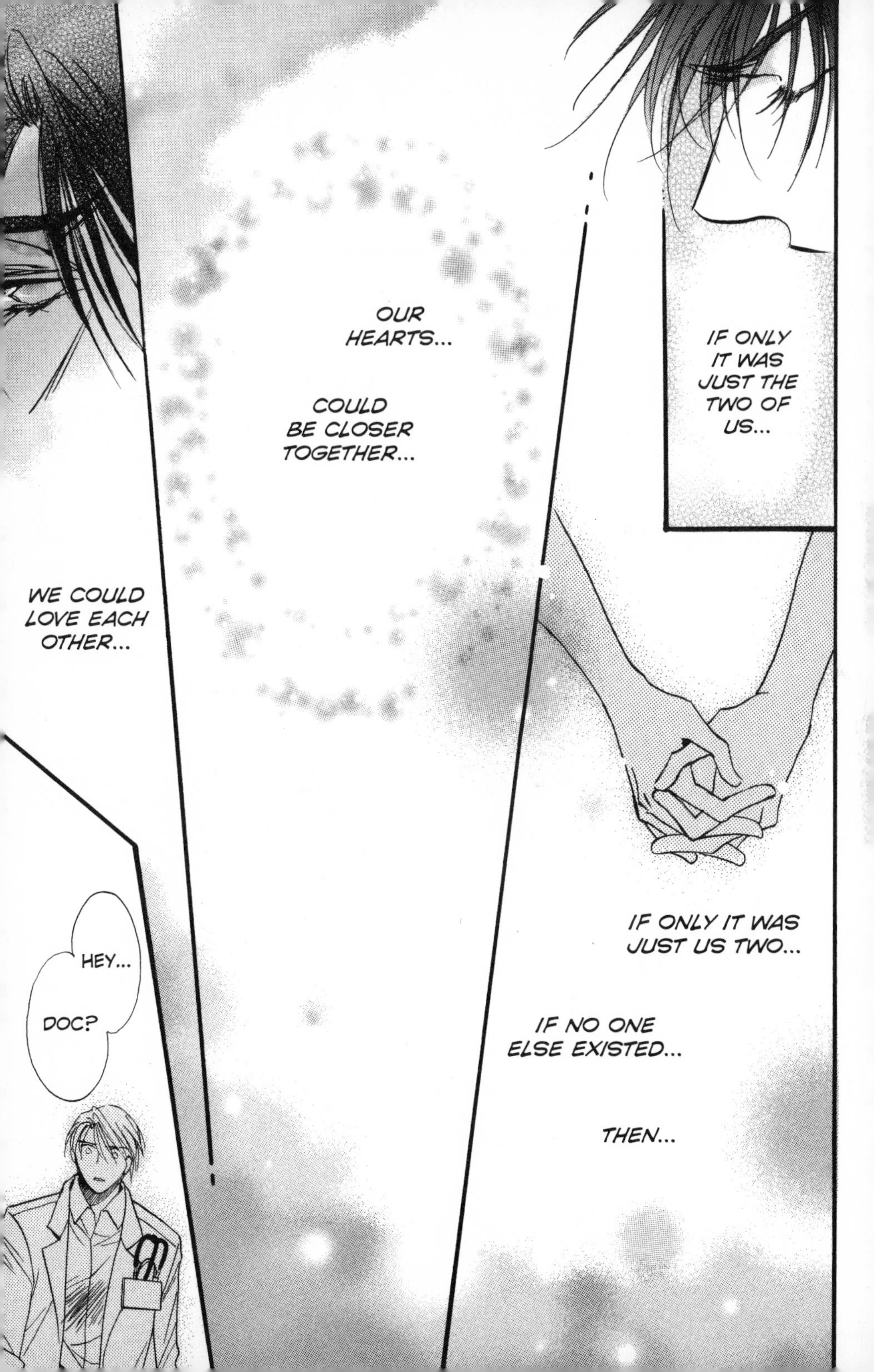
IF ONLY IT WAS JUST THE TWO OF US...
IF ONLY IT WAS JUST US TWO...
IF NO ONE ELSE EXISTED...
THEN...
OUR HEARTS...
COULD BE CLOSER TOGETHER...
WE COULD LOVE EACH OTHER...
HEY...
DOC?

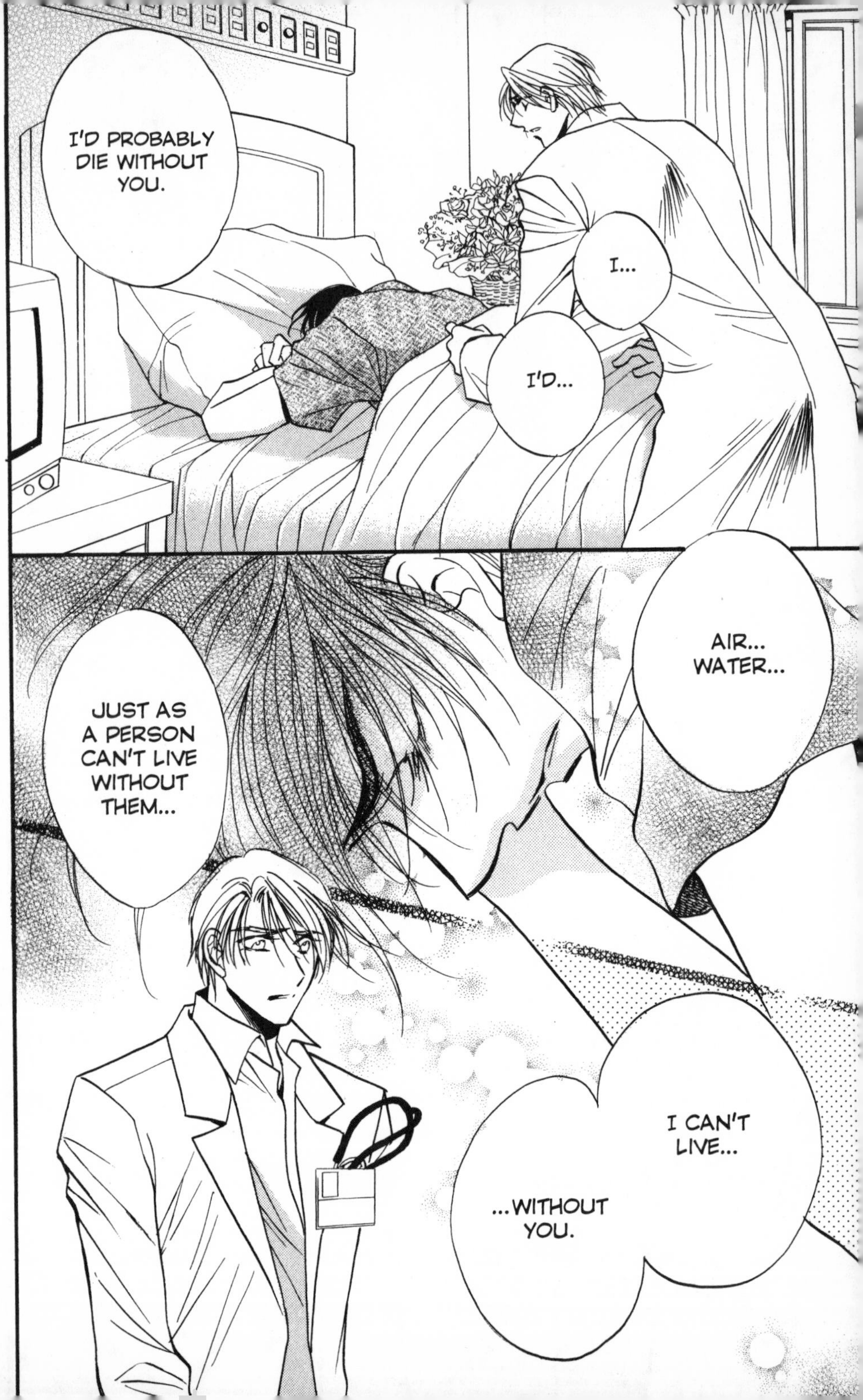
I...
I'D...
I'D PROBABLY DIE WITHOUT YOU.
AIR... WATER...
JUST AS A PERSON CAN'T LIVE WITHOUT THEM...
I CAN'T LIVE...
...WITHOUT YOU.

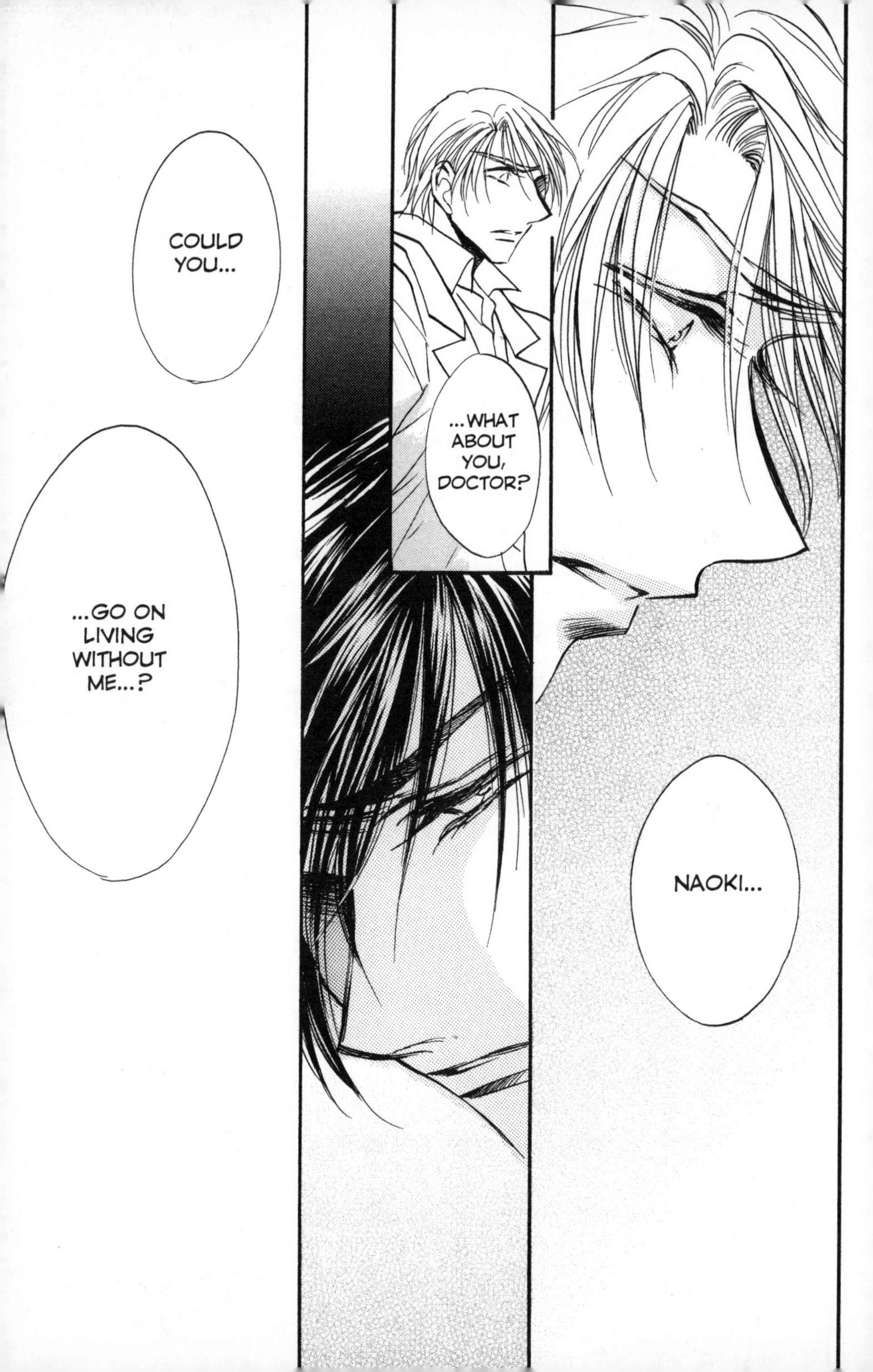
NAOKI...
...WHAT ABOUT YOU, DOCTOR?
COULD YOU...
...GO ON LIVING WITHOUT ME...?

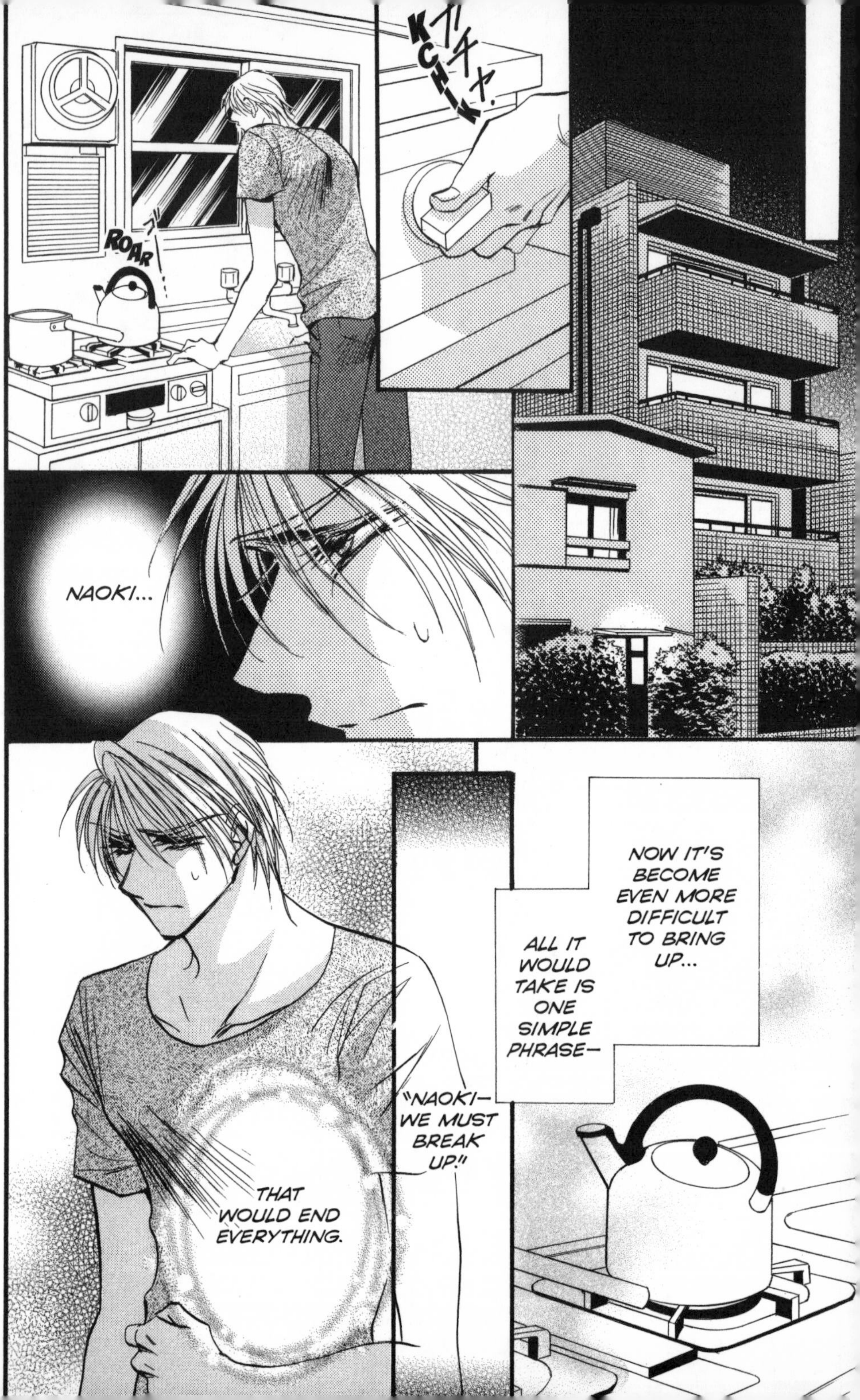
KCHIK
ガチャ.
ROAR
ゴ
NAOKI...
NOW IT'S BECOME EVEN MORE DIFFICULT TO BRING UP...
ALL IT WOULD TAKE IS ONE SIMPLE PHRASE—
"NAOKI— WE MUST BREAK UP."
THAT WOULD END EVERYTHING.

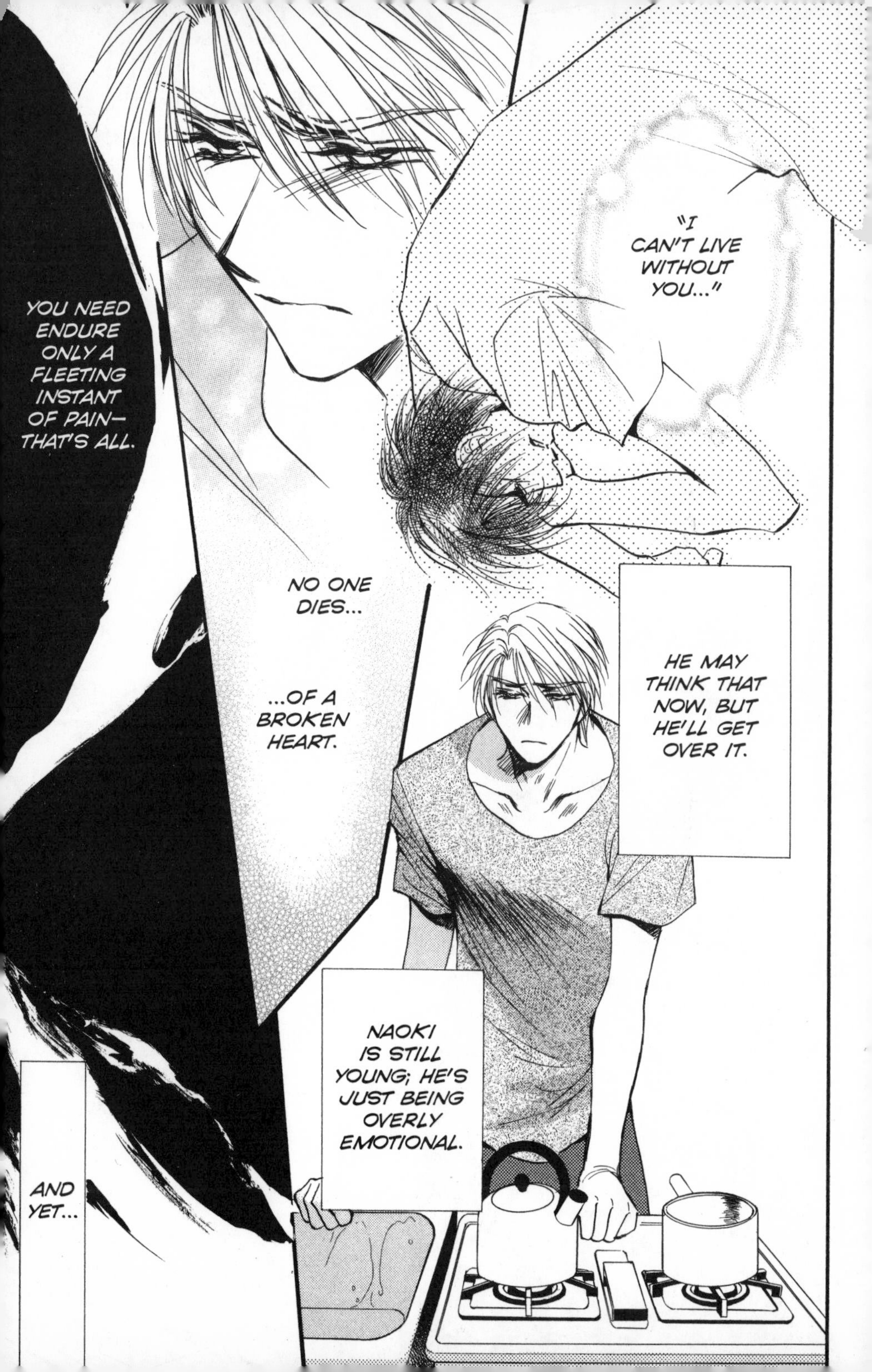
"I CAN'T LIVE WITHOUT YOU..."
YOU NEED ENDURE ONLY A FLEETING INSTANT OF PAIN—THAT'S ALL.
NO ONE DIES...
...OF A BROKEN HEART.
HE MAY THINK THAT NOW, BUT HE'LL GET OVER IT.
NAOKI IS STILL YOUNG; HE'S JUST BEING OVERLY EMOTIONAL.
AND YET...

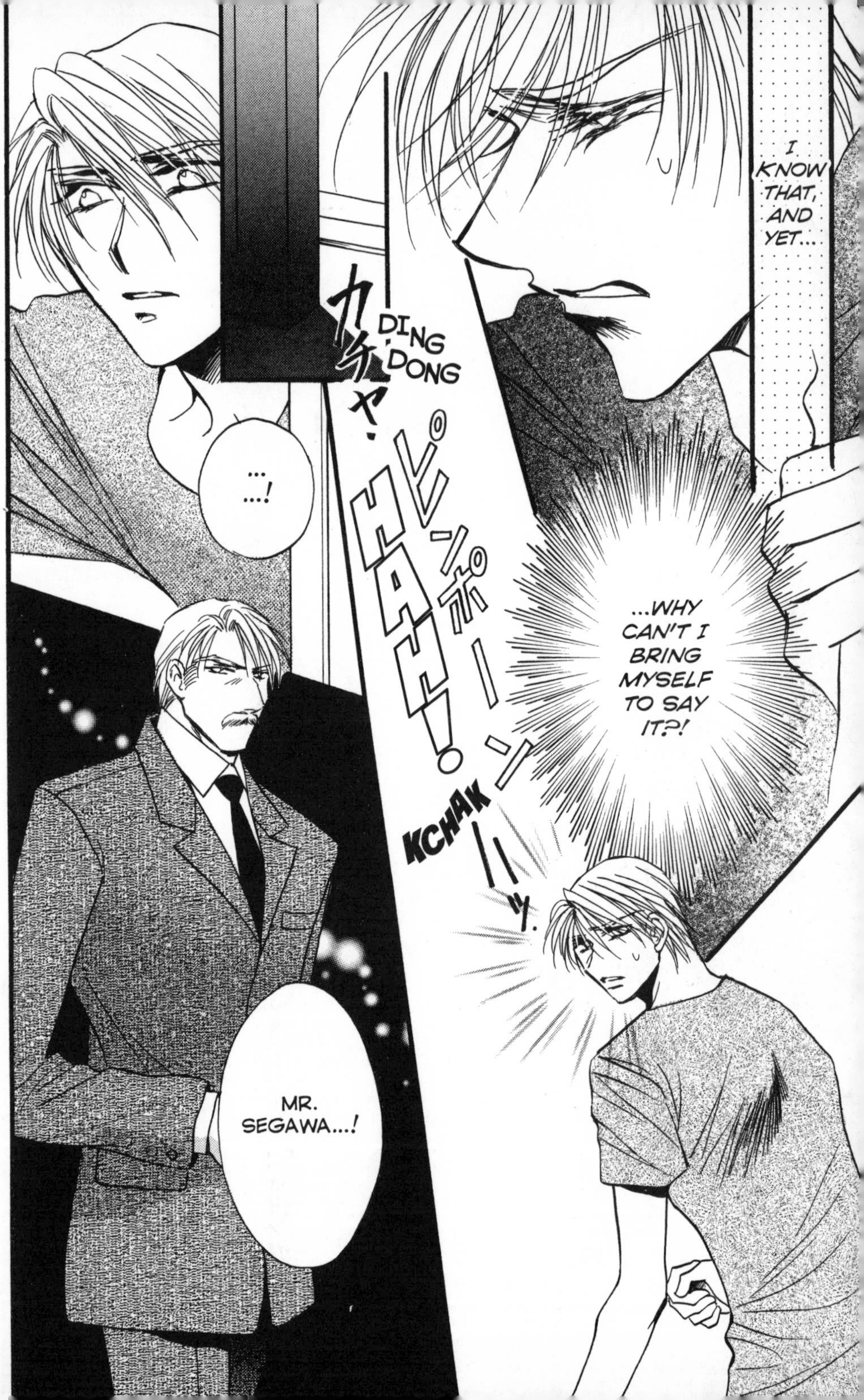
I KNOW THAT, AND YET...
...WHY CAN'T I BRING MYSELF TO SAY IT?!
DING DONG
HAAH!
KCHAK
... ...!
MR. SEGAWA...!

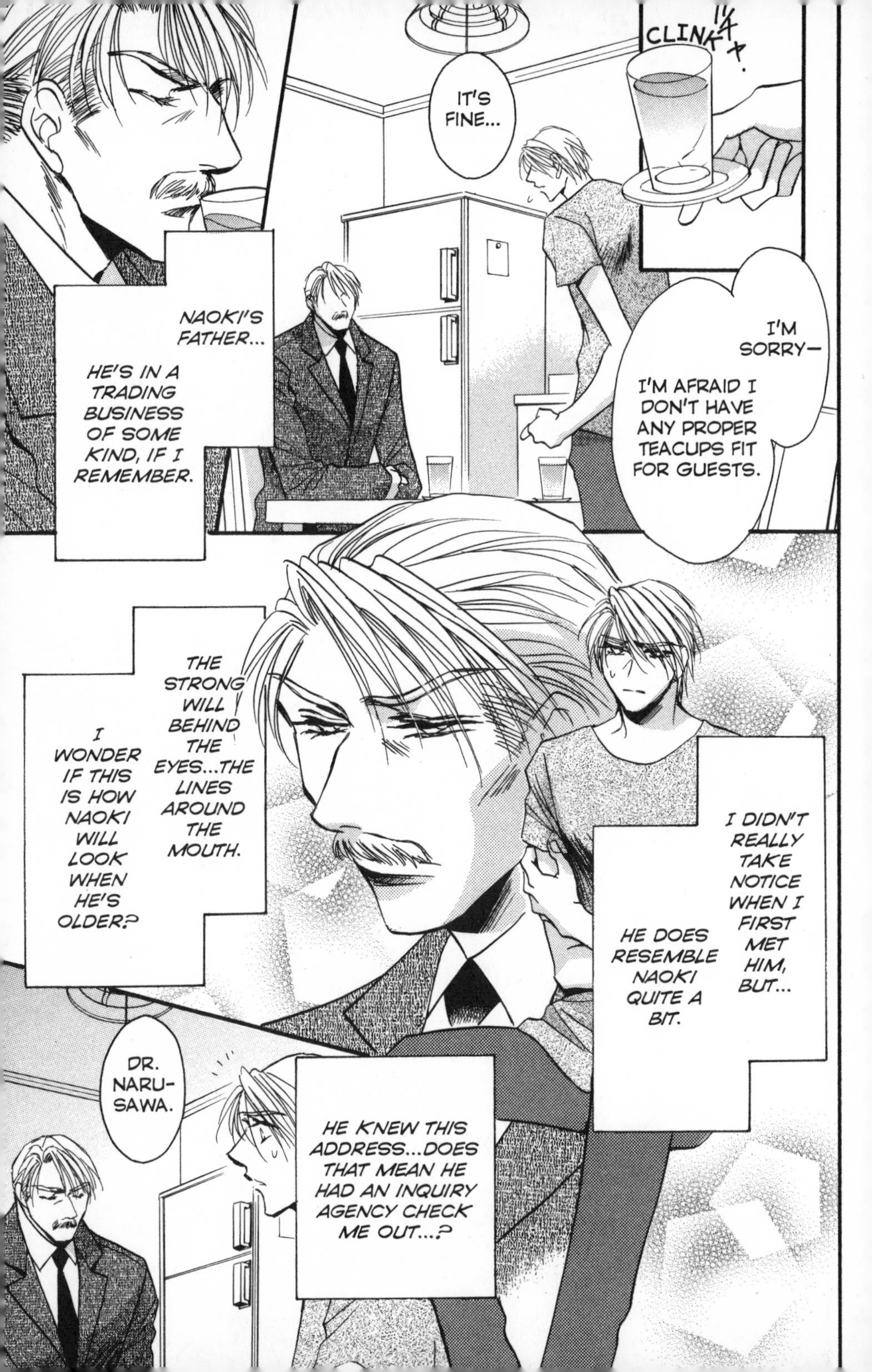
CLINK
I'M SORRY—
I'M AFRAID I DON'T HAVE ANY PROPER TEACUPS FIT FOR GUESTS.
IT'S FINE...
NAOKI'S FATHER...
HE'S IN A TRADING BUSINESS OF SOME KIND, IF I REMEMBER.
I DIDN'T REALLY TAKE NOTICE WHEN I FIRST MET HIM, BUT...
HE DOES RESEMBLE NAOKI QUITE A BIT.
THE STRONG WILL BEHIND THE EYES...THE LINES AROUND THE MOUTH.
I WONDER IF THIS IS HOW NAOKI WILL LOOK WHEN HE'S OLDER?
HE KNEW THIS ADDRESS...DOES THAT MEAN HE HAD AN INQUIRY AGENCY CHECK ME OUT...?
DR. NARU-SAWA.

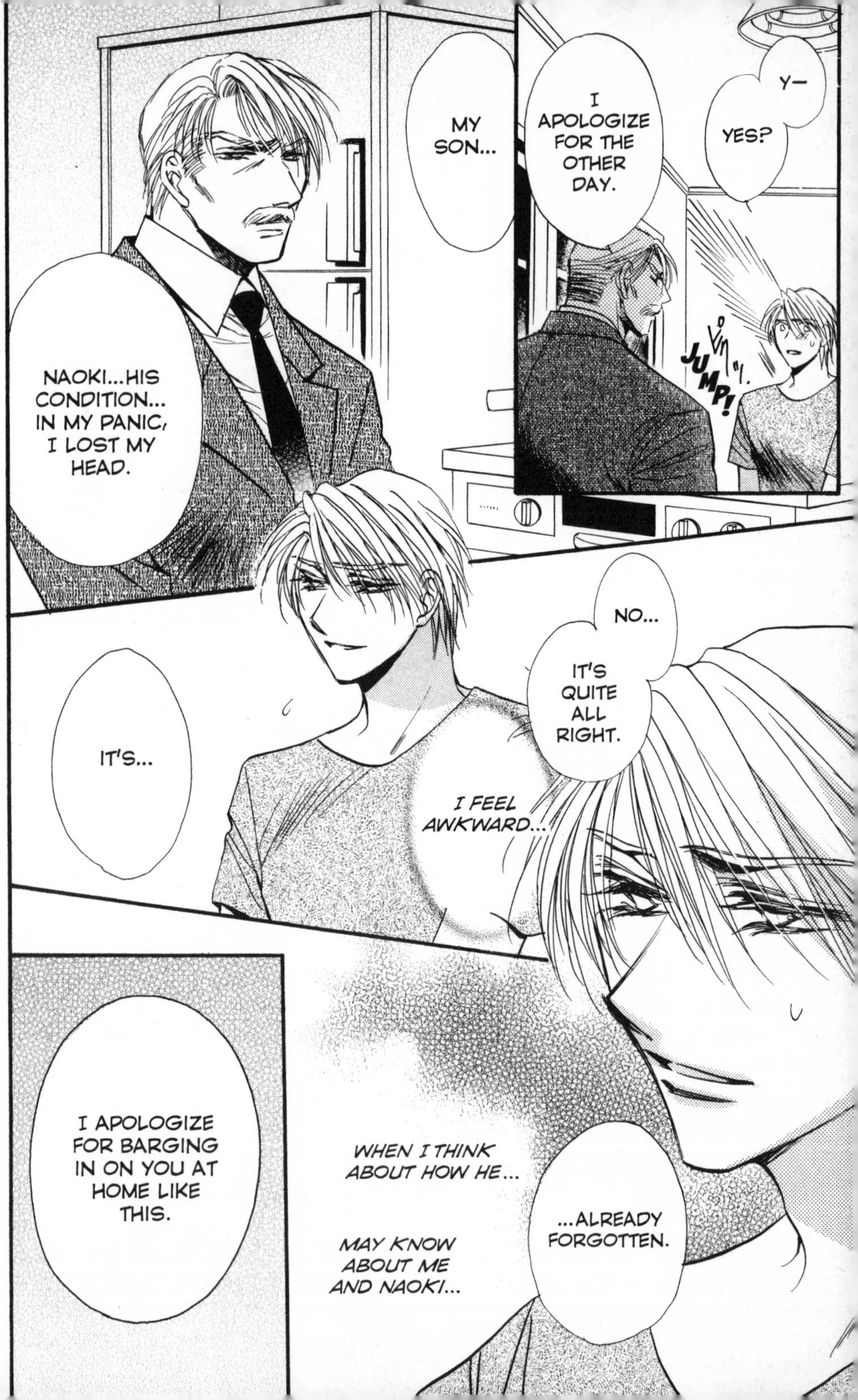
Y—
YES?
I APOLOGIZE FOR THE OTHER DAY.
JUMP!
MY SON...
NAOKI...HIS CONDITION... IN MY PANIC, I LOST MY HEAD.
NO...
IT'S QUITE ALL RIGHT.
I FEEL AWKWARD...
IT'S...
...ALREADY FORGOTTEN.
WHEN I THINK ABOUT HOW HE...
MAY KNOW ABOUT ME AND NAOKI...
I APOLOGIZE FOR BARGING IN ON YOU AT HOME LIKE THIS.

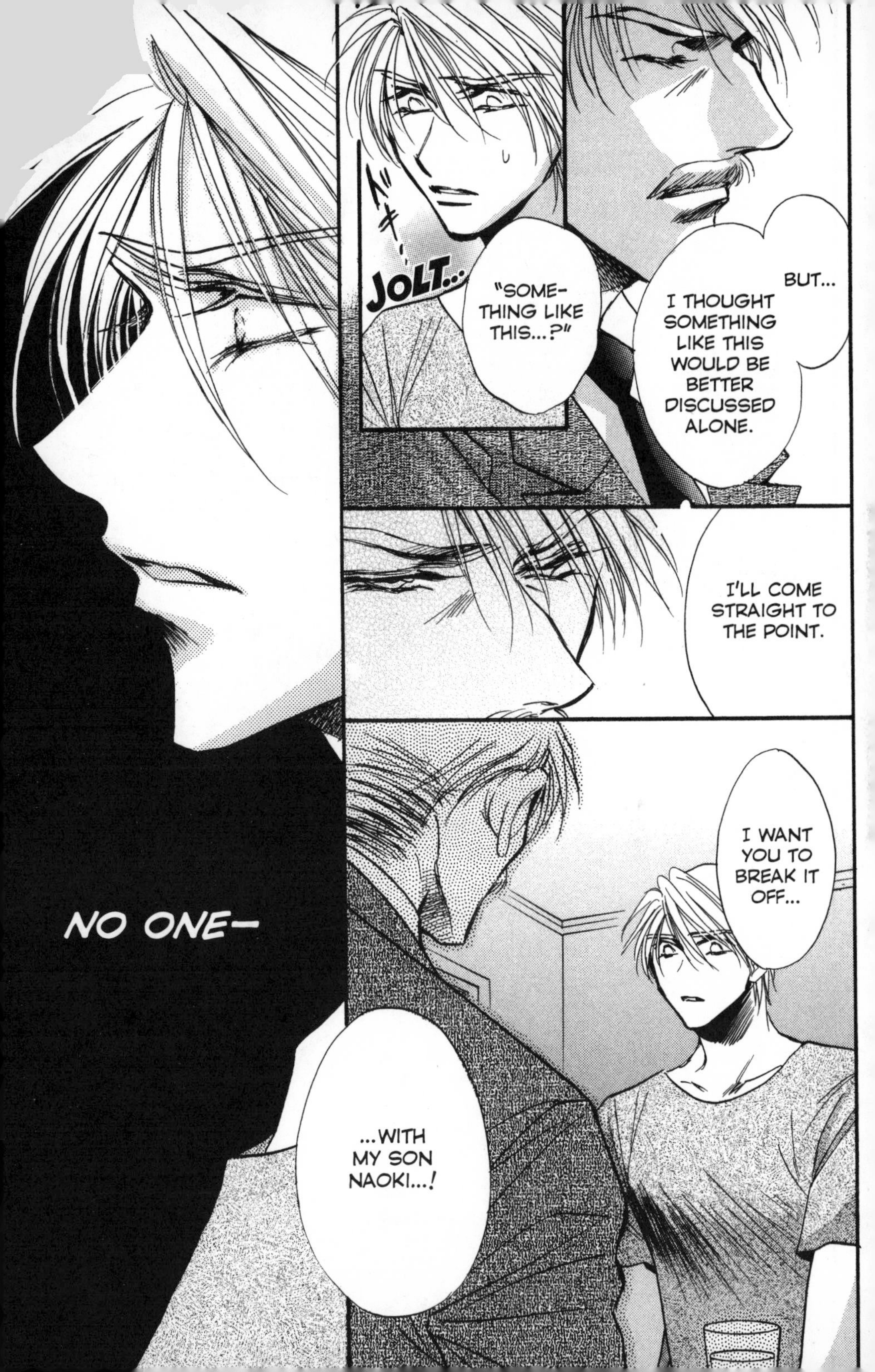
BUT...
I THOUGHT SOMETHING LIKE THIS WOULD BE BETTER DISCUSSED ALONE.
ドキ
JOLT...
"SOME-THING LIKE THIS...?"
I'LL COME STRAIGHT TO THE POINT.
I WANT YOU TO BREAK IT OFF...
...WITH MY SON NAOKI...!
NO ONE–

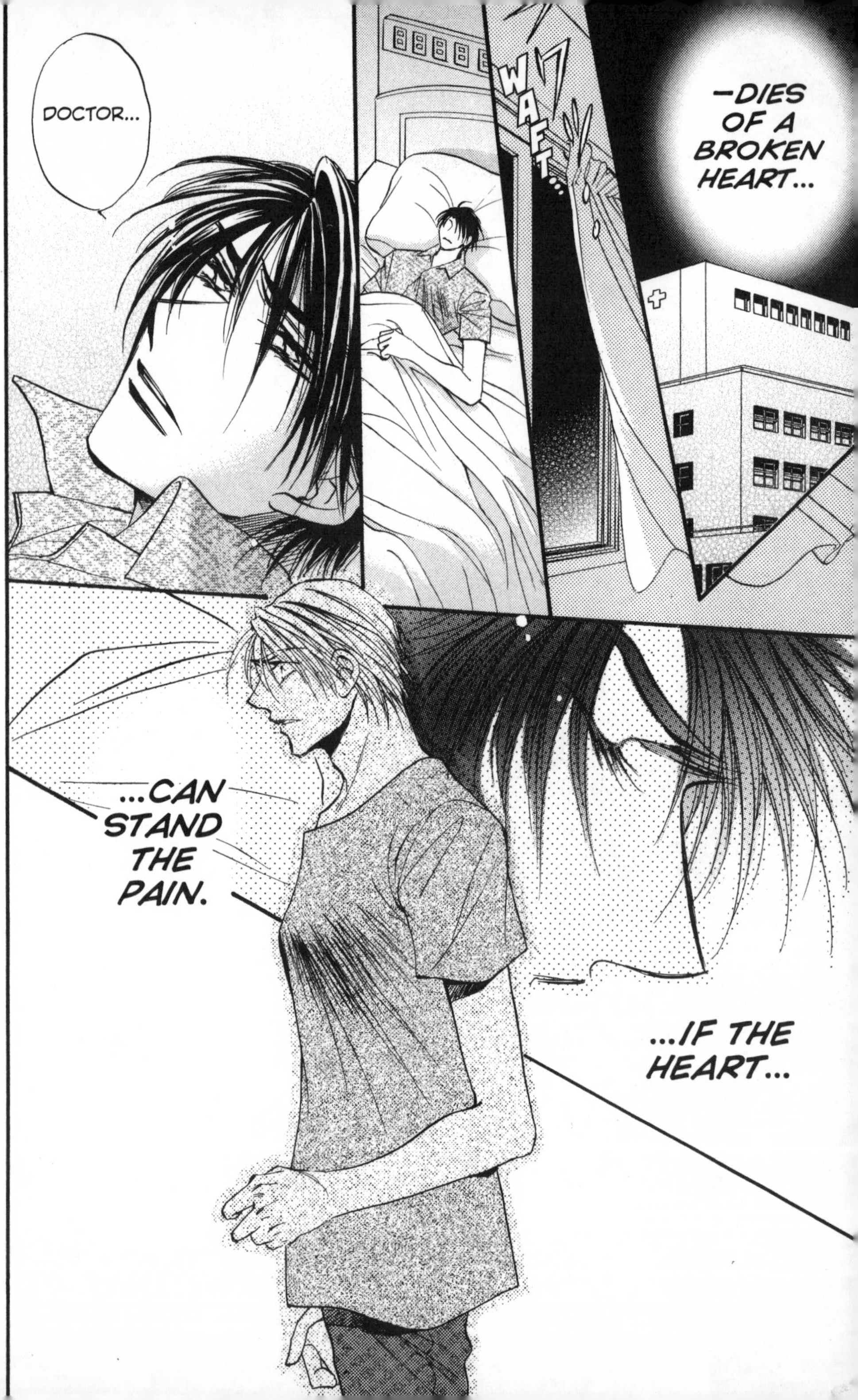
—DIES OF A BROKEN HEART...
WAFT...
DOCTOR...
...IF THE HEART...
...CAN STAND THE PAIN.

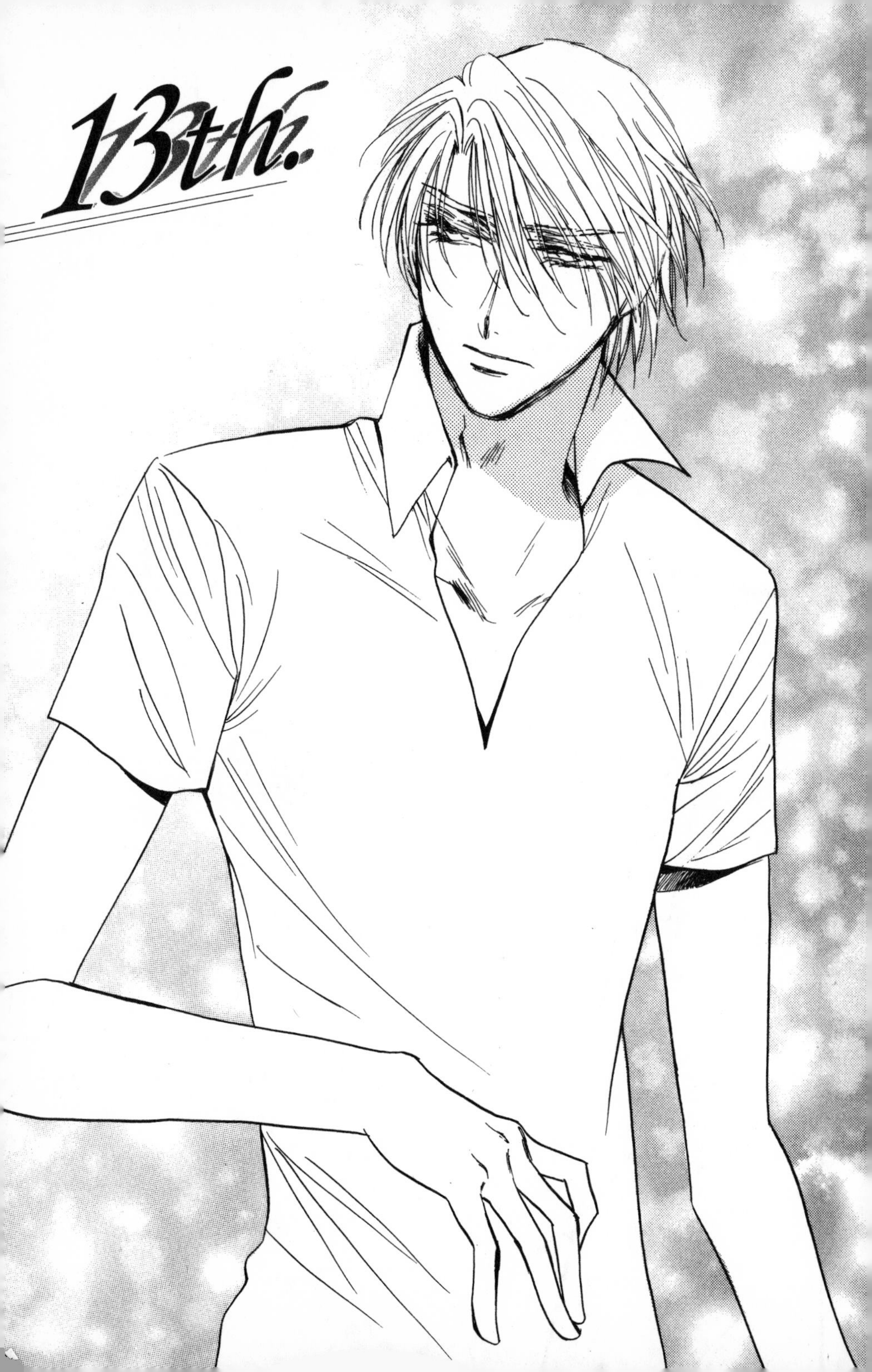
13th.

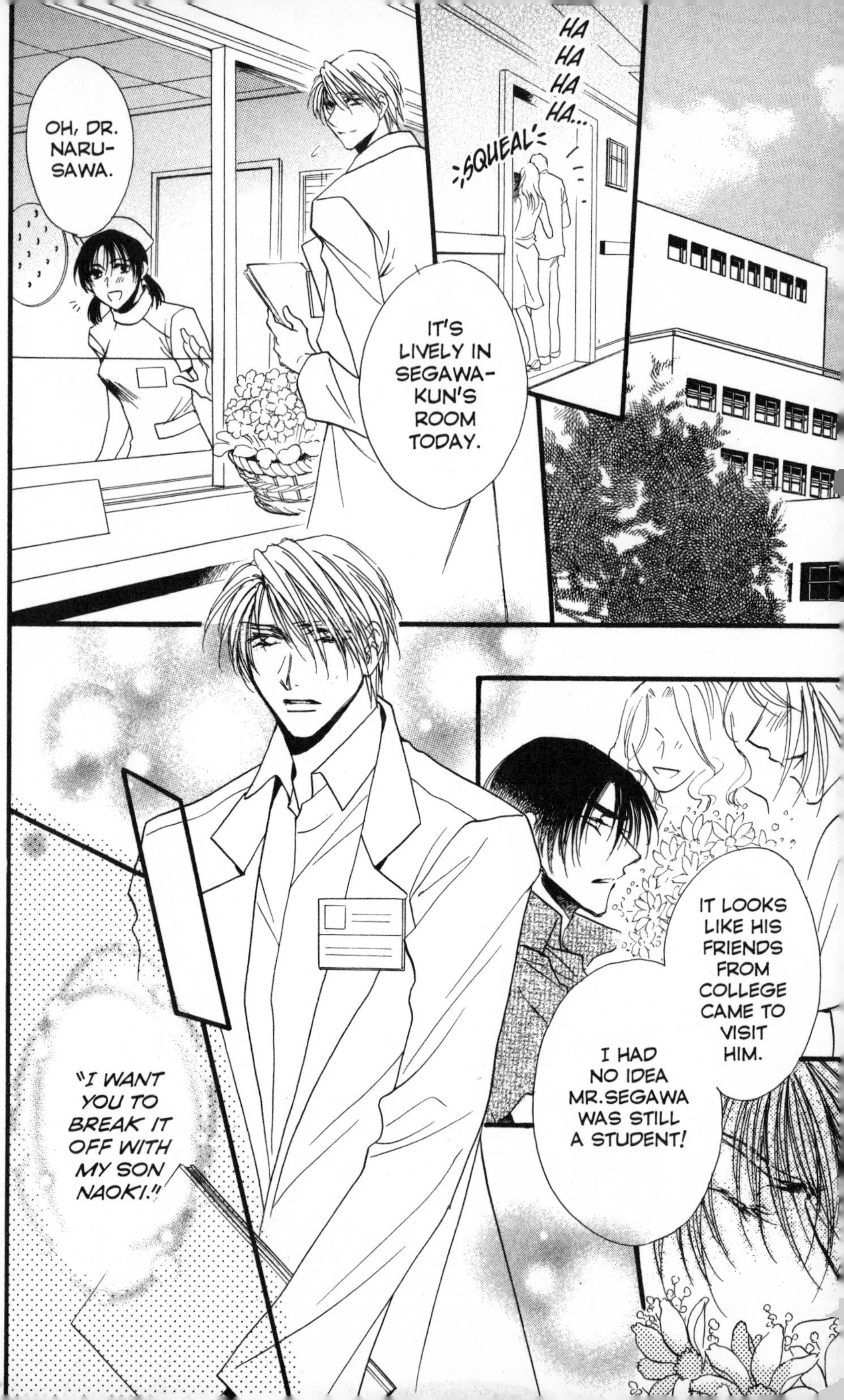
HA HA HA HA...
SQUEAL
OH, DR. NARUSAWA.
IT'S LIVELY IN SEGAWA-KUN'S ROOM TODAY.
IT LOOKS LIKE HIS FRIENDS FROM COLLEGE CAME TO VISIT HIM.
I HAD NO IDEA MR.SEGAWA WAS STILL A STUDENT!
"I WANT YOU TO BREAK IT OFF WITH MY SON NAOKI."

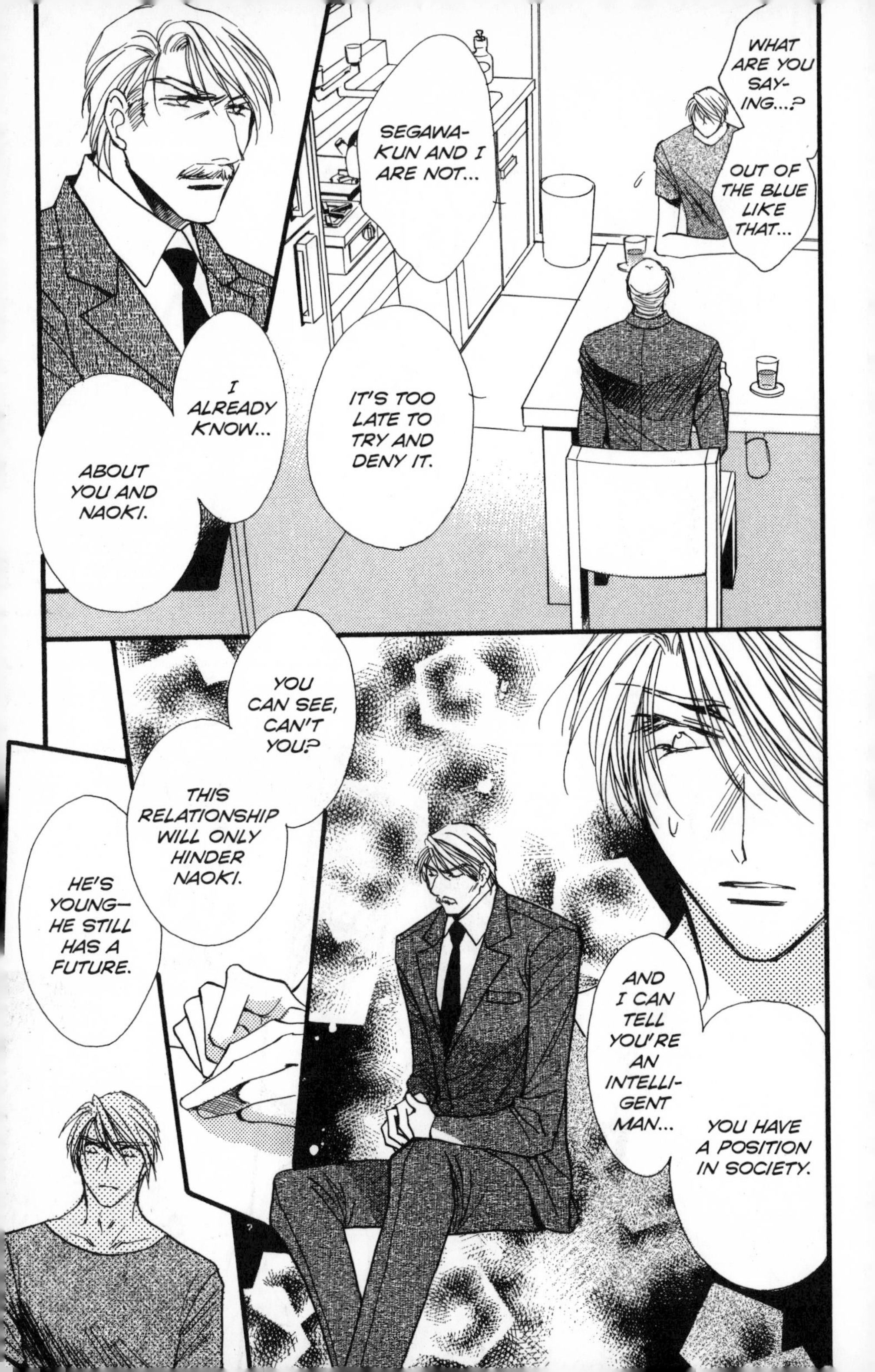
WHAT ARE YOU SAYING...?
OUT OF THE BLUE LIKE THAT...
SEGAWA-KUN AND I ARE NOT...
IT'S TOO LATE TO TRY AND DENY IT.
I ALREADY KNOW...
ABOUT YOU AND NAOKI.
AND I CAN TELL YOU'RE AN INTELLIGENT MAN...
YOU HAVE A POSITION IN SOCIETY.
YOU CAN SEE, CAN'T YOU?
THIS RELATIONSHIP WILL ONLY HINDER NAOKI.
HE'S YOUNG— HE STILL HAS A FUTURE.

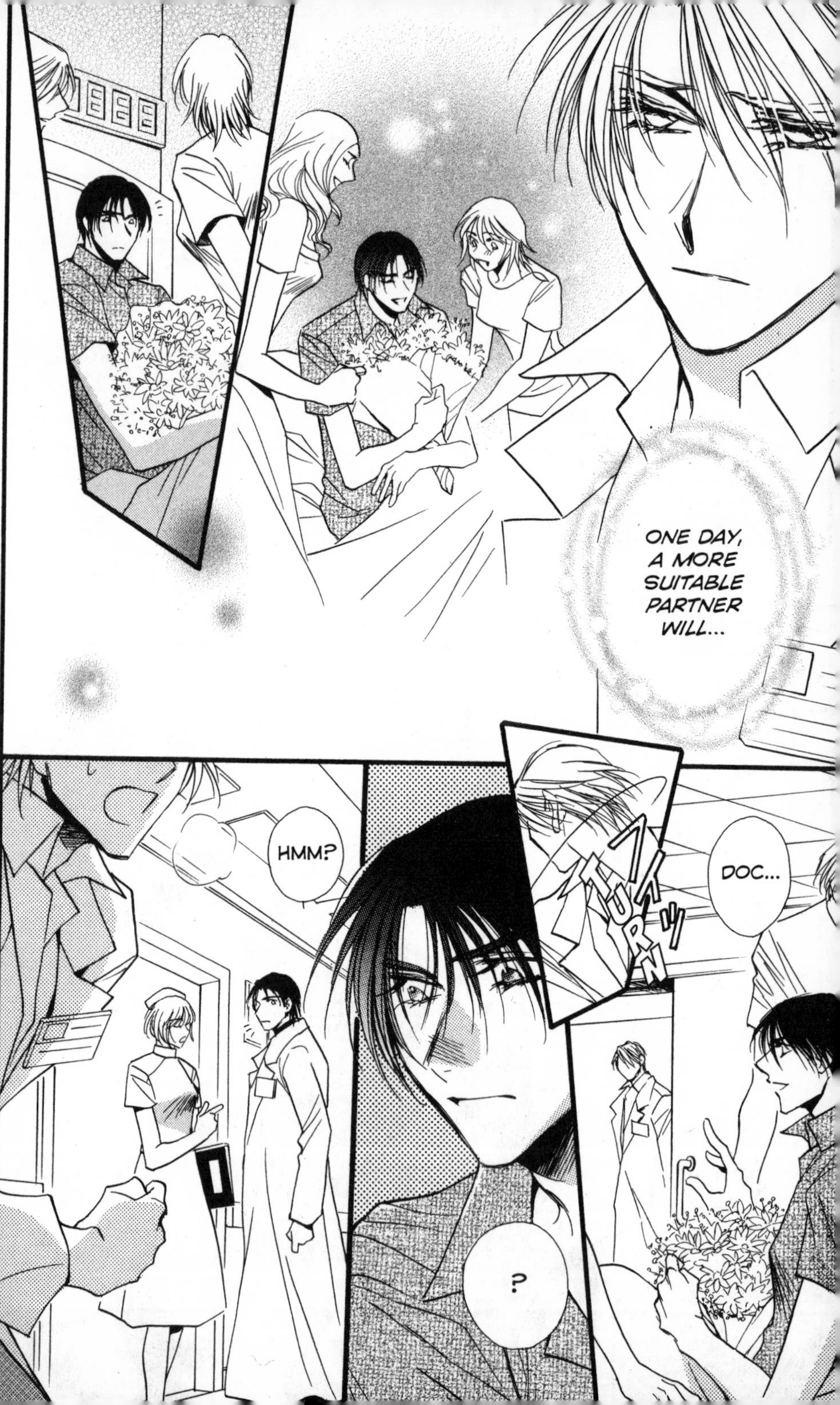
ONE DAY, A MORE SUITABLE PARTNER WILL...
DOC...
TURN
?
HMM?

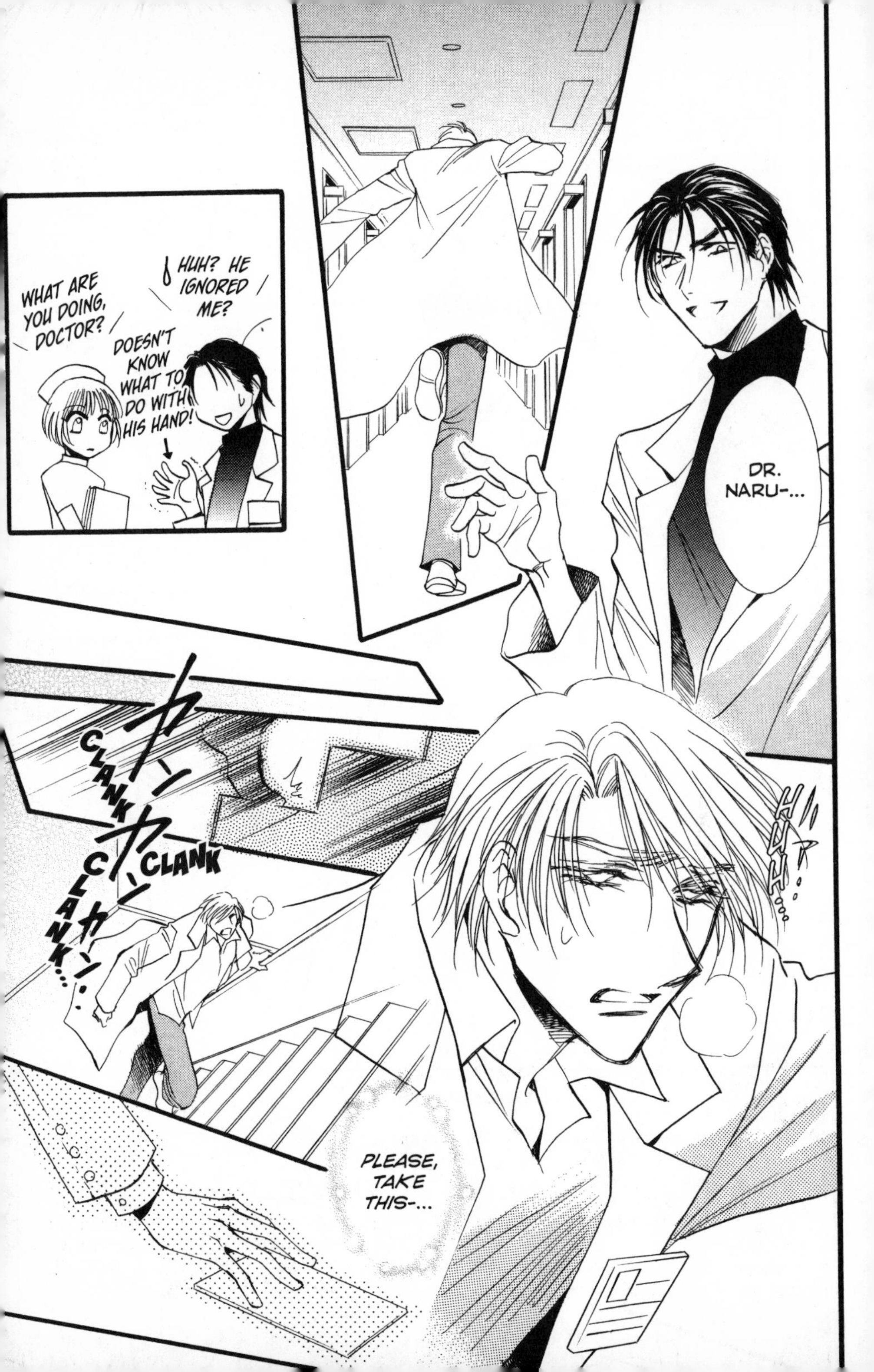
DR. NARU-...
HUH? HE IGNORED ME?
WHAT ARE YOU DOING, DOCTOR?
DOESN'T KNOW WHAT TO DO WITH HIS HAND!
HUFF HUFF...
PLEASE, TAKE THIS-...
CLANK
CLANK
CLANK
CLANK...

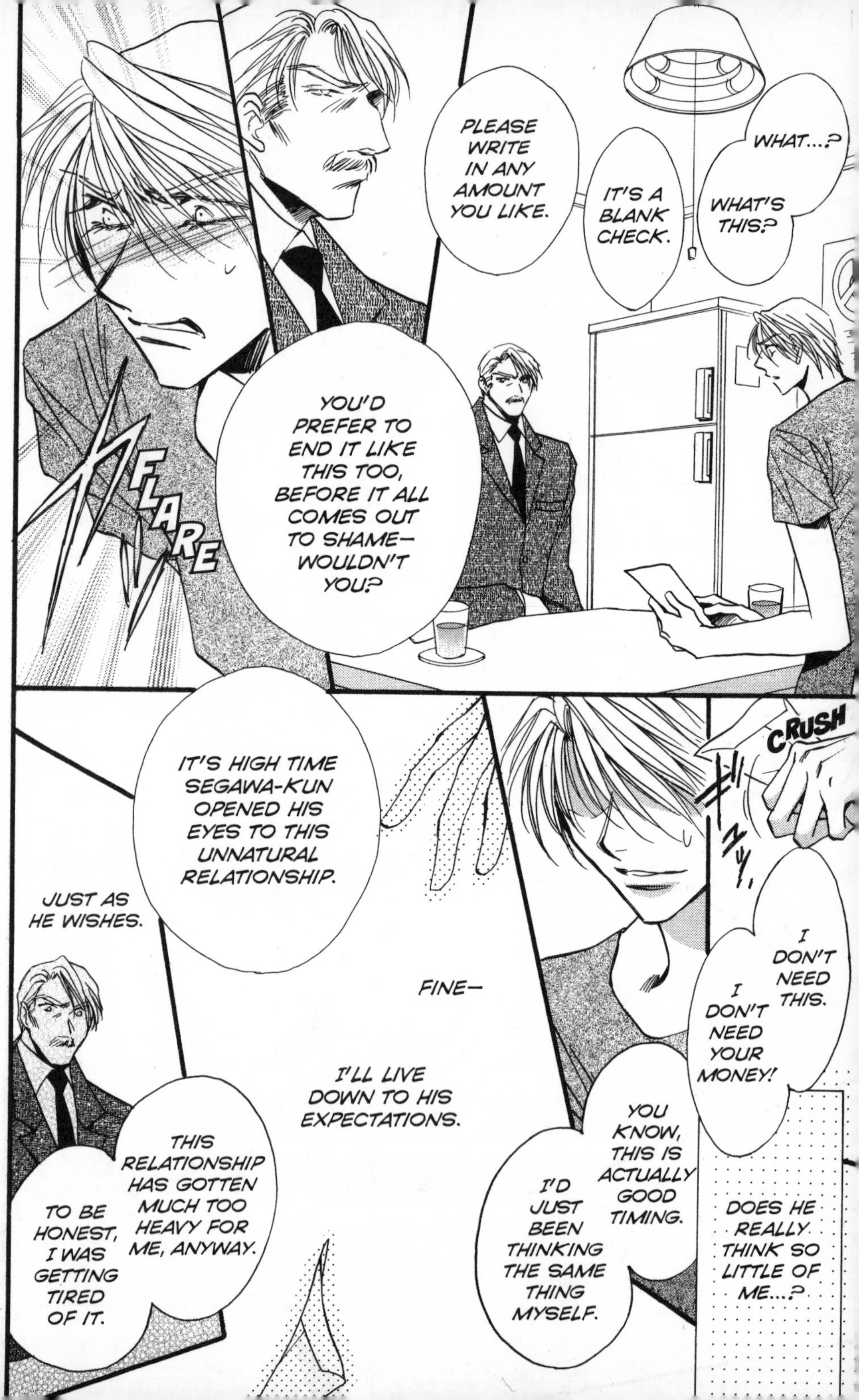
WHAT...?
WHAT'S THIS?
IT'S A BLANK CHECK.
PLEASE WRITE IN ANY AMOUNT YOU LIKE.
YOU'D PREFER TO END IT LIKE THIS TOO, BEFORE IT ALL COMES OUT TO SHAME—WOULDN'T YOU?
FLARE
CRUSH
I DON'T NEED THIS.
I DON'T NEED YOUR MONEY!
DOES HE REALLY THINK SO LITTLE OF ME...?
IT'S HIGH TIME SEGAWA-KUN OPENED HIS EYES TO THIS UNNATURAL RELATIONSHIP.
FINE—
I'LL LIVE DOWN TO HIS EXPECTATIONS.
YOU KNOW, THIS IS ACTUALLY GOOD TIMING.
I'D JUST BEEN THINKING THE SAME THING MYSELF.
JUST AS HE WISHES.
THIS RELATIONSHIP HAS GOTTEN MUCH TOO HEAVY FOR ME, ANYWAY.
TO BE HONEST, I WAS GETTING TIRED OF IT.

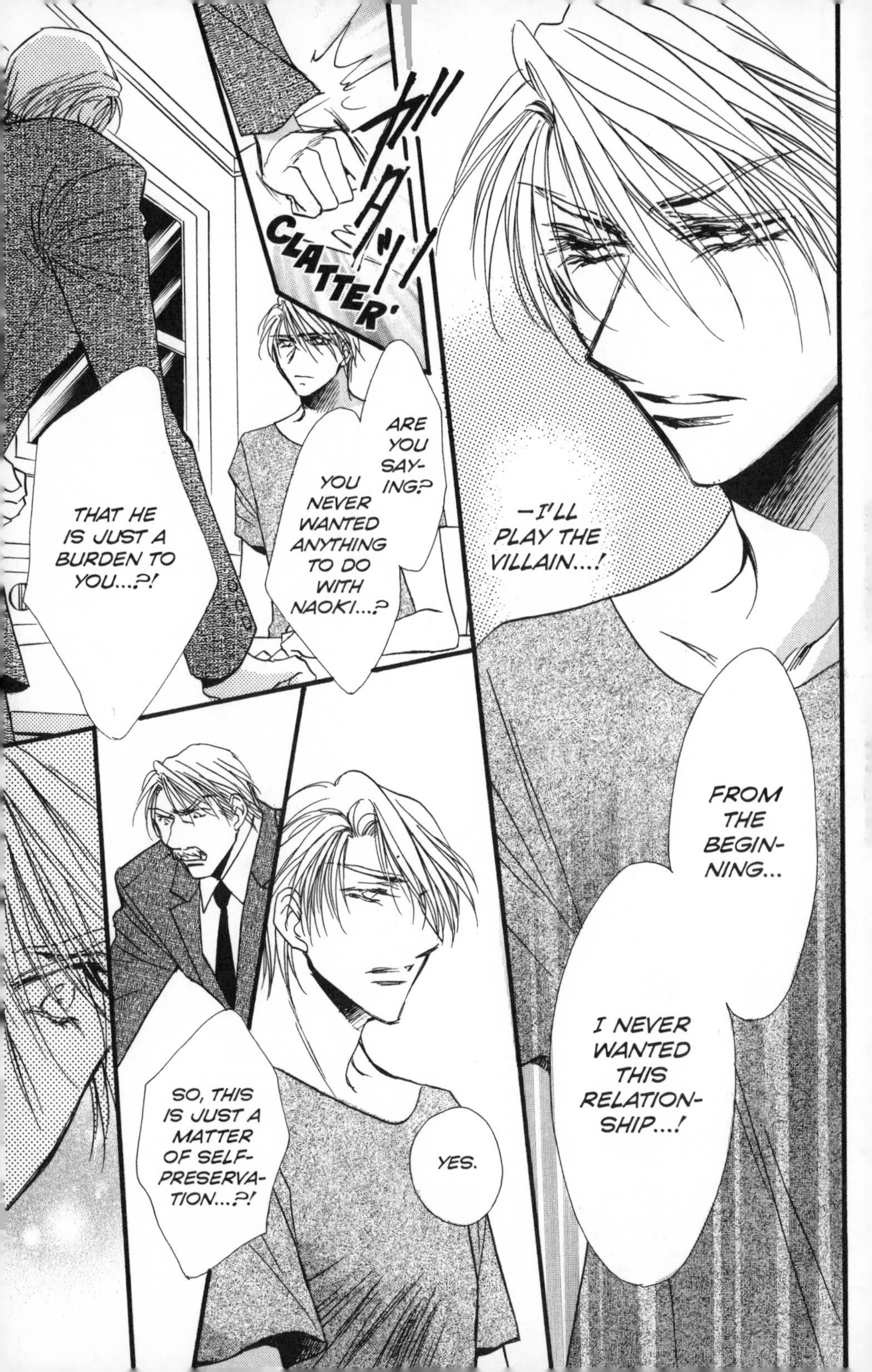
—I'LL PLAY THE VILLAIN...!
FROM THE BEGINNING...
I NEVER WANTED THIS RELATIONSHIP...!
CLATTER
ARE YOU SAYING? YOU NEVER WANTED ANYTHING TO DO WITH NAOKI...?
THAT HE IS JUST A BURDEN TO YOU...?!
SO, THIS IS JUST A MATTER OF SELF-PRESERVATION...?!
YES.

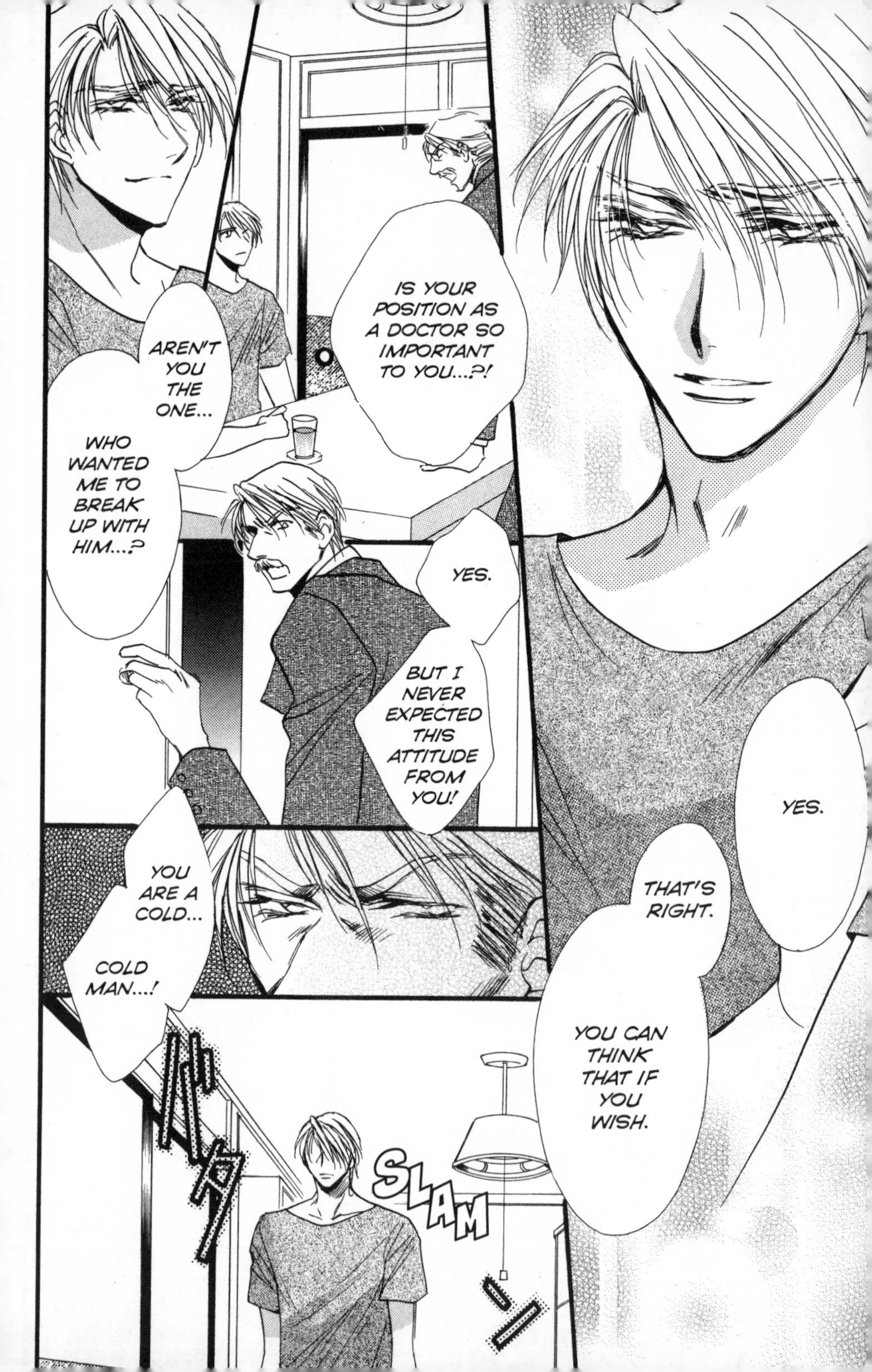
IS YOUR POSITION AS A DOCTOR SO IMPORTANT TO YOU...?!
AREN'T YOU THE ONE...
WHO WANTED ME TO BREAK UP WITH HIM...?
YES.
BUT I NEVER EXPECTED THIS ATTITUDE FROM YOU!
YOU ARE A COLD...
COLD MAN...!
YES.
THAT'S RIGHT.
YOU CAN THINK THAT IF YOU WISH.
SLAM

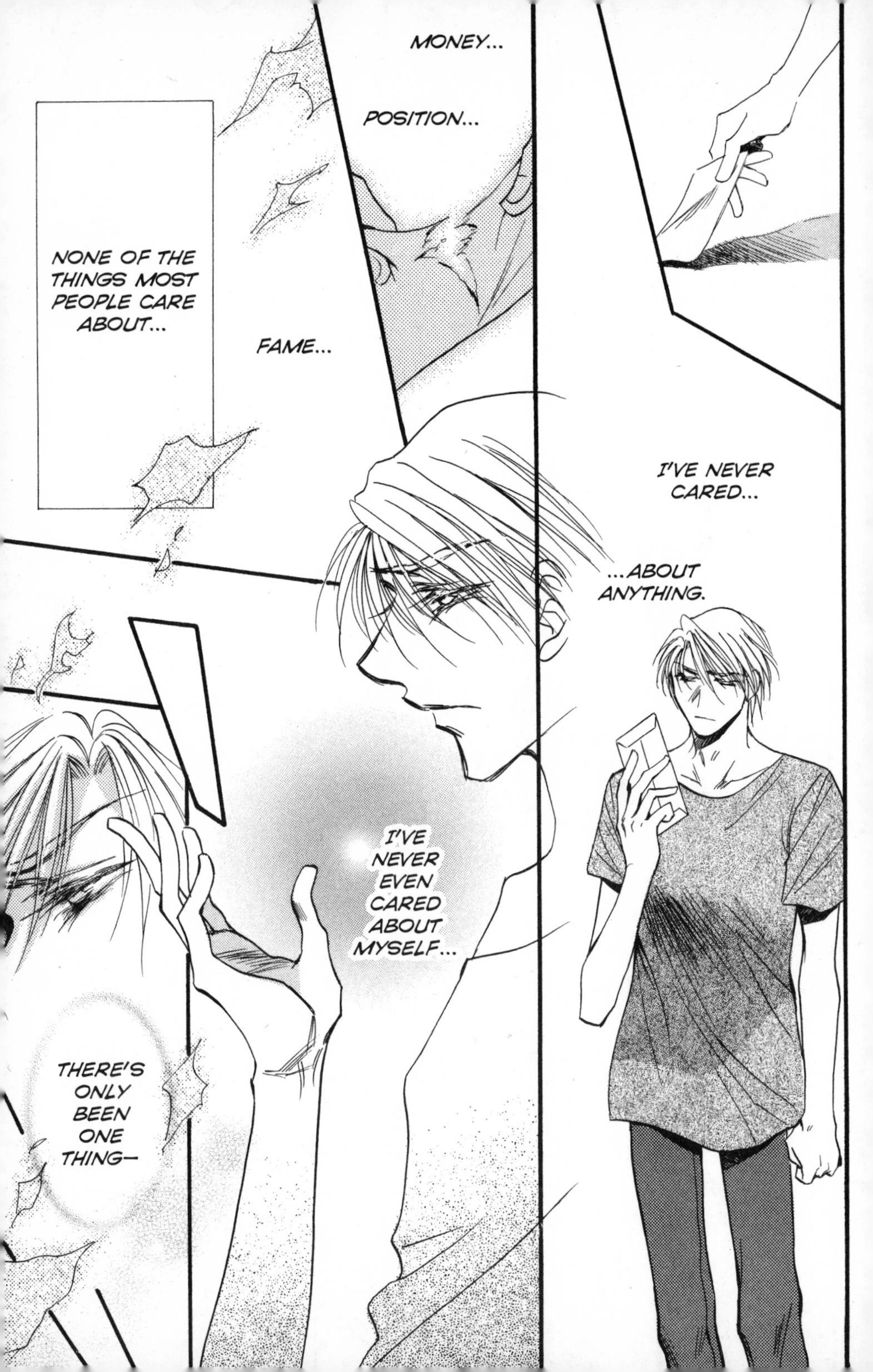
I'VE NEVER CARED...
...ABOUT ANYTHING.
MONEY...
POSITION...
FAME...
NONE OF THE THINGS MOST PEOPLE CARE ABOUT...
I'VE NEVER EVEN CARED ABOUT MYSELF...
THERE'S ONLY BEEN ONE THING—

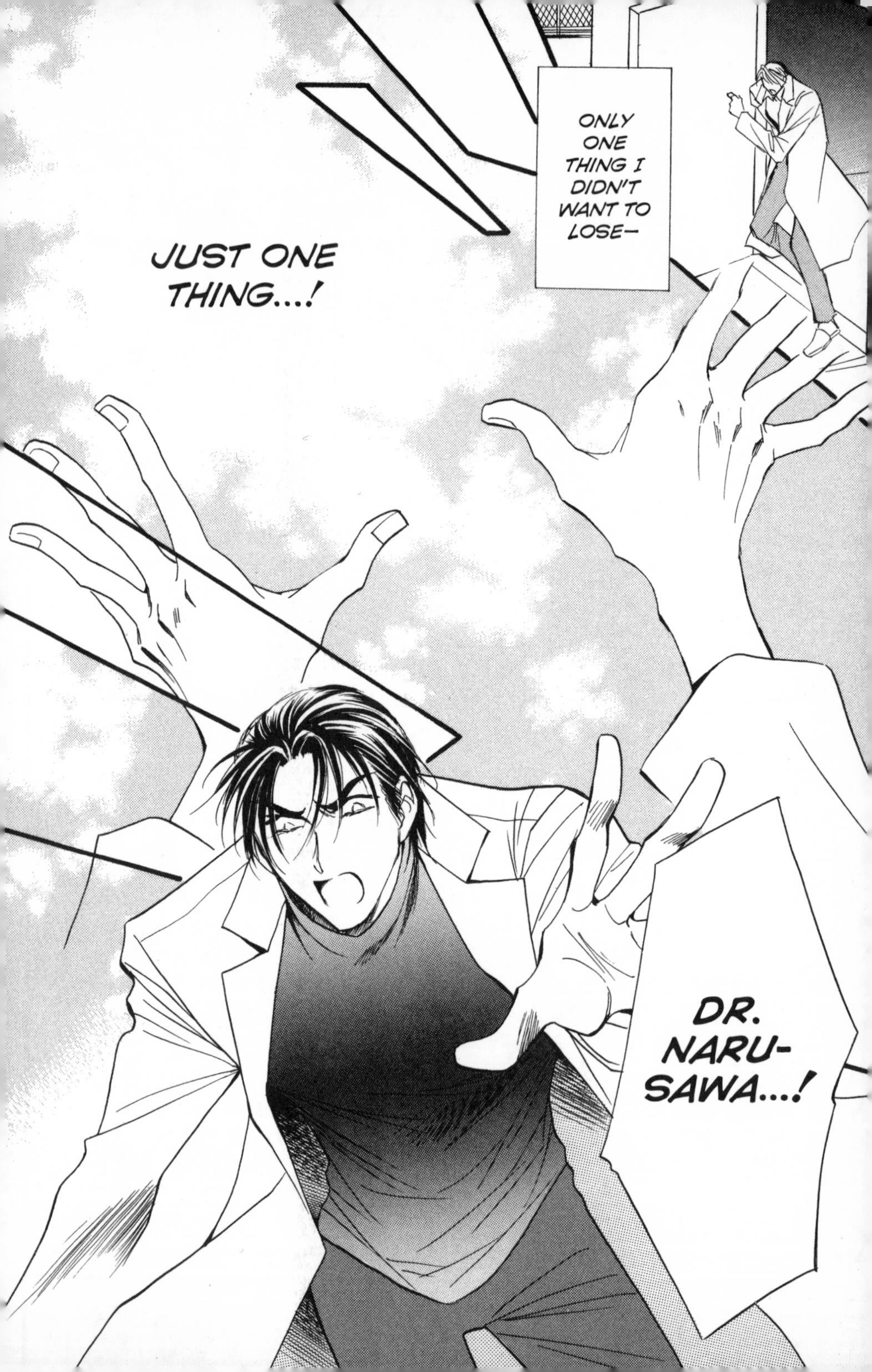
ONLY ONE THING I DIDN'T WANT TO LOSE—
JUST ONE THING...!
DR. NARU-SAWA...!

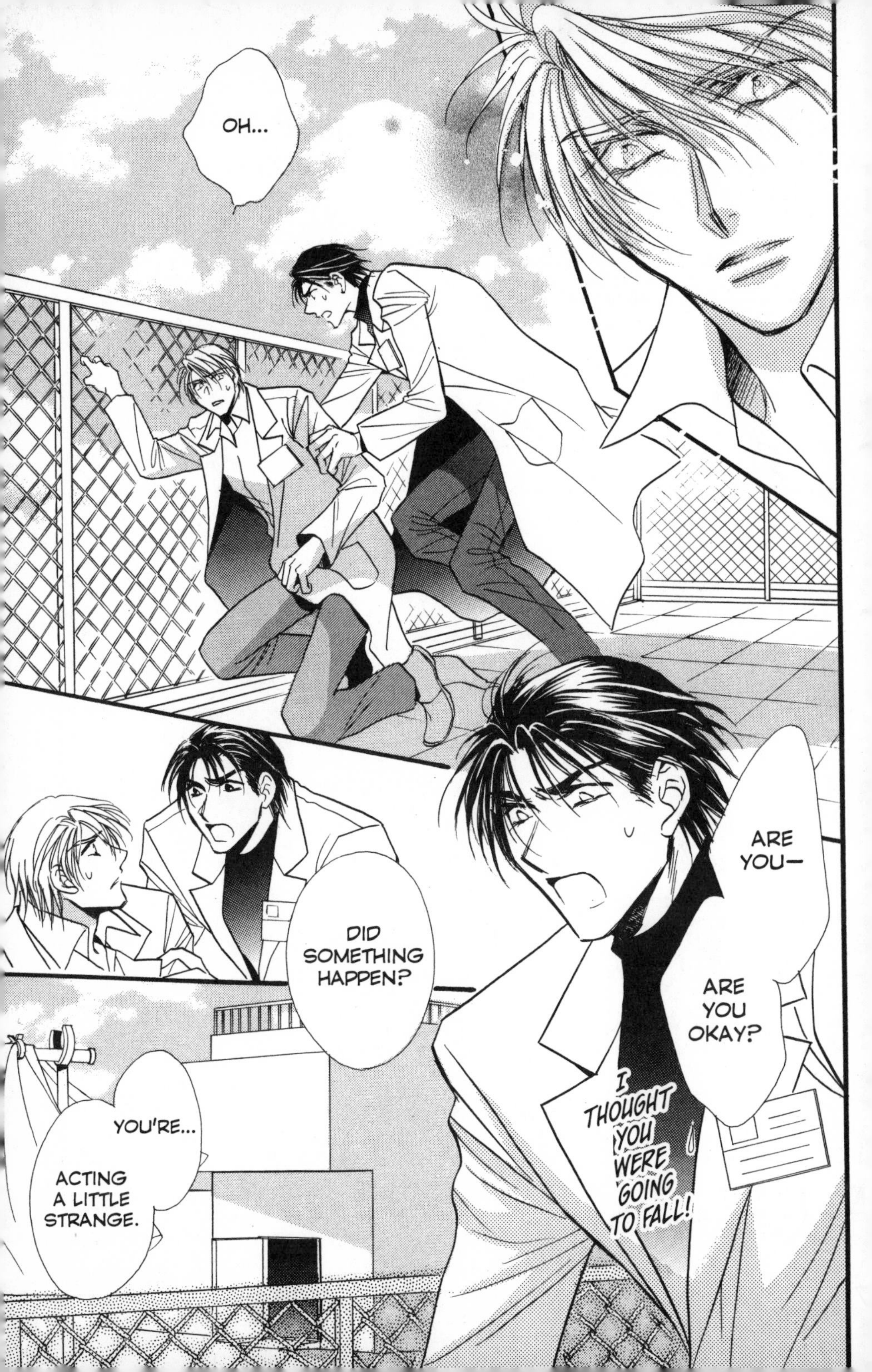
OH...
ARE YOU—
ARE YOU OKAY?
I THOUGHT YOU WERE GOING TO FALL!
DID SOMETHING HAPPEN?
YOU'RE...
ACTING A LITTLE STRANGE.

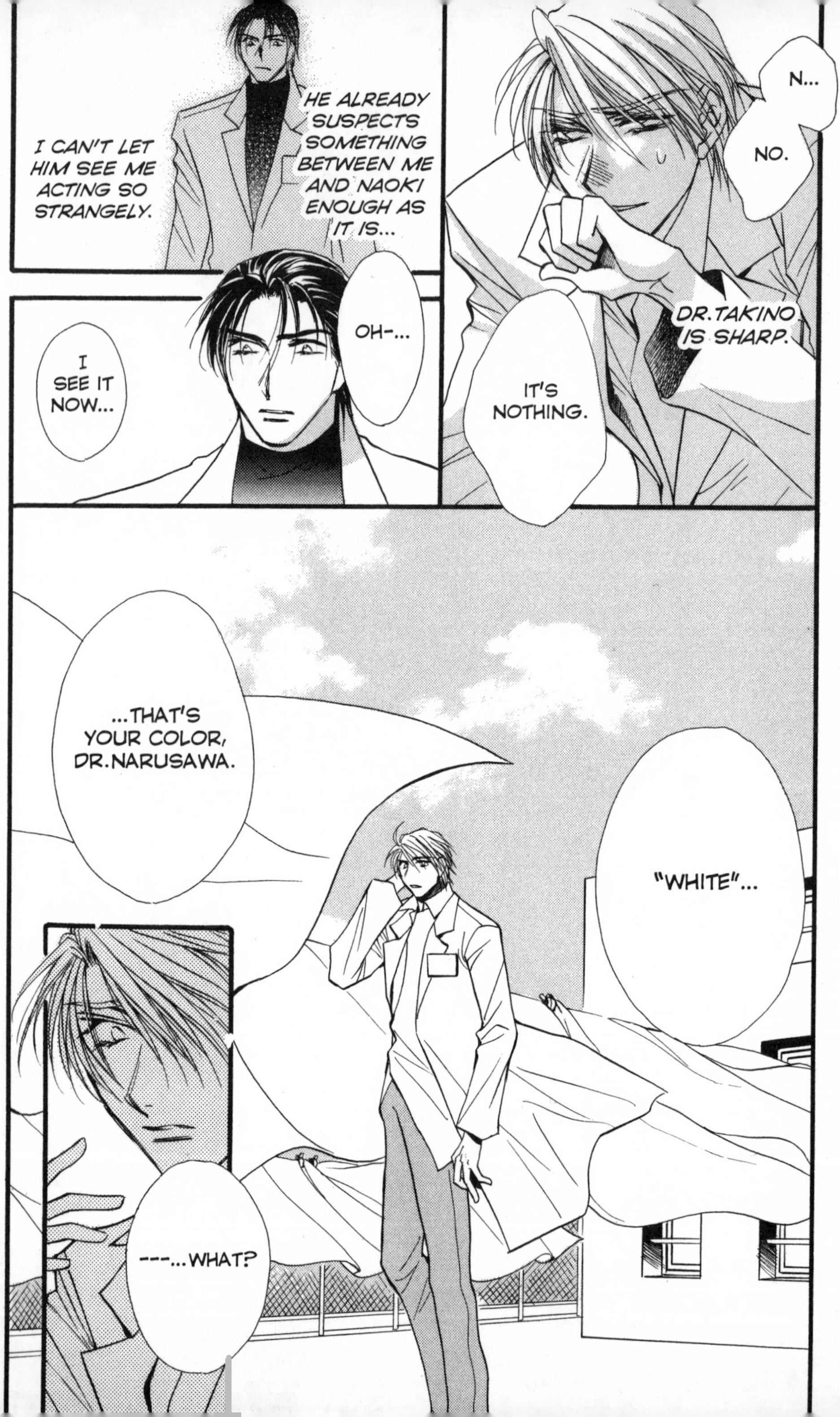
N...
NO.
DR.TAKINO IS SHARP.
IT'S NOTHING.
HE ALREADY SUSPECTS SOMETHING BETWEEN ME AND NAOKI ENOUGH AS IT IS...
I CAN'T LET HIM SEE ME ACTING SO STRANGELY.
OH-...
I SEE IT NOW...
"WHITE"...
...THAT'S YOUR COLOR, DR.NARUSAWA.
---...WHAT?

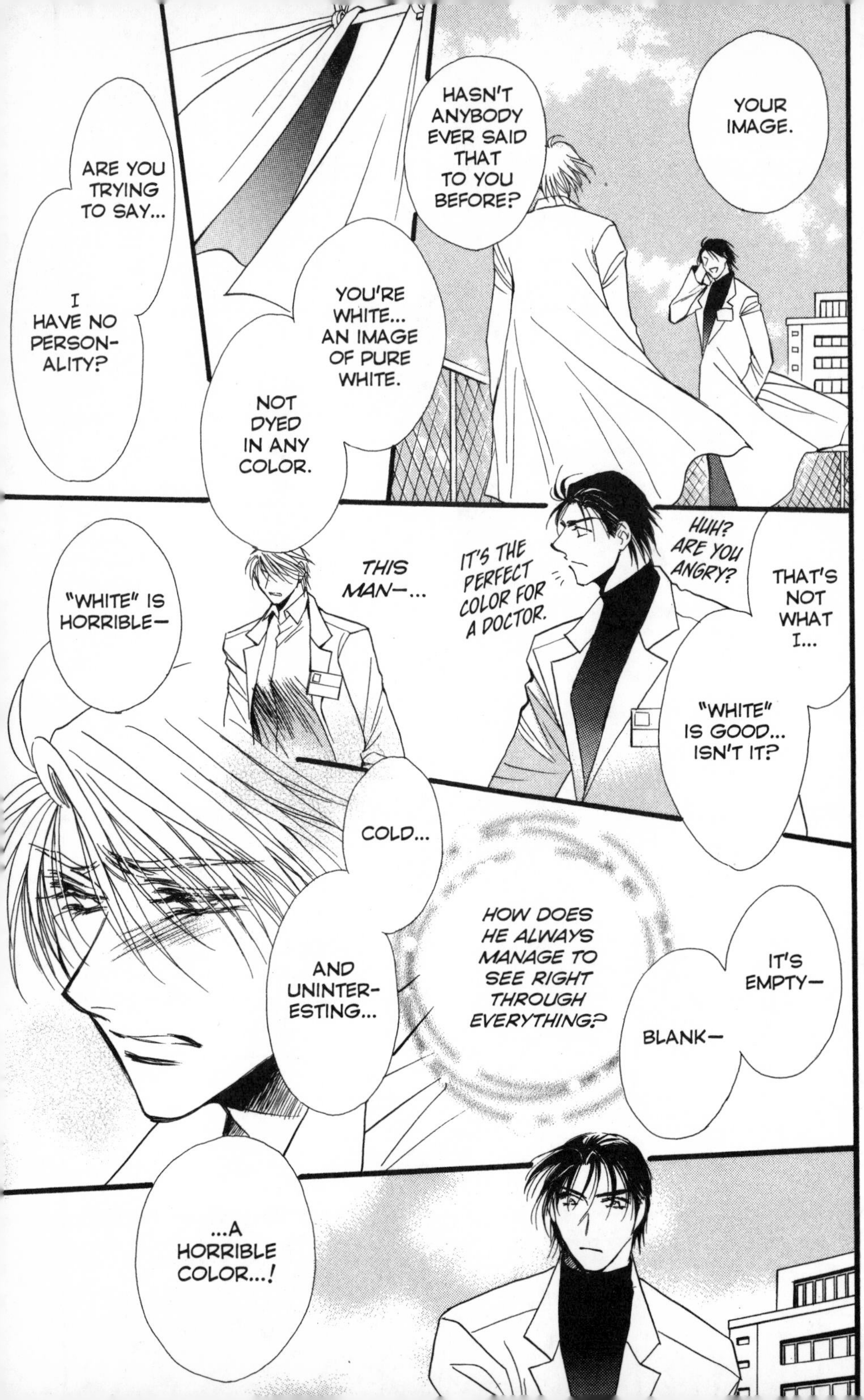
YOUR IMAGE.
HASN'T ANYBODY EVER SAID THAT TO YOU BEFORE?
YOU'RE WHITE... AN IMAGE OF PURE WHITE.
NOT DYED IN ANY COLOR.
ARE YOU TRYING TO SAY...
I HAVE NO PERSONALITY?
THAT'S NOT WHAT I...
HUH? ARE YOU ANGRY?
IT'S THE PERFECT COLOR FOR A DOCTOR.
"WHITE" IS GOOD... ISN'T IT?
THIS MAN—...
"WHITE" IS HORRIBLE—
IT'S EMPTY—
BLANK—
HOW DOES HE ALWAYS MANAGE TO SEE RIGHT THROUGH EVERYTHING?
COLD...
AND UNINTERESTING...
...A HORRIBLE COLOR...!

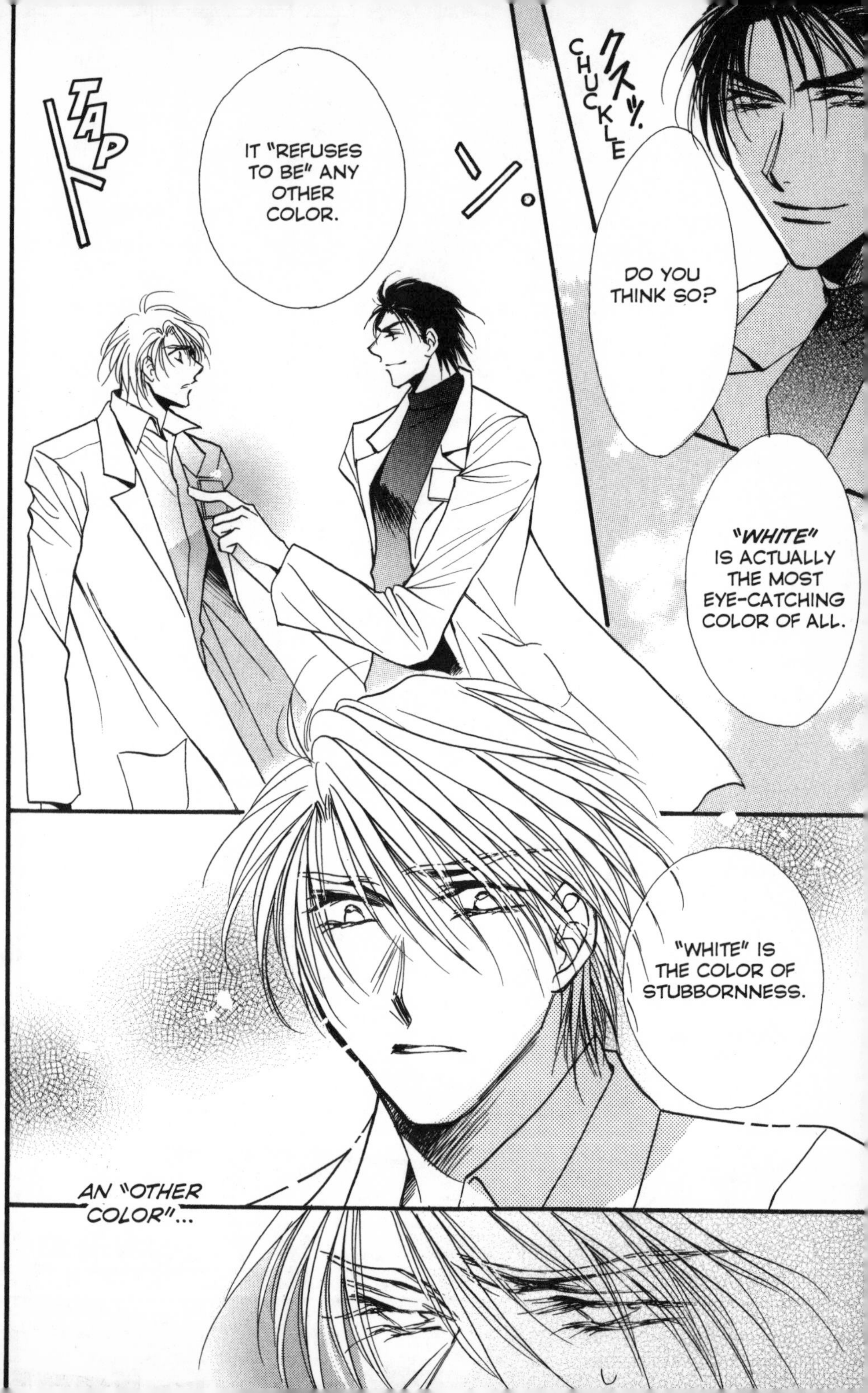
クスッ。
CHUCKLE
DO YOU THINK SO?
"WHITE" IS ACTUALLY THE MOST EYE-CATCHING COLOR OF ALL.
IT "REFUSES TO BE" ANY OTHER COLOR.
TAP
"WHITE" IS THE COLOR OF STUBBORNNESS.
AN "OTHER COLOR"...

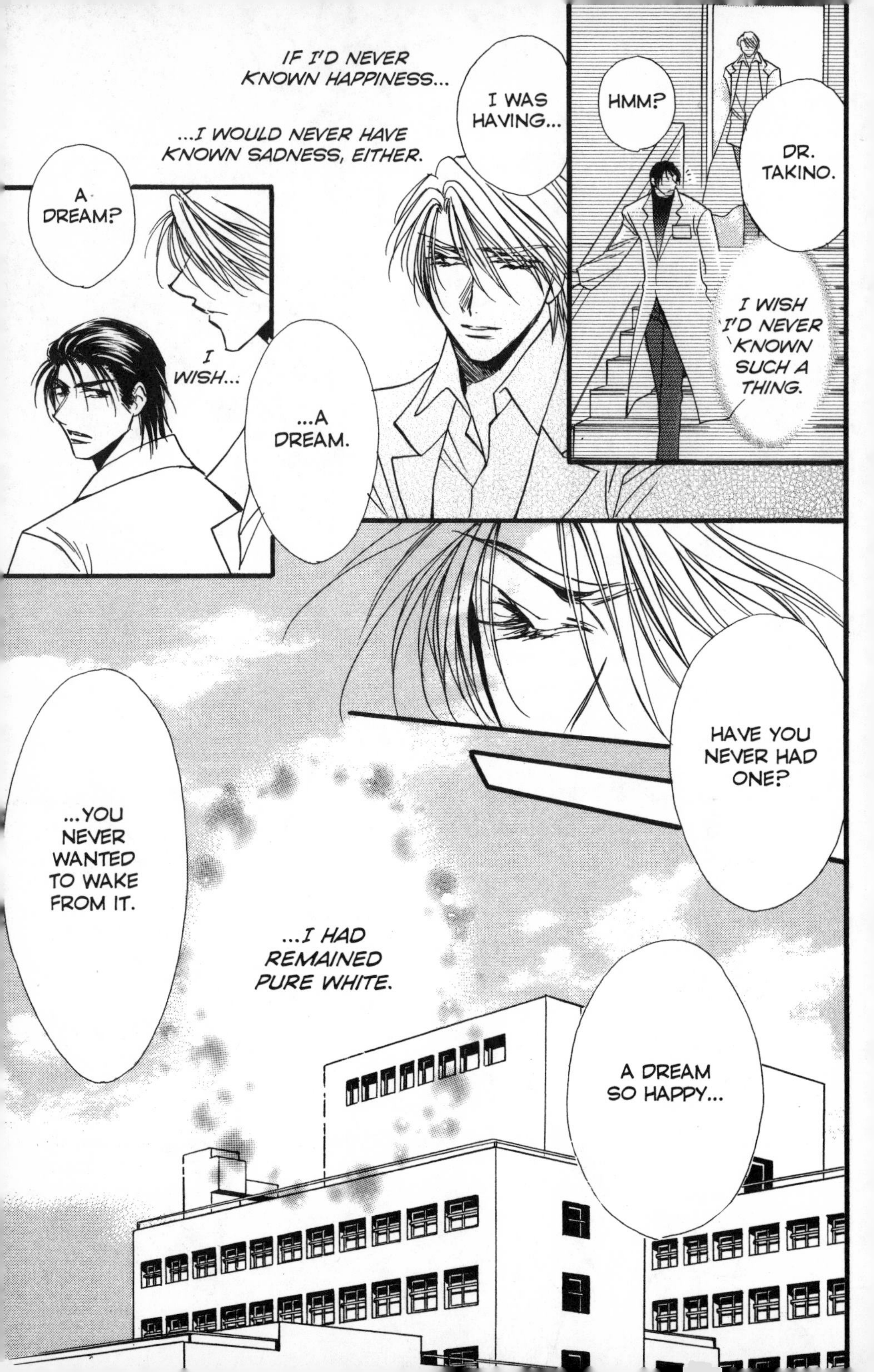
DR. TAKINO.
HMM?
I WISH I'D NEVER KNOWN SUCH A THING.
IF I'D NEVER KNOWN HAPPINESS...
...I WOULD NEVER HAVE KNOWN SADNESS, EITHER.
I WAS HAVING...
...A DREAM.
A DREAM?
I WISH...
HAVE YOU NEVER HAD ONE?
A DREAM SO HAPPY...
...I HAD REMAINED PURE WHITE.
...YOU NEVER WANTED TO WAKE FROM IT.

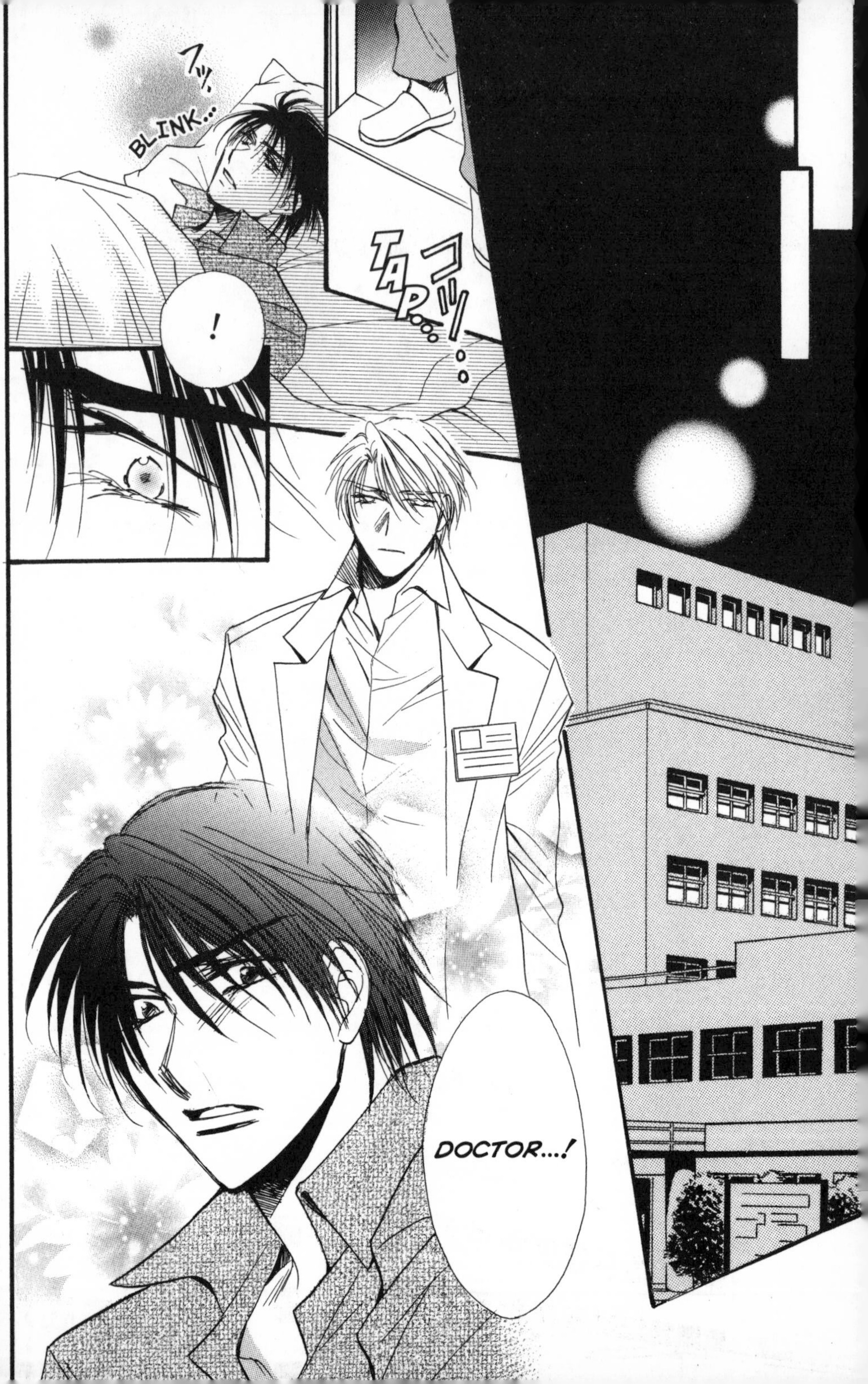
フッ
BLINK...
コツ
TAP...
!
DOCTOR...!

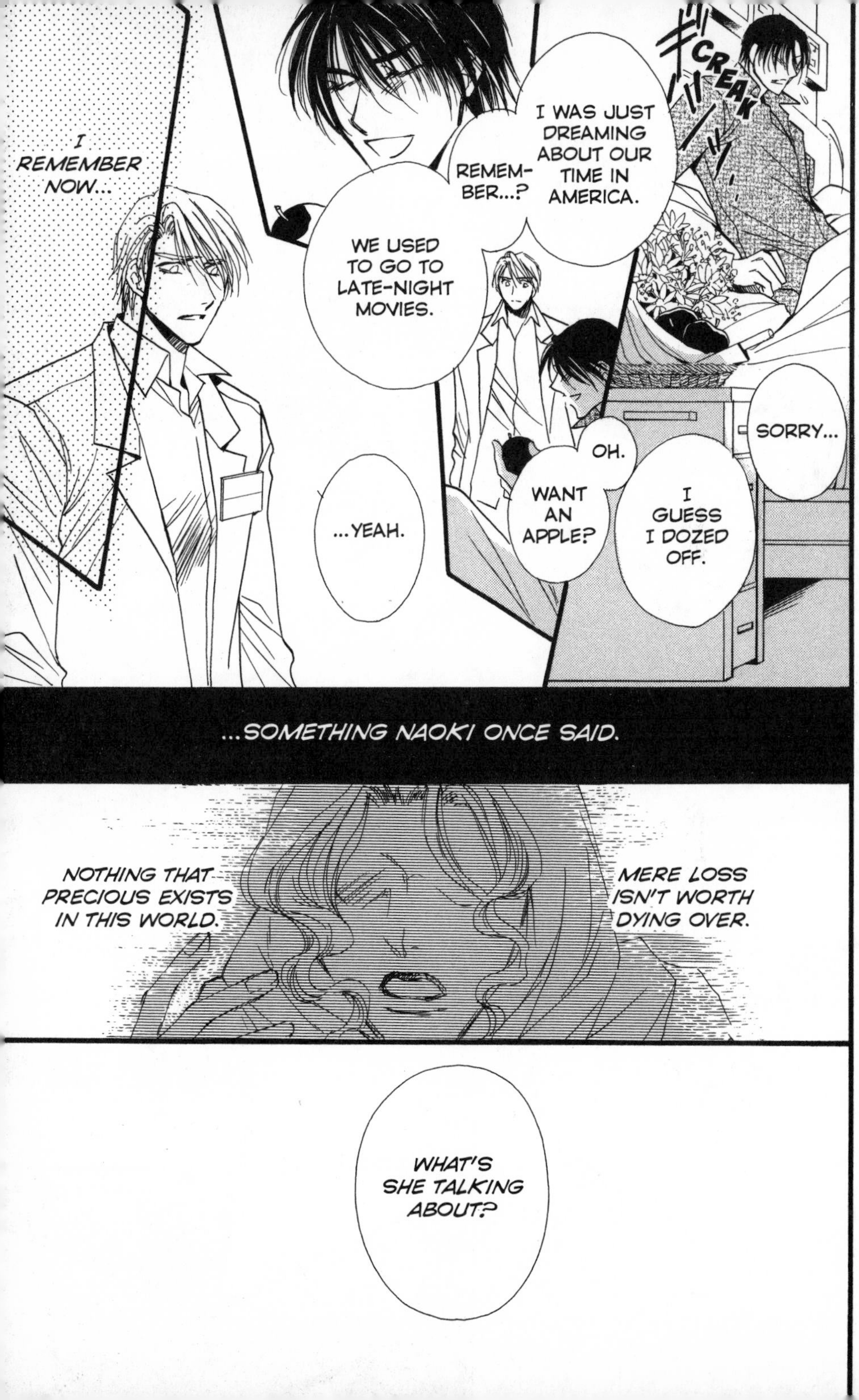
CREAK
SORRY...
I GUESS I DOZED OFF.
OH.
WANT AN APPLE?
I WAS JUST DREAMING ABOUT OUR TIME IN AMERICA.
REMEMBER...?
WE USED TO GO TO LATE-NIGHT MOVIES.
...YEAH.
I REMEMBER NOW...
...SOMETHING NAOKI ONCE SAID.
MERE LOSS ISN'T WORTH DYING OVER.
NOTHING THAT PRECIOUS EXISTS IN THIS WORLD.
WHAT'S SHE TALKING ABOUT?

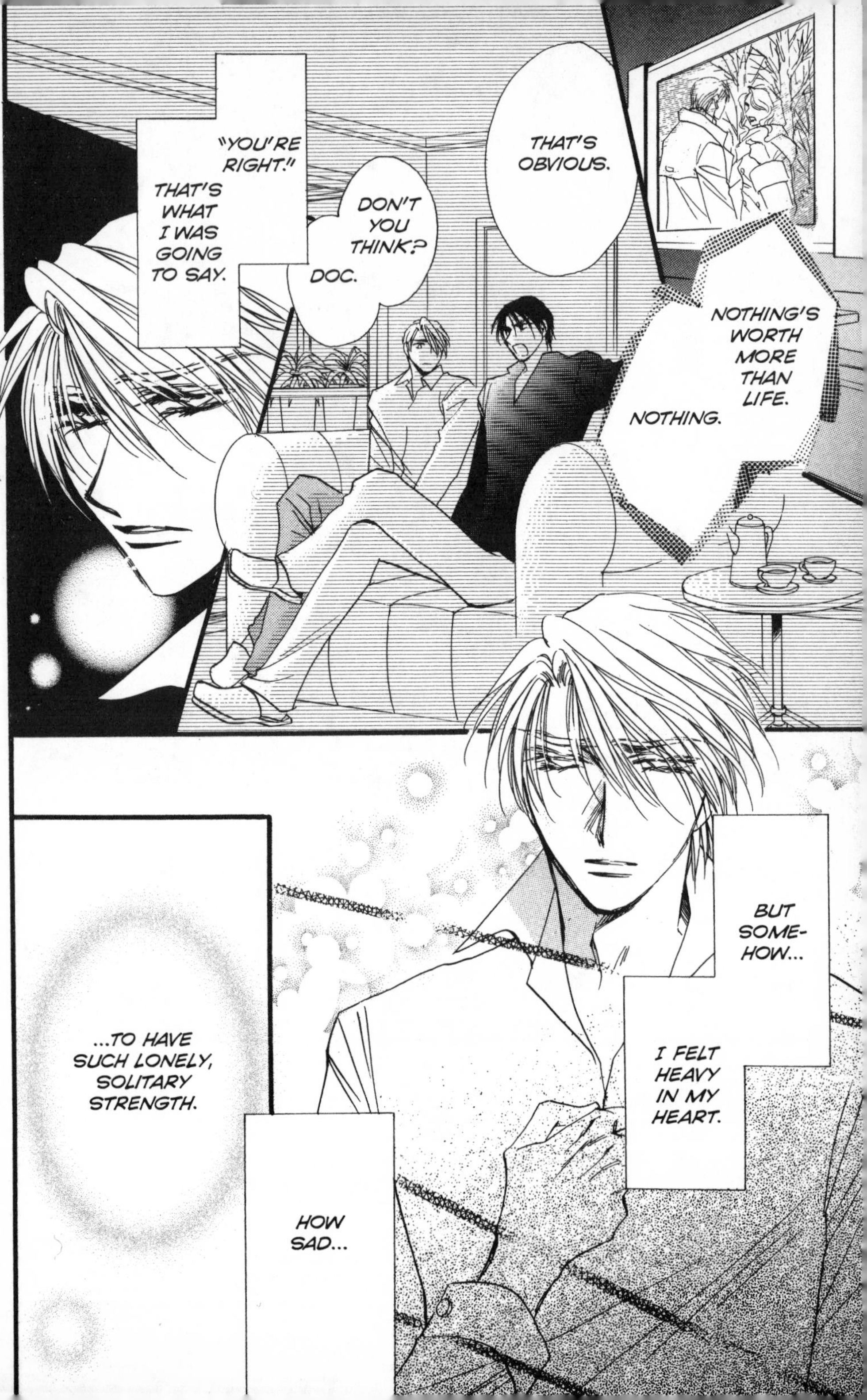
THAT'S OBVIOUS.
NOTHING'S WORTH MORE THAN LIFE.
NOTHING.
DON'T YOU THINK?
DOC.
"YOU'RE RIGHT!"
THAT'S WHAT I WAS GOING TO SAY.
BUT SOME-HOW...
I FELT HEAVY IN MY HEART.
HOW SAD...
...TO HAVE SUCH LONELY, SOLITARY STRENGTH.

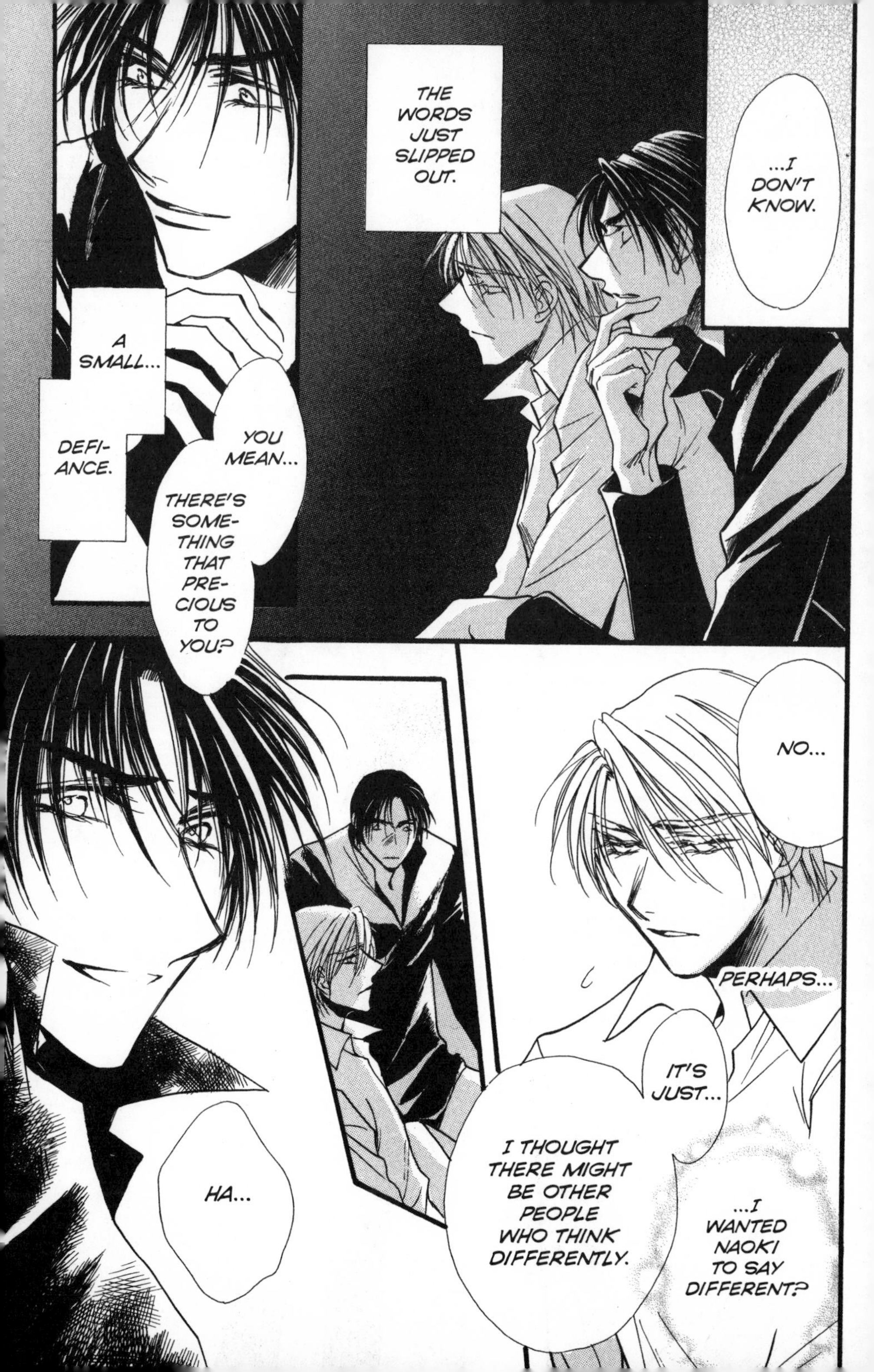
...I DON'T KNOW.
THE WORDS JUST SLIPPED OUT.
A SMALL...
DEFIANCE.
YOU MEAN...
THERE'S SOMETHING THAT PRECIOUS TO YOU?
NO...
PERHAPS...
IT'S JUST...
...I WANTED NAOKI TO SAY DIFFERENT?
I THOUGHT THERE MIGHT BE OTHER PEOPLE WHO THINK DIFFERENTLY.
HA...

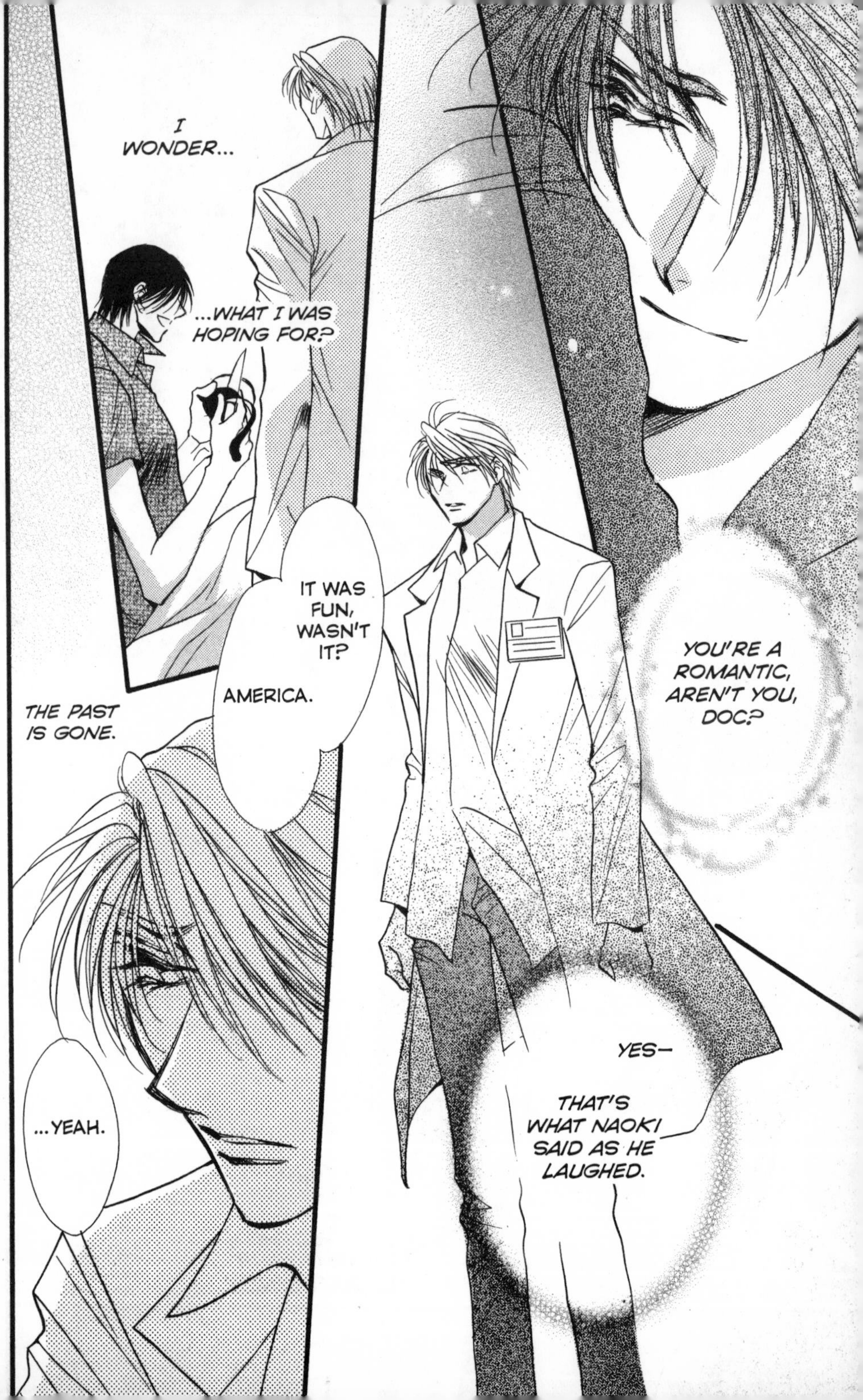
YOU'RE A ROMANTIC, AREN'T YOU, DOC?
YES—
THAT'S WHAT NAOKI SAID AS HE LAUGHED.
IT WAS FUN, WASN'T IT?
AMERICA.
I WONDER...
...WHAT I WAS HOPING FOR?
THE PAST IS GONE.
...YEAH.

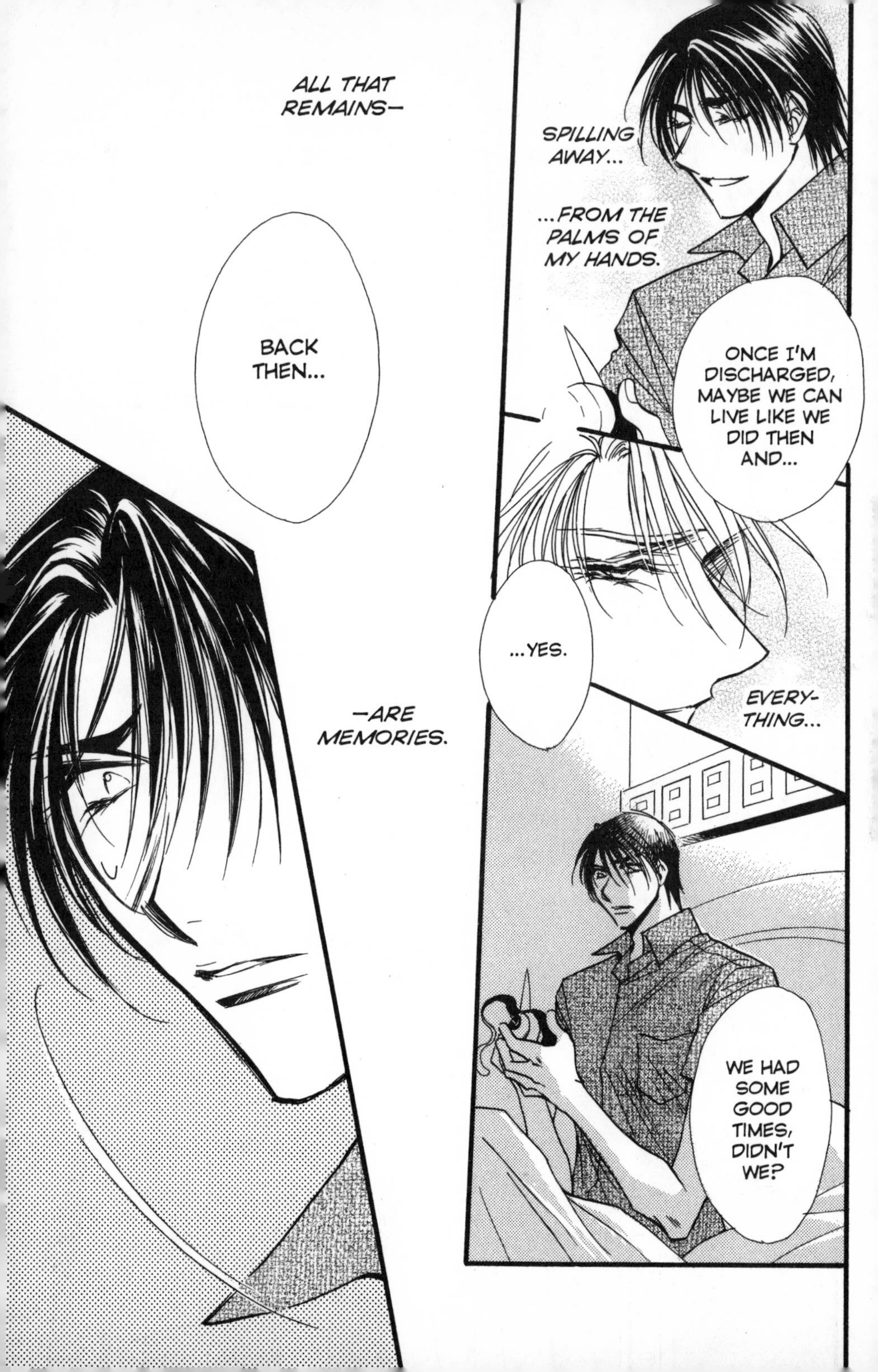
SPILLING AWAY...
...FROM THE PALMS OF MY HANDS.
ONCE I'M DISCHARGED, MAYBE WE CAN LIVE LIKE WE DID THEN AND...
...YES.
EVERY-THING...
WE HAD SOME GOOD TIMES, DIDN'T WE?
ALL THAT REMAINS—
BACK THEN...
—ARE MEMORIES.

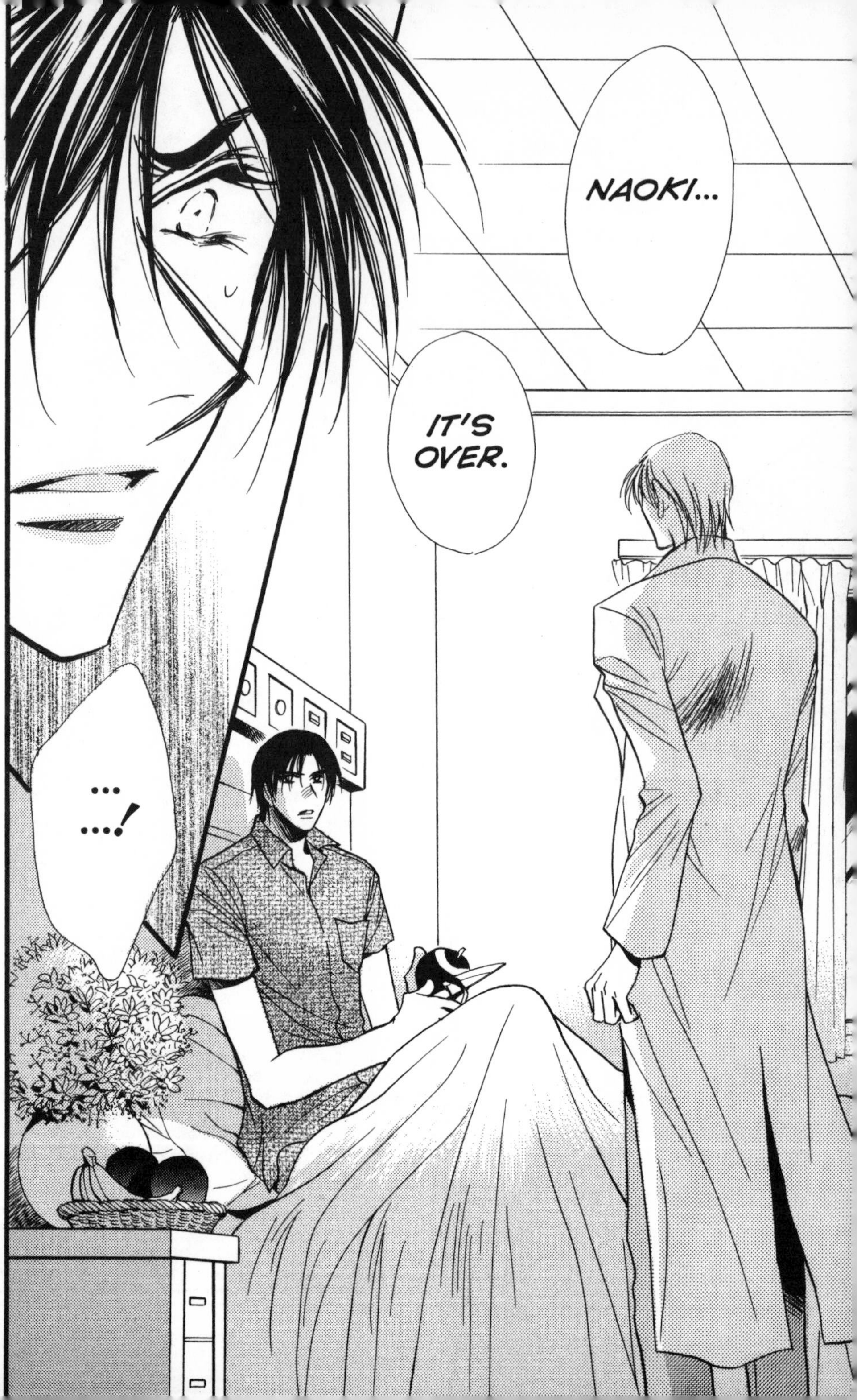
NAOKI...
IT'S OVER.
... ...!

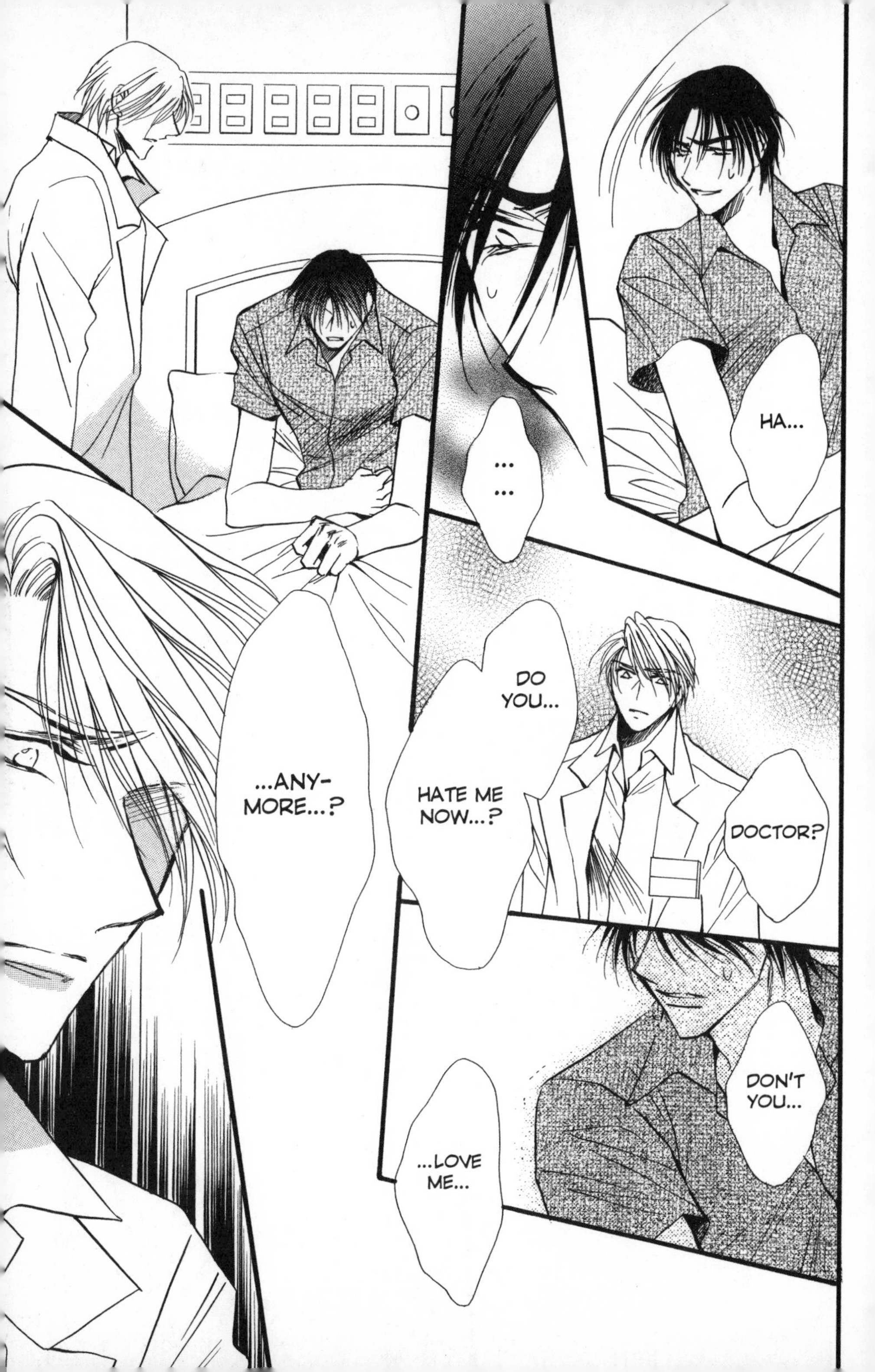
HA...
...
...
DOCTOR?
DO YOU...
HATE ME NOW...?
DON'T YOU...
...LOVE ME...
...ANY-MORE...?

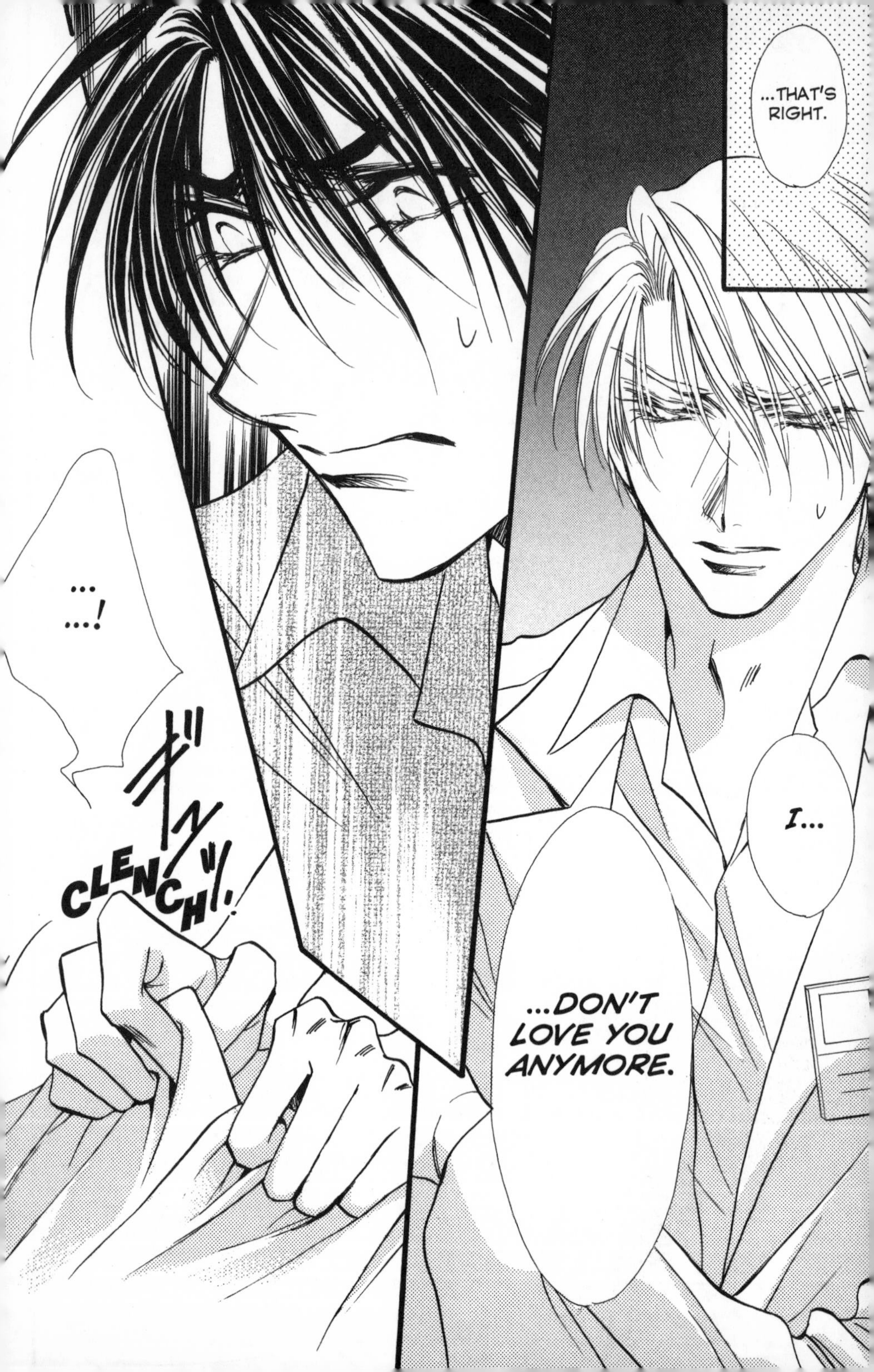
...THAT'S RIGHT.
I...
...DON'T LOVE YOU ANYMORE.
... ...!
CLENCH!!

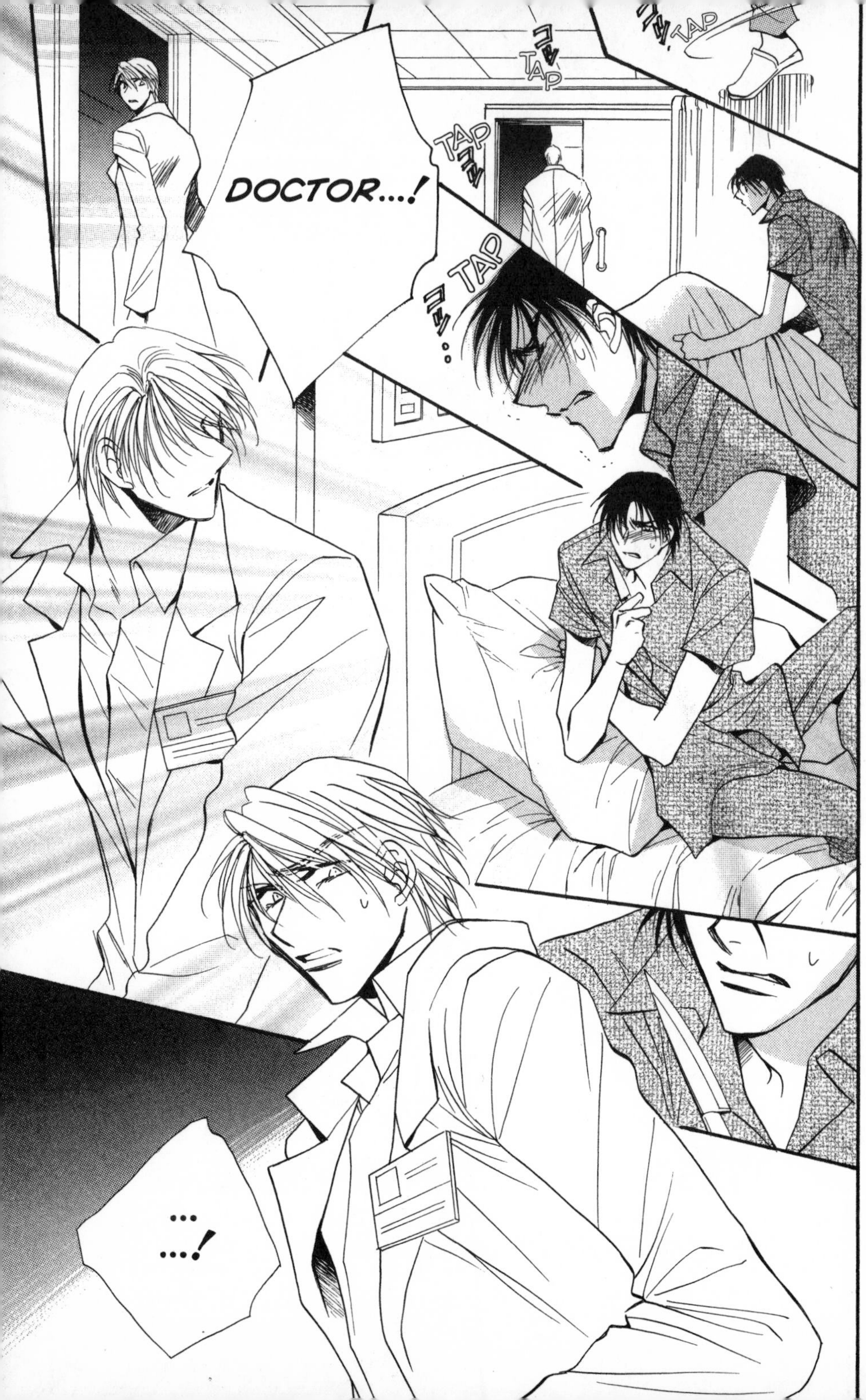
TAP
TAP TAP
TAP
DOCTOR...!
TAP
......!

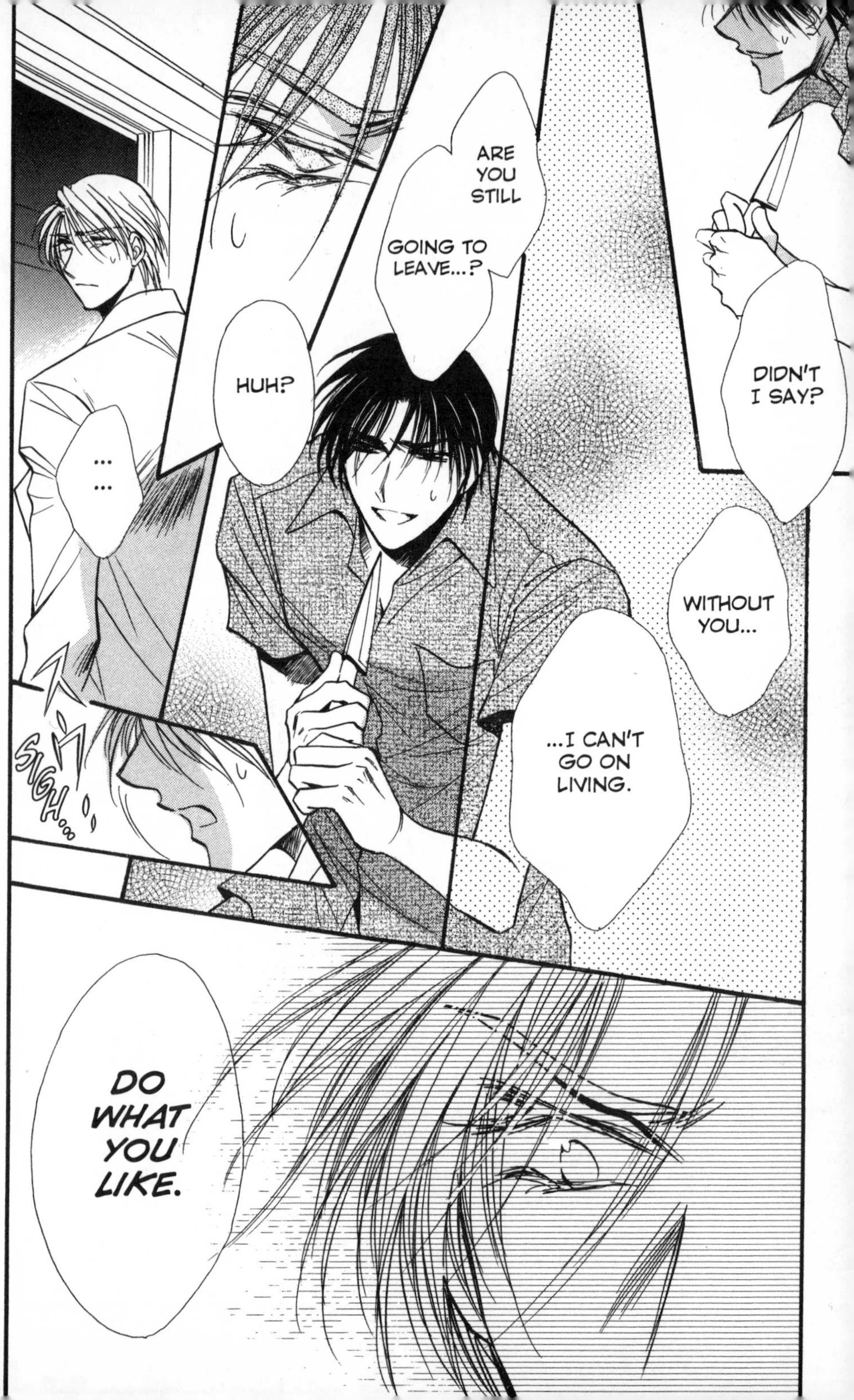
DIDN'T I SAY?
WITHOUT YOU...
...I CAN'T GO ON LIVING.
ARE YOU STILL GOING TO LEAVE...?
HUH?
......
SIGH...
DO WHAT YOU LIKE.

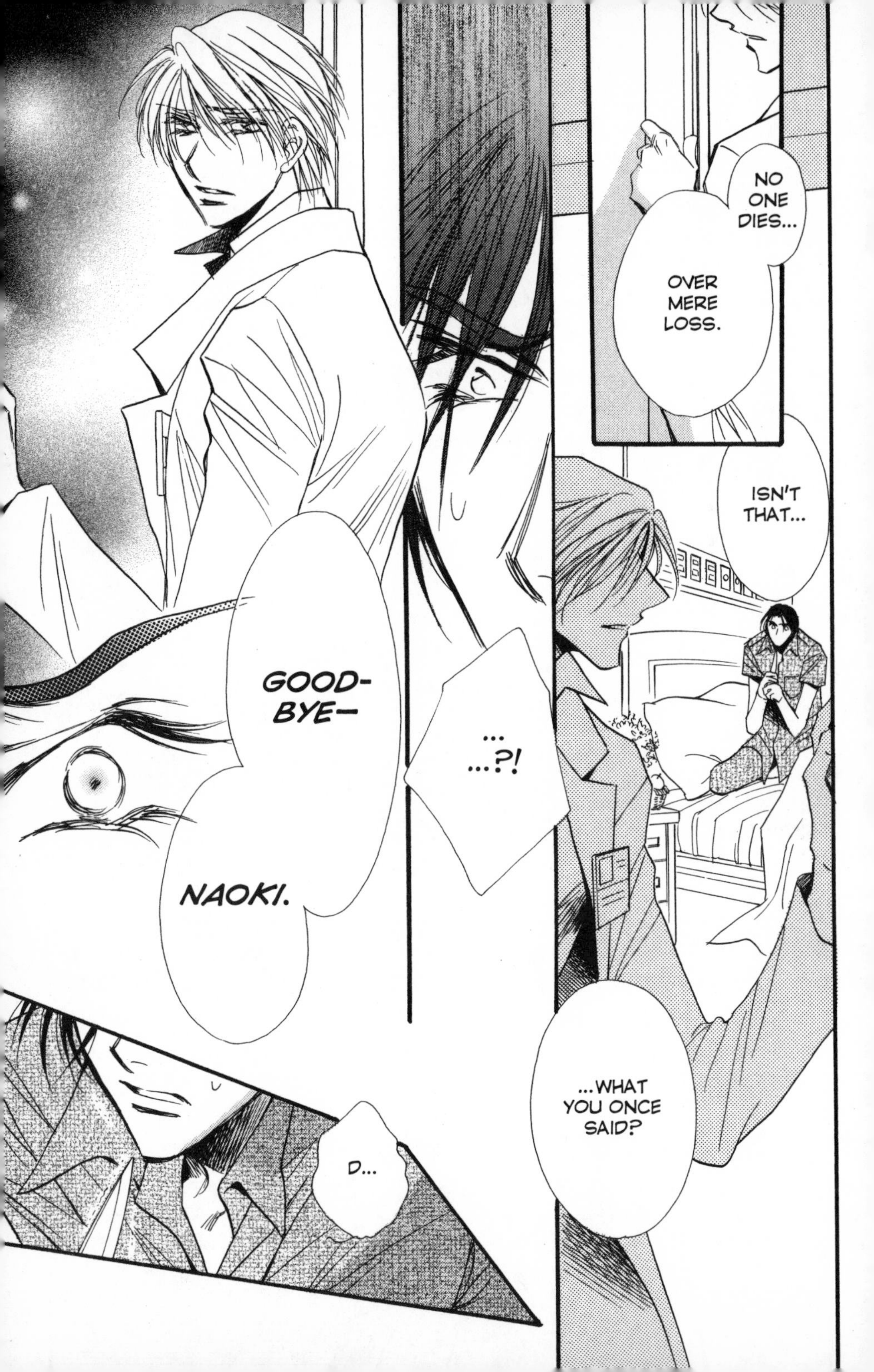
NO ONE DIES...
OVER MERE LOSS.
ISN'T THAT...
...WHAT YOU ONCE SAID?
... ...?!
GOOD-BYE—
NAOKI.
D...

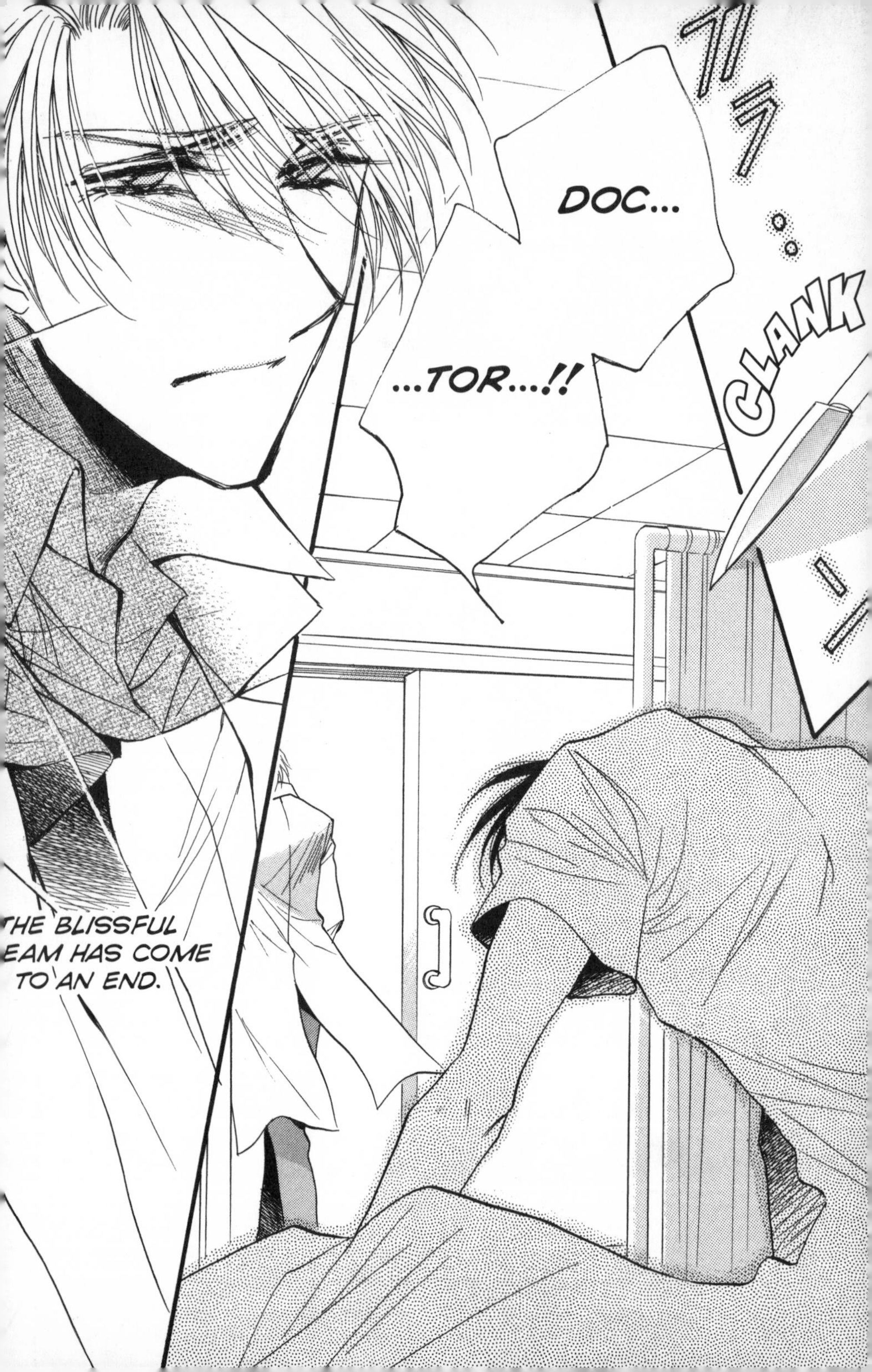
ガラ
CLANK
DOC...
...TOR...!!
THE BLISSFUL
EAM HAS COME
TO AN END.

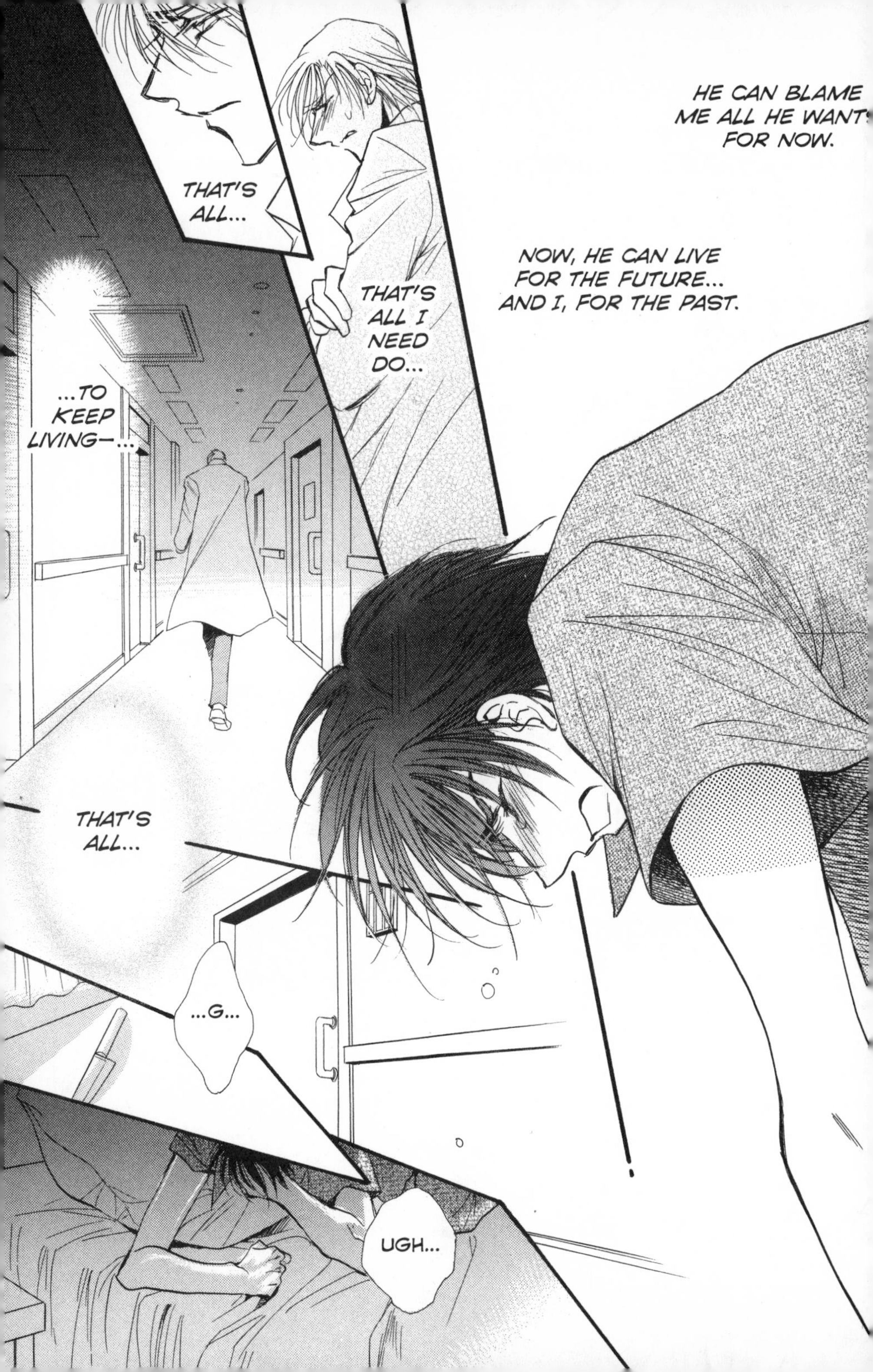
HE CAN BLAME ME ALL HE WANTS FOR NOW.
NOW, HE CAN LIVE FOR THE FUTURE... AND I, FOR THE PAST.
THAT'S ALL...
THAT'S ALL I NEED DO...
...TO KEEP LIVING—...
THAT'S ALL...
...G...
UGH...

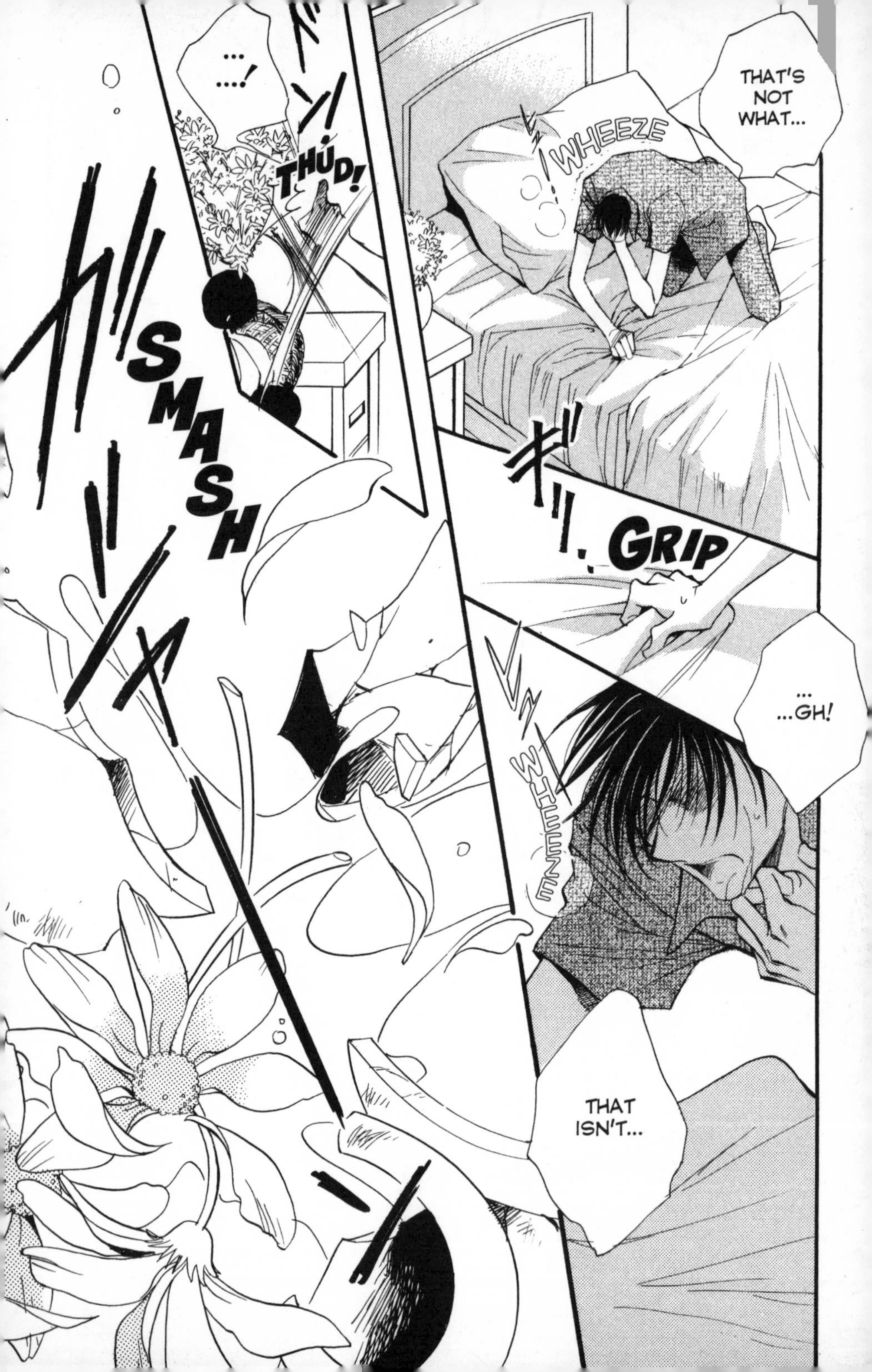
THAT'S NOT WHAT...
WHEEZE
GRIP
... ...GH!
WHEEZE
THAT ISN'T...
... ...!
THUD!
SMASH

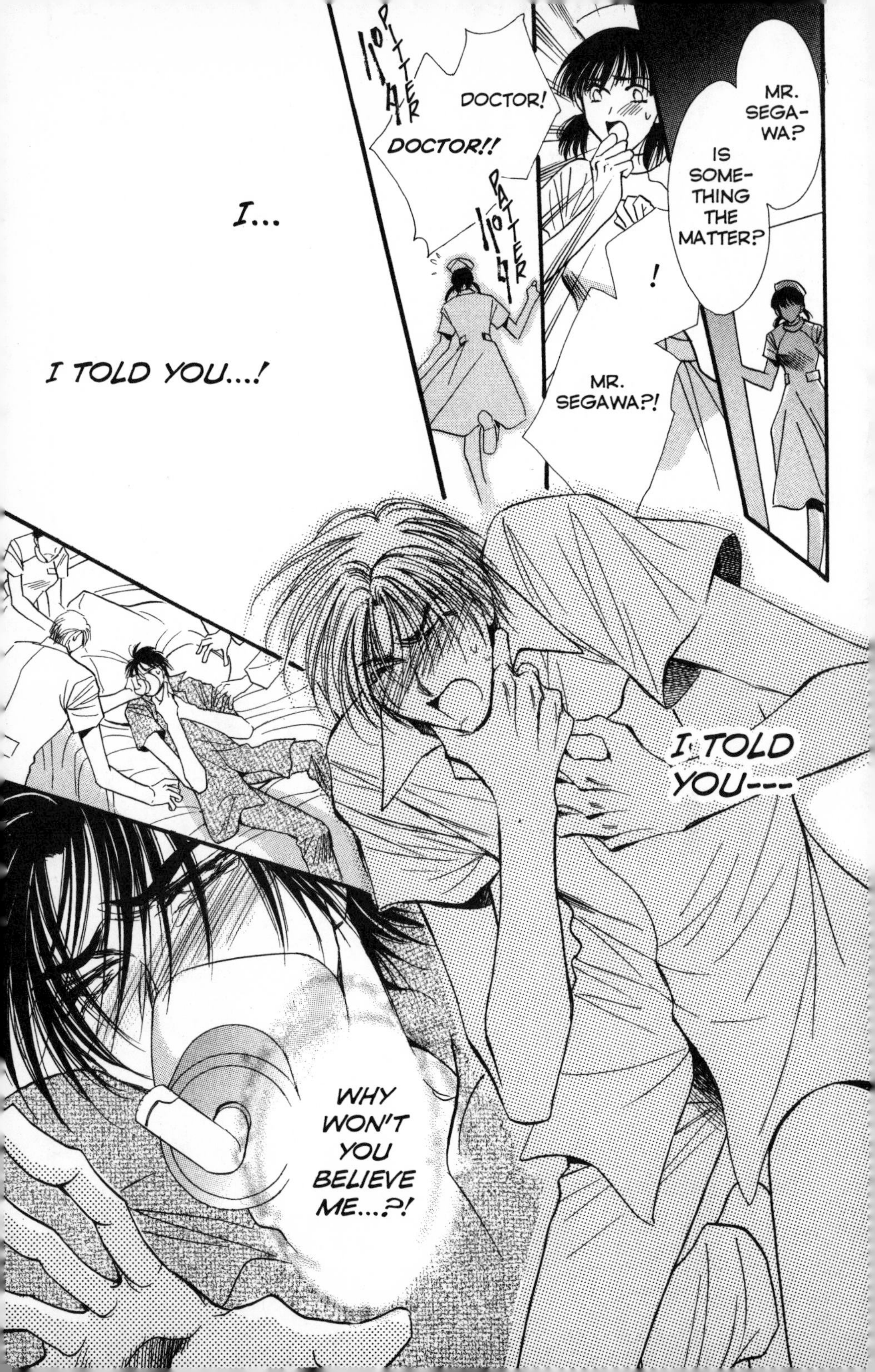
MR. SEGAWA?
IS SOMETHING THE MATTER?
!
MR. SEGAWA?!
PITTER
DOCTOR!
DOCTOR!!
PATTER
I...
I TOLD YOU...!
I TOLD YOU---
WHY WON'T YOU BELIEVE ME...?!

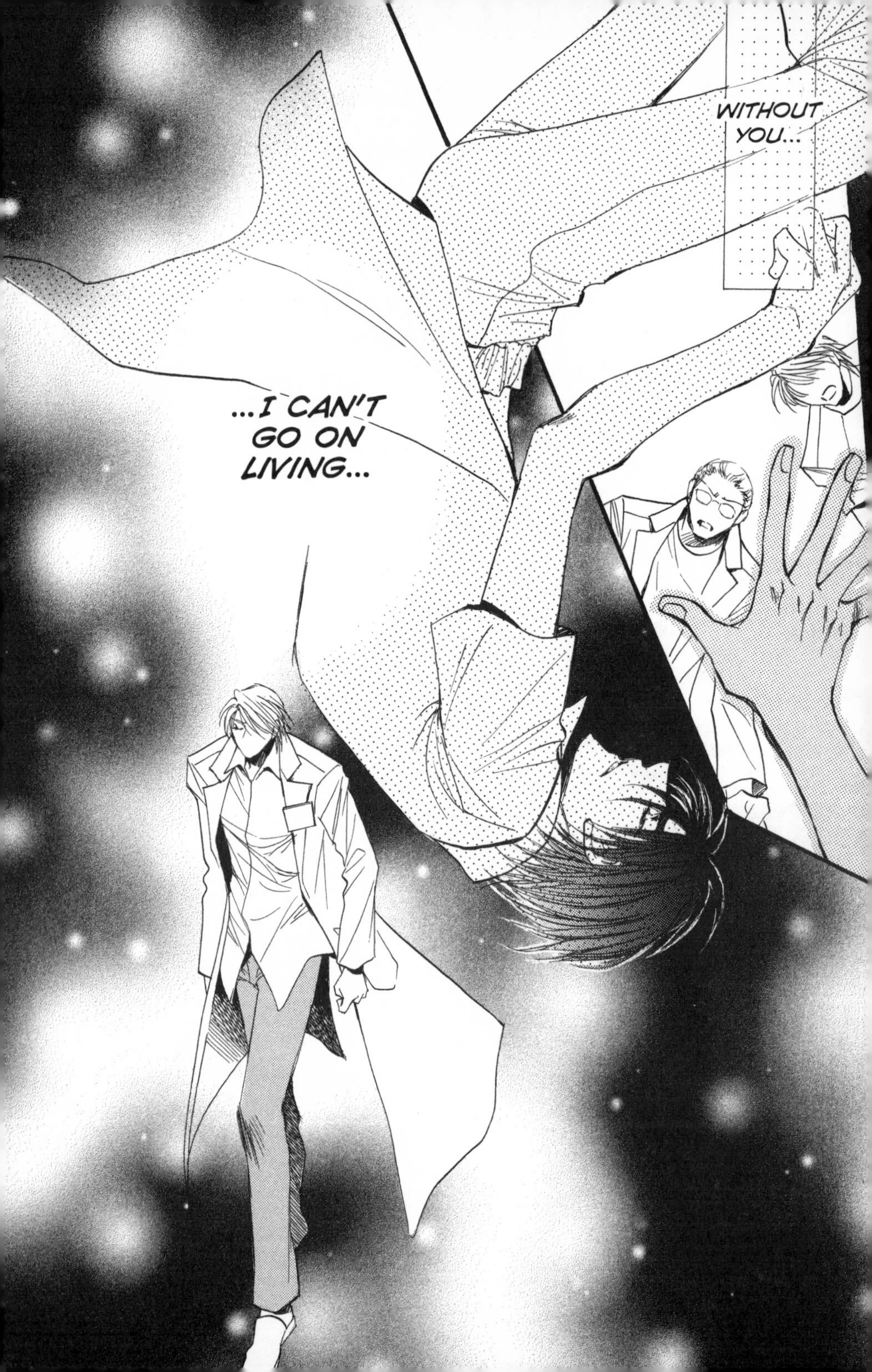
WITHOUT YOU...
...I CAN'T GO ON LIVING...

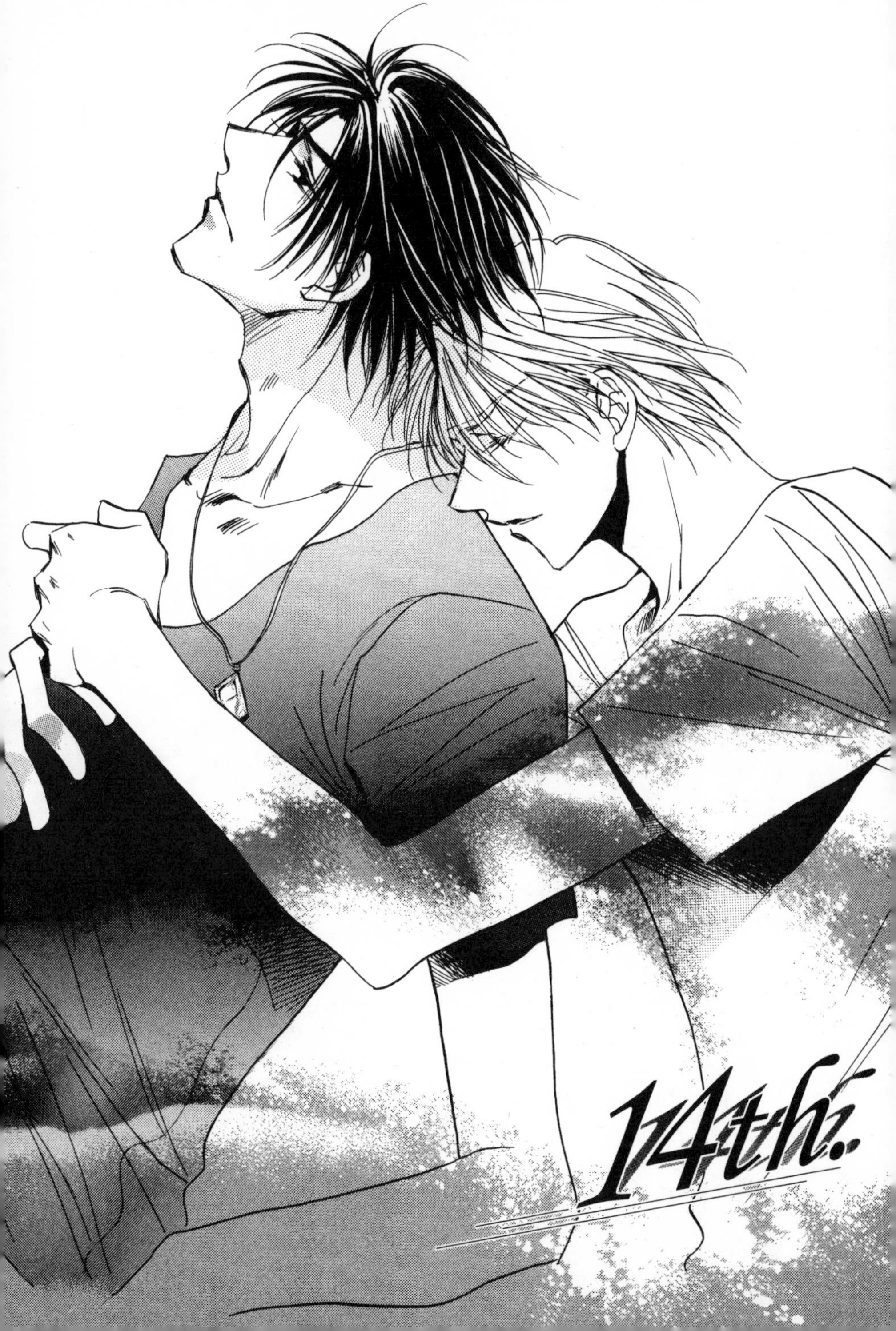
14th.

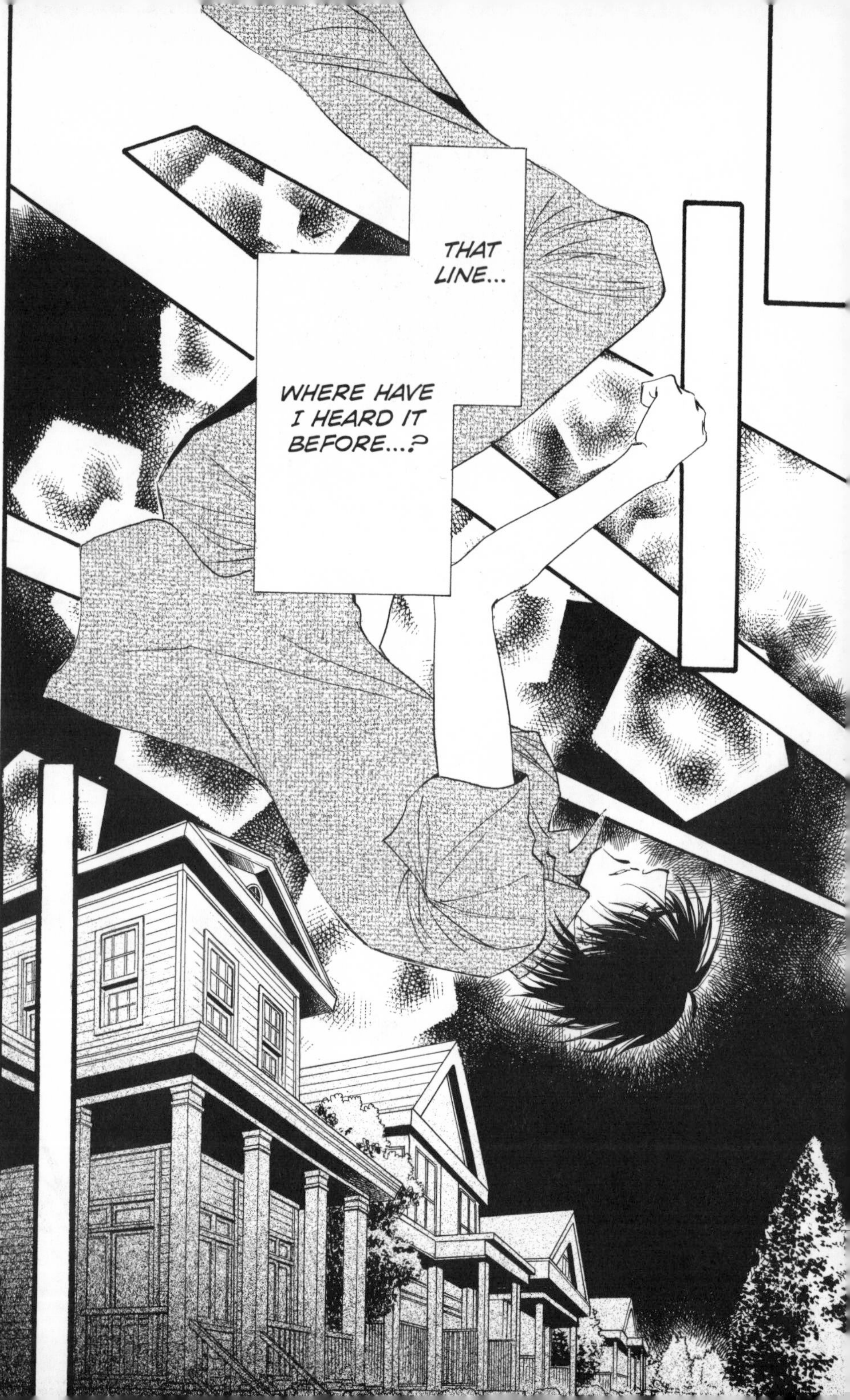
THAT LINE...
WHERE HAVE I HEARD IT BEFORE...?

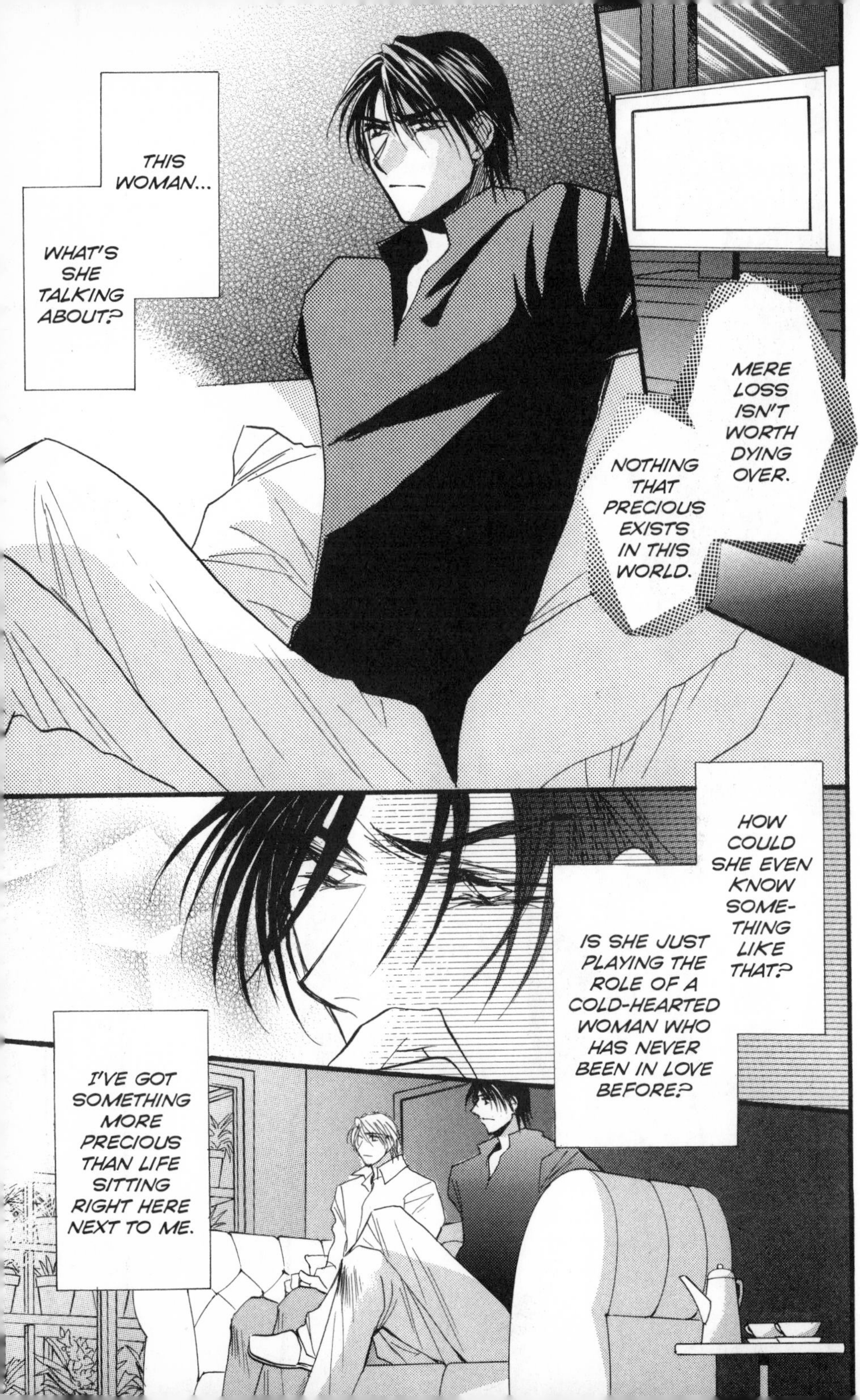
MERE LOSS ISN'T WORTH DYING OVER.
NOTHING THAT PRECIOUS EXISTS IN THIS WORLD.
THIS WOMAN...
WHAT'S SHE TALKING ABOUT?
HOW COULD SHE EVEN KNOW SOME-THING LIKE THAT?
IS SHE JUST PLAYING THE ROLE OF A COLD-HEARTED WOMAN WHO HAS NEVER BEEN IN LOVE BEFORE?
I'VE GOT SOMETHING MORE PRECIOUS THAN LIFE SITTING RIGHT HERE NEXT TO ME.

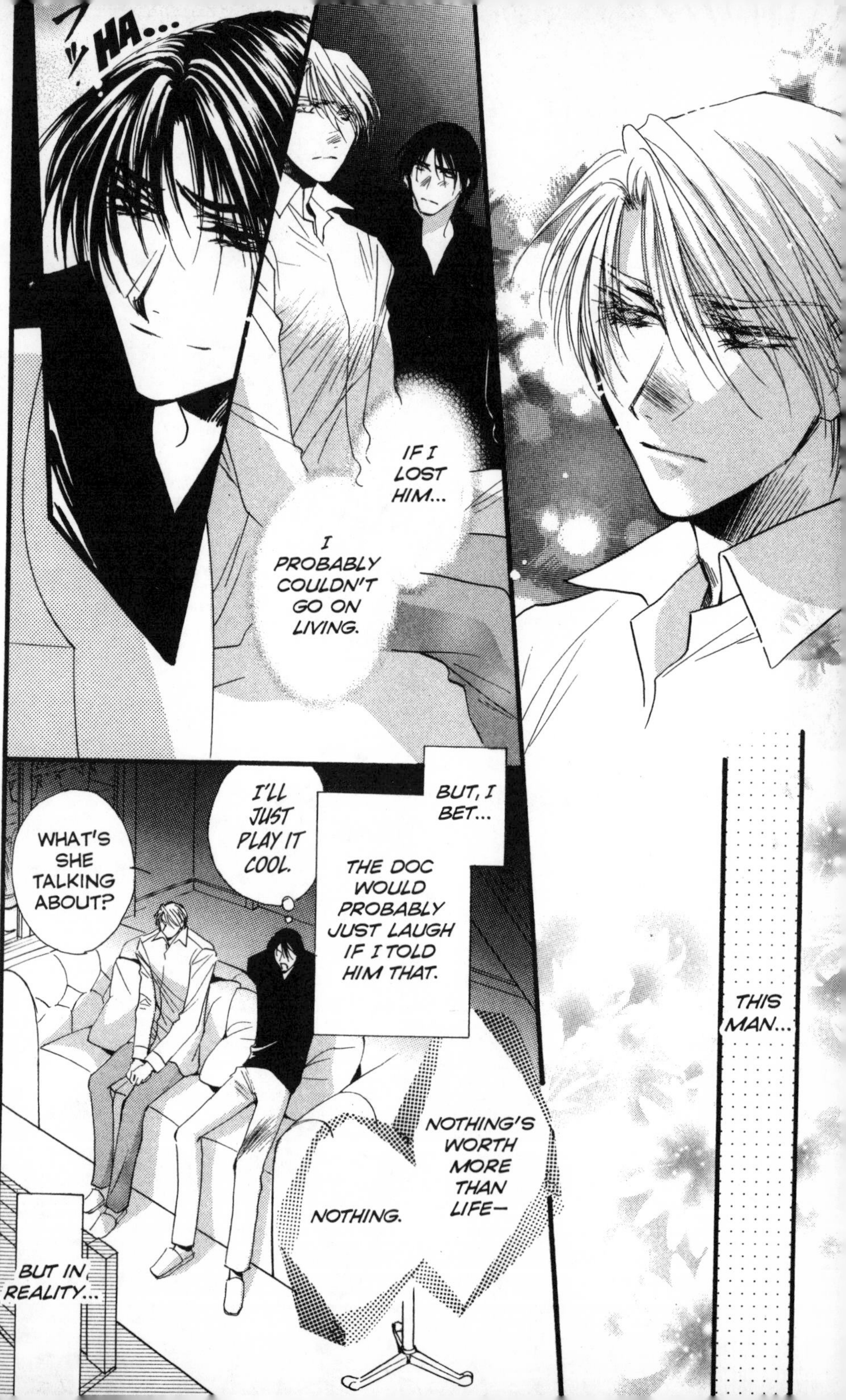
HA...
IF I LOST HIM...
I PROBABLY COULDN'T GO ON LIVING.
THIS MAN...
BUT, I BET...
THE DOC WOULD PROBABLY JUST LAUGH IF I TOLD HIM THAT.
I'LL JUST PLAY IT COOL.
WHAT'S SHE TALKING ABOUT?
NOTHING'S WORTH MORE THAN LIFE—
NOTHING.
BUT IN, REALITY...

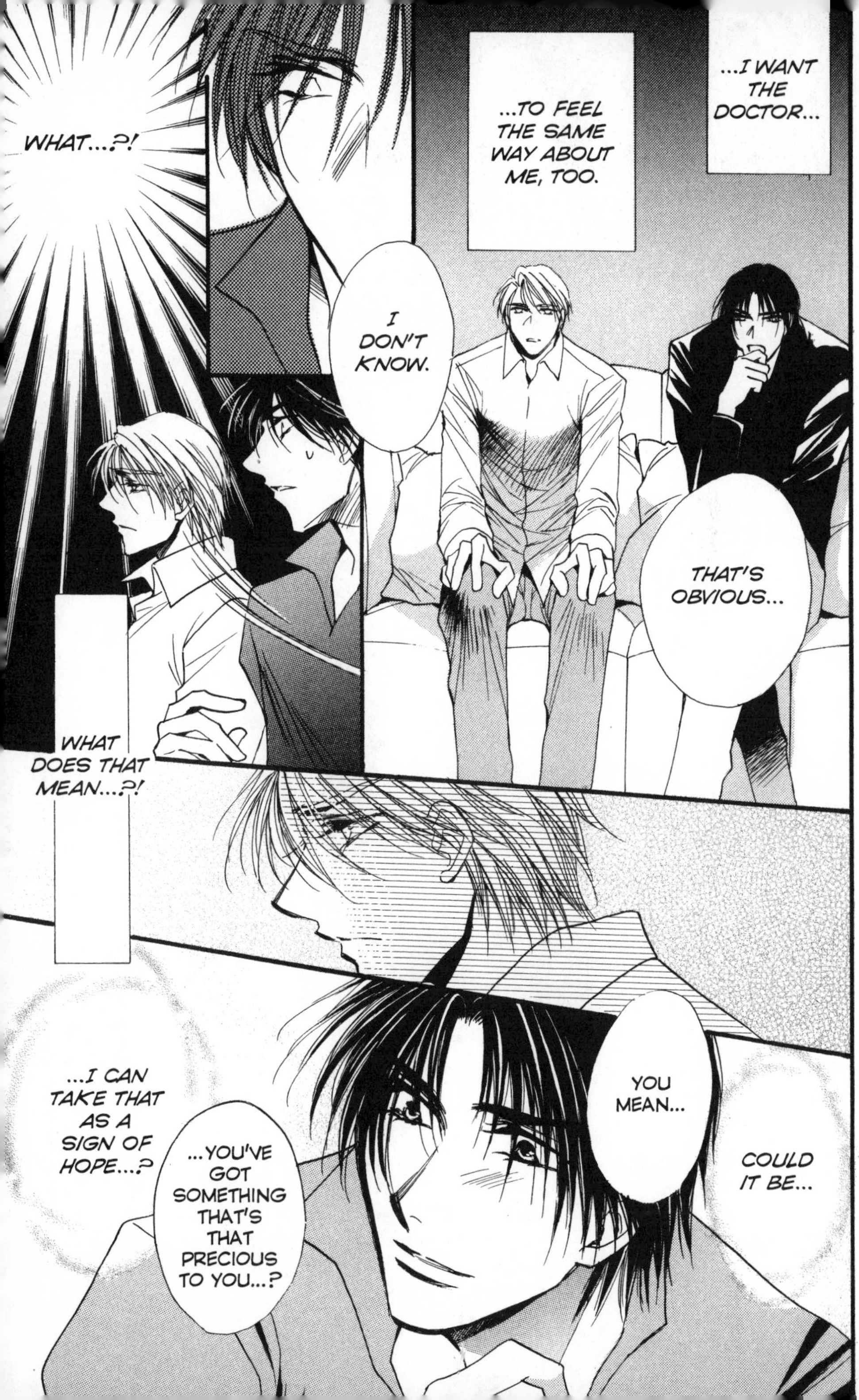
...I WANT THE DOCTOR...
...TO FEEL THE SAME WAY ABOUT ME, TOO.
I DON'T KNOW.
THAT'S OBVIOUS...
WHAT...?!
WHAT DOES THAT MEAN...?!
YOU MEAN...
COULD IT BE...
...YOU'VE GOT SOMETHING THAT'S THAT PRECIOUS TO YOU...?
...I CAN TAKE THAT AS A SIGN OF HOPE...?

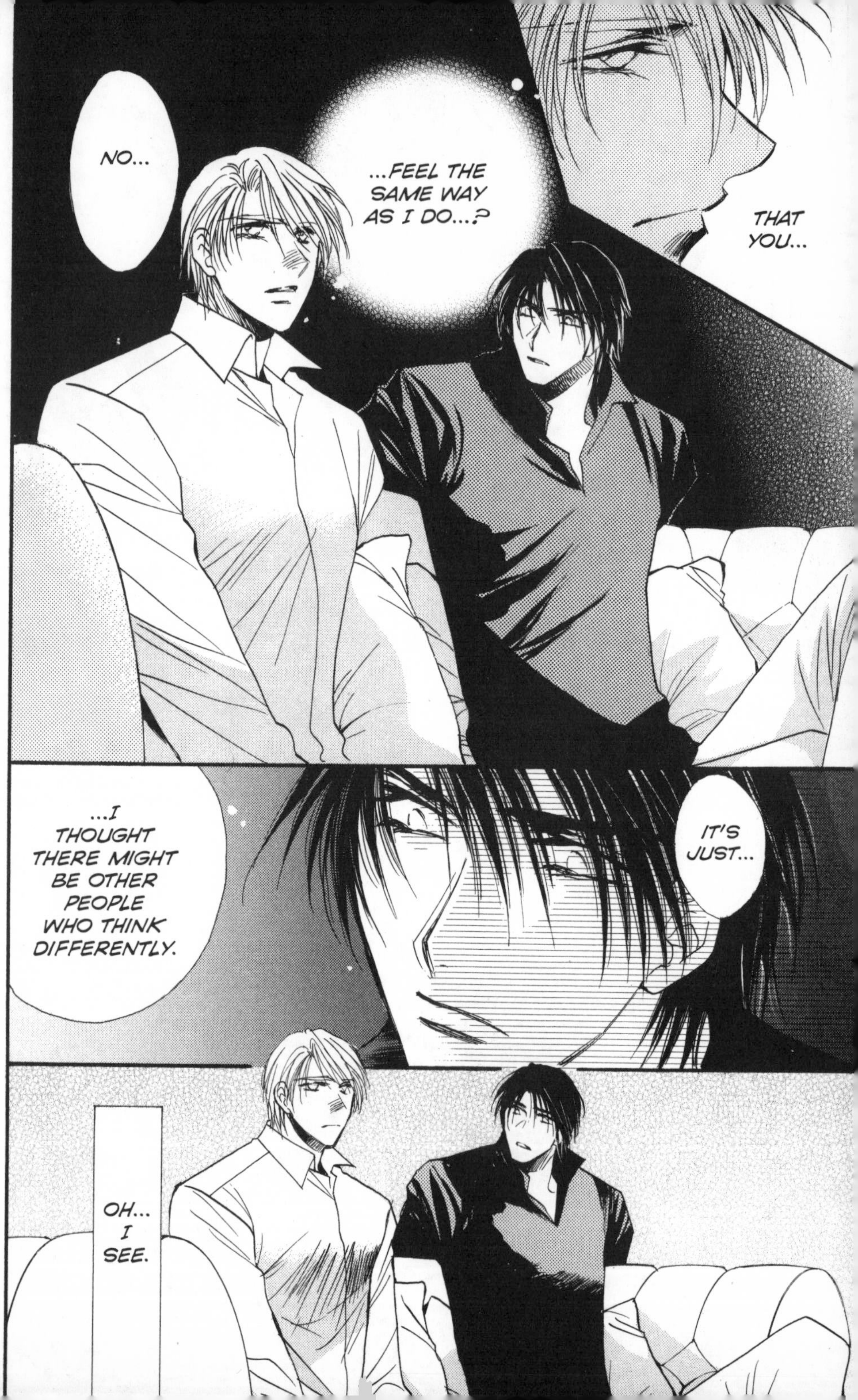
THAT YOU...
...FEEL THE SAME WAY AS I DO...?
NO...
IT'S JUST...
...I THOUGHT THERE MIGHT BE OTHER PEOPLE WHO THINK DIFFERENTLY.
OH... I SEE.

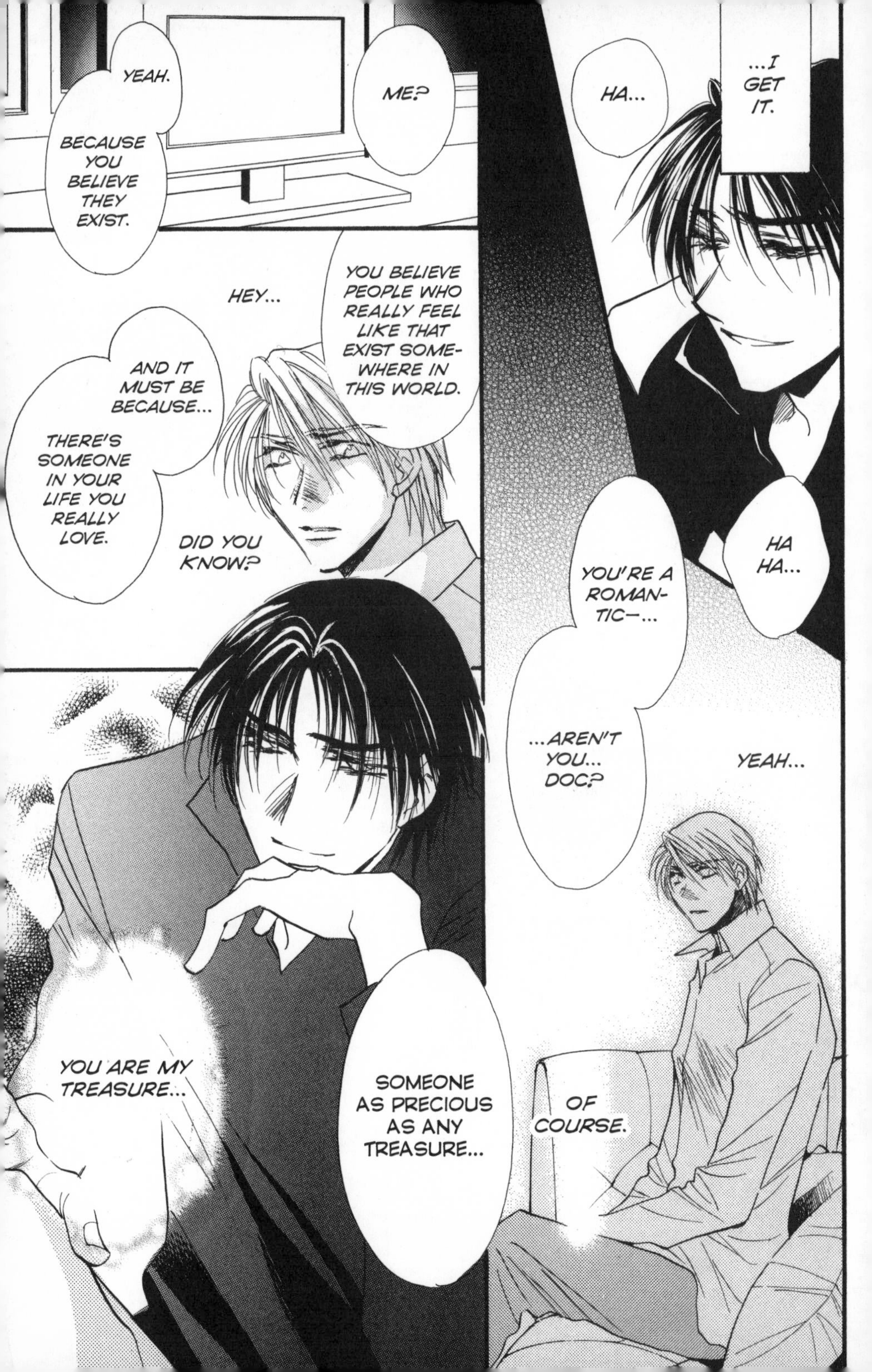
...I GET IT.
HA...
HA HA...
YOU'RE A ROMAN-TIC—...
...AREN'T YOU... DOC?
YEAH...
OF COURSE.
ME?
YEAH.
BECAUSE YOU BELIEVE THEY EXIST.
YOU BELIEVE PEOPLE WHO REALLY FEEL LIKE THAT EXIST SOME-WHERE IN THIS WORLD.
HEY...
AND IT MUST BE BECAUSE...
THERE'S SOMEONE IN YOUR LIFE YOU REALLY LOVE.
DID YOU KNOW?
SOMEONE AS PRECIOUS AS ANY TREASURE...
YOU ARE MY TREASURE...

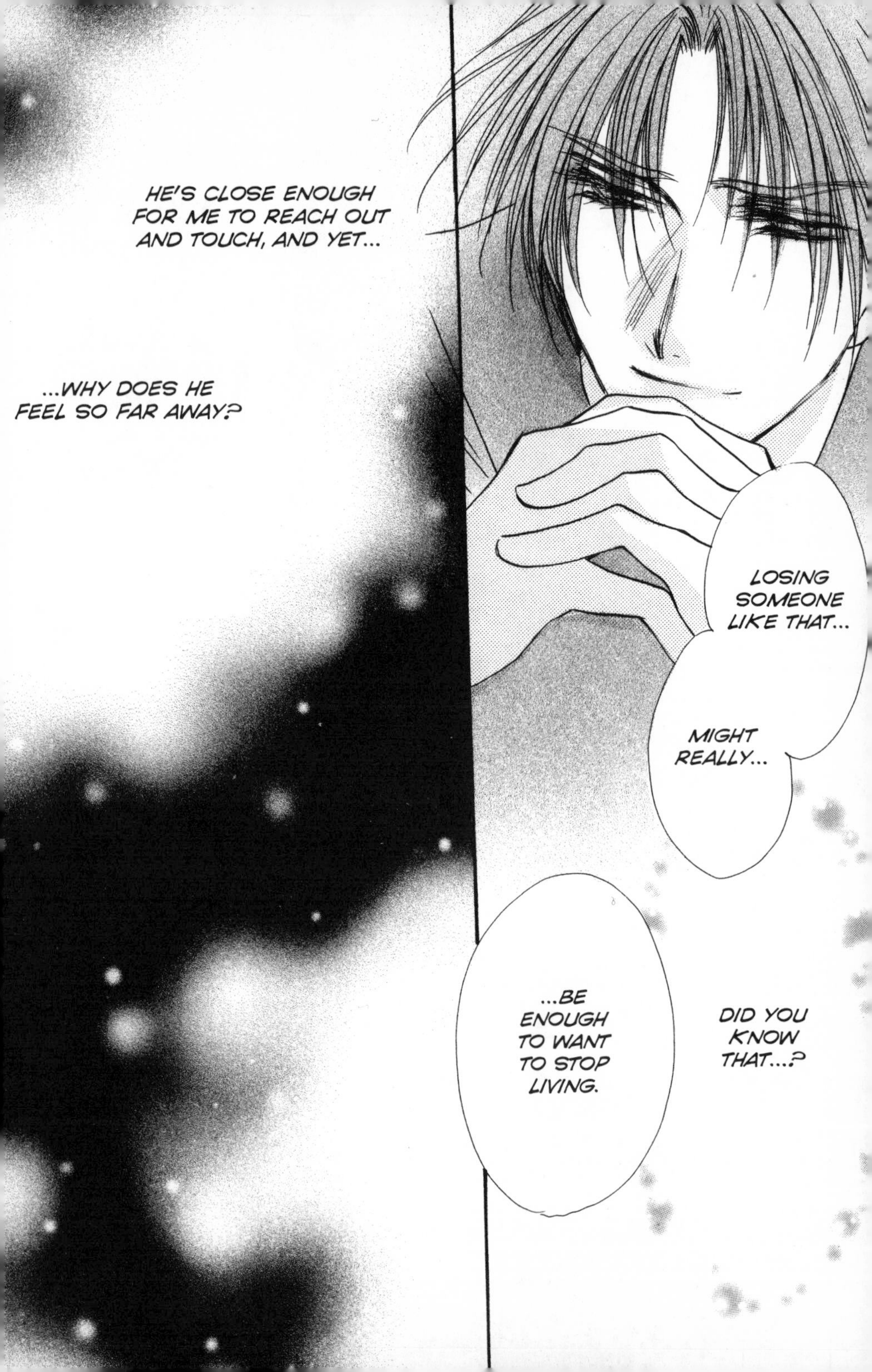
LOSING SOMEONE LIKE THAT...
MIGHT REALLY...
...BE ENOUGH TO WANT TO STOP LIVING.
DID YOU KNOW THAT...?
HE'S CLOSE ENOUGH FOR ME TO REACH OUT AND TOUCH, AND YET...
...WHY DOES HE FEEL SO FAR AWAY?

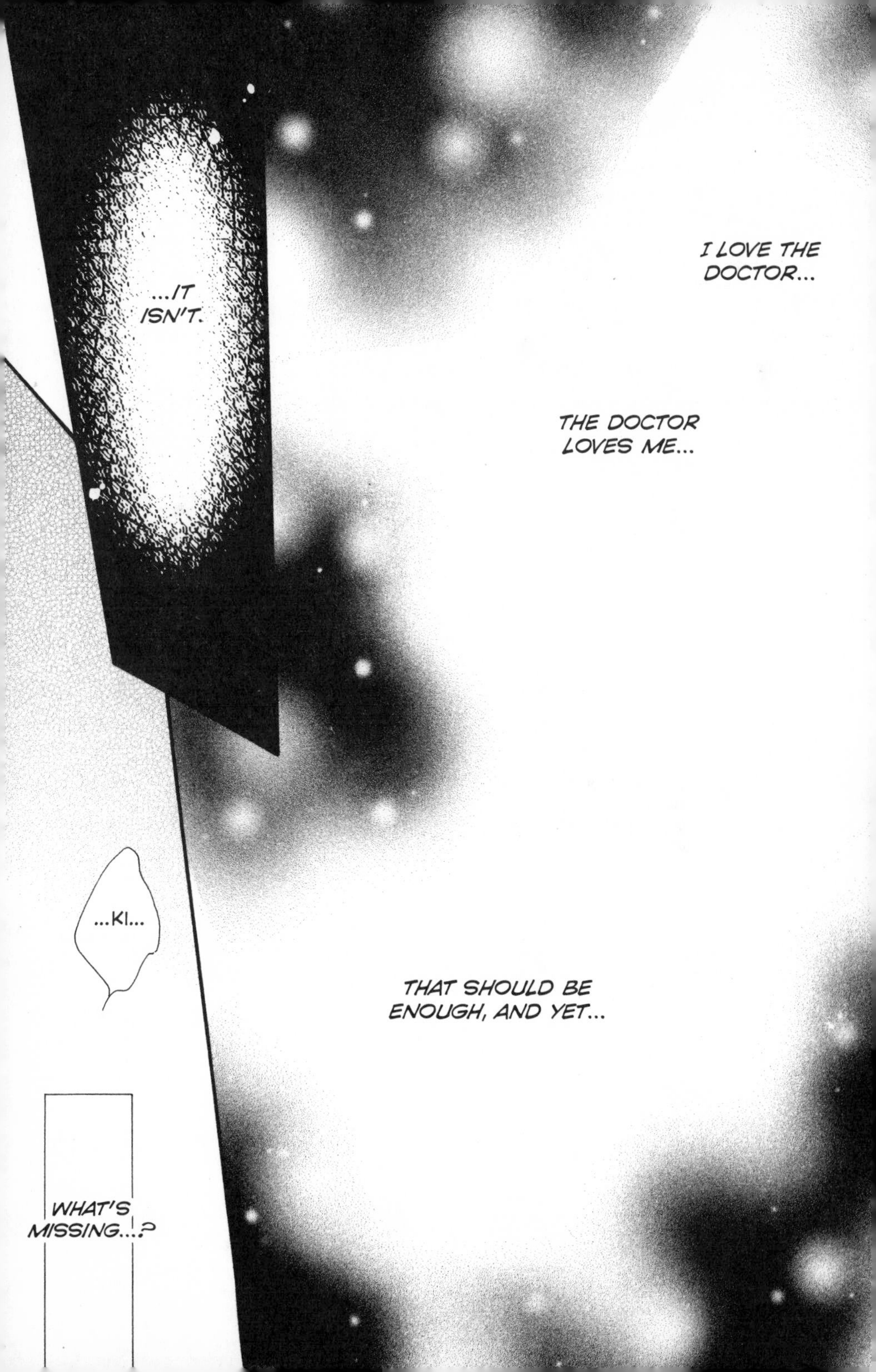
I LOVE THE DOCTOR...
THE DOCTOR LOVES ME...
THAT SHOULD BE ENOUGH, AND YET...
...IT ISN'T.
...KI...
WHAT'S MISSING...?

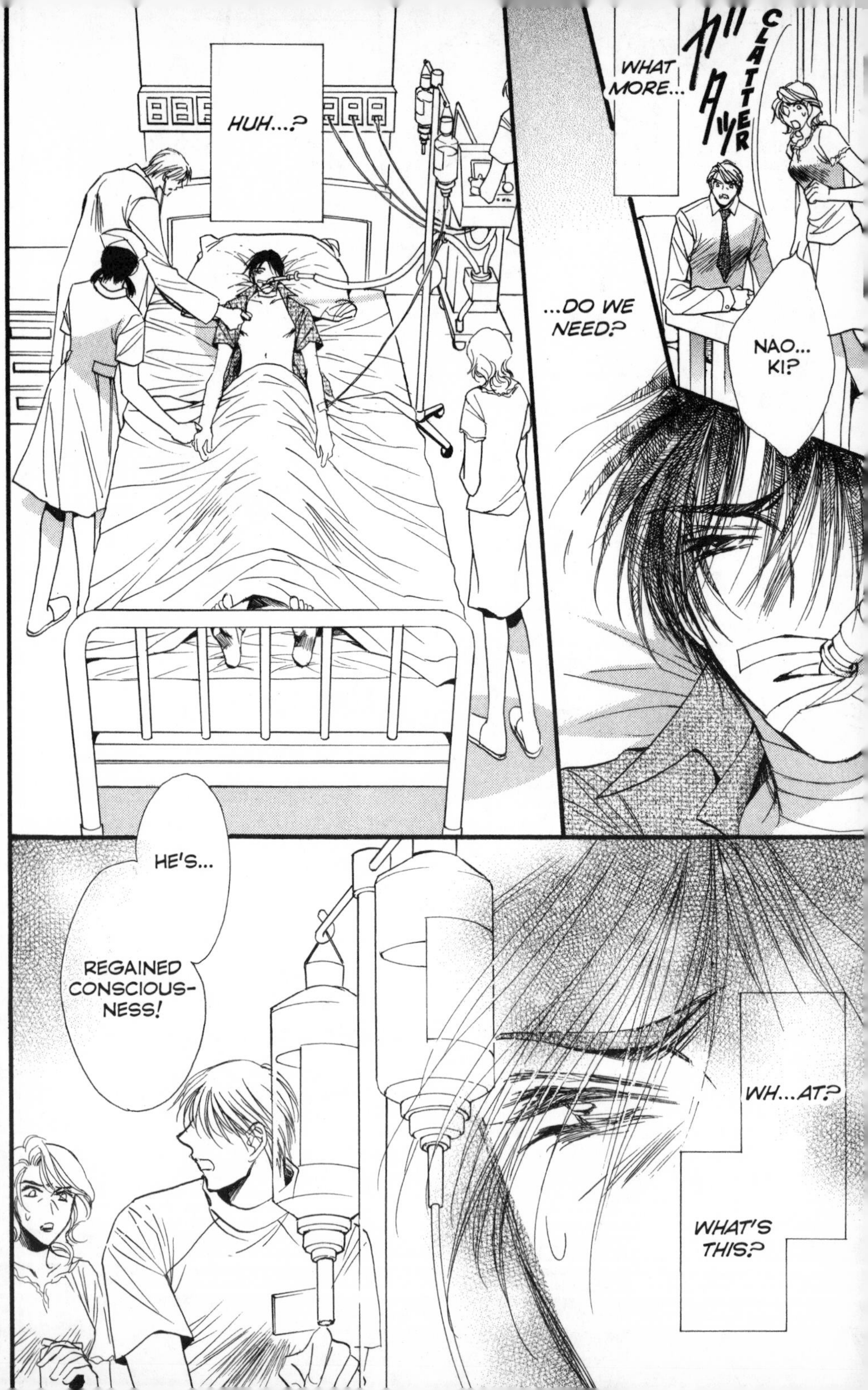
WHAT MORE...
ガタッ
CLATTER
...DO WE NEED?
NAO... KI?
HUH...?
WH...AT?
WHAT'S THIS?
HE'S...
REGAINED CONSCIOUS-NESS!

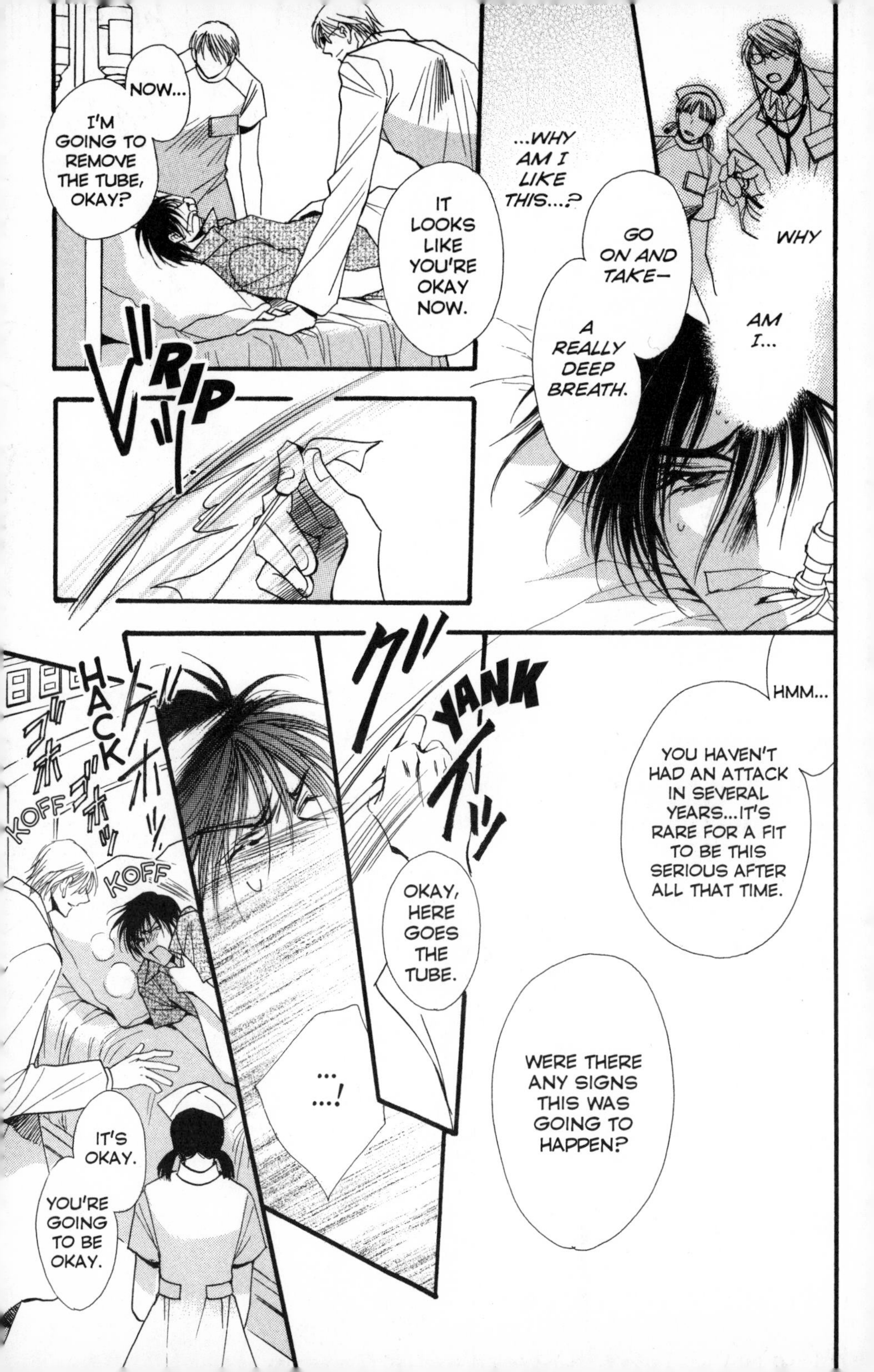
WHY
AM I...
...WHY AM I LIKE THIS...?
GO ON AND TAKE—
A REALLY DEEP BREATH.
IT LOOKS LIKE YOU'RE OKAY NOW.
NOW...
I'M GOING TO REMOVE THE TUBE, OKAY?
RIP
HMM...
YOU HAVEN'T HAD AN ATTACK IN SEVERAL YEARS...IT'S RARE FOR A FIT TO BE THIS SERIOUS AFTER ALL THAT TIME.
WERE THERE ANY SIGNS THIS WAS GOING TO HAPPEN?
YANK
OKAY, HERE GOES THE TUBE.
...
...!
HACK
KOFF
KOFF
IT'S OKAY.
YOU'RE GOING TO BE OKAY.

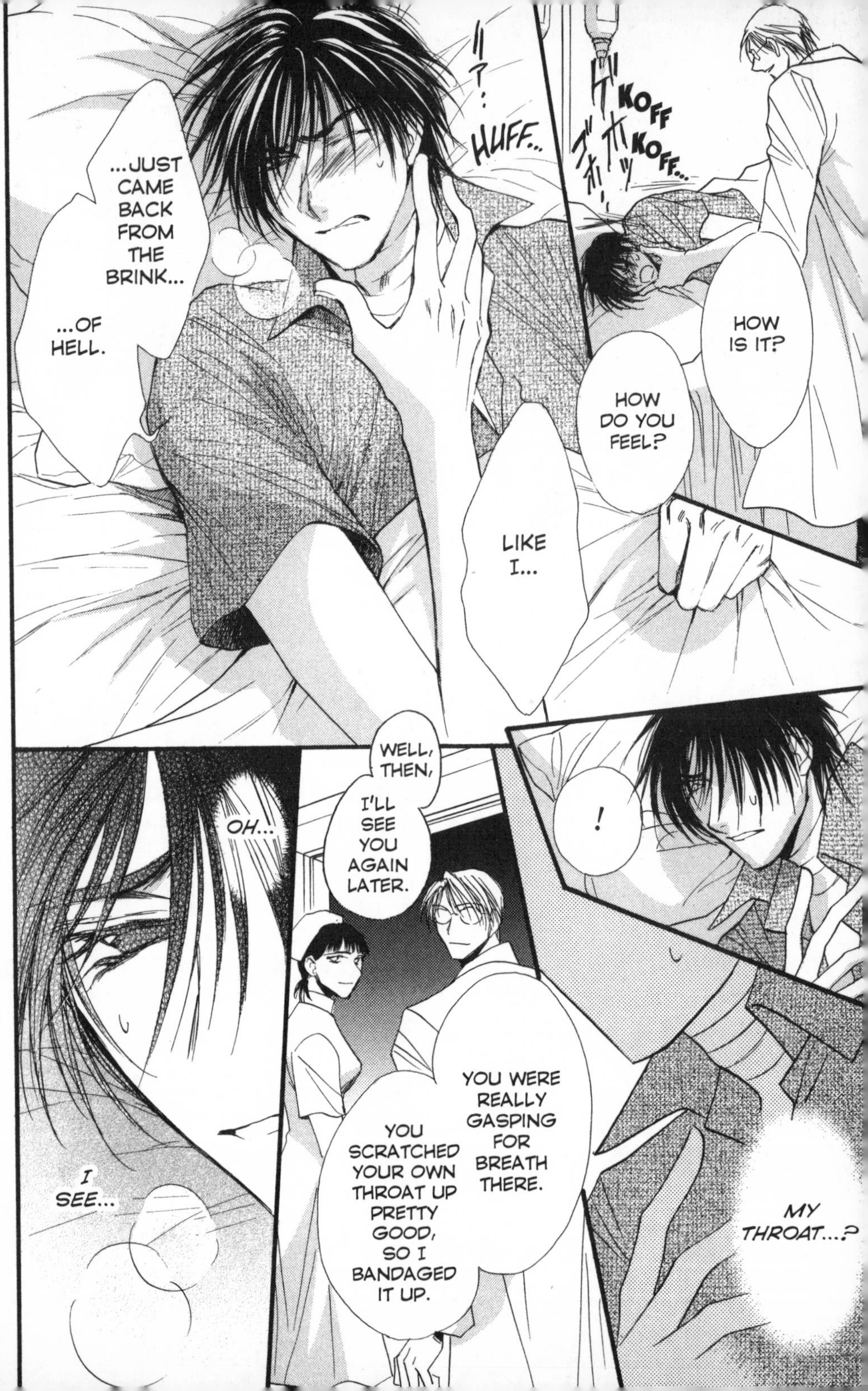
KOFF KOFF...
HOW IS IT?
HOW DO YOU FEEL?
HUFF...
LIKE I...
...JUST CAME BACK FROM THE BRINK...
...OF HELL.
!
MY THROAT...?
YOU WERE REALLY GASPING FOR BREATH THERE.
YOU SCRATCHED YOUR OWN THROAT UP PRETTY GOOD, SO I BANDAGED IT UP.
WELL, THEN, I'LL SEE YOU AGAIN LATER.
OH...
I SEE...

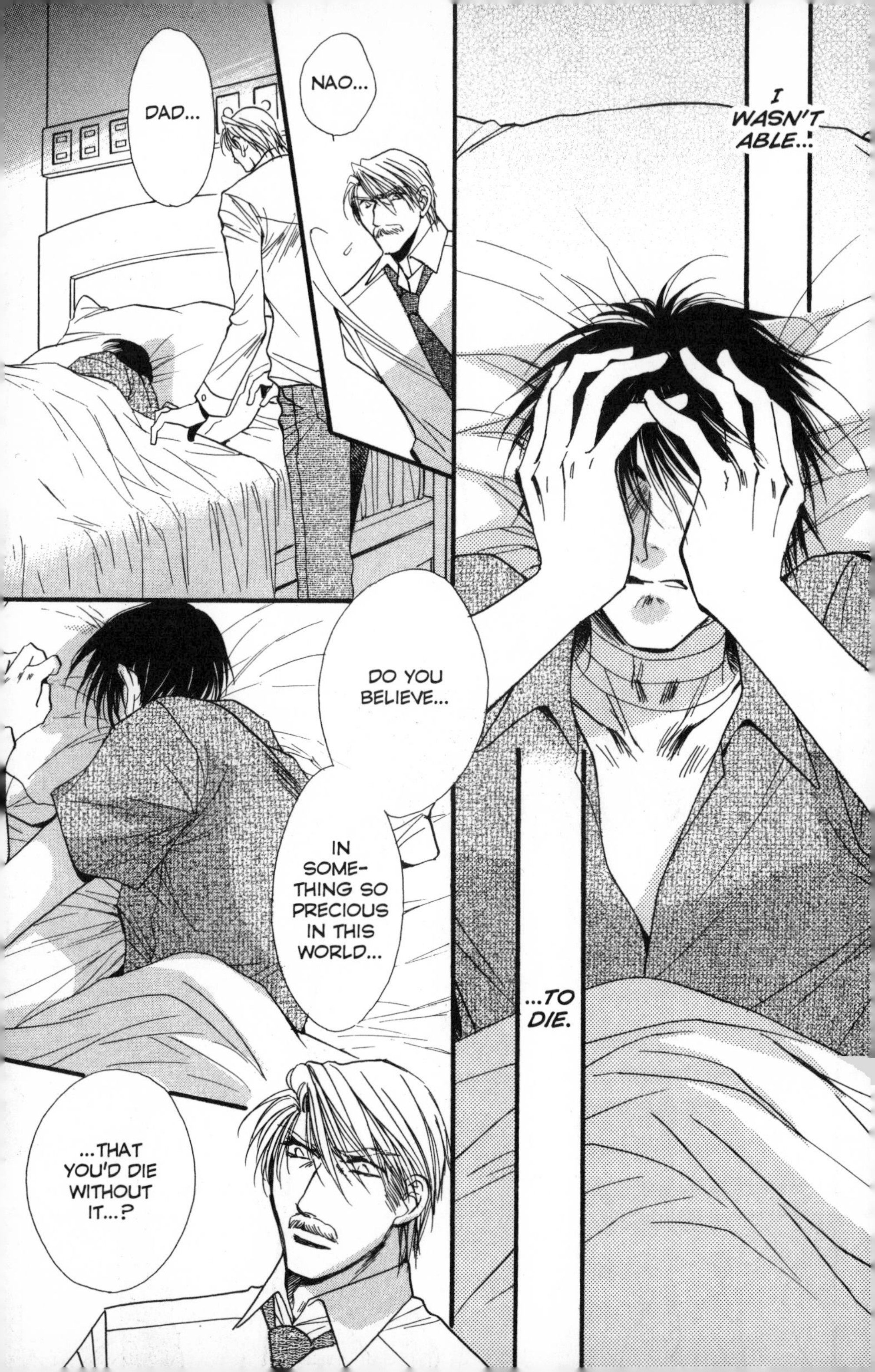
I WASN'T ABLE...
...TO DIE.
NAO...
DAD...
DO YOU BELIEVE...
IN SOMETHING SO PRECIOUS IN THIS WORLD...
...THAT YOU'D DIE WITHOUT IT...?

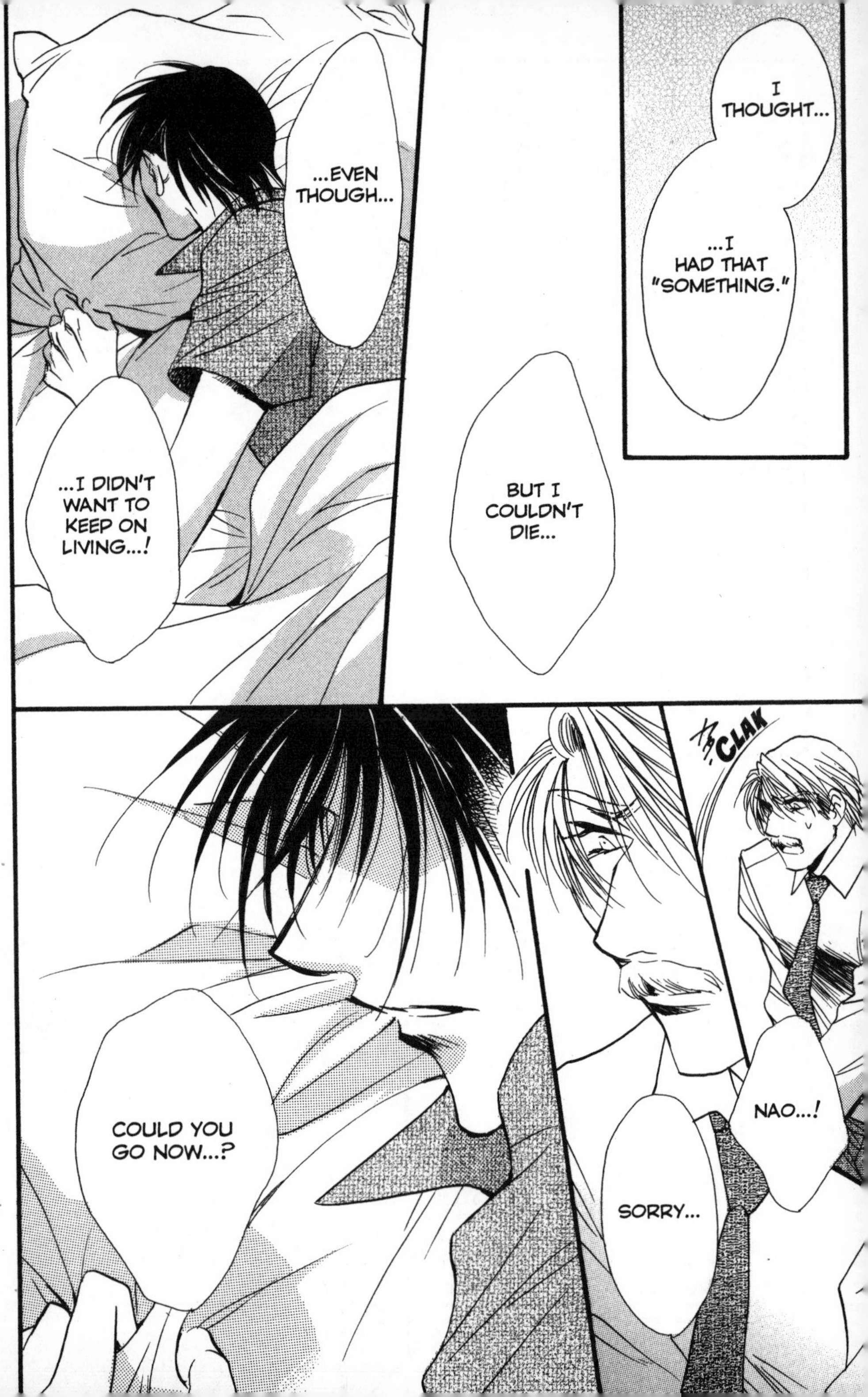
I THOUGHT...
...I HAD THAT "SOMETHING."
BUT I COULDN'T DIE...
...EVEN THOUGH...
...I DIDN'T WANT TO KEEP ON LIVING...!
CLAK
NAO...!
SORRY...
COULD YOU GO NOW...?

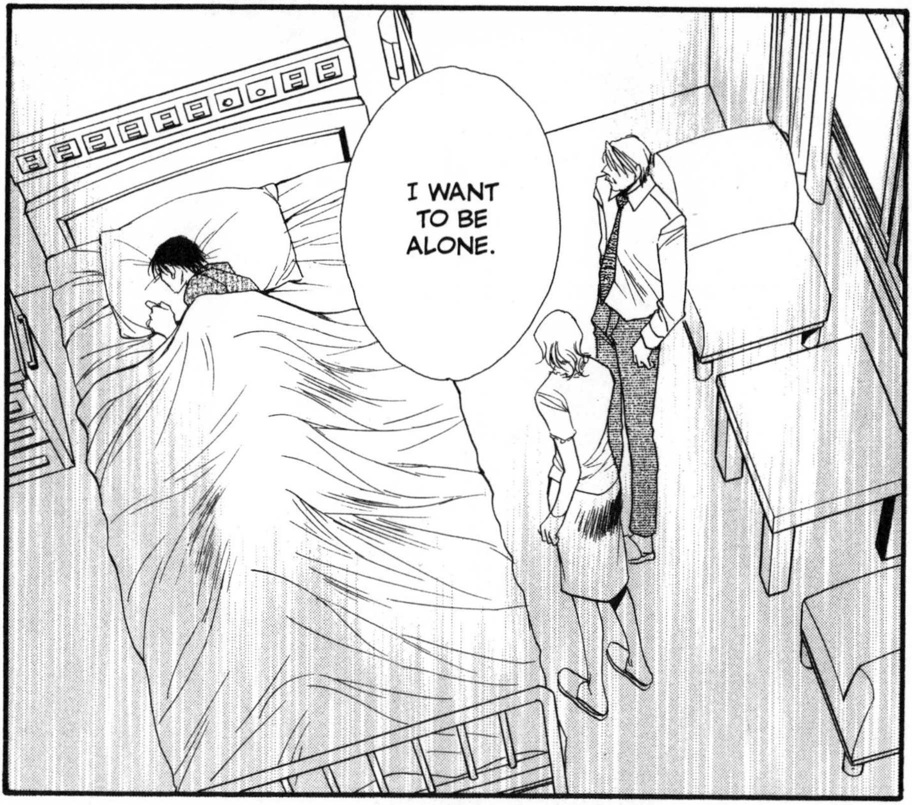
I WANT TO BE ALONE.

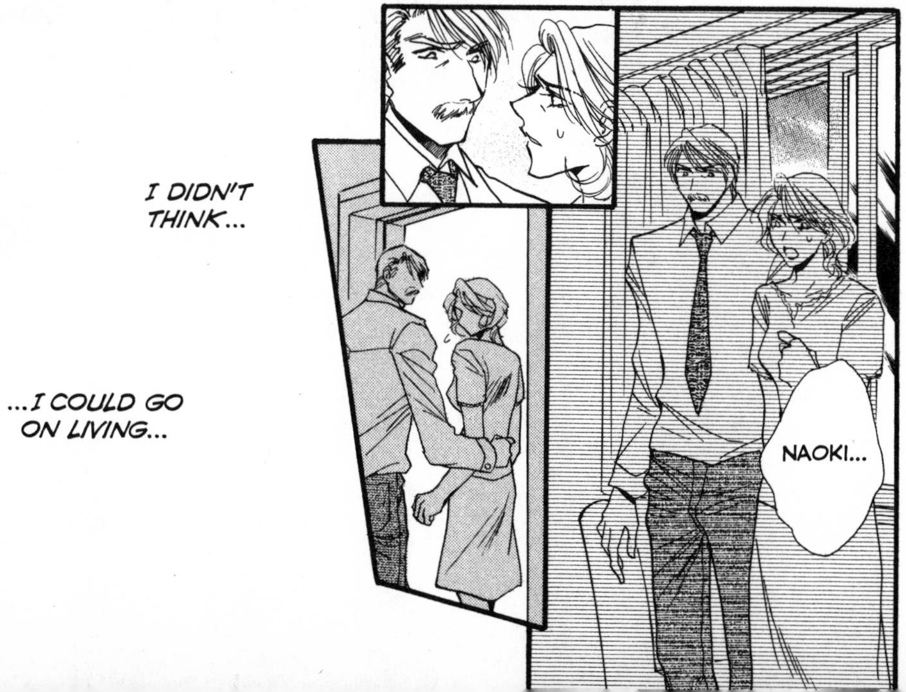
NAOKI...
I DIDN'T THINK...
...I COULD GO ON LIVING...

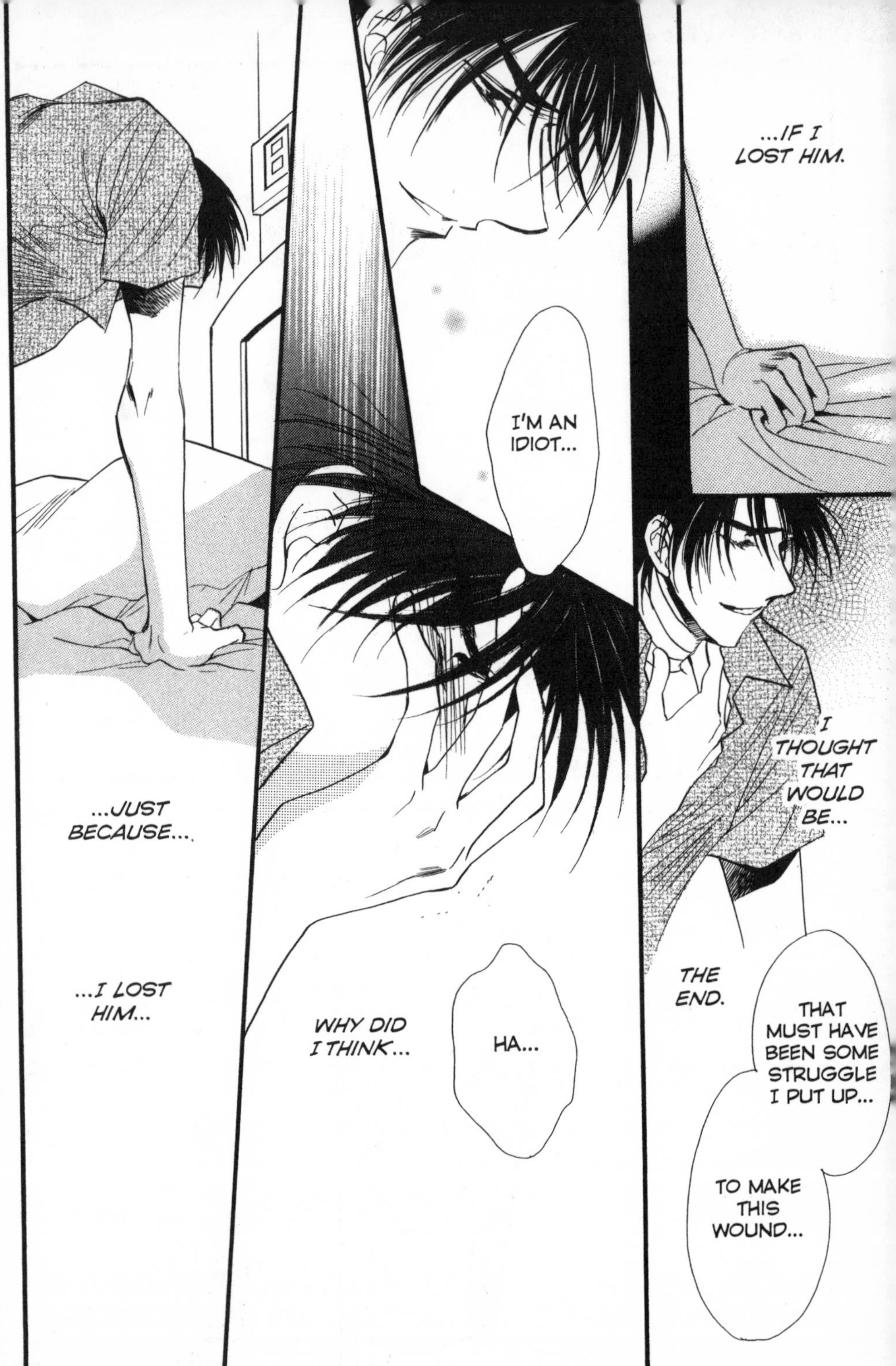

...IF I LOST HIM.
I THOUGHT THAT WOULD BE...
THE END.
THAT MUST HAVE BEEN SOME STRUGGLE I PUT UP...
TO MAKE THIS WOUND...
I'M AN IDIOT...
HA...
WHY DID I THINK...
...JUST BECAUSE...
...I LOST HIM...

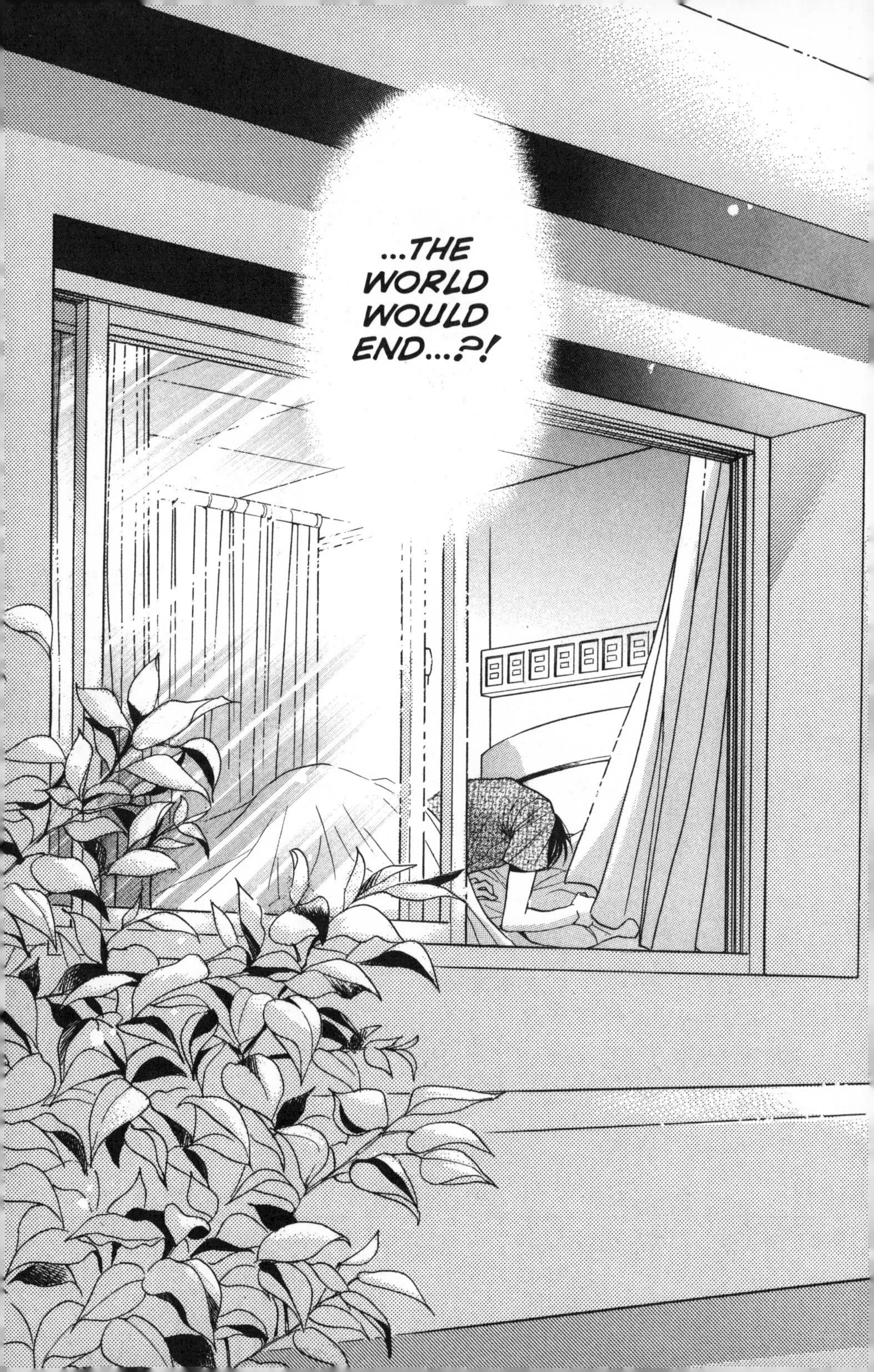
...THE WORLD WOULD END...?!

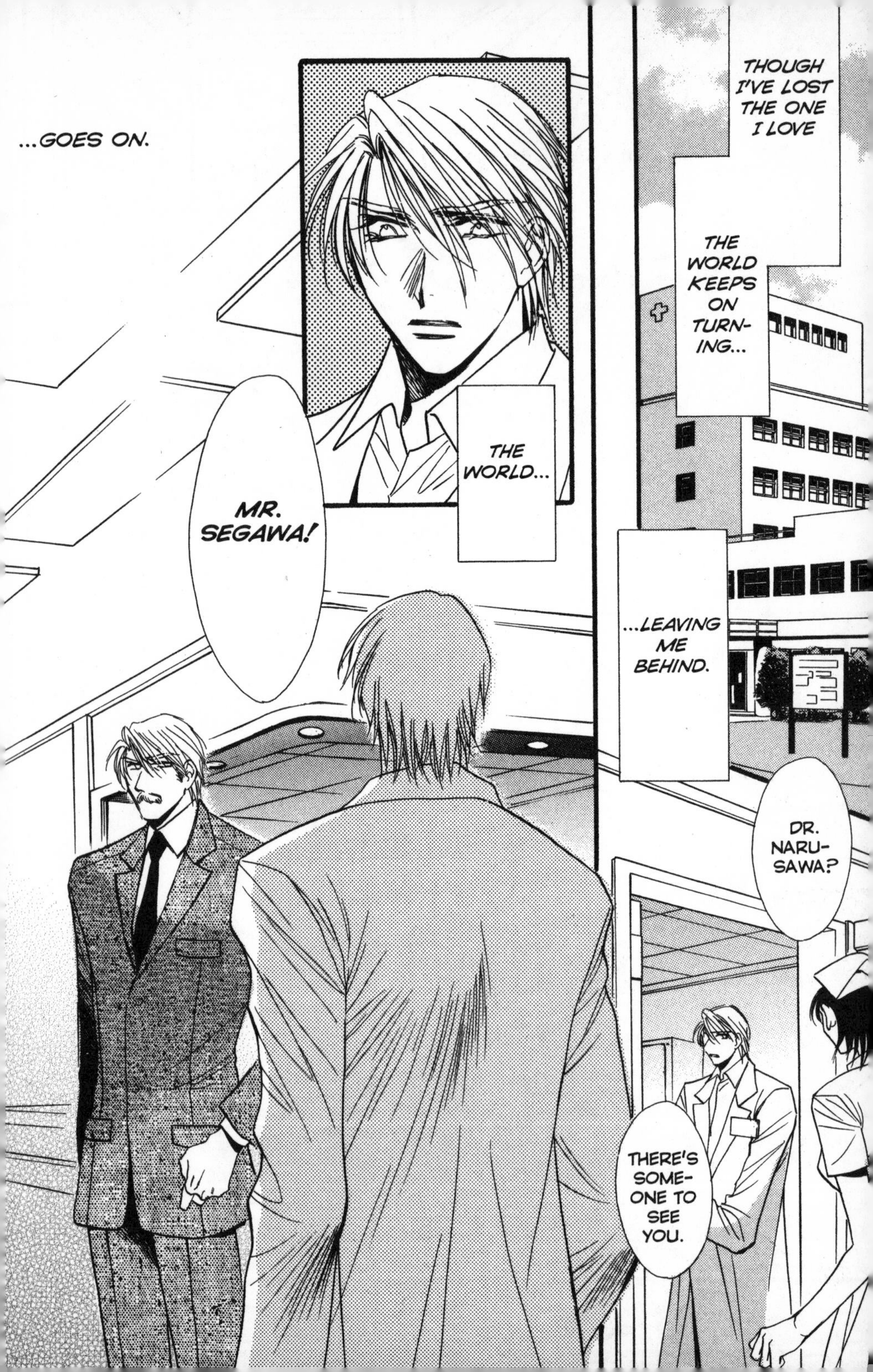
THOUGH I'VE LOST THE ONE I LOVE
THE WORLD KEEPS ON TURNING...
...LEAVING ME BEHIND.
DR. NARUSAWA?
THERE'S SOMEONE TO SEE YOU.
THE WORLD...
...GOES ON.
MR. SEGAWA!

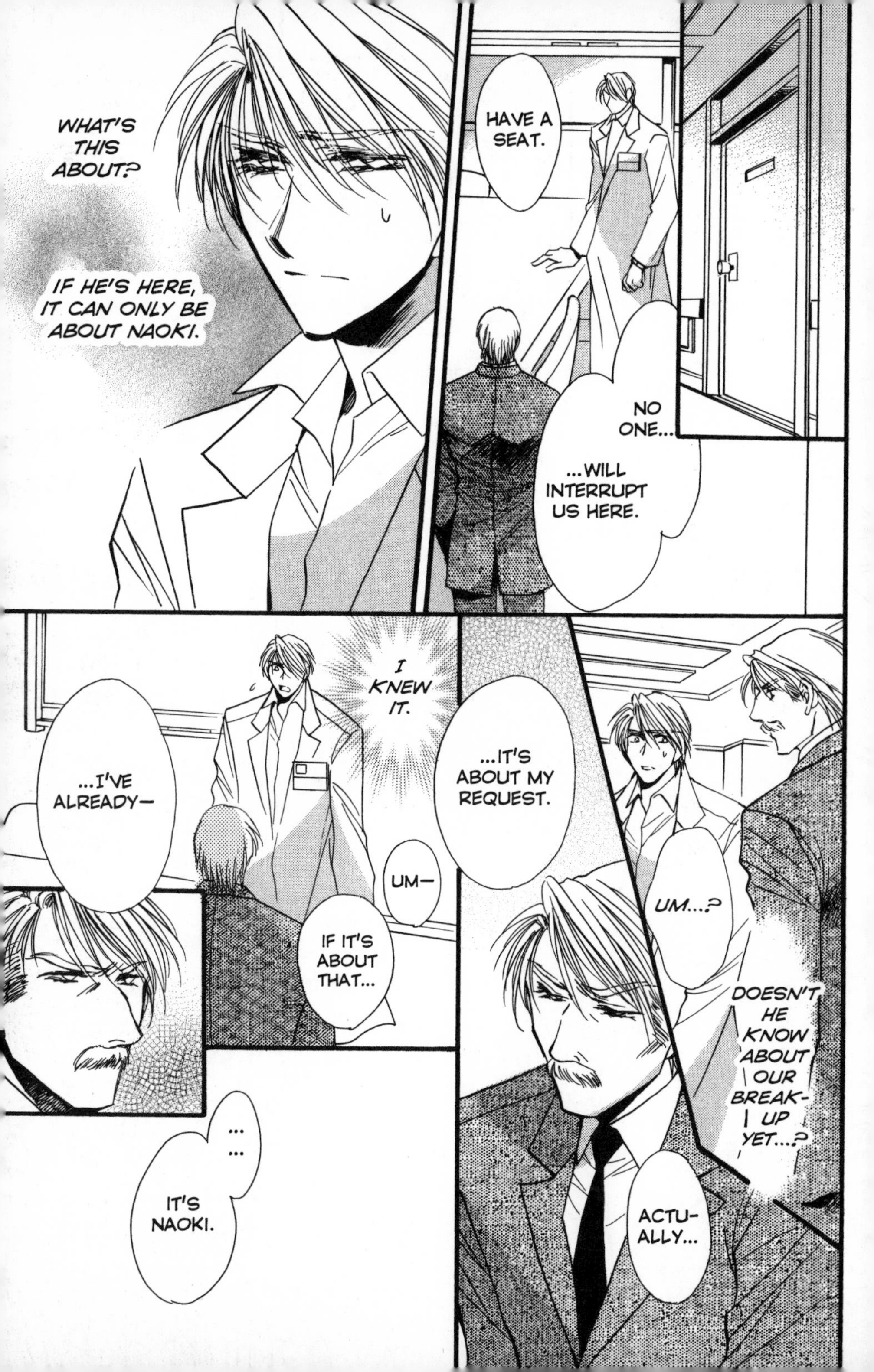
HAVE A SEAT.
NO ONE... ...WILL INTERRUPT US HERE.
WHAT'S THIS ABOUT?
IF HE'S HERE, IT CAN ONLY BE ABOUT NAOKI.
...IT'S ABOUT MY REQUEST.
UM...?
DOESN'T HE KNOW ABOUT OUR BREAK-UP YET...?
ACTU-ALLY...
I KNEW IT.
UM—
IF IT'S ABOUT THAT...
...I'VE ALREADY—
......
IT'S NAOKI.

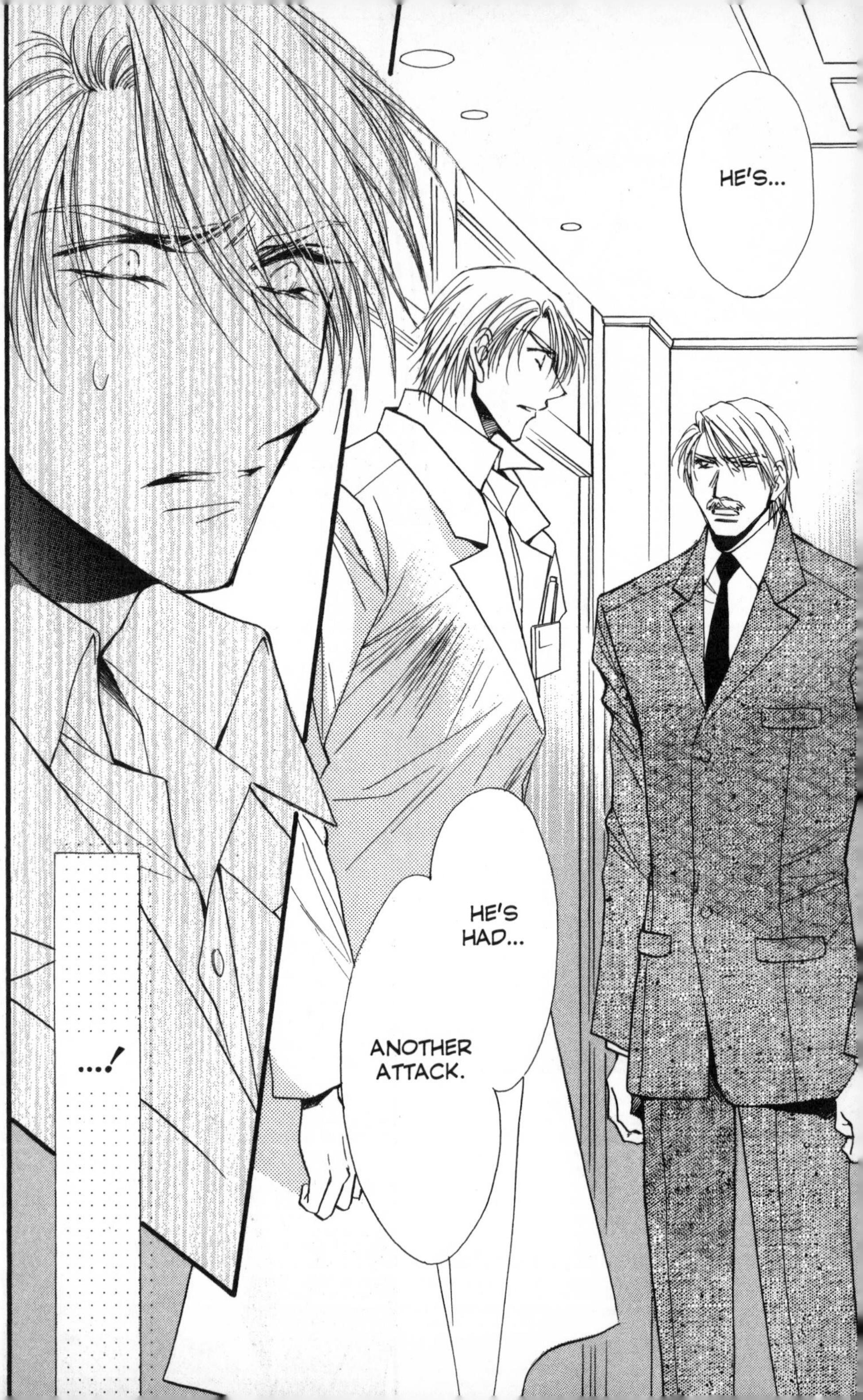
HE'S...
HE'S HAD... ANOTHER ATTACK.
...!

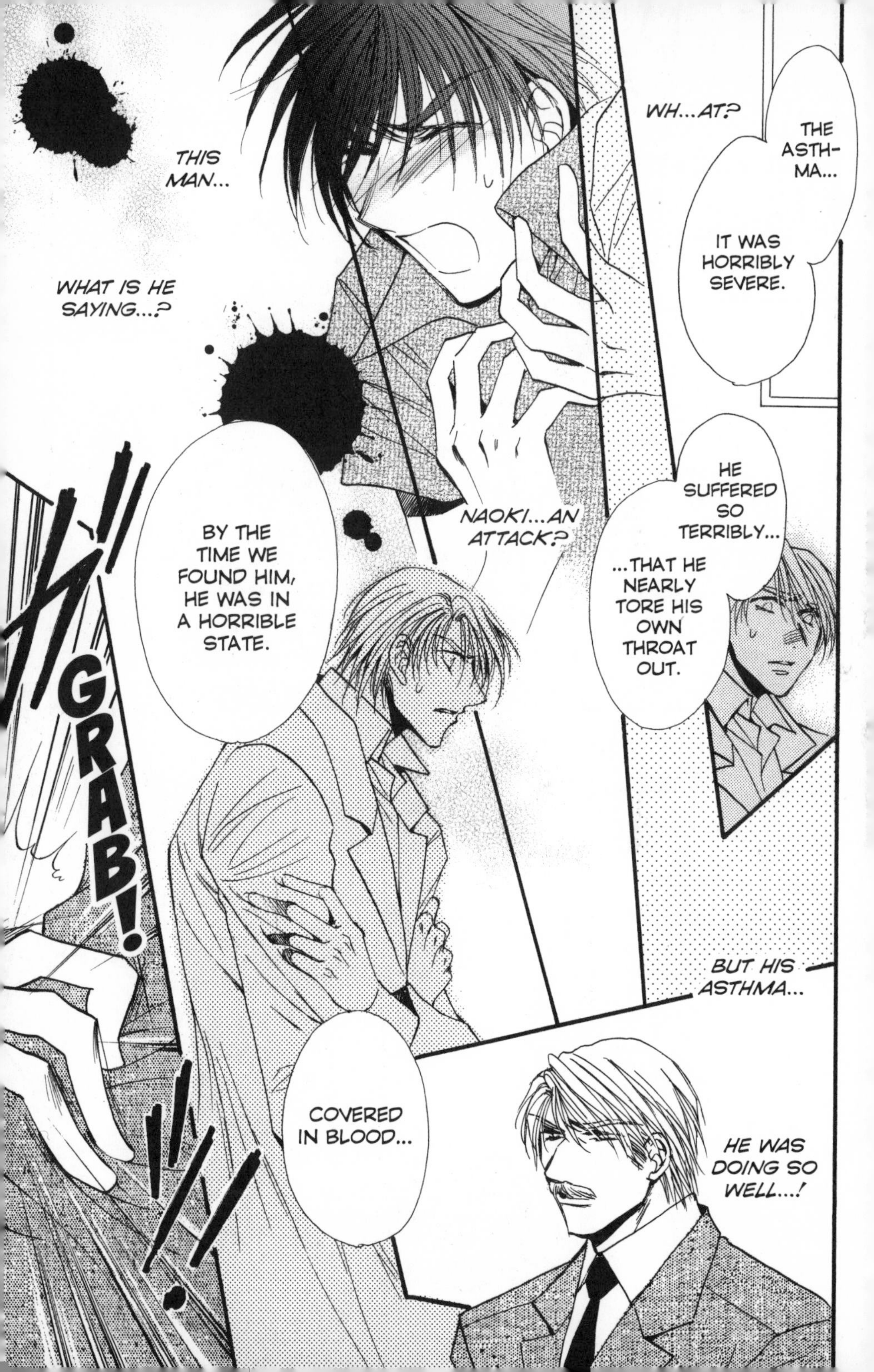
THE ASTHMA...
IT WAS HORRIBLY SEVERE.
WH...AT?
THIS MAN...
WHAT IS HE SAYING...?
HE SUFFERED SO TERRIBLY...
...THAT HE NEARLY TORE HIS OWN THROAT OUT.
NAOKI...AN ATTACK?
BY THE TIME WE FOUND HIM, HE WAS IN A HORRIBLE STATE.
BUT HIS ASTHMA...
HE WAS DOING SO WELL...!
COVERED IN BLOOD...
GRAB!

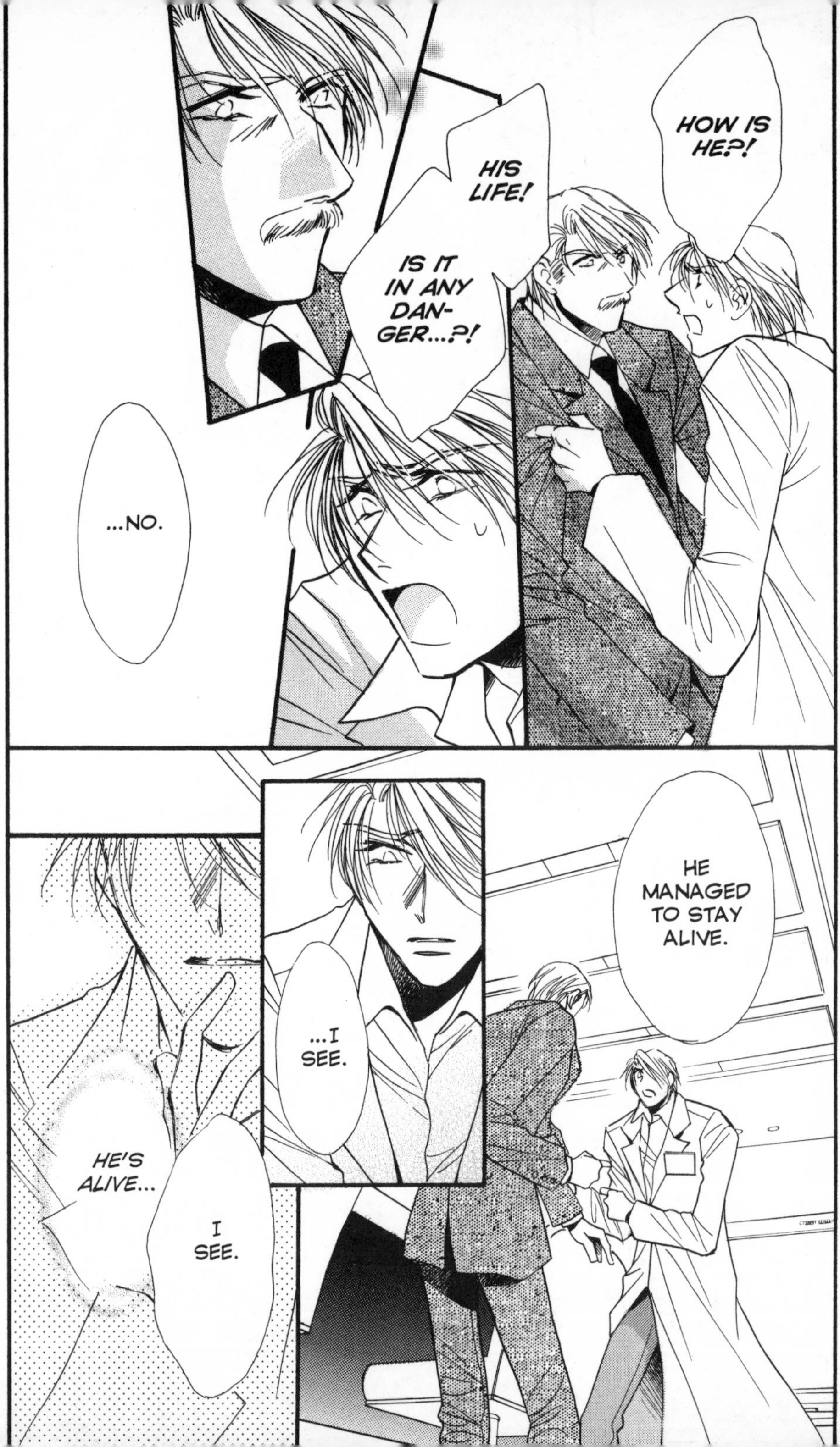
HOW IS HE?!
HIS LIFE!
IS IT IN ANY DAN-GER...?!
...NO.
HE MANAGED TO STAY ALIVE.
...I SEE.
HE'S ALIVE...
I SEE.

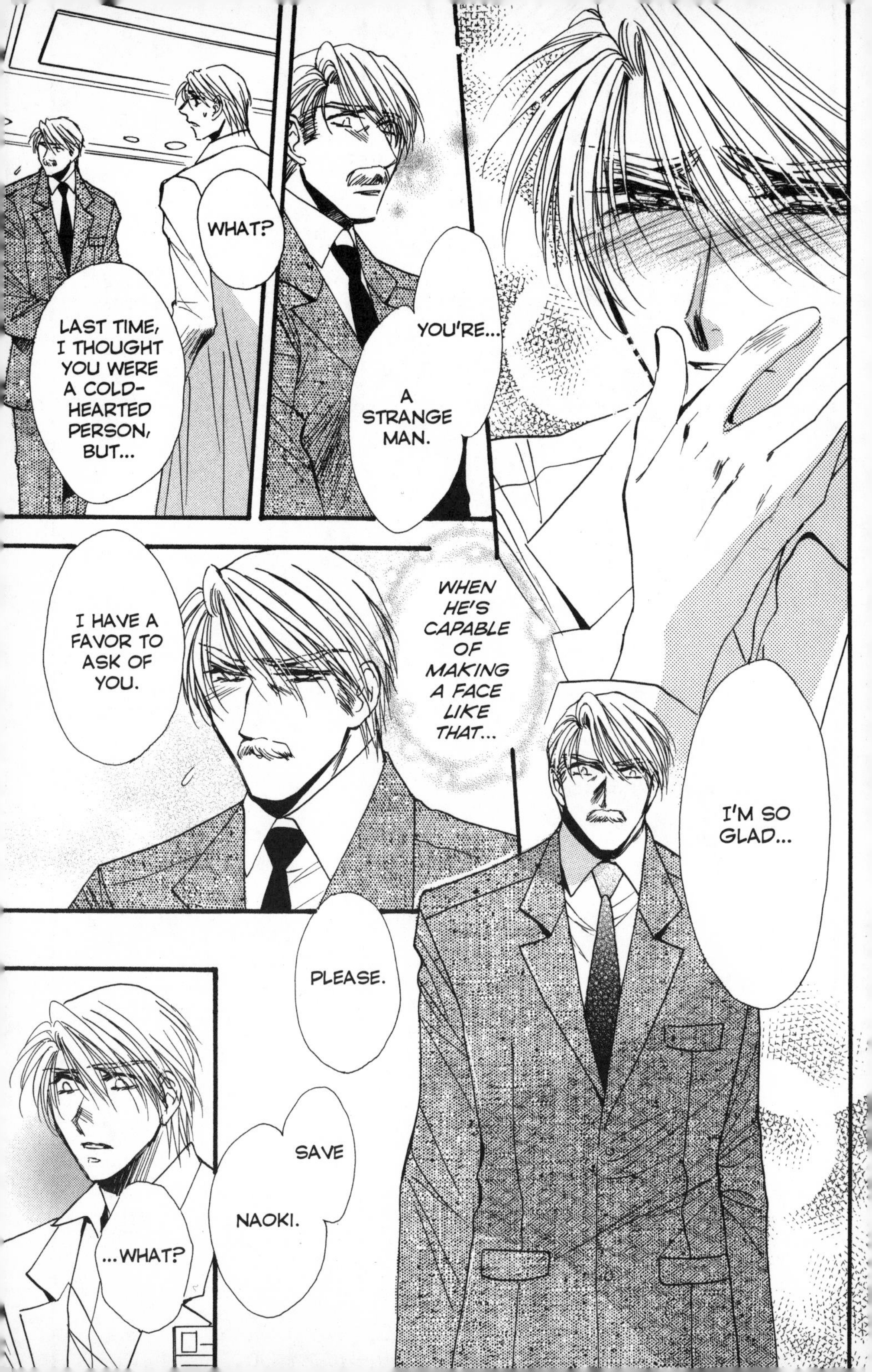
YOU'RE...
A STRANGE MAN.
WHAT?
LAST TIME, I THOUGHT YOU WERE A COLD-HEARTED PERSON, BUT...
I'M SO GLAD...
WHEN HE'S CAPABLE OF MAKING A FACE LIKE THAT...
I HAVE A FAVOR TO ASK OF YOU.
PLEASE.
SAVE NAOKI.
...WHAT?

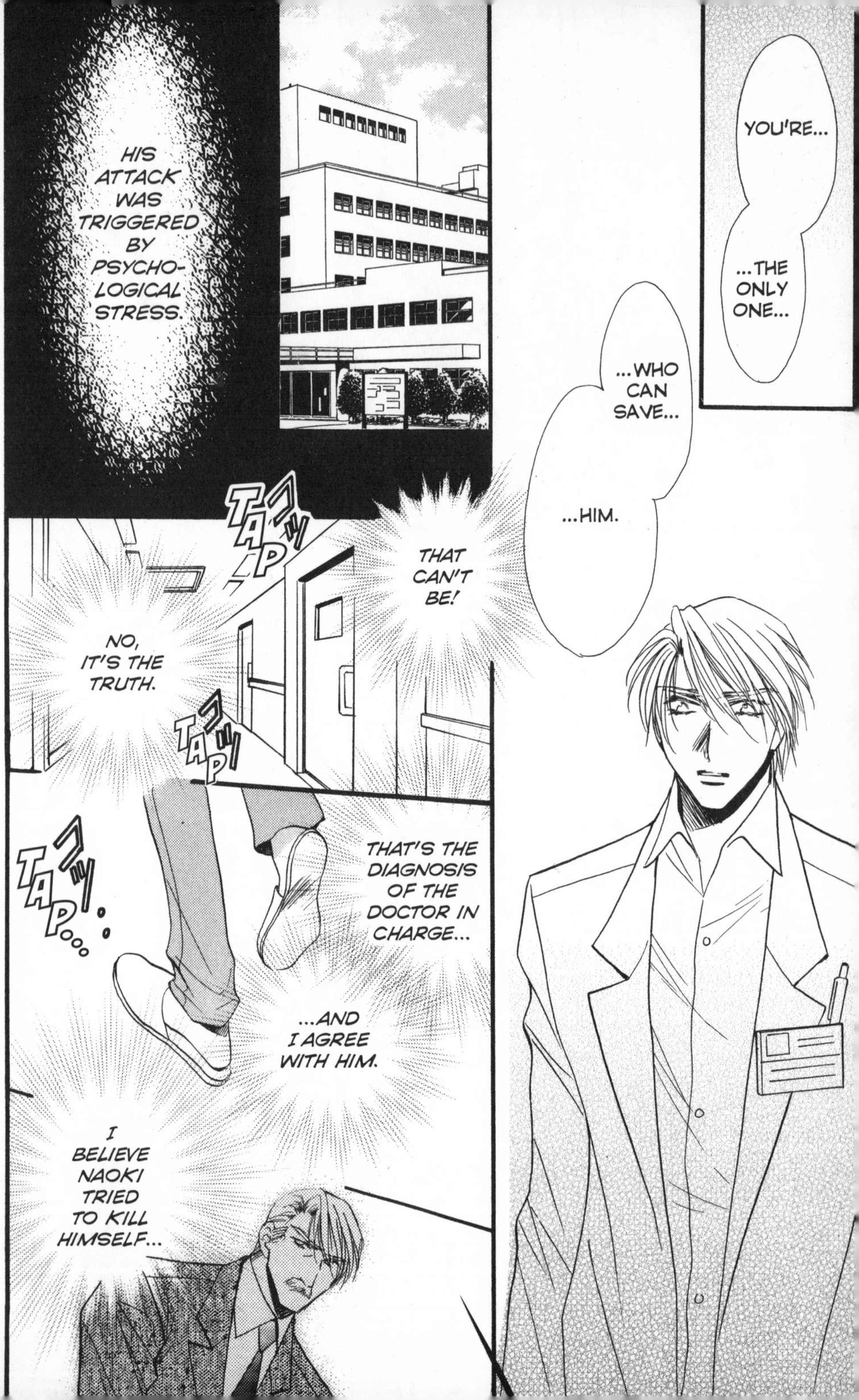
YOU'RE...
...THE ONLY ONE...
...WHO CAN SAVE...
...HIM.
HIS ATTACK WAS TRIGGERED BY PSYCHOLOGICAL STRESS.
TAP
THAT CAN'T BE!
NO, IT'S THE TRUTH.
TAP
THAT'S THE DIAGNOSIS OF THE DOCTOR IN CHARGE...
TAP...
...AND I AGREE WITH HIM.
I BELIEVE NAOKI TRIED TO KILL HIMSELF...

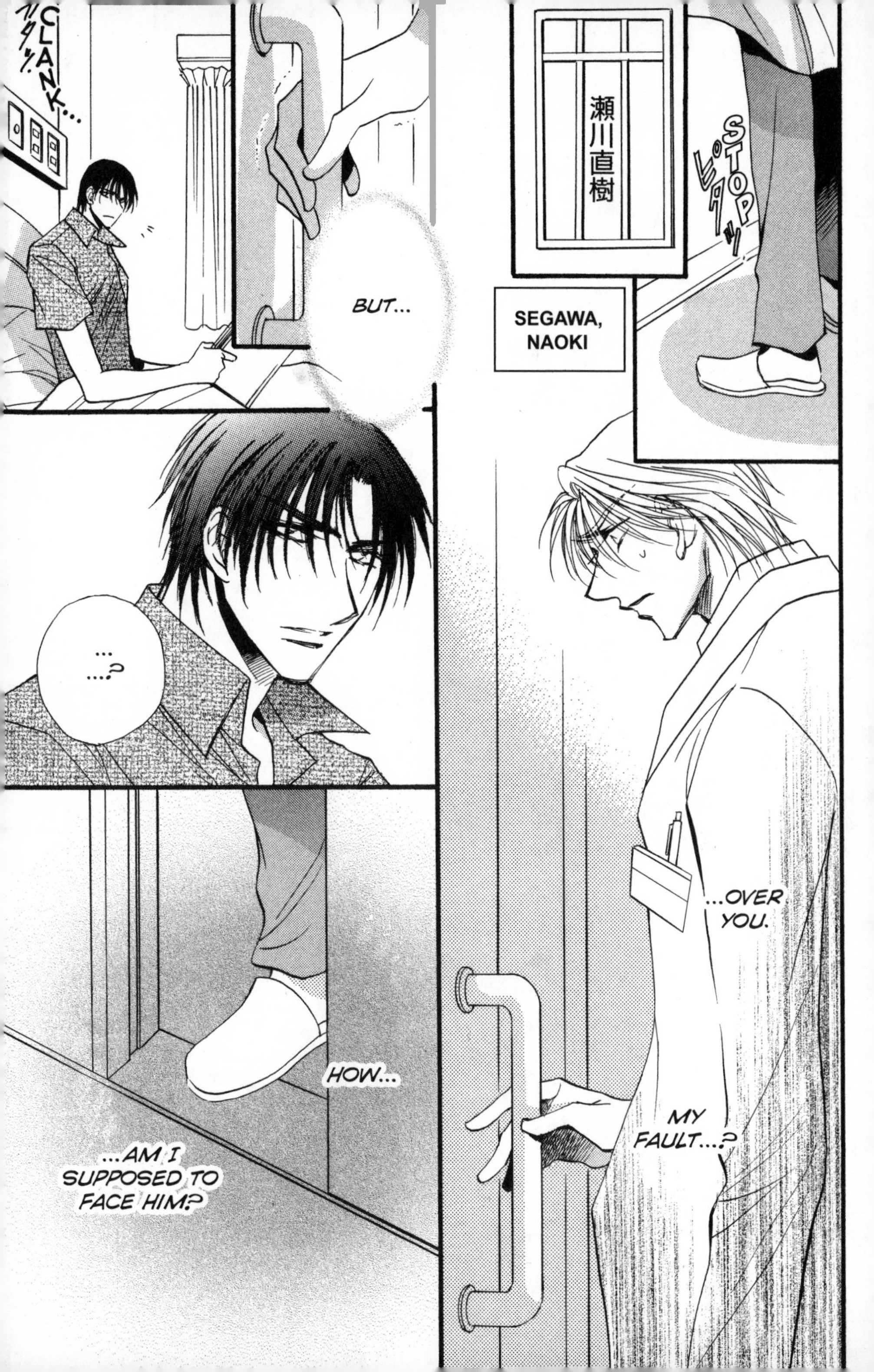
ピタッ
STOP
瀬川直樹
SEGAWA, NAOKI
...OVER YOU.
MY FAULT...?
ガタッ
CLANK...
BUT...
...
...?
HOW...
...AM I SUPPOSED TO FACE HIM?

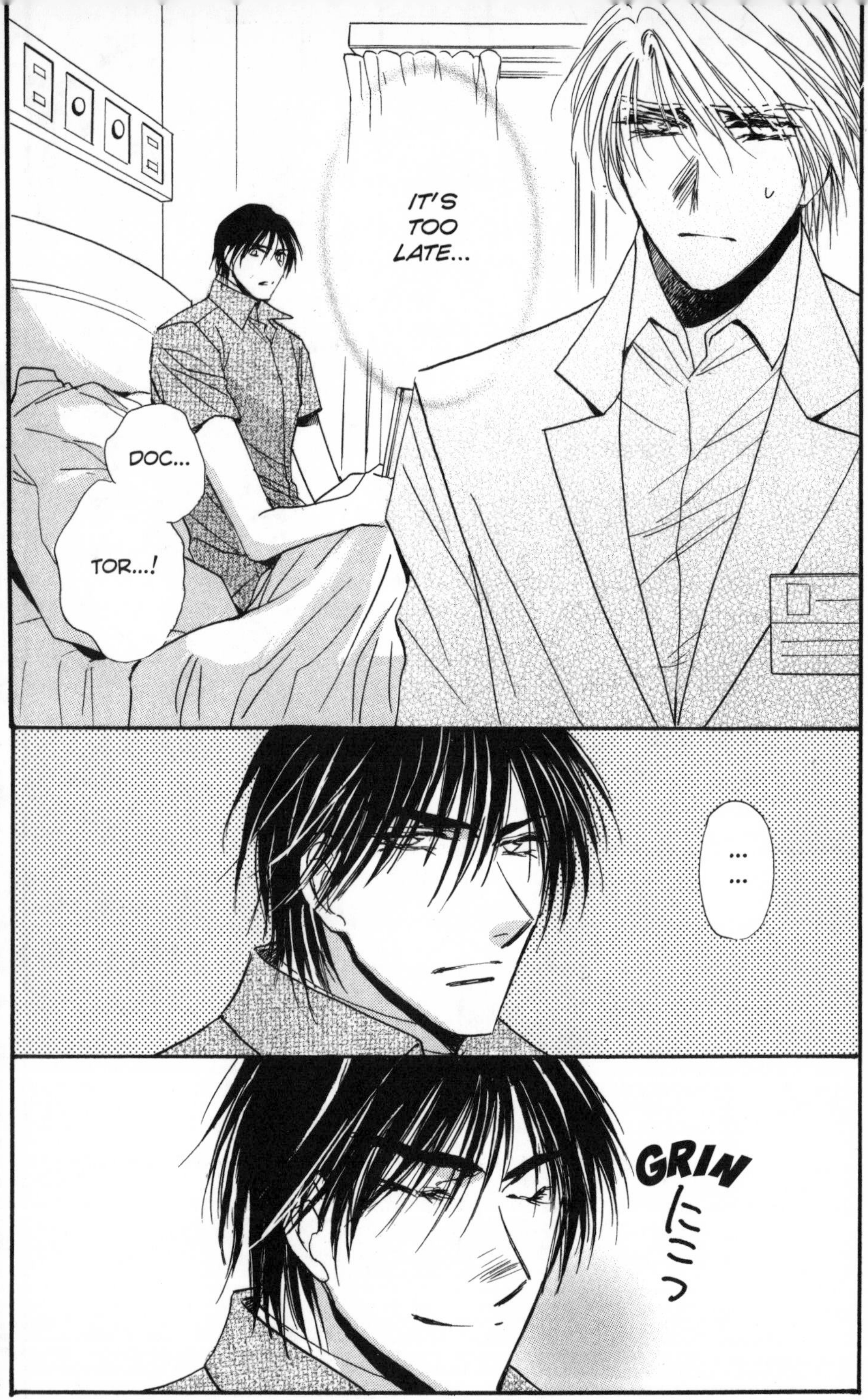
IT'S TOO LATE...
DOC...
TOR...!
......
GRIN
ニコッ

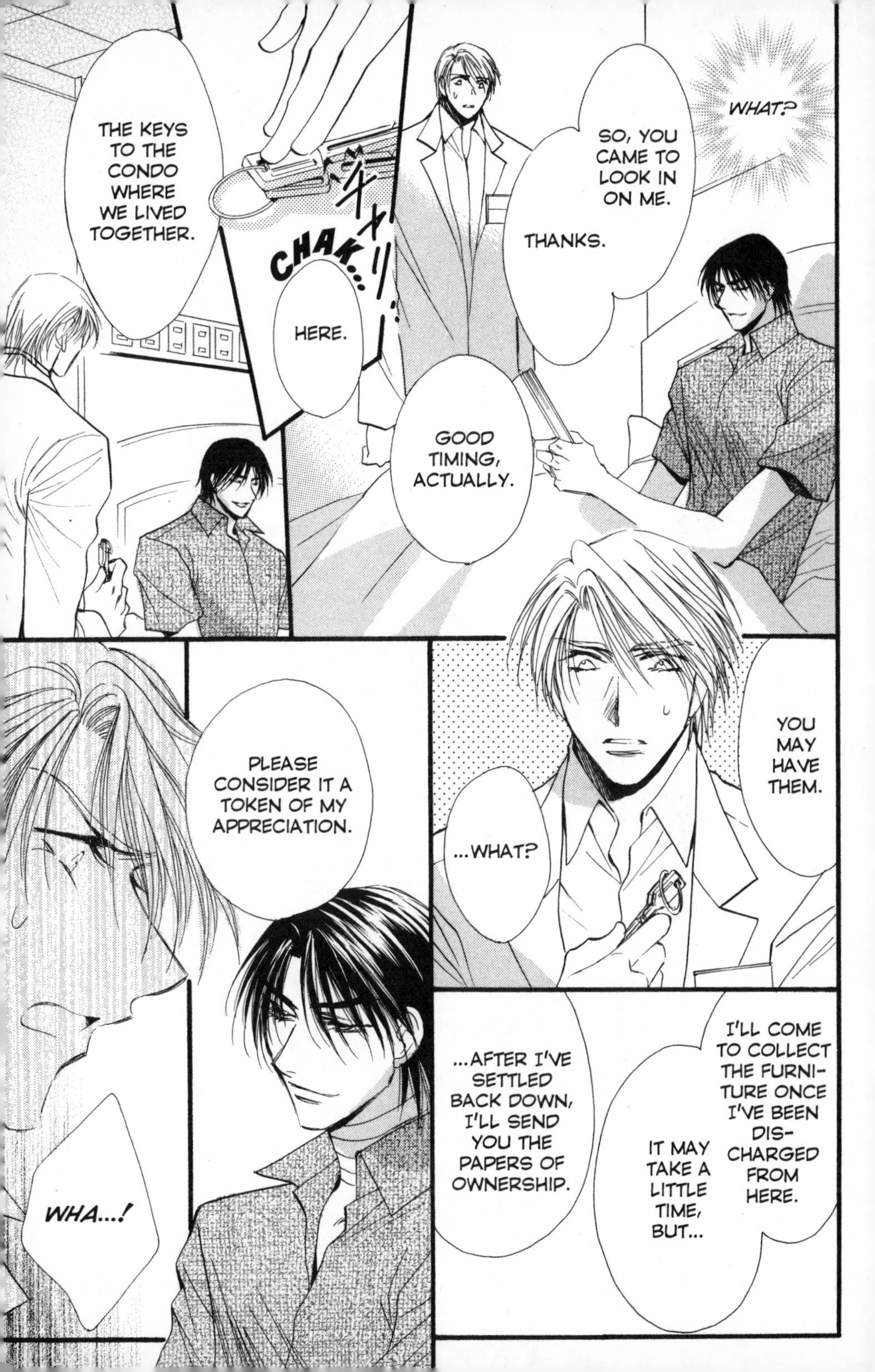
WHAT?
SO, YOU CAME TO LOOK IN ON ME.
THANKS.
GOOD TIMING, ACTUALLY.
CHAK...
HERE.
THE KEYS TO THE CONDO WHERE WE LIVED TOGETHER.
YOU MAY HAVE THEM.
...WHAT?
I'LL COME TO COLLECT THE FURNITURE ONCE I'VE BEEN DISCHARGED FROM HERE.
IT MAY TAKE A LITTLE TIME, BUT...
...AFTER I'VE SETTLED BACK DOWN, I'LL SEND YOU THE PAPERS OF OWNERSHIP.
PLEASE CONSIDER IT A TOKEN OF MY APPRECIATION.
WHA...!

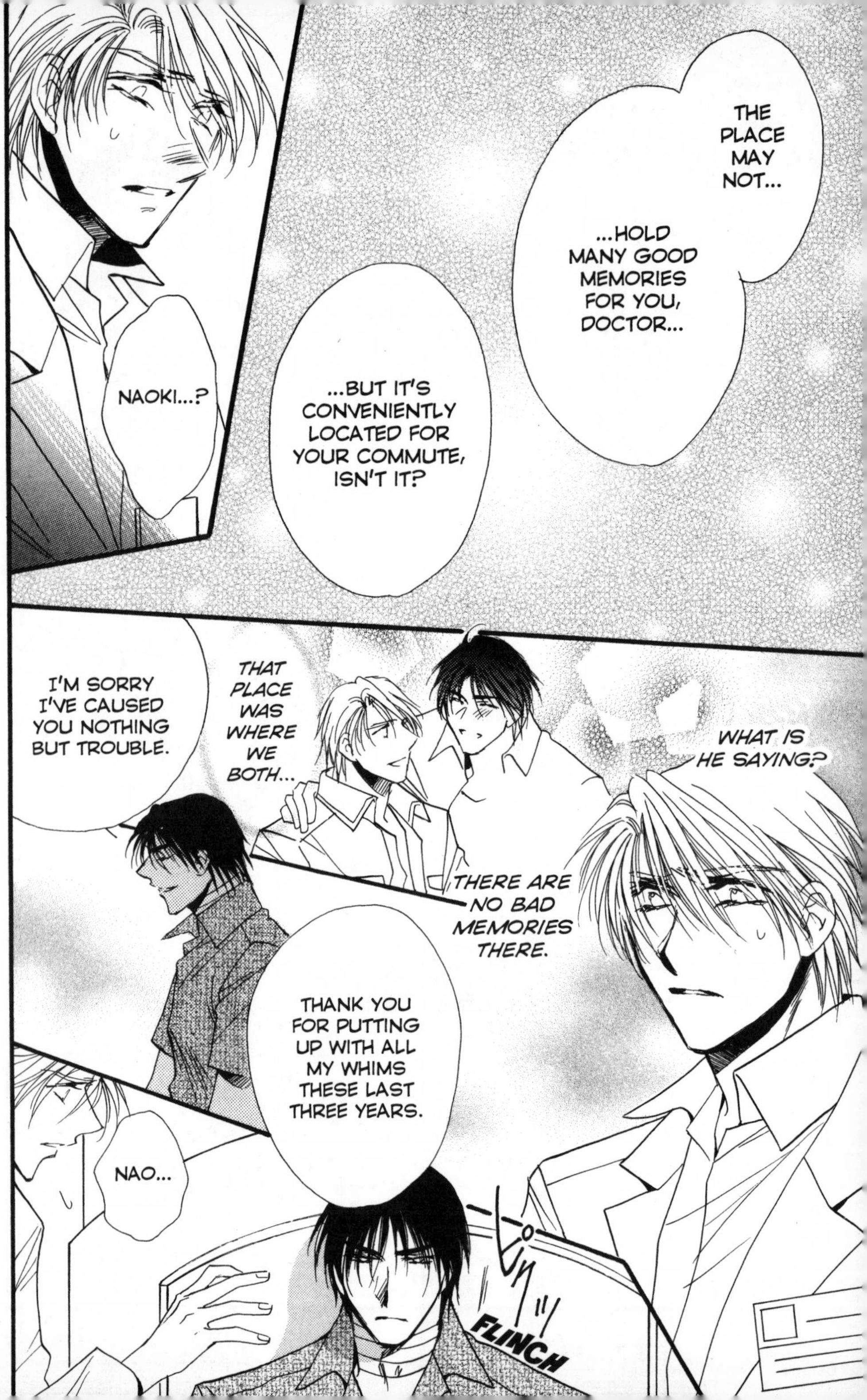
THE PLACE MAY NOT...
...HOLD MANY GOOD MEMORIES FOR YOU, DOCTOR...
...BUT IT'S CONVENIENTLY LOCATED FOR YOUR COMMUTE, ISN'T IT?
NAOKI...?
WHAT IS HE SAYING?
THAT PLACE WAS WHERE WE BOTH...
THERE ARE NO BAD MEMORIES THERE.
I'M SORRY I'VE CAUSED YOU NOTHING BUT TROUBLE.
THANK YOU FOR PUTTING UP WITH ALL MY WHIMS THESE LAST THREE YEARS.
FLINCH
NAO...

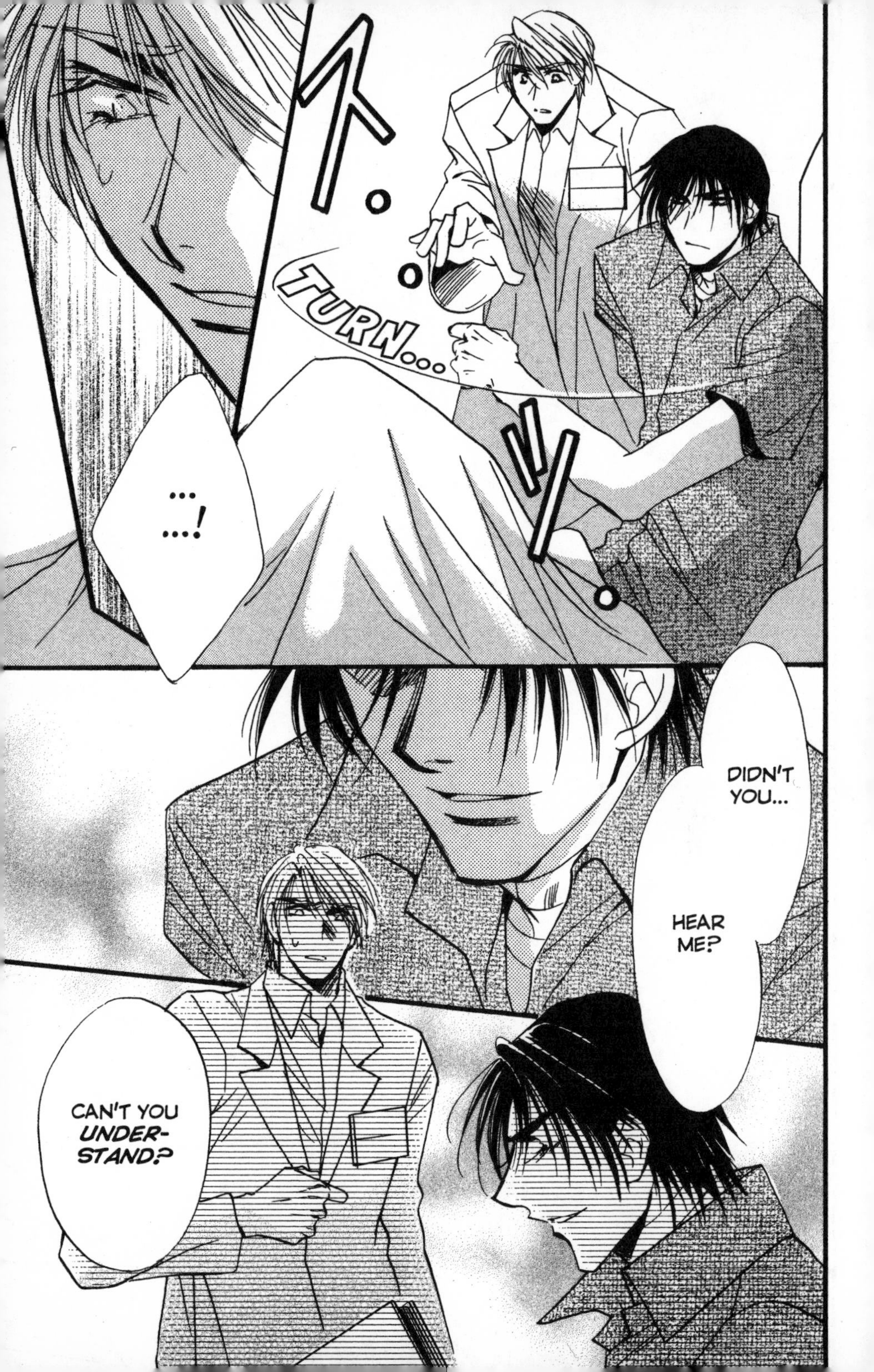
TURN...
... ...!
DIDN'T YOU... HEAR ME?
CAN'T YOU UNDERSTAND?

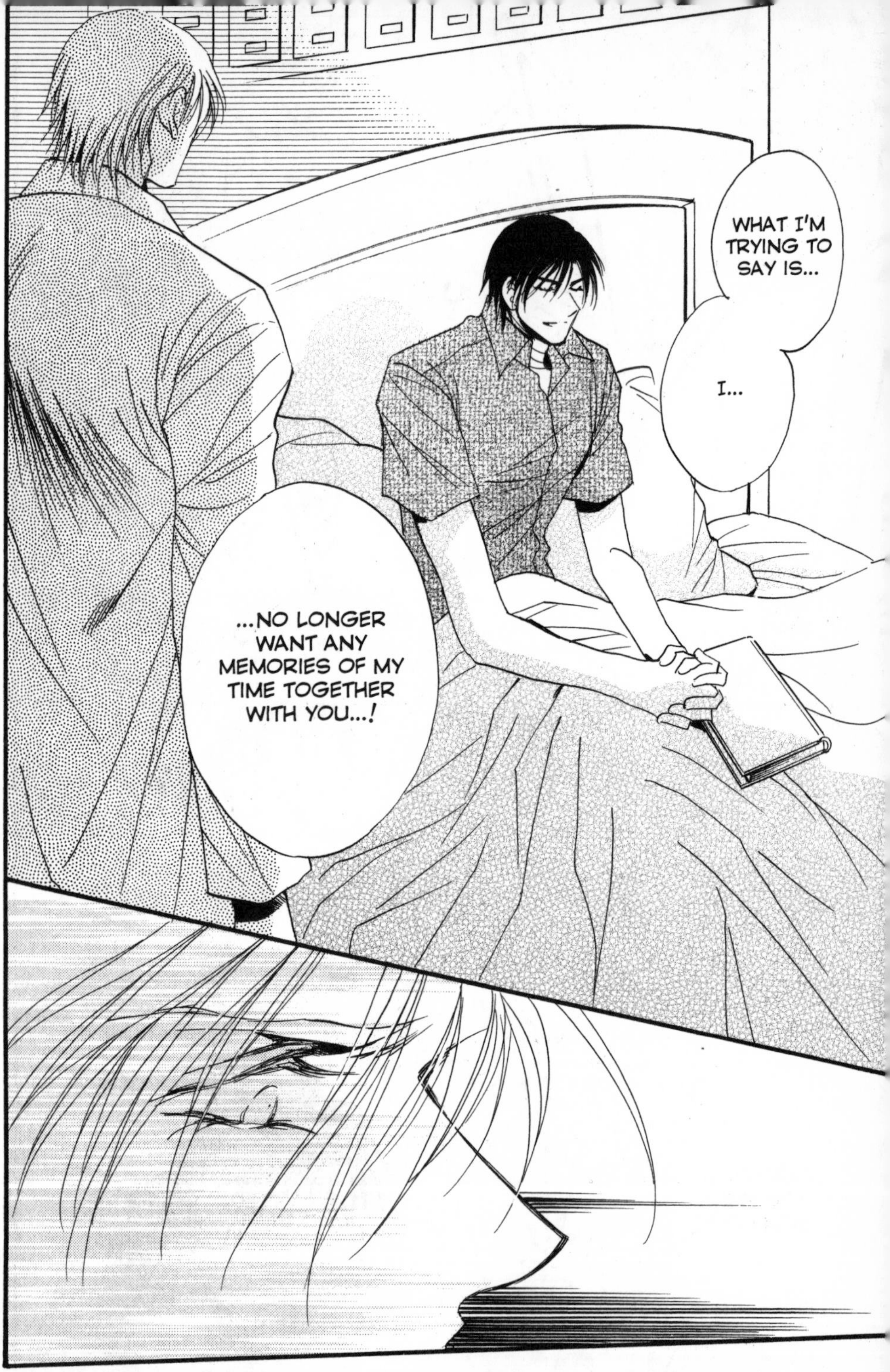
WHAT I'M TRYING TO SAY IS...
I...
...NO LONGER WANT ANY MEMORIES OF MY TIME TOGETHER WITH YOU...!

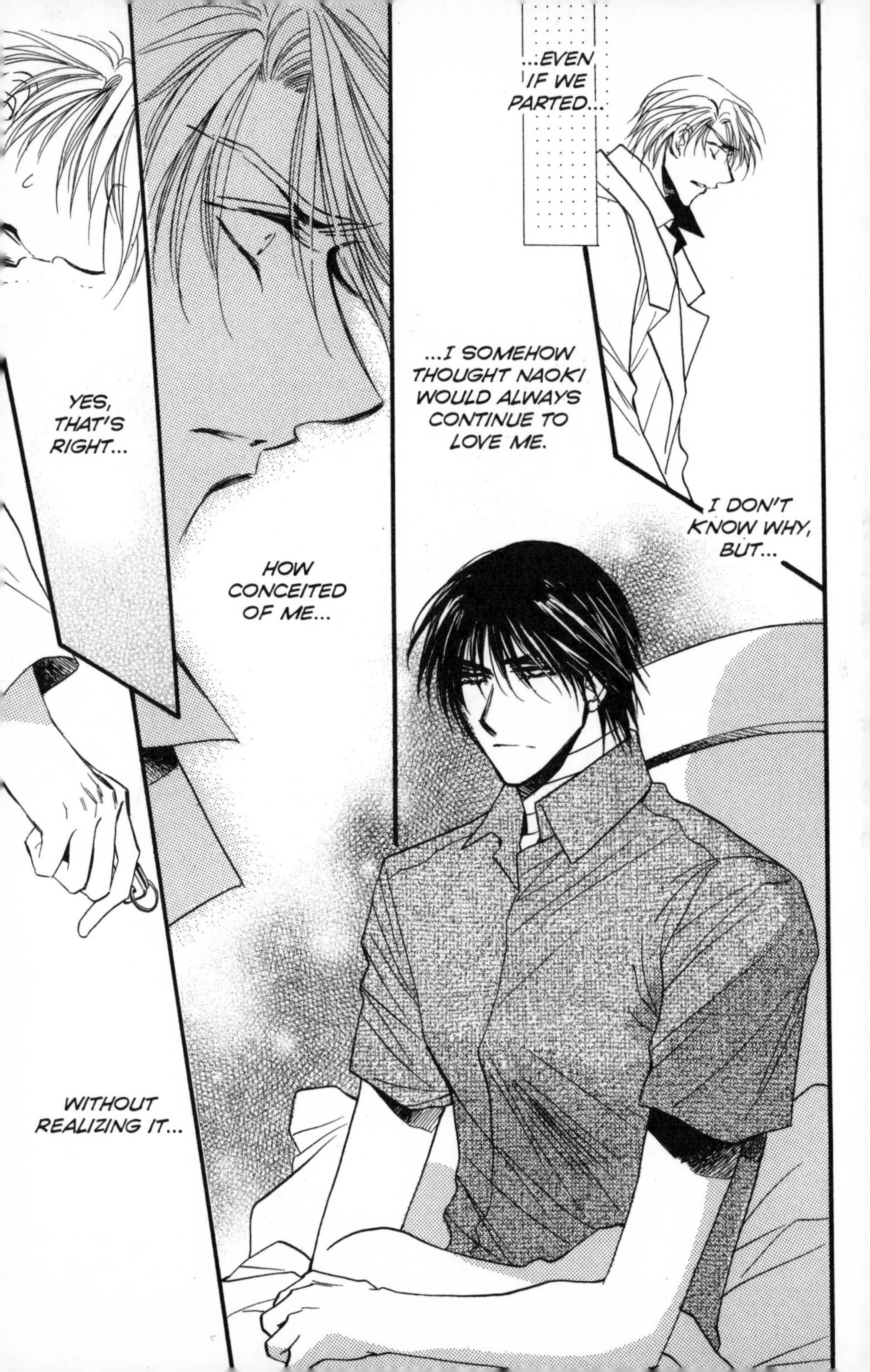
I DON'T KNOW WHY, BUT...
...EVEN IF WE PARTED...
...I SOMEHOW THOUGHT NAOKI WOULD ALWAYS CONTINUE TO LOVE ME.
HOW CONCEITED OF ME...
YES, THAT'S RIGHT...
WITHOUT REALIZING IT...

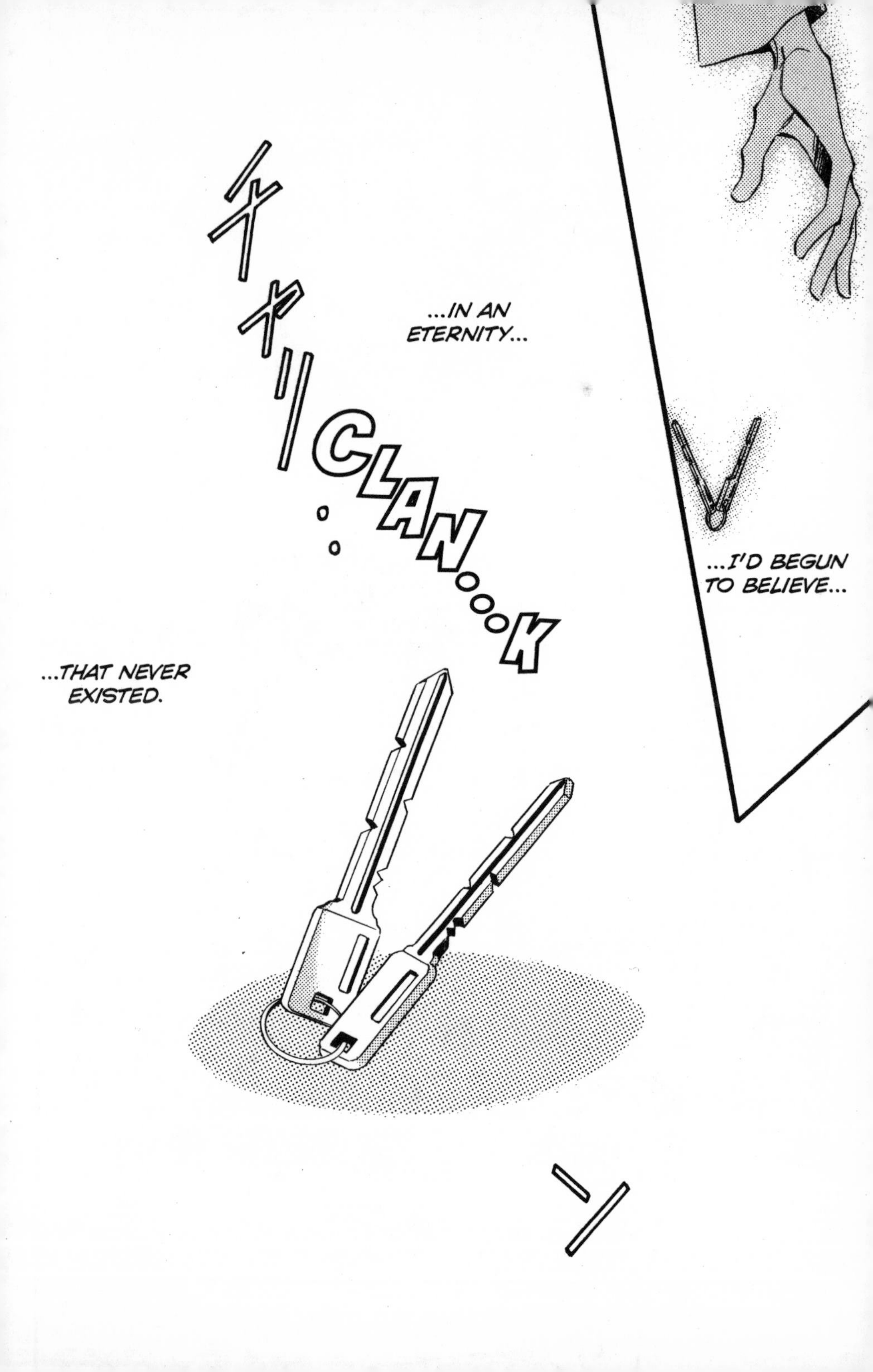
...I'D BEGUN TO BELIEVE...
...IN AN ETERNITY...
CLANOOOK
...THAT NEVER EXISTED.

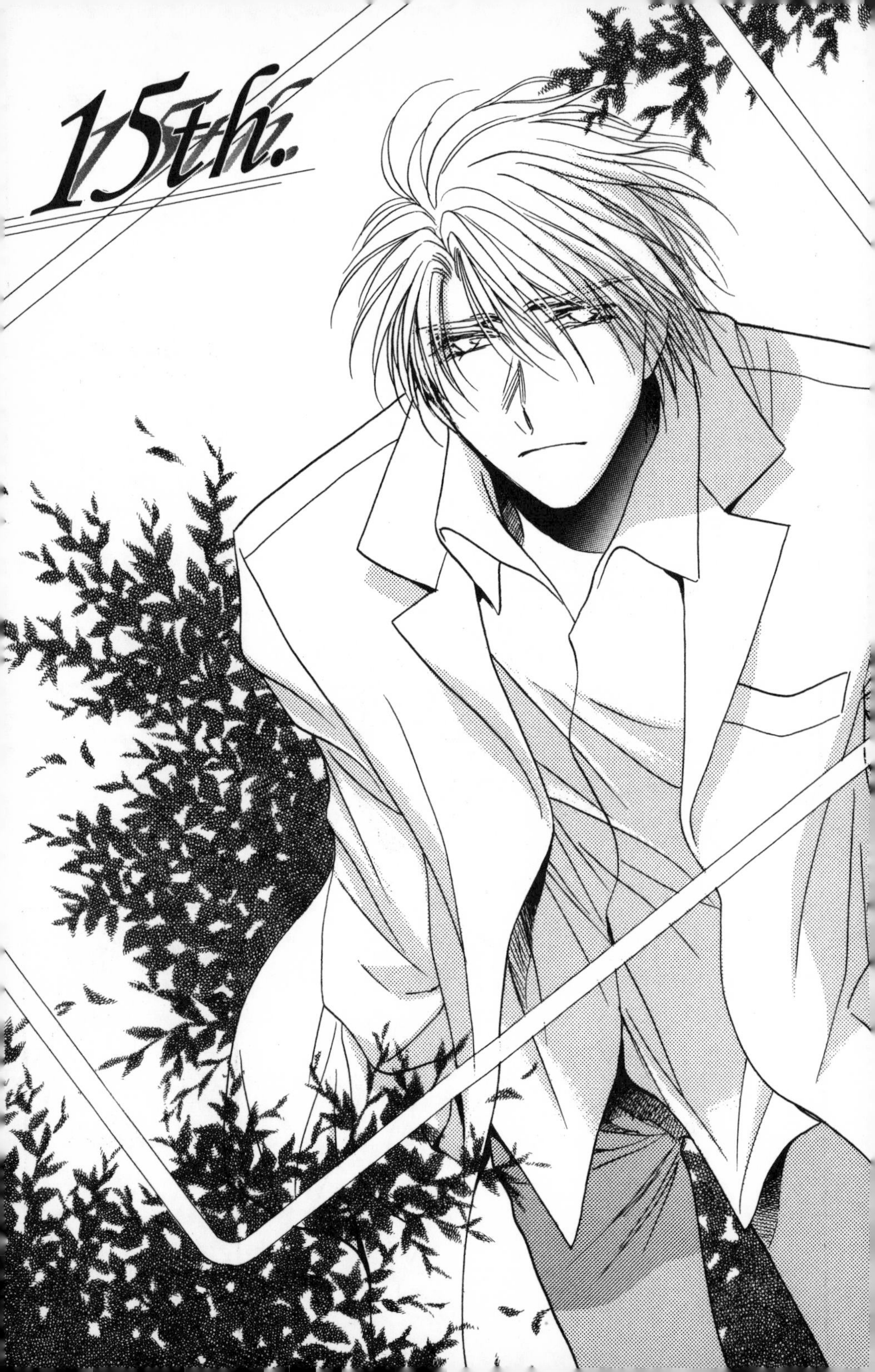
15th.

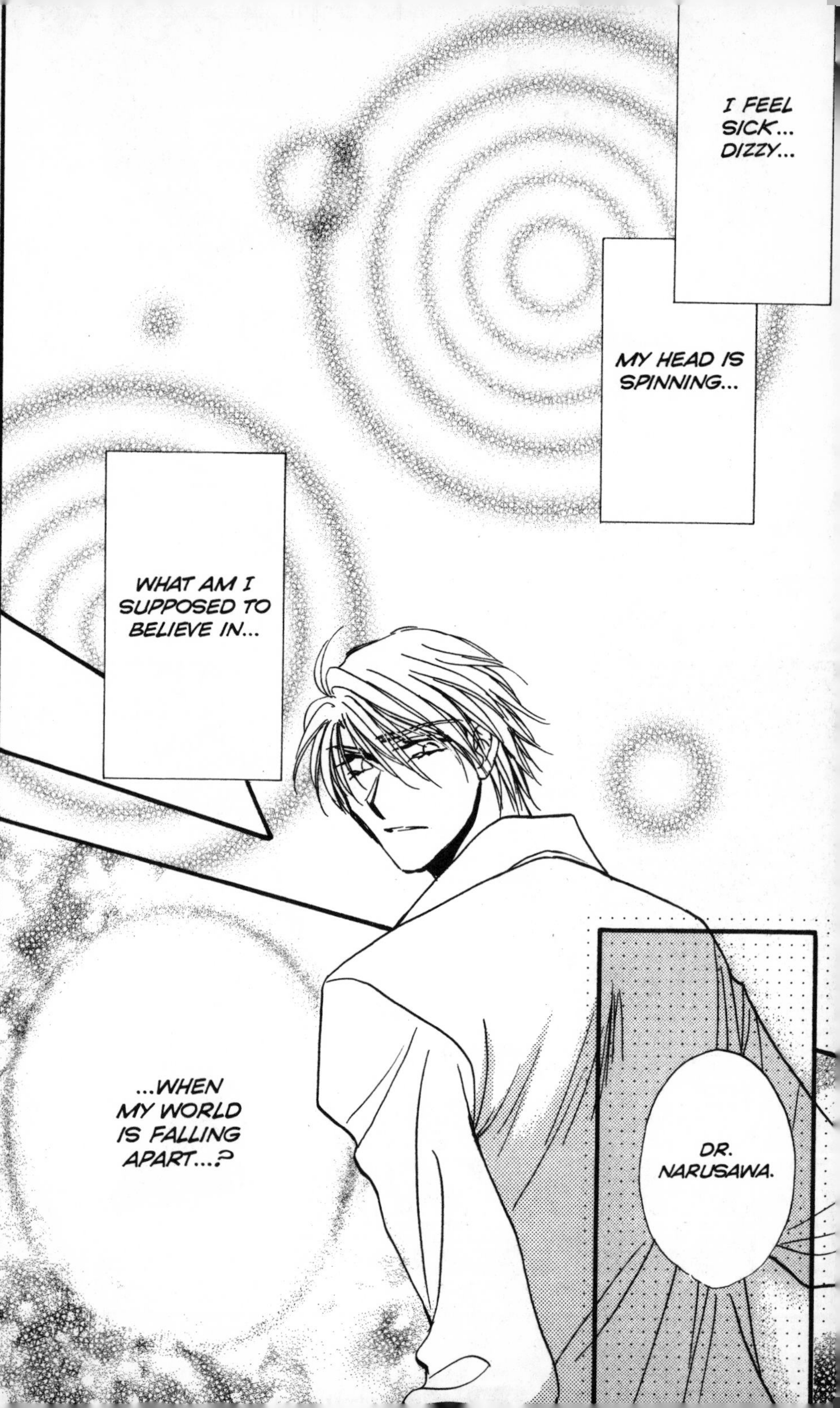
I FEEL SICK... DIZZY...
MY HEAD IS SPINNING...
WHAT AM I SUPPOSED TO BELIEVE IN...
DR. NARUSAWA.
...WHEN MY WORLD IS FALLING APART...?

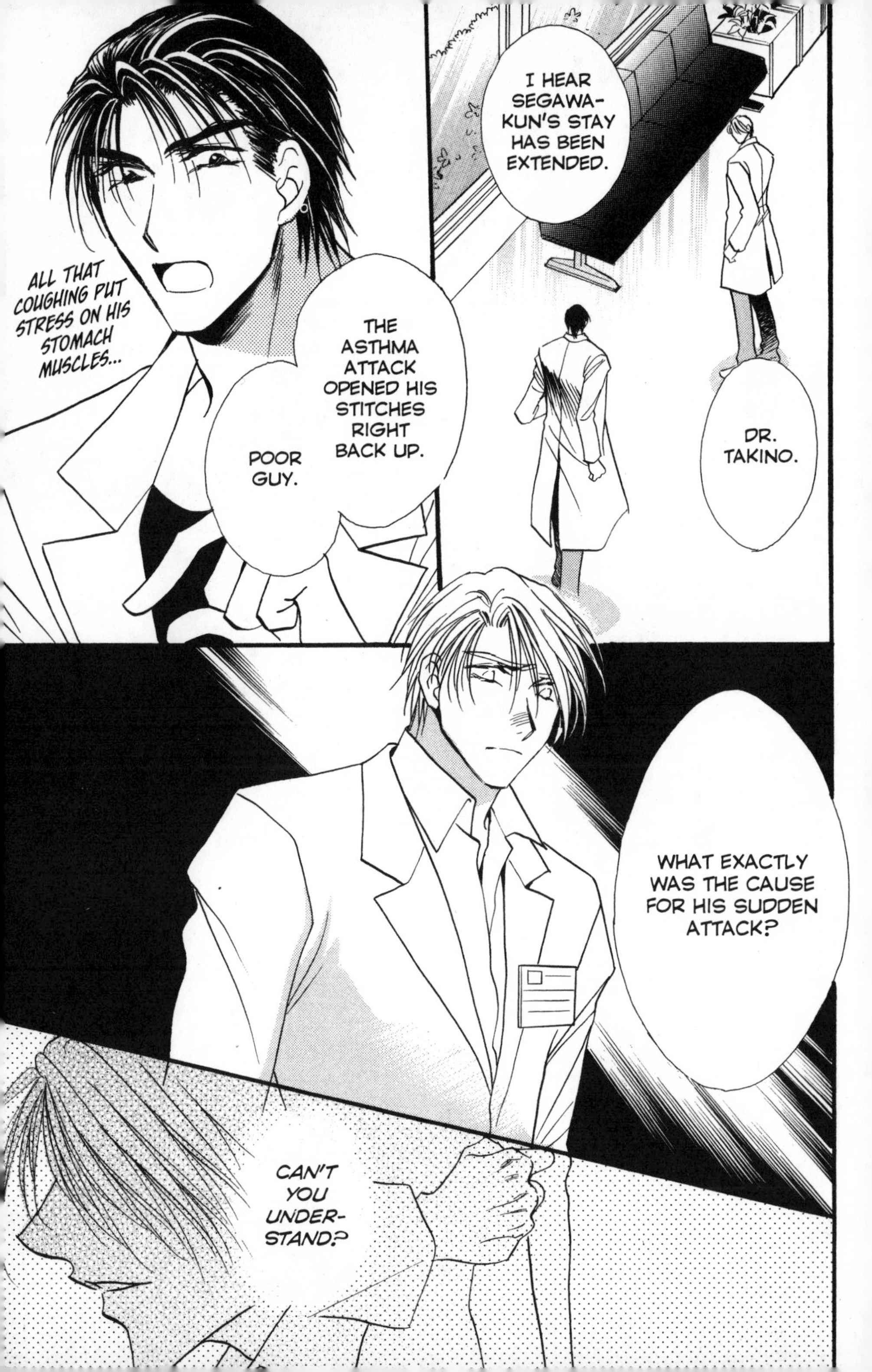
I HEAR SEGAWA-KUN'S STAY HAS BEEN EXTENDED.
DR. TAKINO.
THE ASTHMA ATTACK OPENED HIS STITCHES RIGHT BACK UP.
POOR GUY.
ALL THAT COUGHING PUT STRESS ON HIS STOMACH MUSCLES...
WHAT EXACTLY WAS THE CAUSE FOR HIS SUDDEN ATTACK?
CAN'T YOU UNDER-STAND?

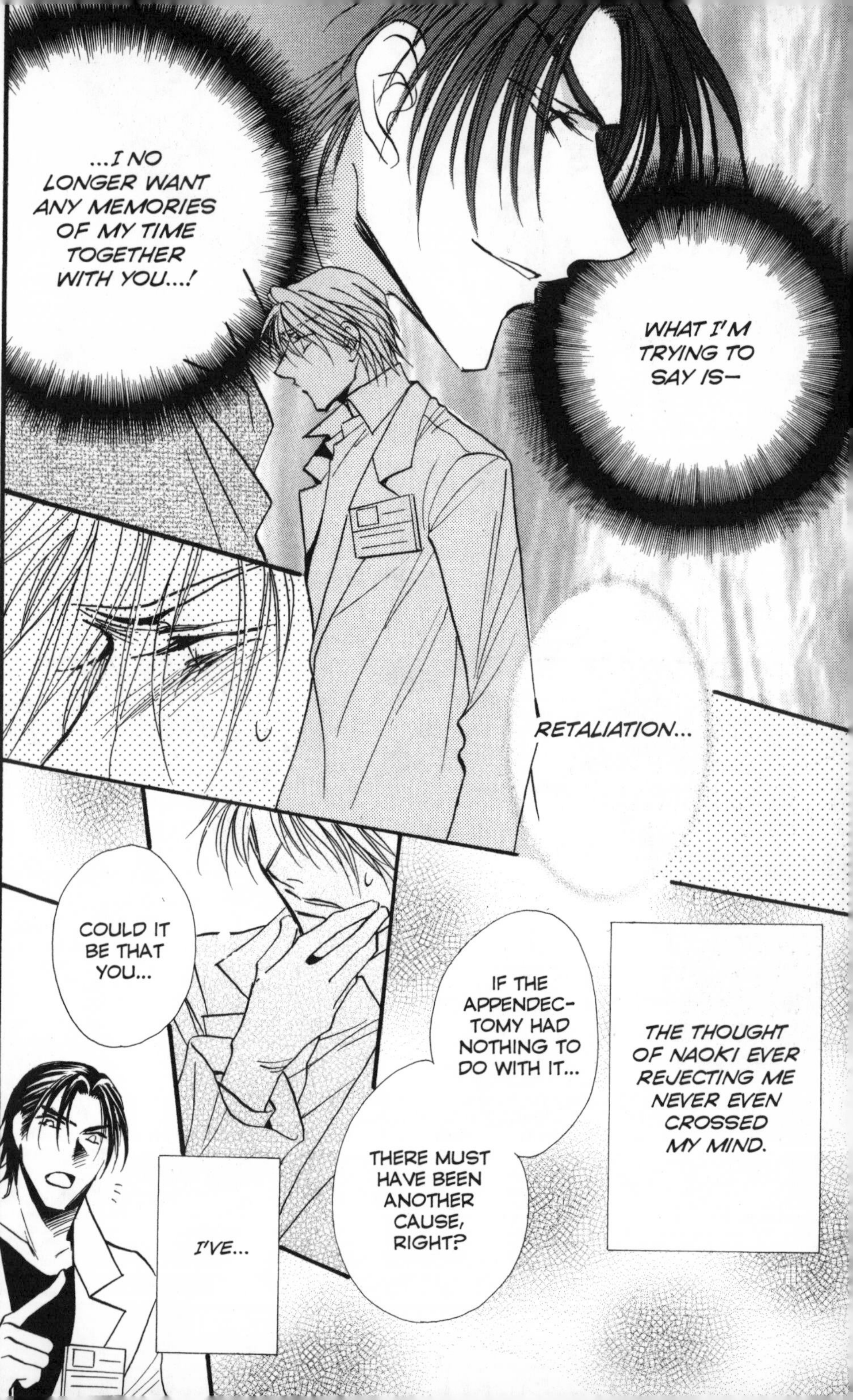
WHAT I'M TRYING TO SAY IS—
...I NO LONGER WANT ANY MEMORIES OF MY TIME TOGETHER WITH YOU...!
RETALIATION...
THE THOUGHT OF NAOKI EVER REJECTING ME NEVER EVEN CROSSED MY MIND.
COULD IT BE THAT YOU...
IF THE APPENDEC-TOMY HAD NOTHING TO DO WITH IT...
THERE MUST HAVE BEEN ANOTHER CAUSE, RIGHT?
I'VE...

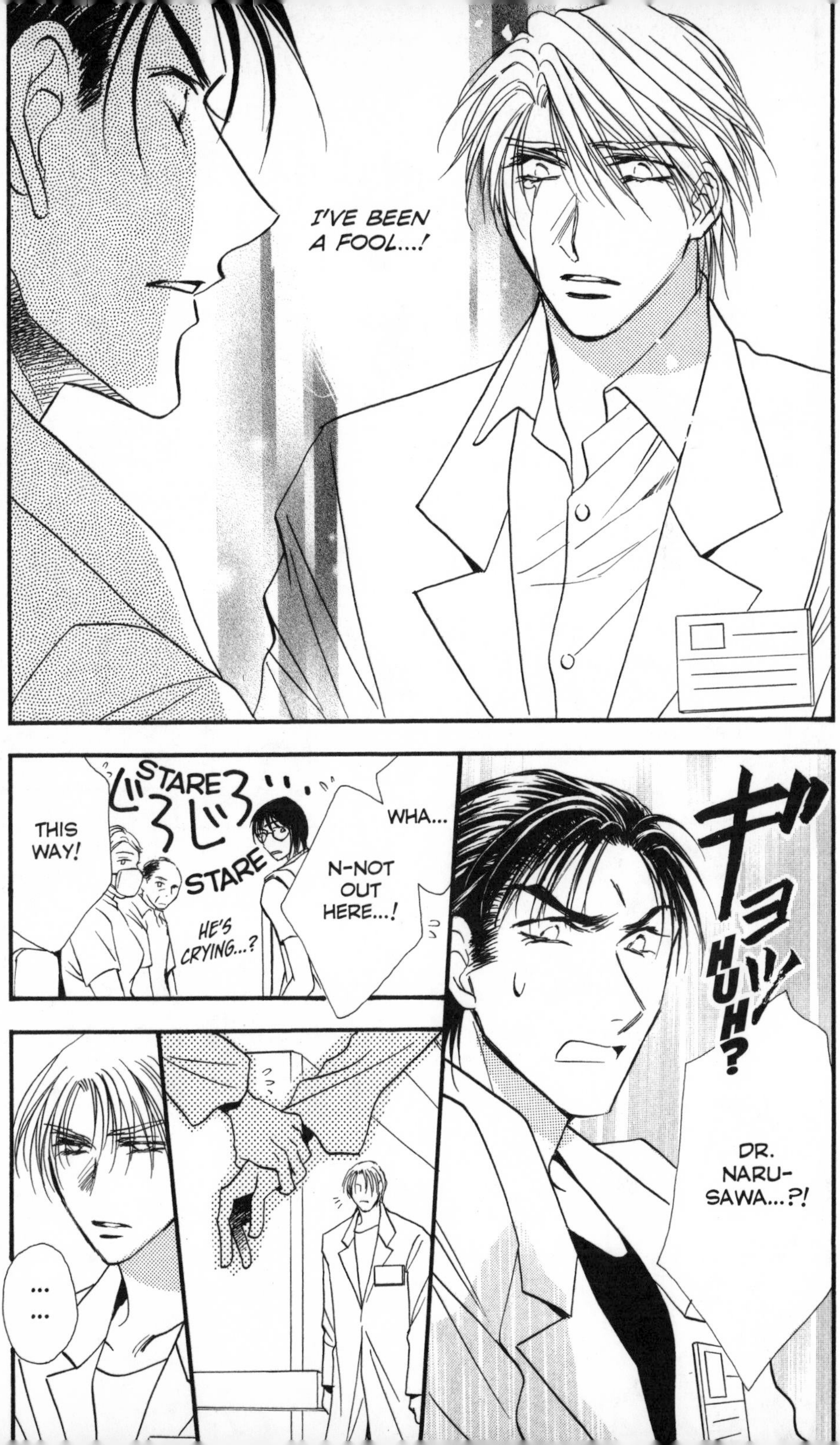

I'VE BEEN A FOOL...!
ギョッ
UH?
DR. NARU-SAWA...?!
WHA...
N-NOT OUT HERE...!
STARE
じろじろ
STARE
HE'S CRYING...?
THIS WAY!
......

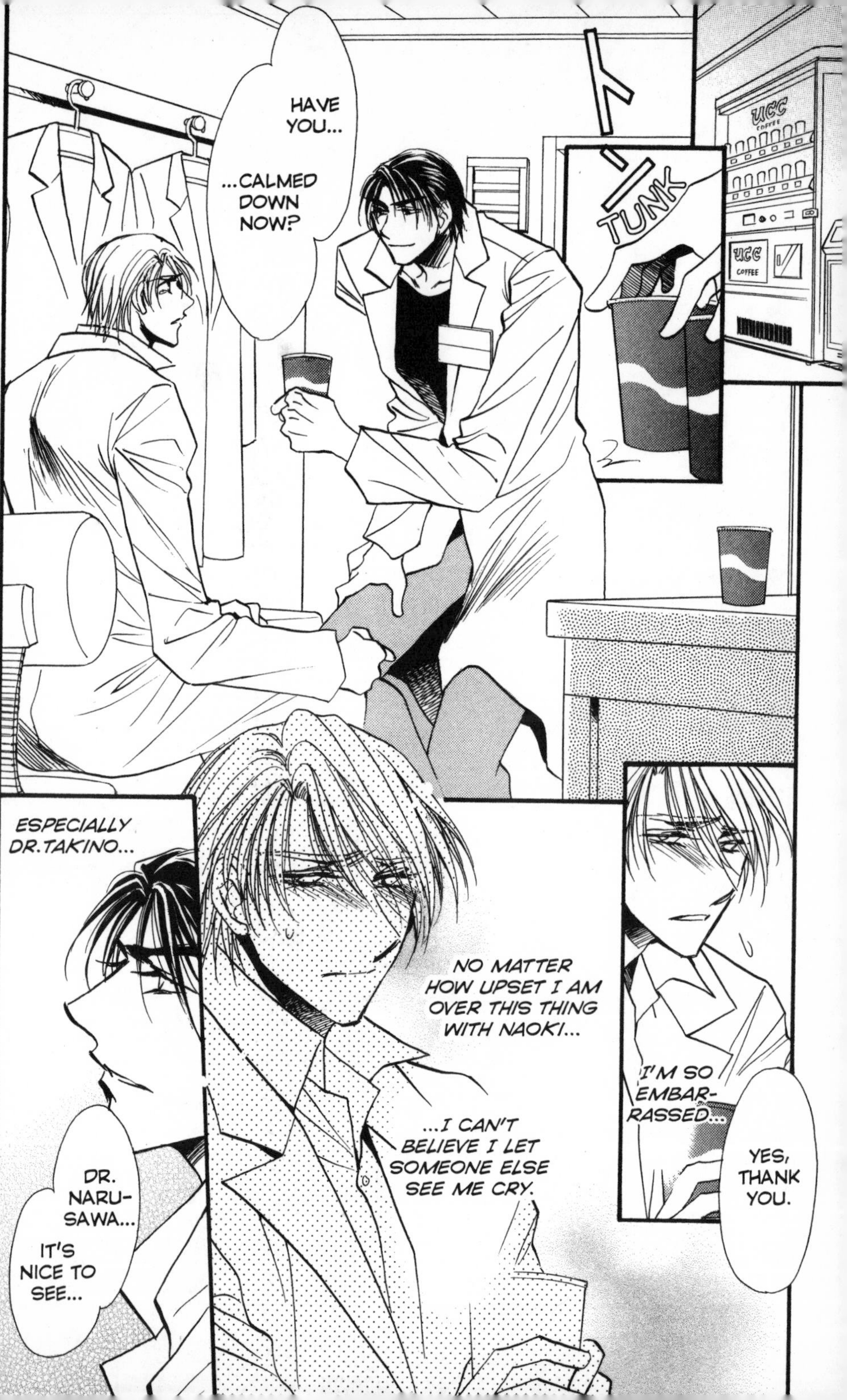
TUNK
HAVE YOU...
...CALMED DOWN NOW?
I'M SO EMBARRASSED...
YES, THANK YOU.
NO MATTER HOW UPSET I AM OVER THIS THING WITH NAOKI...
...I CAN'T BELIEVE I LET SOMEONE ELSE SEE ME CRY.
ESPECIALLY DR.TAKINO...
DR. NARUSAWA...
IT'S NICE TO SEE...

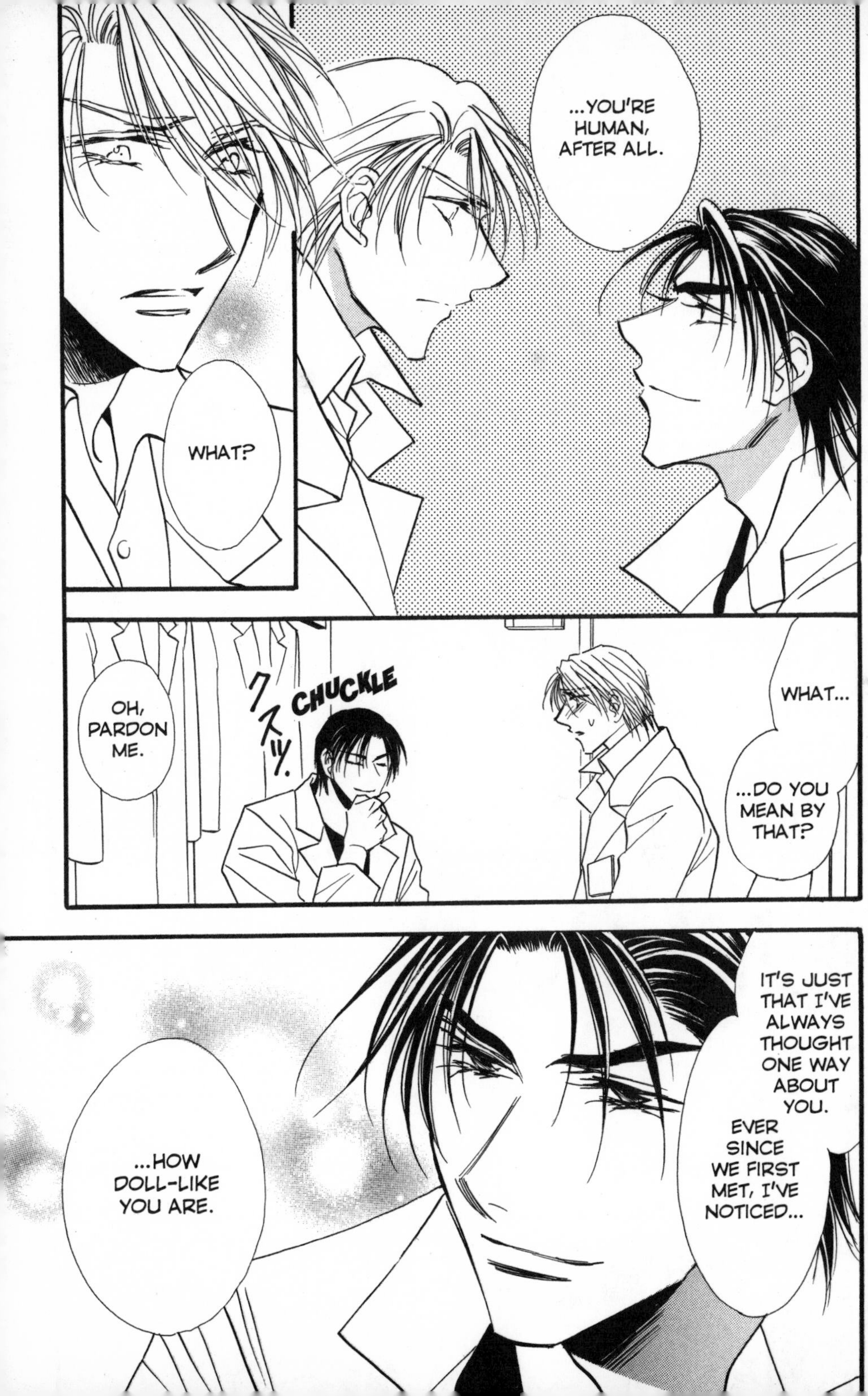
...YOU'RE HUMAN, AFTER ALL.
WHAT?
WHAT...
...DO YOU MEAN BY THAT?
クスッ
CHUCKLE
OH, PARDON ME.
IT'S JUST THAT I'VE ALWAYS THOUGHT ONE WAY ABOUT YOU.
EVER SINCE WE FIRST MET, I'VE NOTICED...
...HOW DOLL-LIKE YOU ARE.

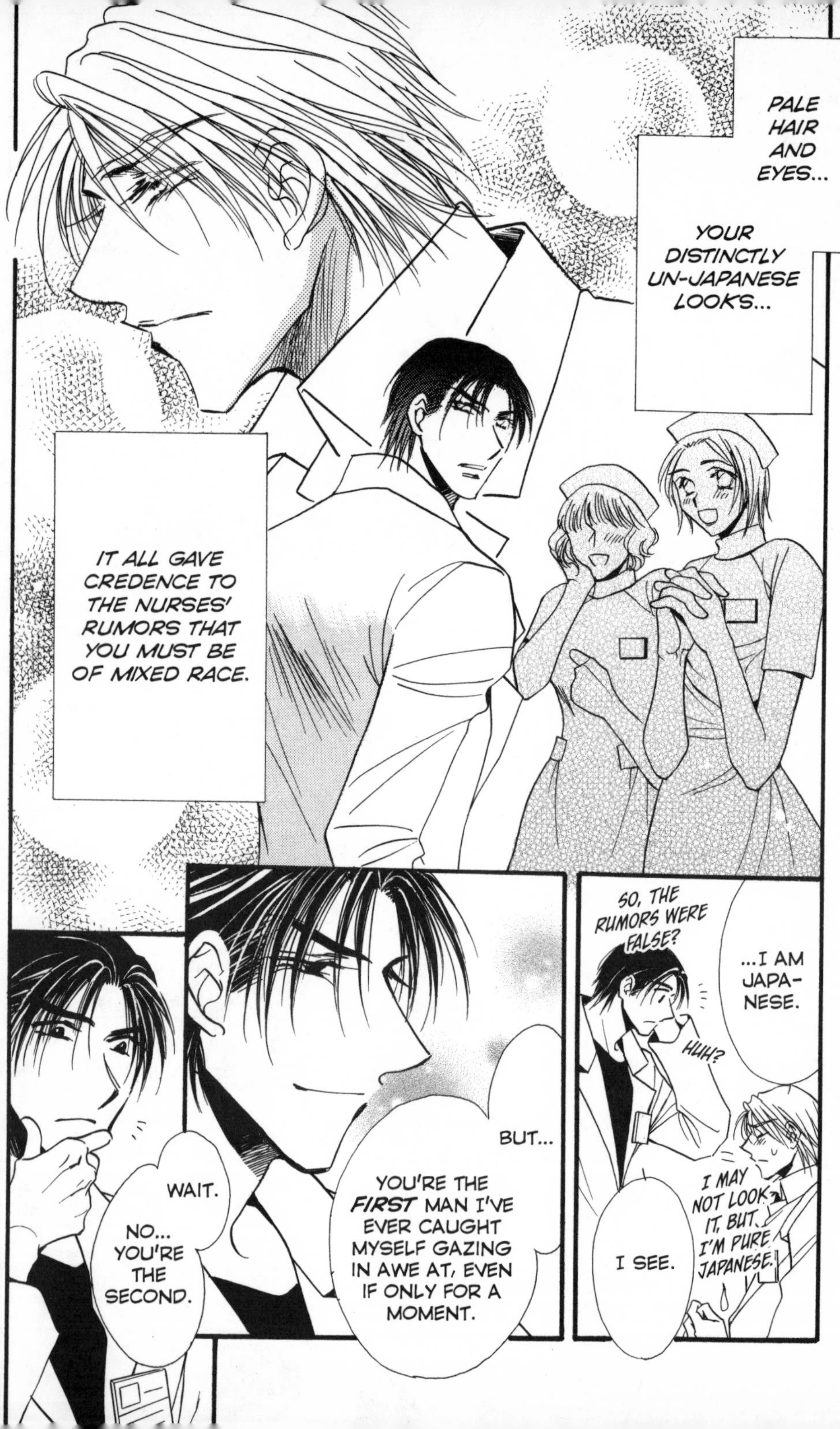
PALE HAIR AND EYES...
YOUR DISTINCTLY UN-JAPANESE LOOKS...
IT ALL GAVE CREDENCE TO THE NURSES' RUMORS THAT YOU MUST BE OF MIXED RACE.
SO, THE RUMORS WERE FALSE?
...I AM JAPA-NESE.
HUH?
I MAY NOT LOOK IT, BUT I'M PURE JAPANESE.
I SEE.
BUT...
YOU'RE THE *FIRST* MAN I'VE EVER CAUGHT MYSELF GAZING IN AWE AT, EVEN IF ONLY FOR A MOMENT.
WAIT.
NO... YOU'RE THE SECOND.

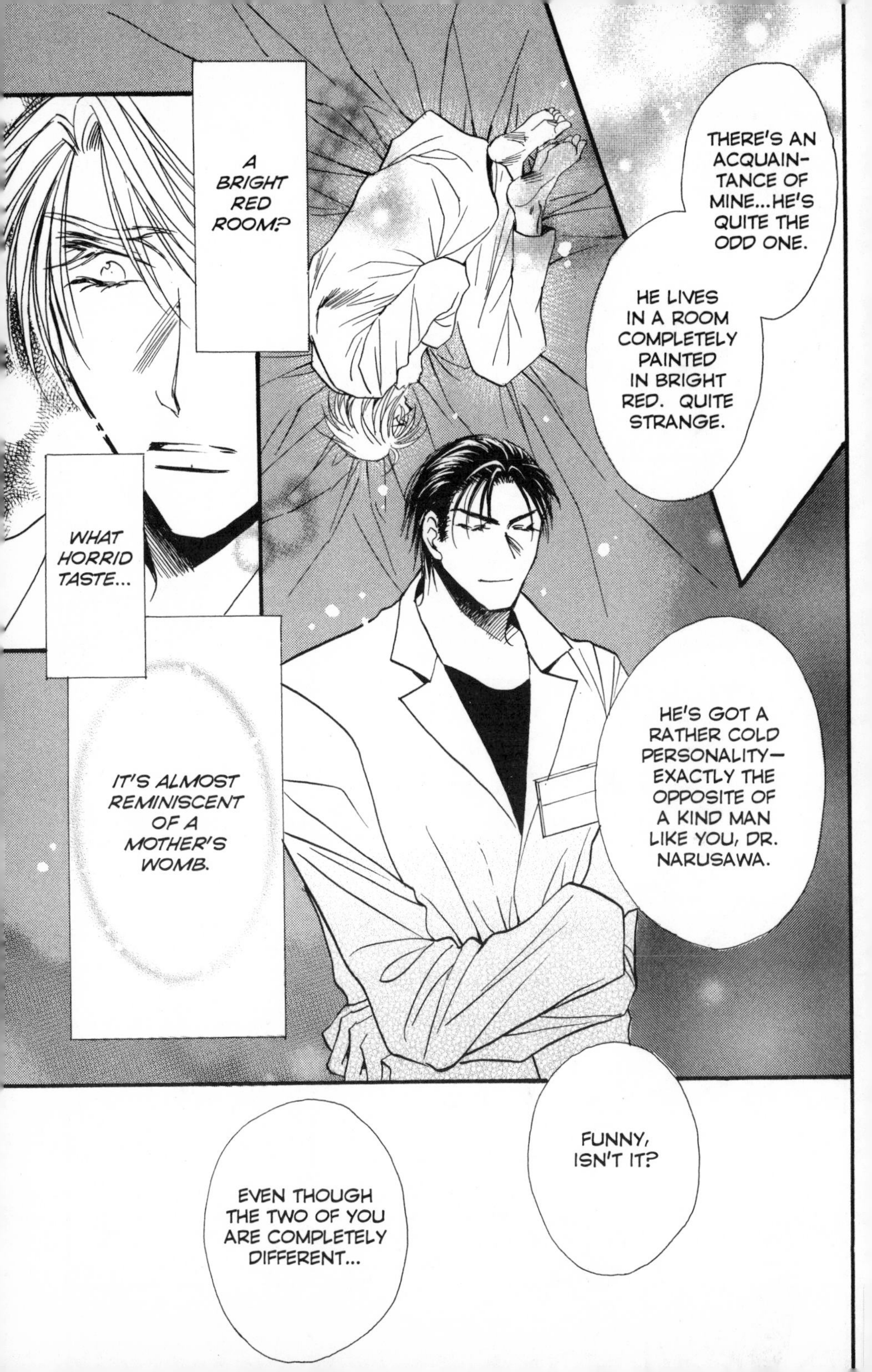
THERE'S AN ACQUAINTANCE OF MINE...HE'S QUITE THE ODD ONE.
HE LIVES IN A ROOM COMPLETELY PAINTED IN BRIGHT RED. QUITE STRANGE.
A BRIGHT RED ROOM?
WHAT HORRID TASTE...
HE'S GOT A RATHER COLD PERSONALITY—EXACTLY THE OPPOSITE OF A KIND MAN LIKE YOU, DR. NARUSAWA.
IT'S ALMOST REMINISCENT OF A MOTHER'S WOMB.
FUNNY, ISN'T IT?
EVEN THOUGH THE TWO OF YOU ARE COMPLETELY DIFFERENT...

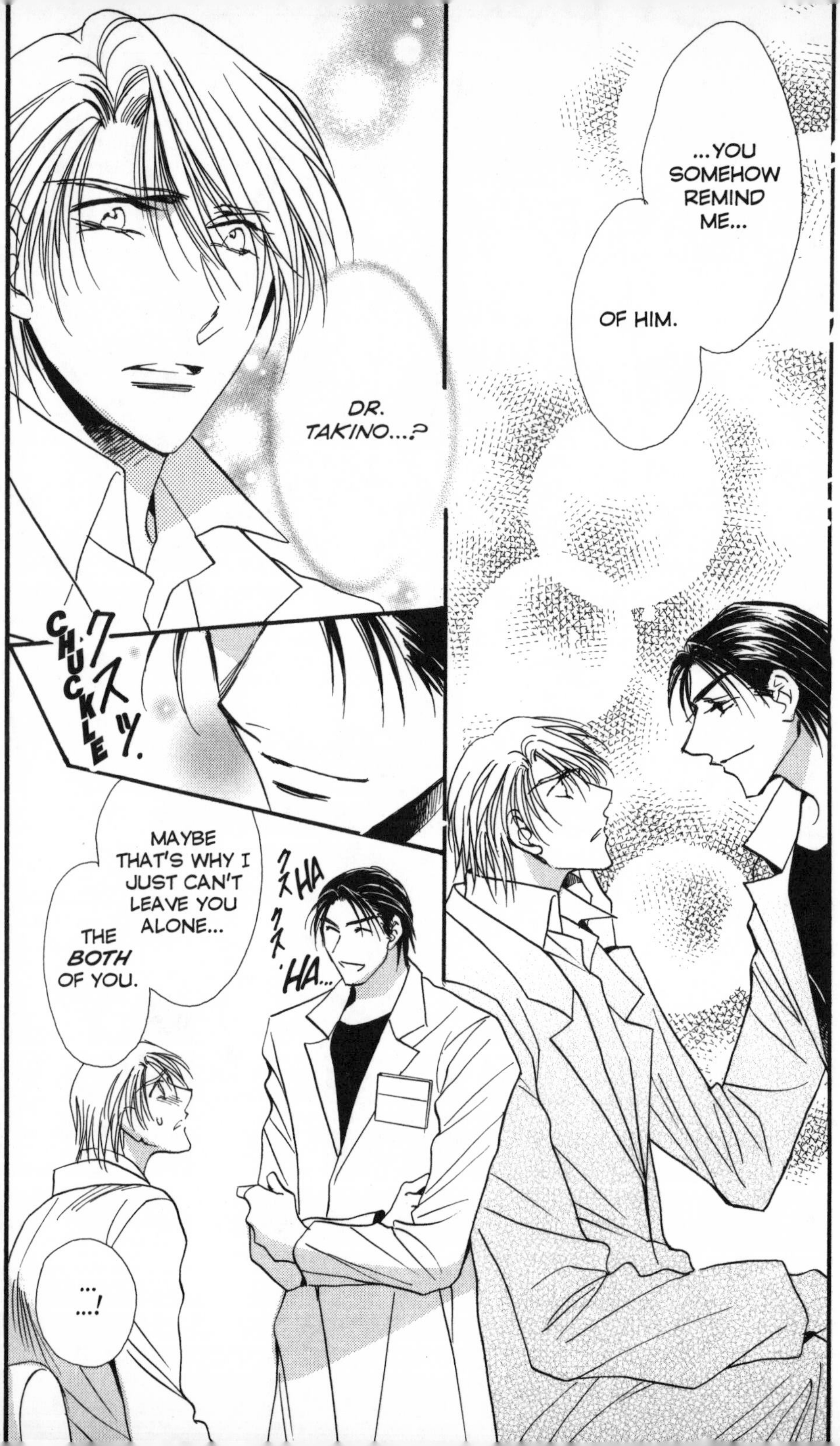
...YOU SOMEHOW REMIND ME...
OF HIM.
DR. TAKINO...?
クスッ.
CHUCKLE
MAYBE THAT'S WHY I JUST CAN'T LEAVE YOU ALONE...
THE BOTH OF YOU.
クスクス...
HA HA...
...
...!

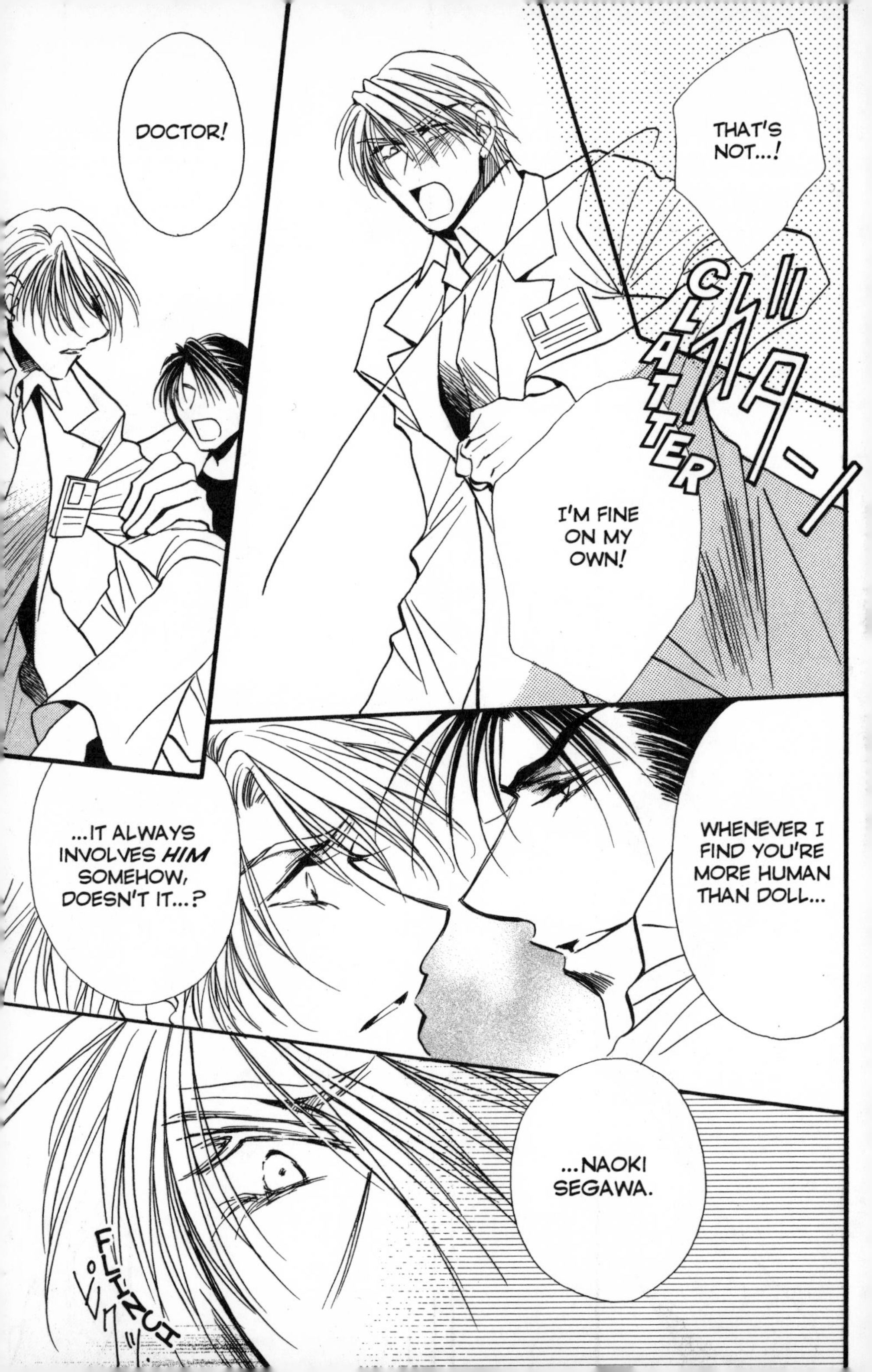
THAT'S NOT...!
CLATTER
I'M FINE ON MY OWN!
DOCTOR!
WHENEVER I FIND YOU'RE MORE HUMAN THAN DOLL...
...IT ALWAYS INVOLVES *HIM* SOMEHOW, DOESN'T IT...?
...NAOKI SEGAWA.
FLINCH

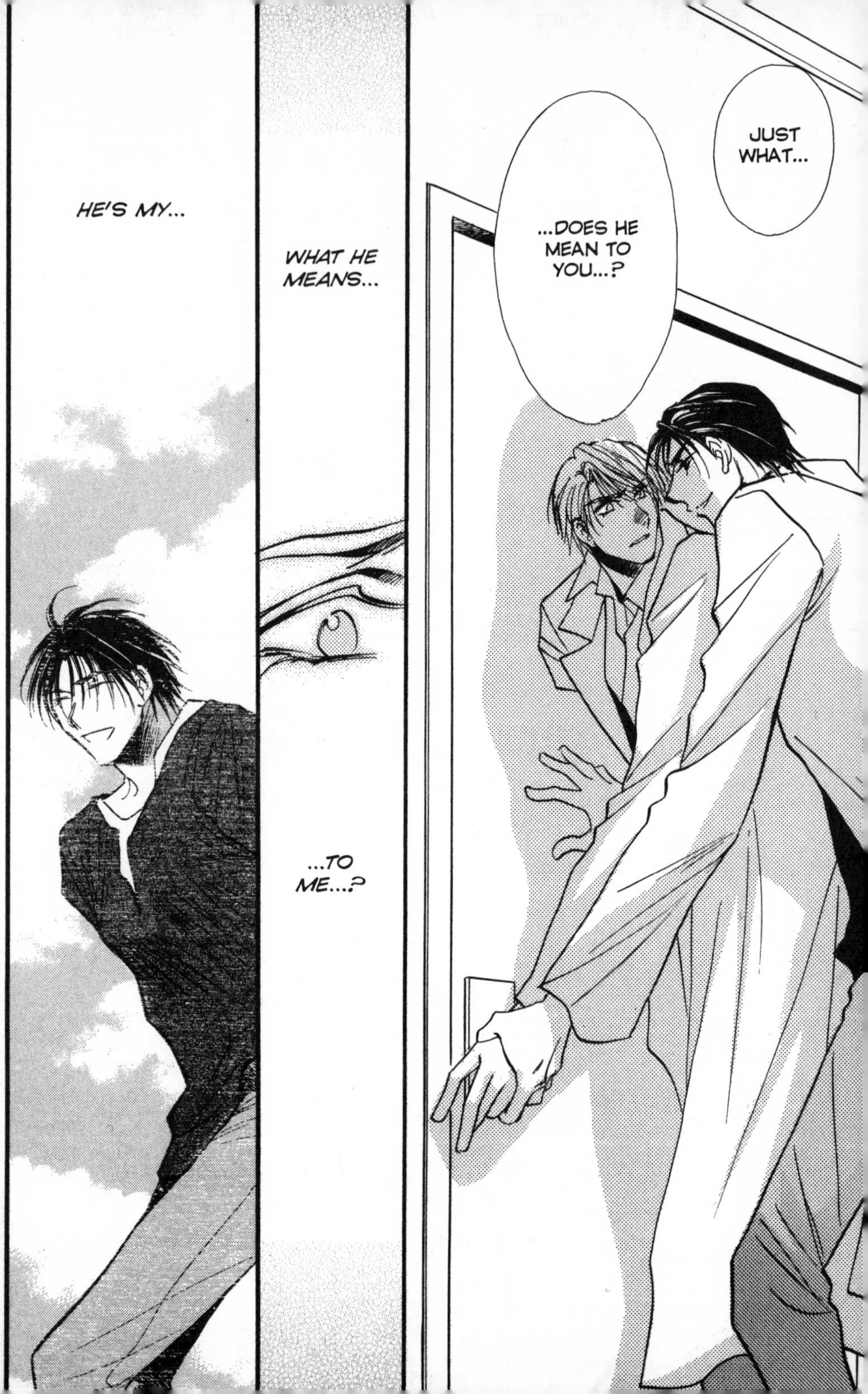

JUST WHAT...
...DOES HE MEAN TO YOU...?
WHAT HE MEANS...
...TO ME...?
HE'S MY...

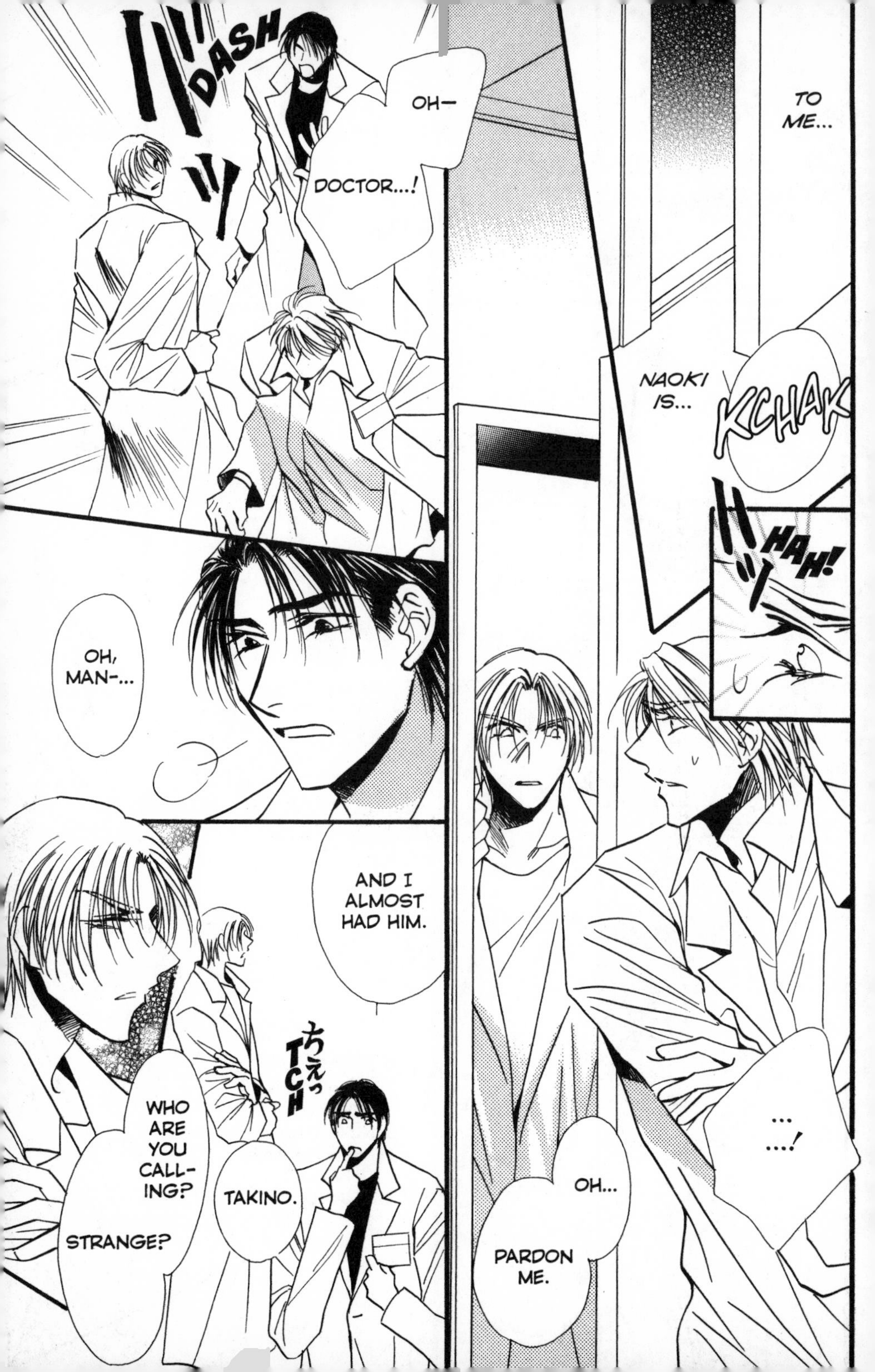
TO ME...
NAOKI IS...
KCHAK
HAH!
... ...!
OH... PARDON ME.
DASH
OH—
DOCTOR...!
OH, MAN-...
AND I ALMOST HAD HIM.
ちぇっ TCH
TAKINO.
WHO ARE YOU CALL-ING?
STRANGE?

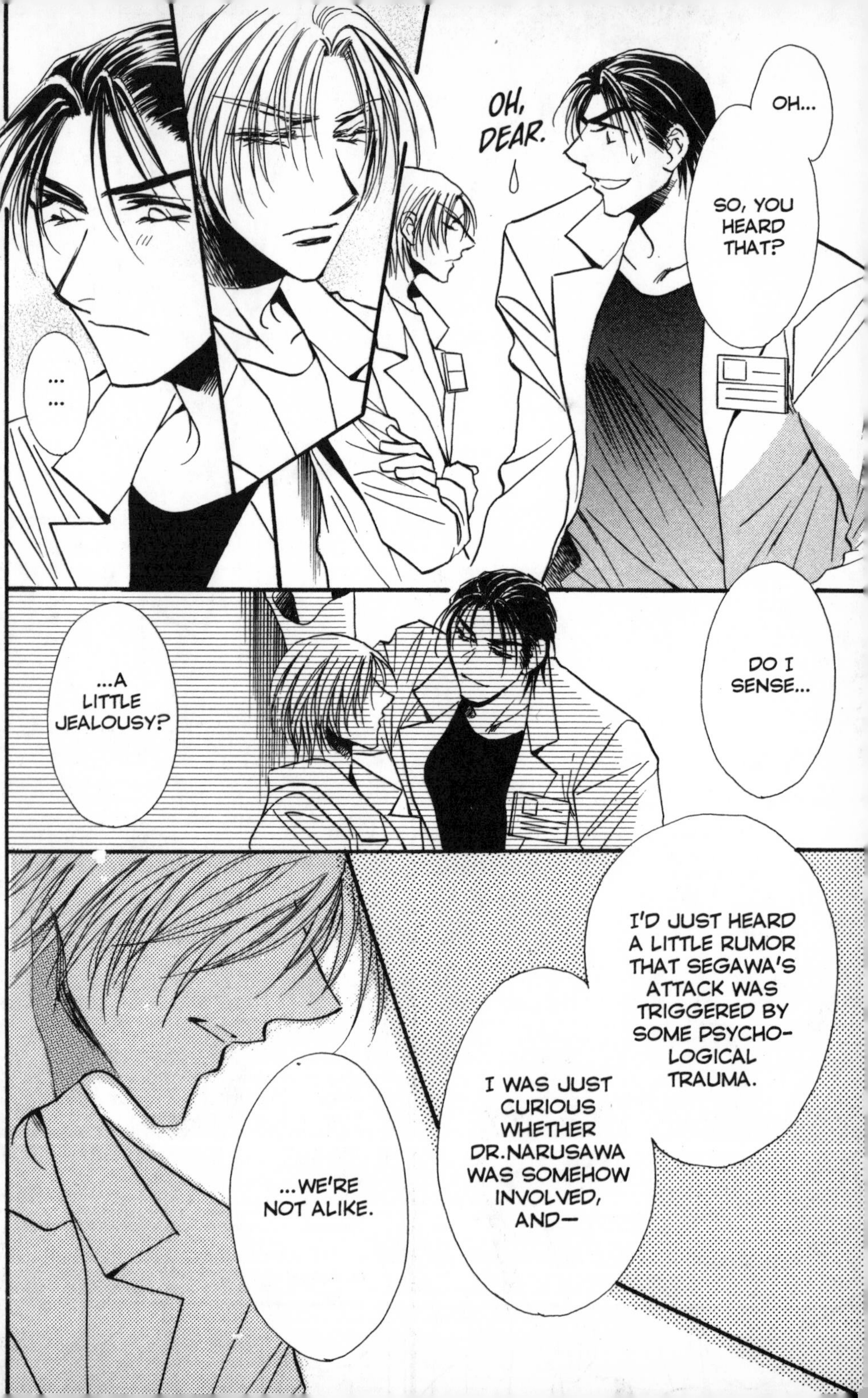
OH...
SO, YOU HEARD THAT?
OH, DEAR.
......
DO I SENSE...
...A LITTLE JEALOUSY?
I'D JUST HEARD A LITTLE RUMOR THAT SEGAWA'S ATTACK WAS TRIGGERED BY SOME PSYCHO-LOGICAL TRAUMA.
I WAS JUST CURIOUS WHETHER DR.NARUSAWA WAS SOMEHOW INVOLVED, AND—
...WE'RE NOT ALIKE.

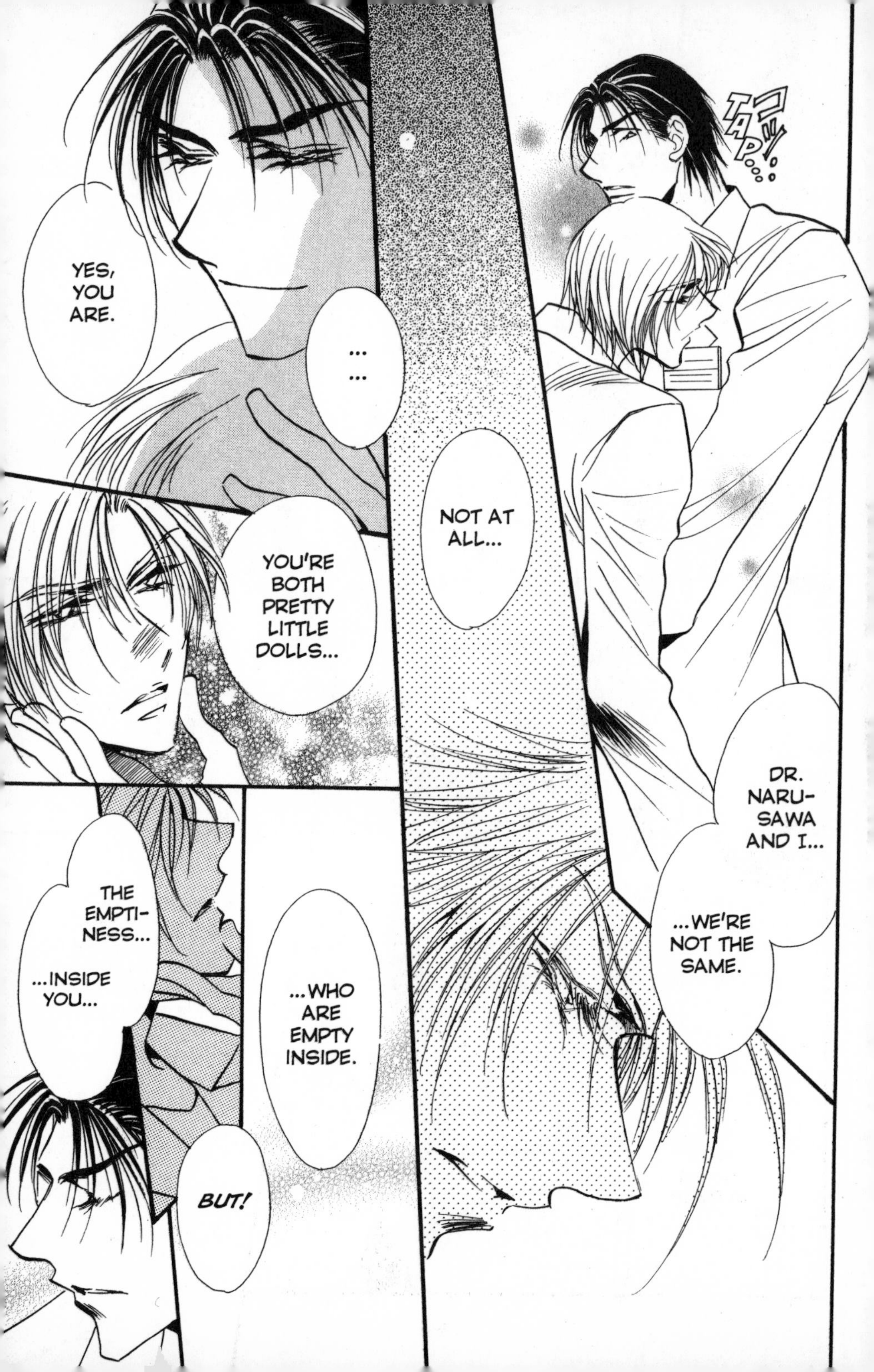
TAP...
DR. NARUSAWA AND I...
...WE'RE NOT THE SAME.
NOT AT ALL...
YES, YOU ARE.
......
YOU'RE BOTH PRETTY LITTLE DOLLS...
...WHO ARE EMPTY INSIDE.
THE EMPTINESS...
...INSIDE YOU...
BUT!

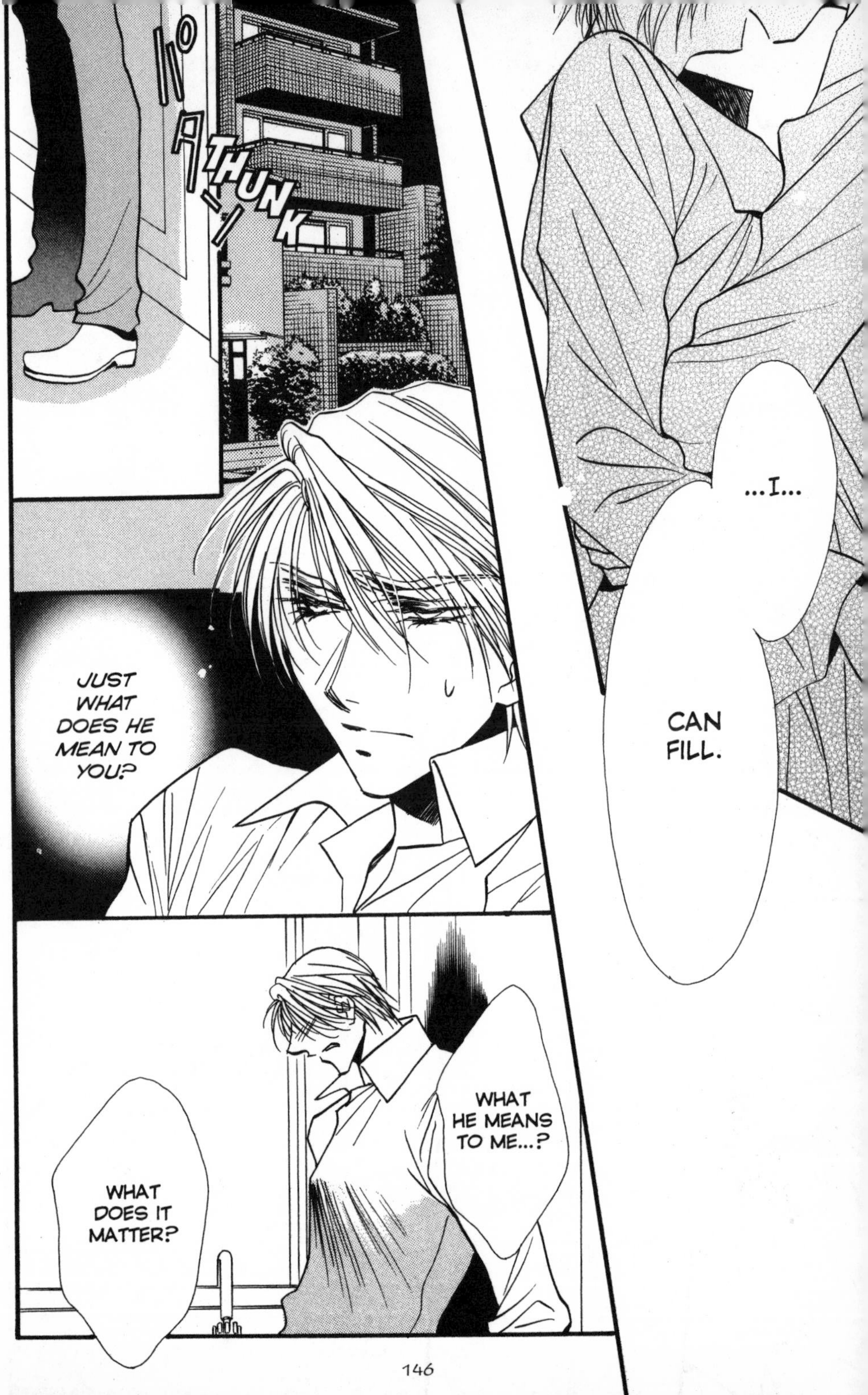
...I...
CAN FILL.
THUNK
JUST WHAT DOES HE MEAN TO YOU?
WHAT HE MEANS TO ME...?
WHAT DOES IT MATTER?

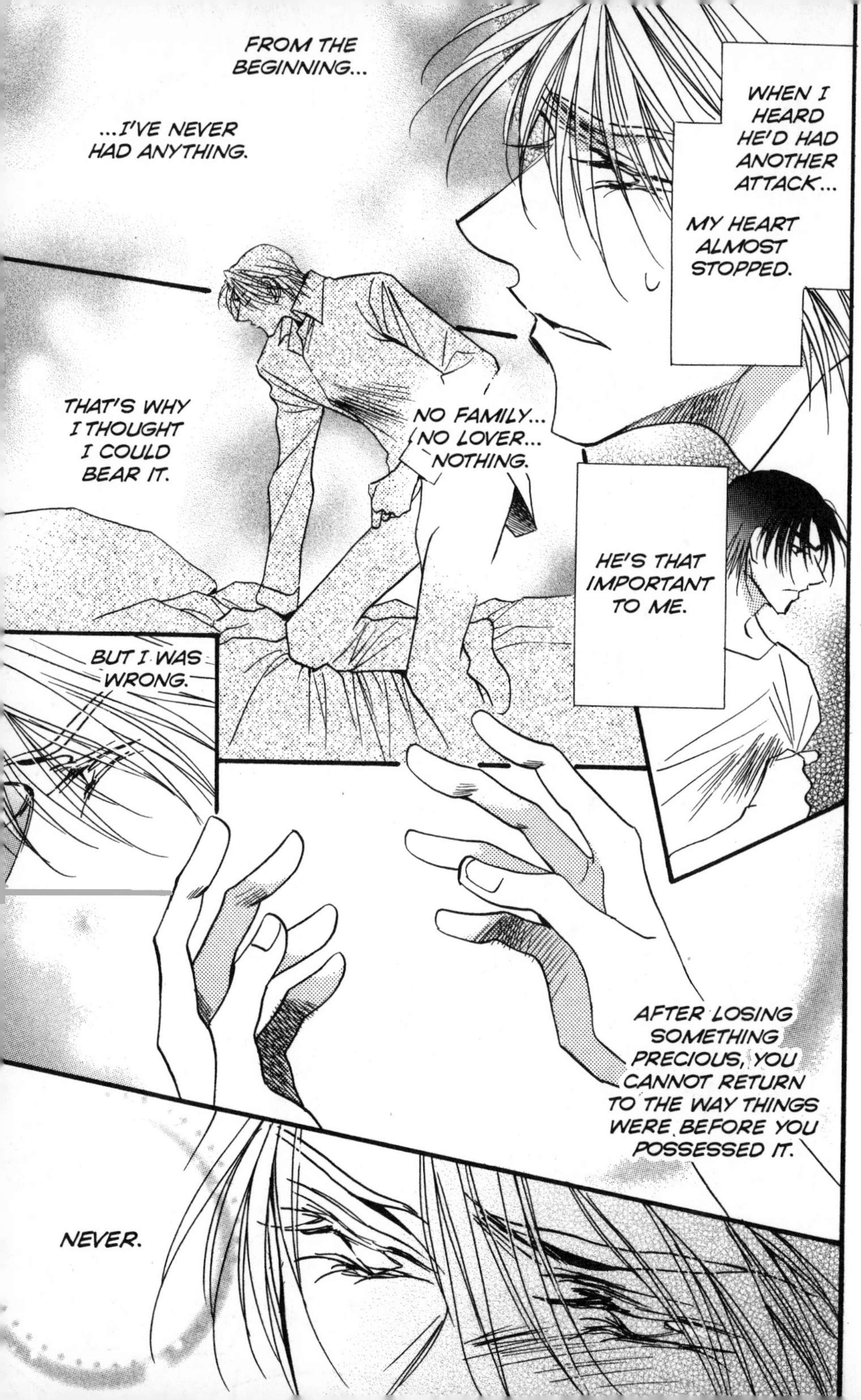
WHEN I HEARD HE'D HAD ANOTHER ATTACK...
MY HEART ALMOST STOPPED.
FROM THE BEGINNING...
...I'VE NEVER HAD ANYTHING.
HE'S THAT IMPORTANT TO ME.
NO FAMILY... NO LOVER... NOTHING.
THAT'S WHY I THOUGHT I COULD BEAR IT.
BUT I WAS WRONG.
AFTER LOSING SOMETHING PRECIOUS, YOU CANNOT RETURN TO THE WAY THINGS WERE BEFORE YOU POSSESSED IT.
NEVER.

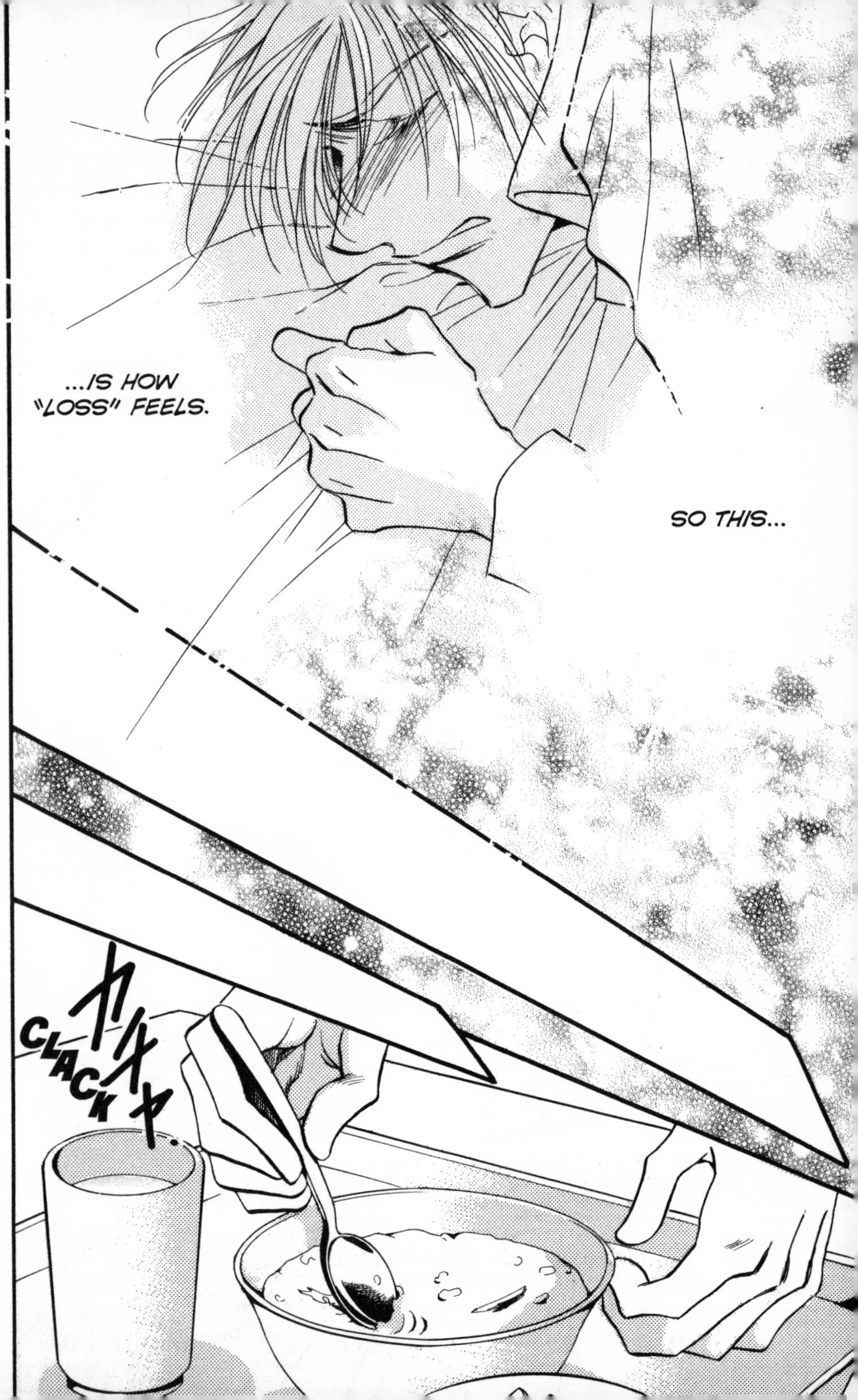
SO THIS...
...IS HOW "LOSS" FEELS.
CLACK

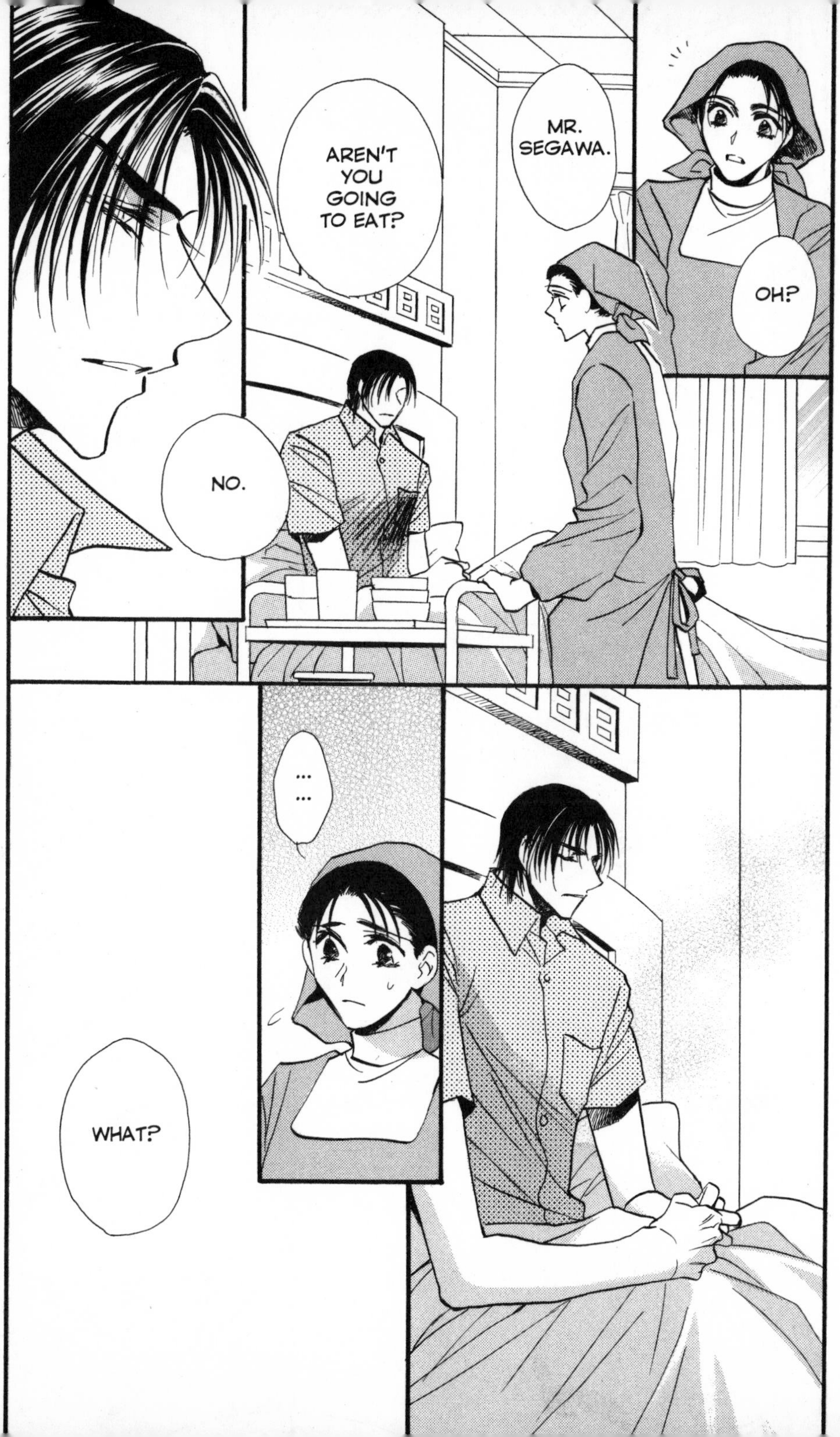
OH?
MR. SEGAWA.
AREN'T YOU GOING TO EAT?
NO.
......
WHAT?

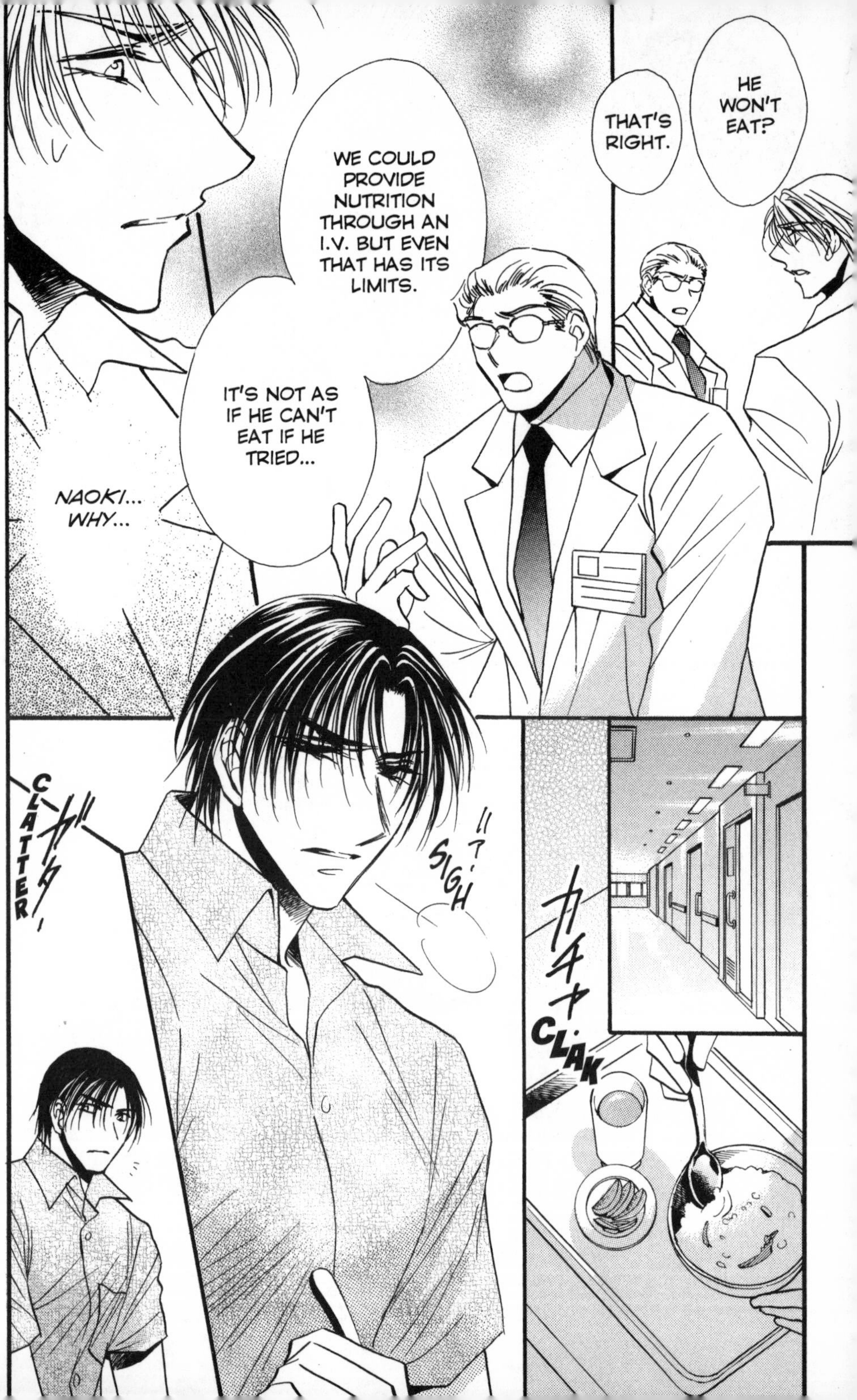
HE WON'T EAT?
THAT'S RIGHT.
WE COULD PROVIDE NUTRITION THROUGH AN I.V. BUT EVEN THAT HAS ITS LIMITS.
IT'S NOT AS IF HE CAN'T EAT IF HE TRIED...
NAOKI... WHY...
CLAK
SIGH
CLATTER

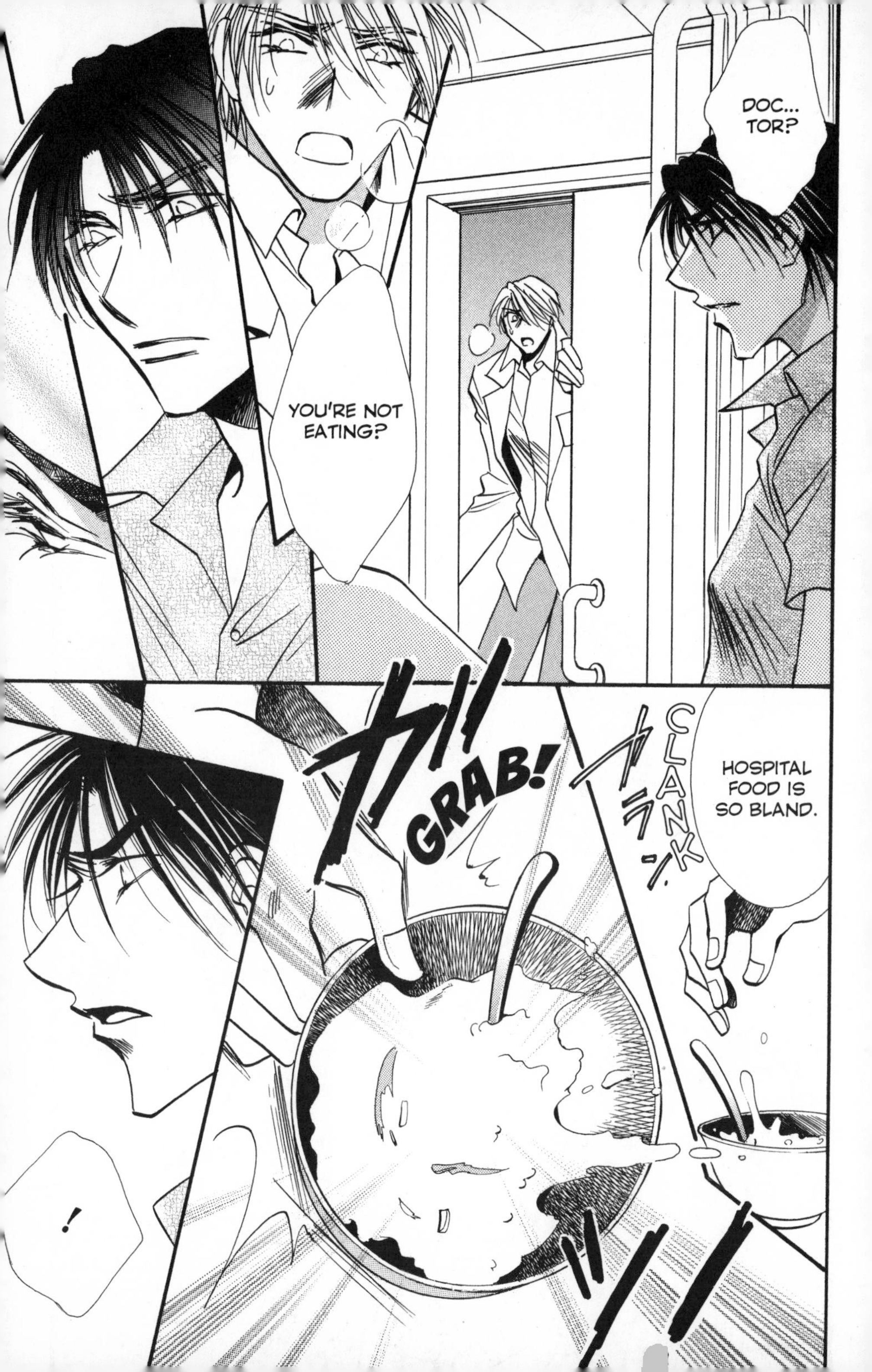
DOC... TOR?
YOU'RE NOT EATING?
HOSPITAL FOOD IS SO BLAND.
CLANK
GRAB!
!

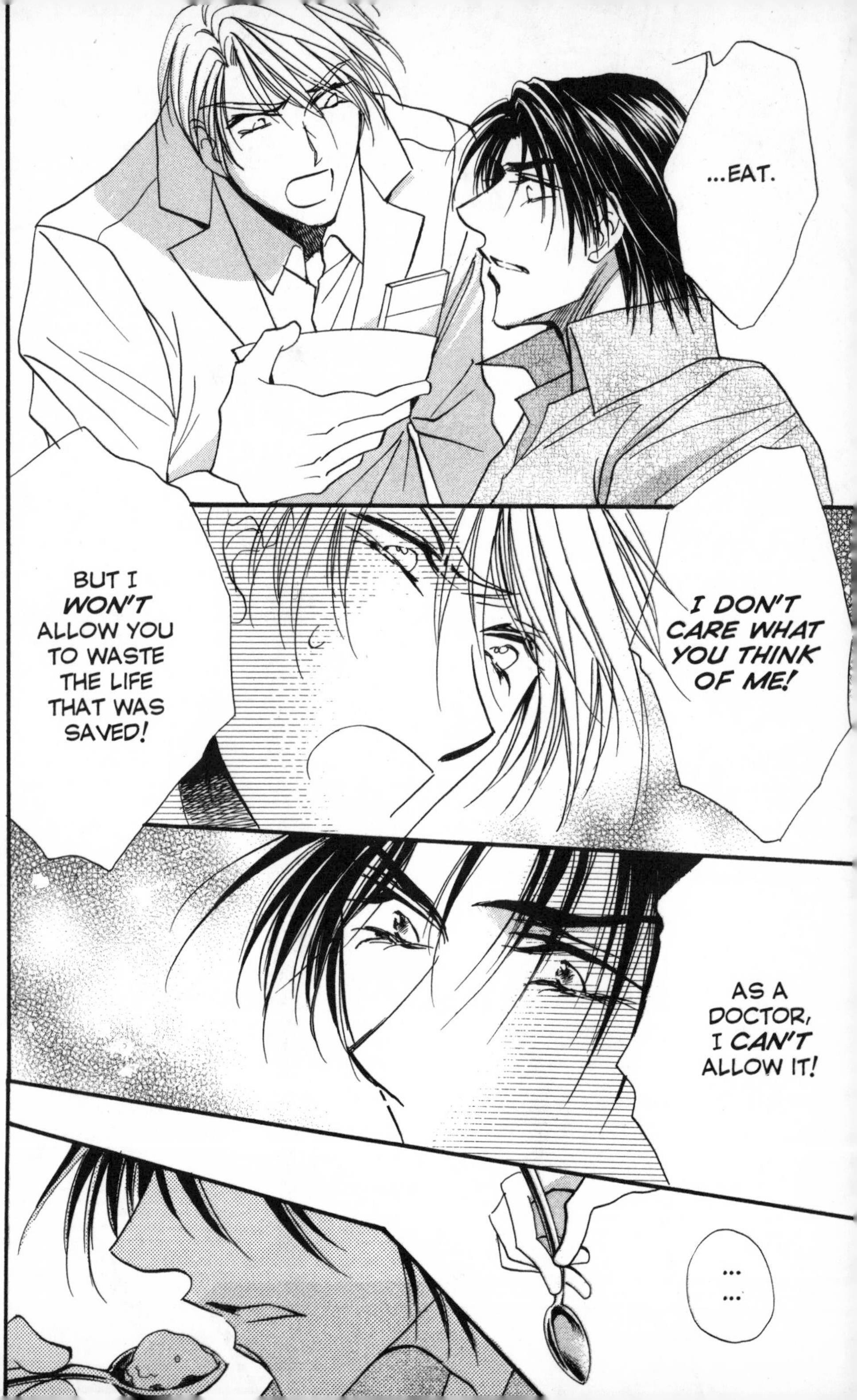
...EAT.
I DON'T CARE WHAT YOU THINK OF ME!
BUT I WON'T ALLOW YOU TO WASTE THE LIFE THAT WAS SAVED!
AS A DOCTOR, I CAN'T ALLOW IT!
... ...

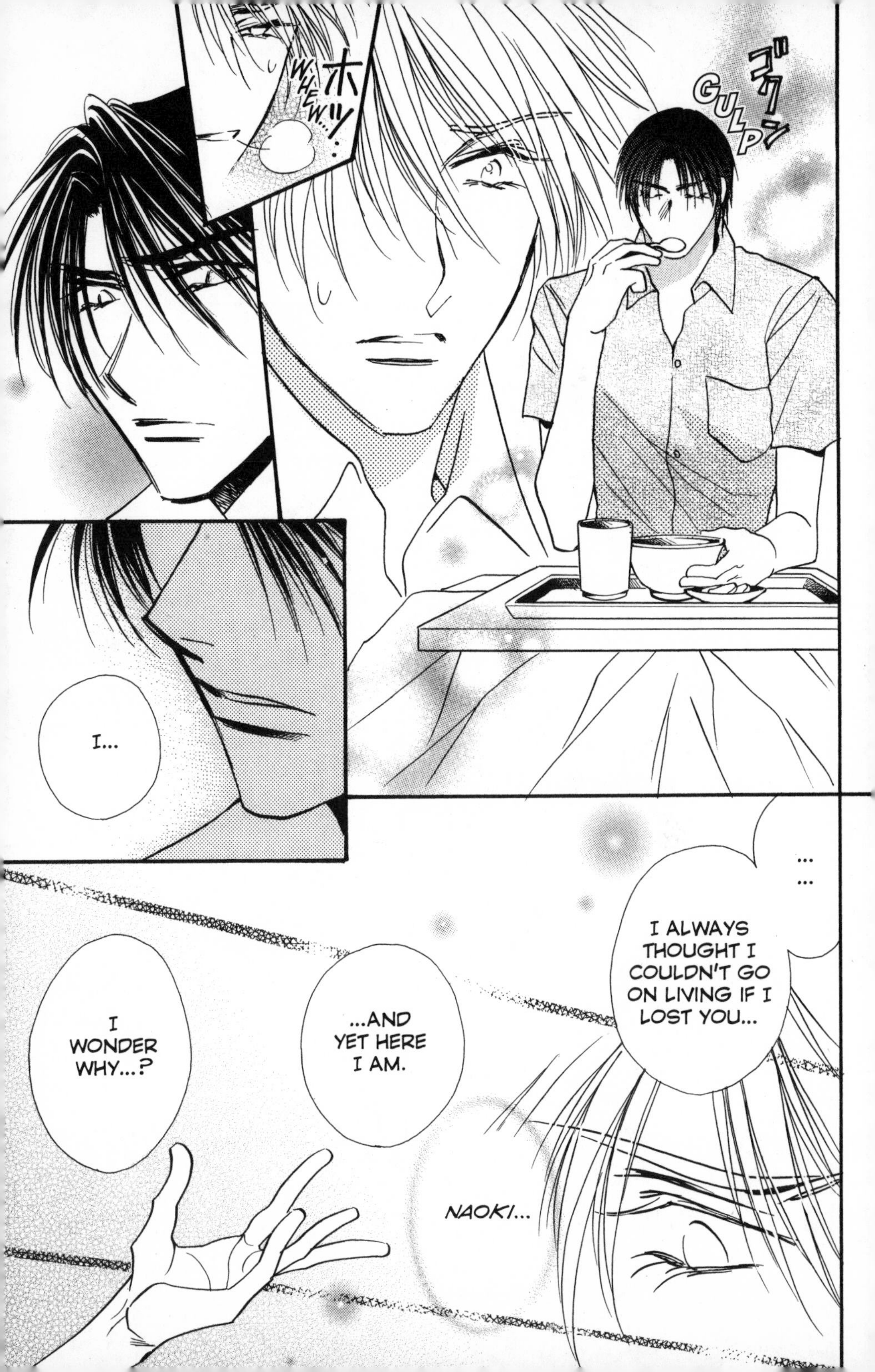
ゴクン
GULP
ホッ
WHEW...
I...
......
I ALWAYS THOUGHT I COULDN'T GO ON LIVING IF I LOST YOU...
...AND YET HERE I AM.
I WONDER WHY...?
NAOKI...

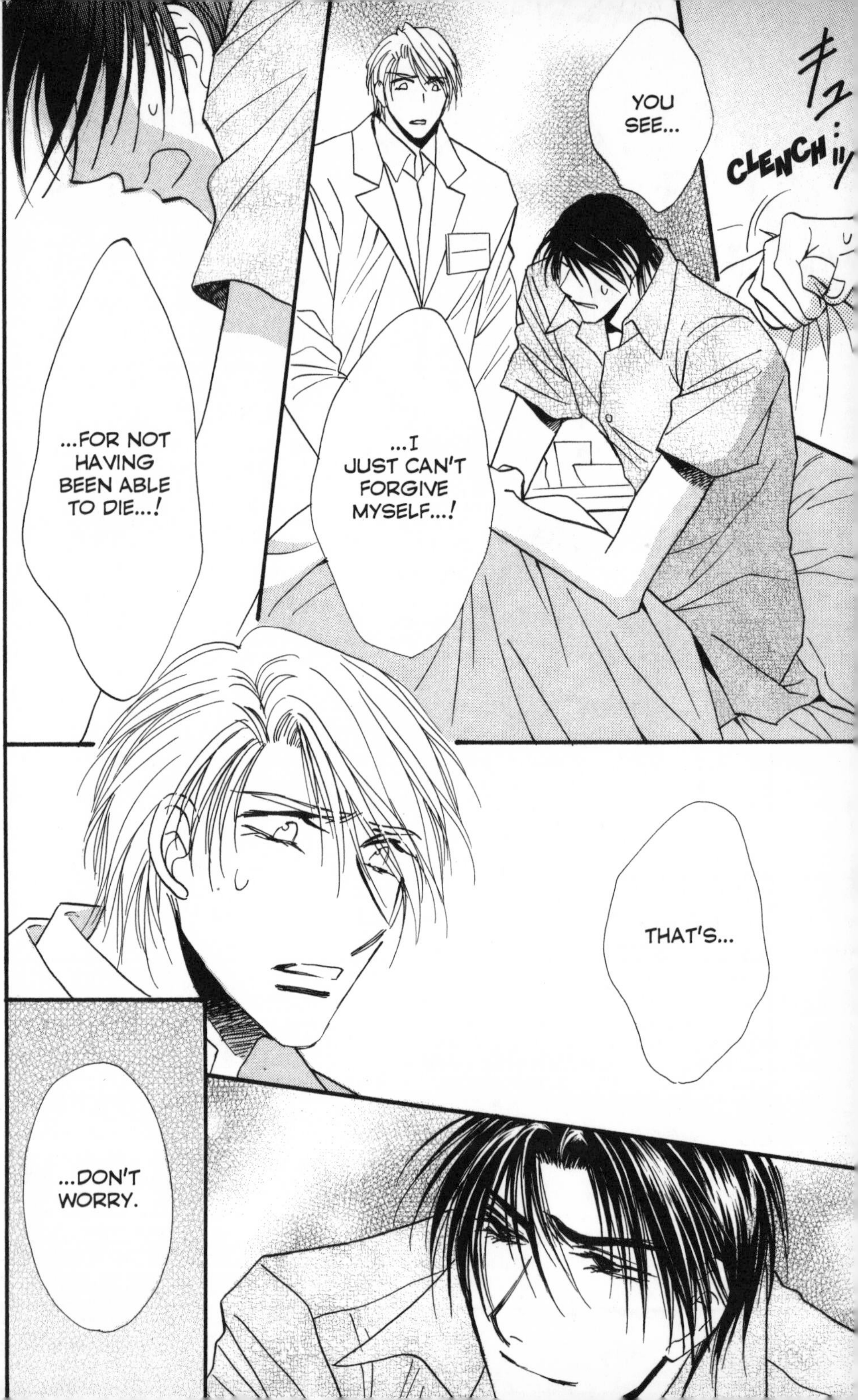
キュ
CLENCH
YOU SEE...
...I JUST CAN'T FORGIVE MYSELF...!
...FOR NOT HAVING BEEN ABLE TO DIE...!
THAT'S...
...DON'T WORRY.

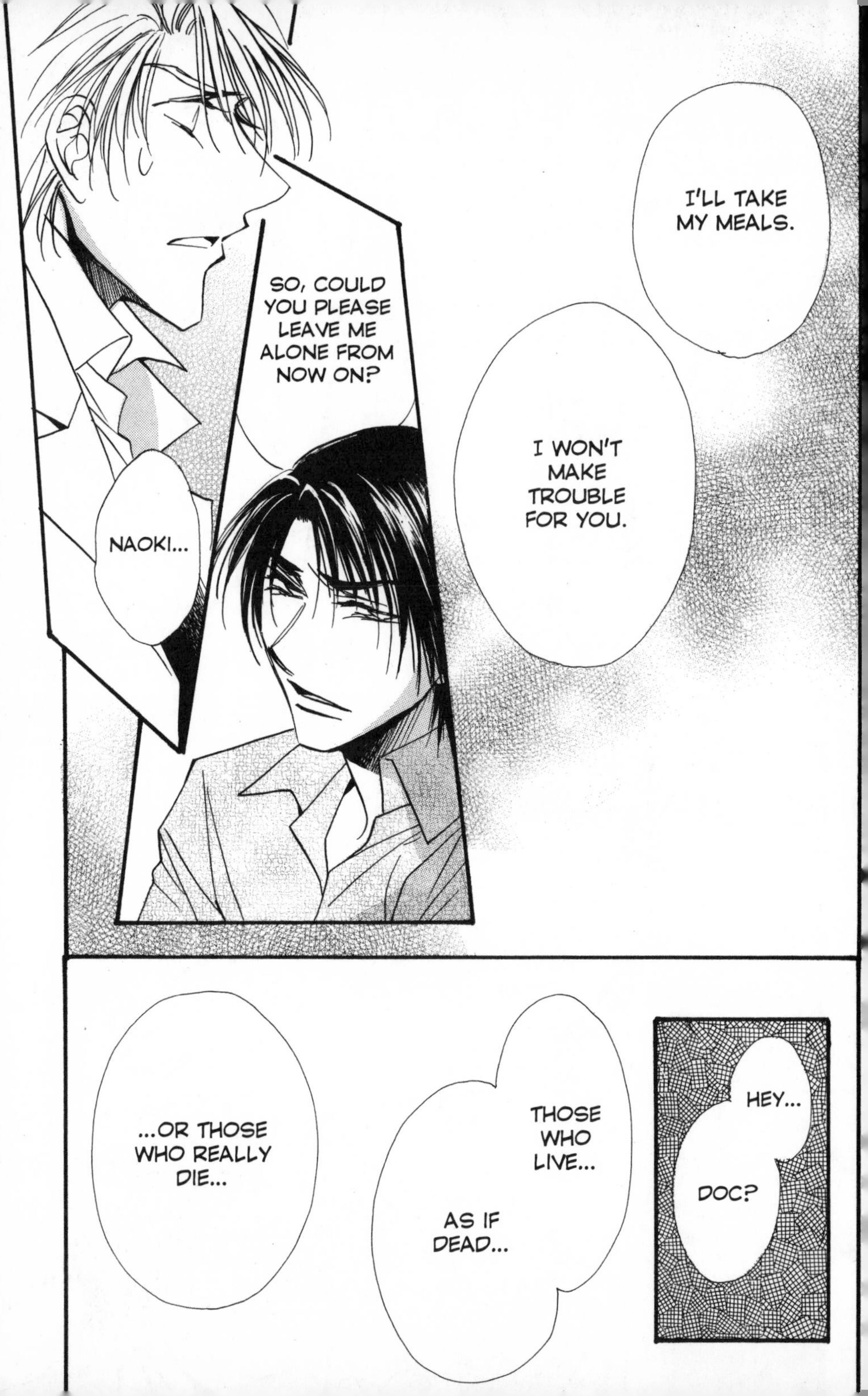
I'LL TAKE MY MEALS.
I WON'T MAKE TROUBLE FOR YOU.
SO, COULD YOU PLEASE LEAVE ME ALONE FROM NOW ON?
NAOKI...
HEY...
DOC?
THOSE WHO LIVE...
AS IF DEAD...
...OR THOSE WHO REALLY DIE...

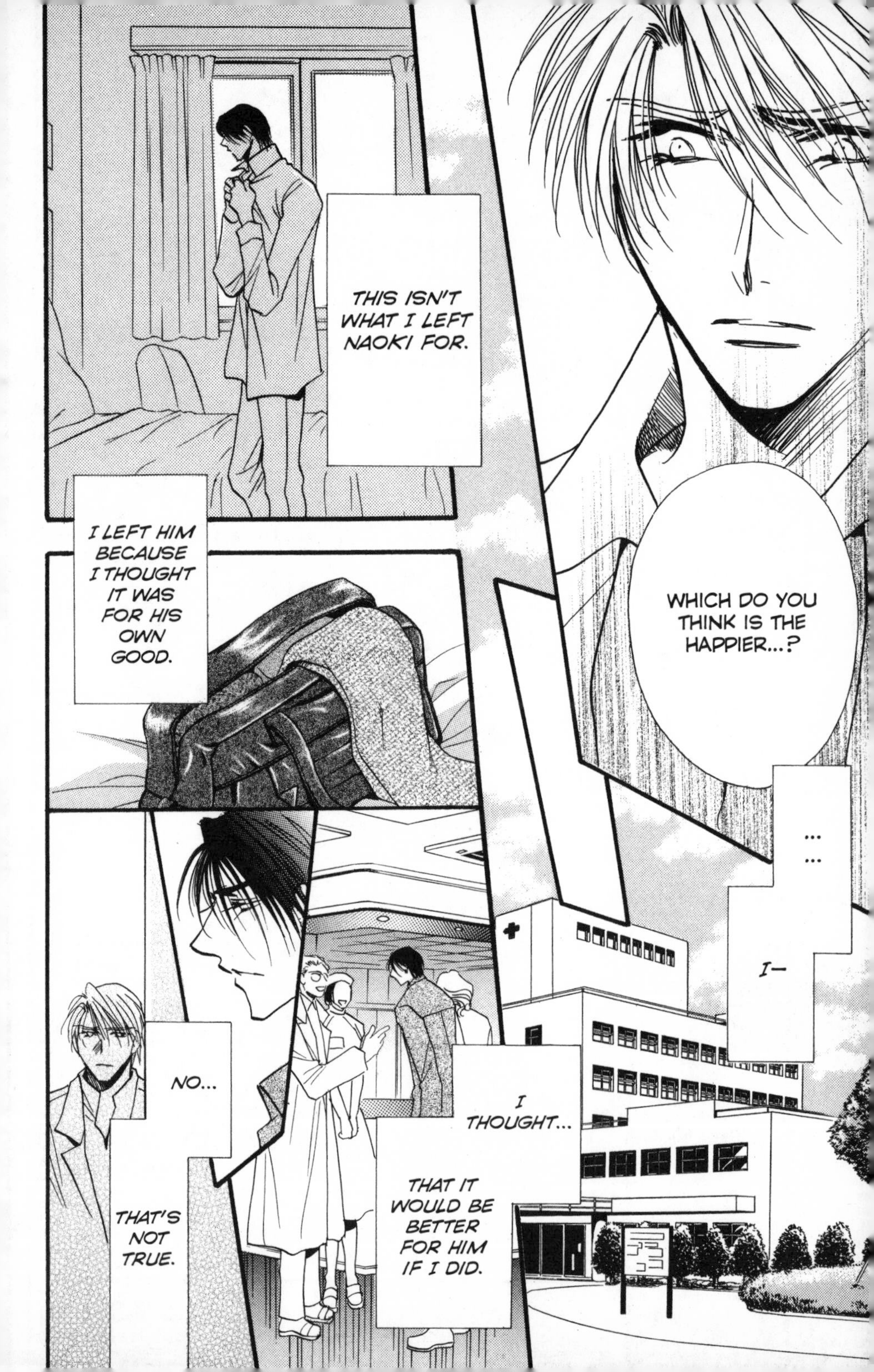
WHICH DO YOU THINK IS THE HAPPIER...?
THIS ISN'T WHAT I LEFT NAOKI FOR.
I LEFT HIM BECAUSE I THOUGHT IT WAS FOR HIS OWN GOOD.
... ...
I—
I THOUGHT...
THAT IT WOULD BE BETTER FOR HIM IF I DID.
NO...
THAT'S NOT TRUE.

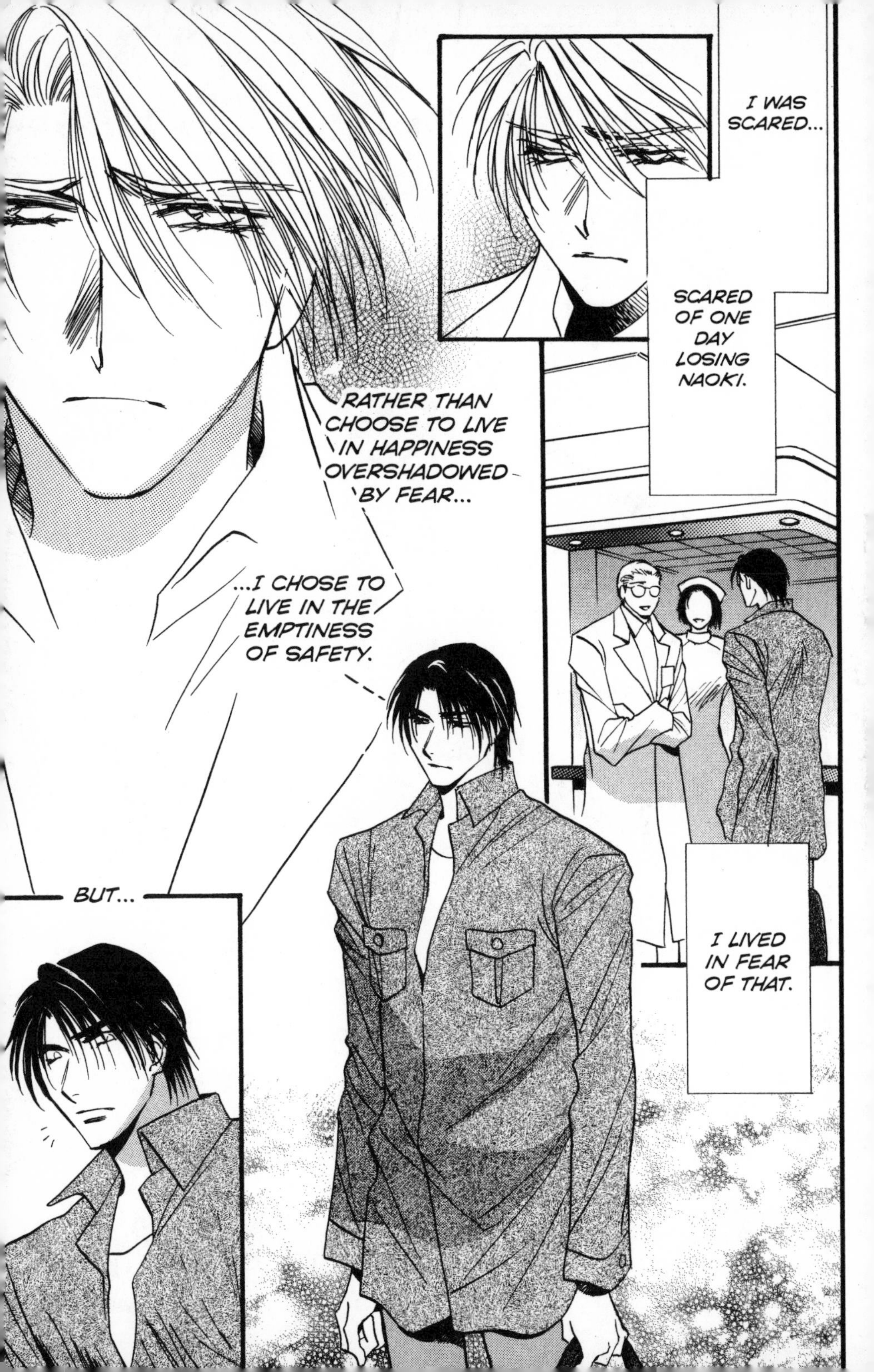
I WAS SCARED...
SCARED OF ONE DAY LOSING NAOKI.
I LIVED IN FEAR OF THAT.
RATHER THAN CHOOSE TO LIVE IN HAPPINESS OVERSHADOWED BY FEAR...
...I CHOSE TO LIVE IN THE EMPTINESS OF SAFETY.
BUT...

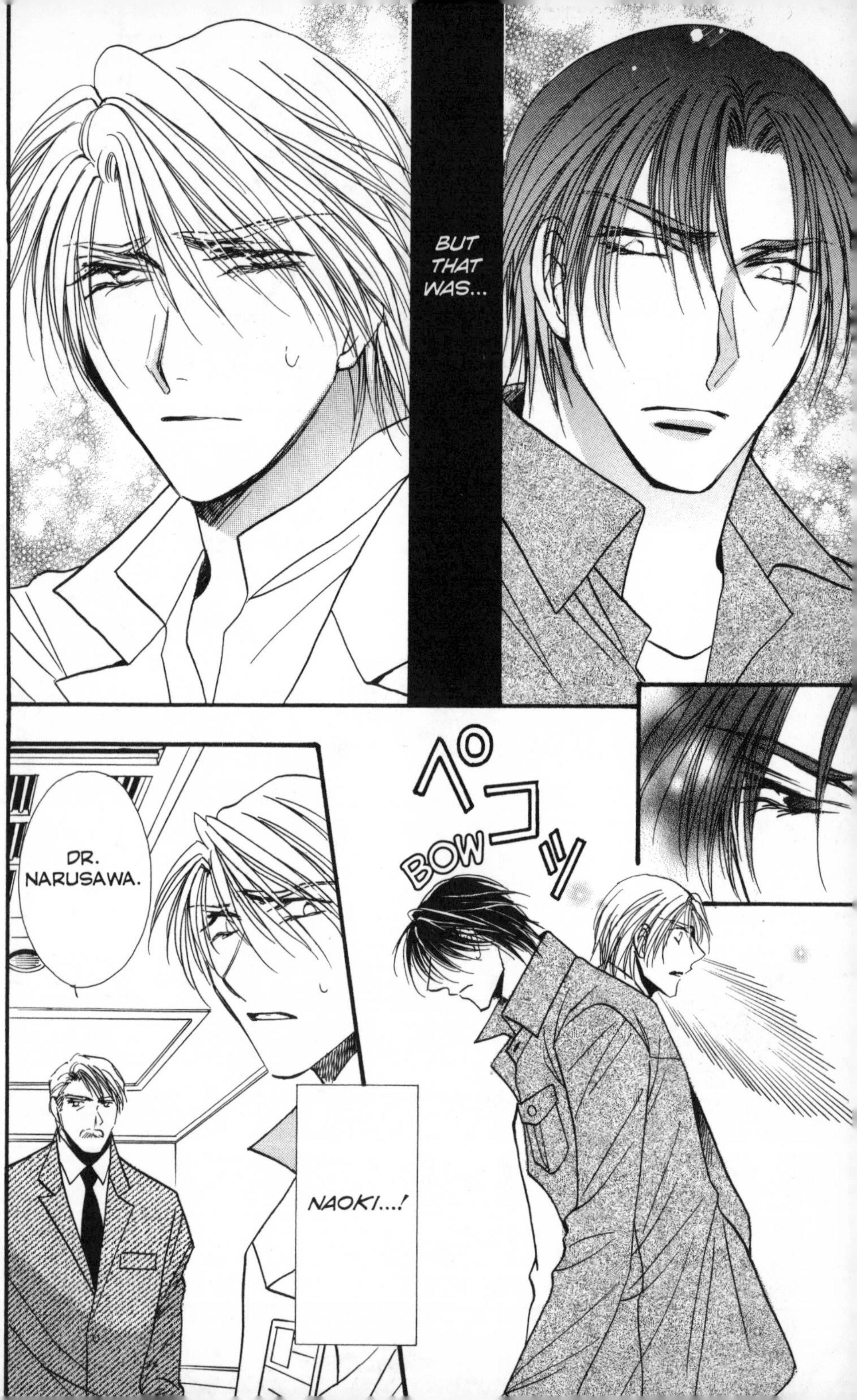
BUT THAT WAS...
ペコッ
BOW
DR. NARUSAWA.
NAOKI...!

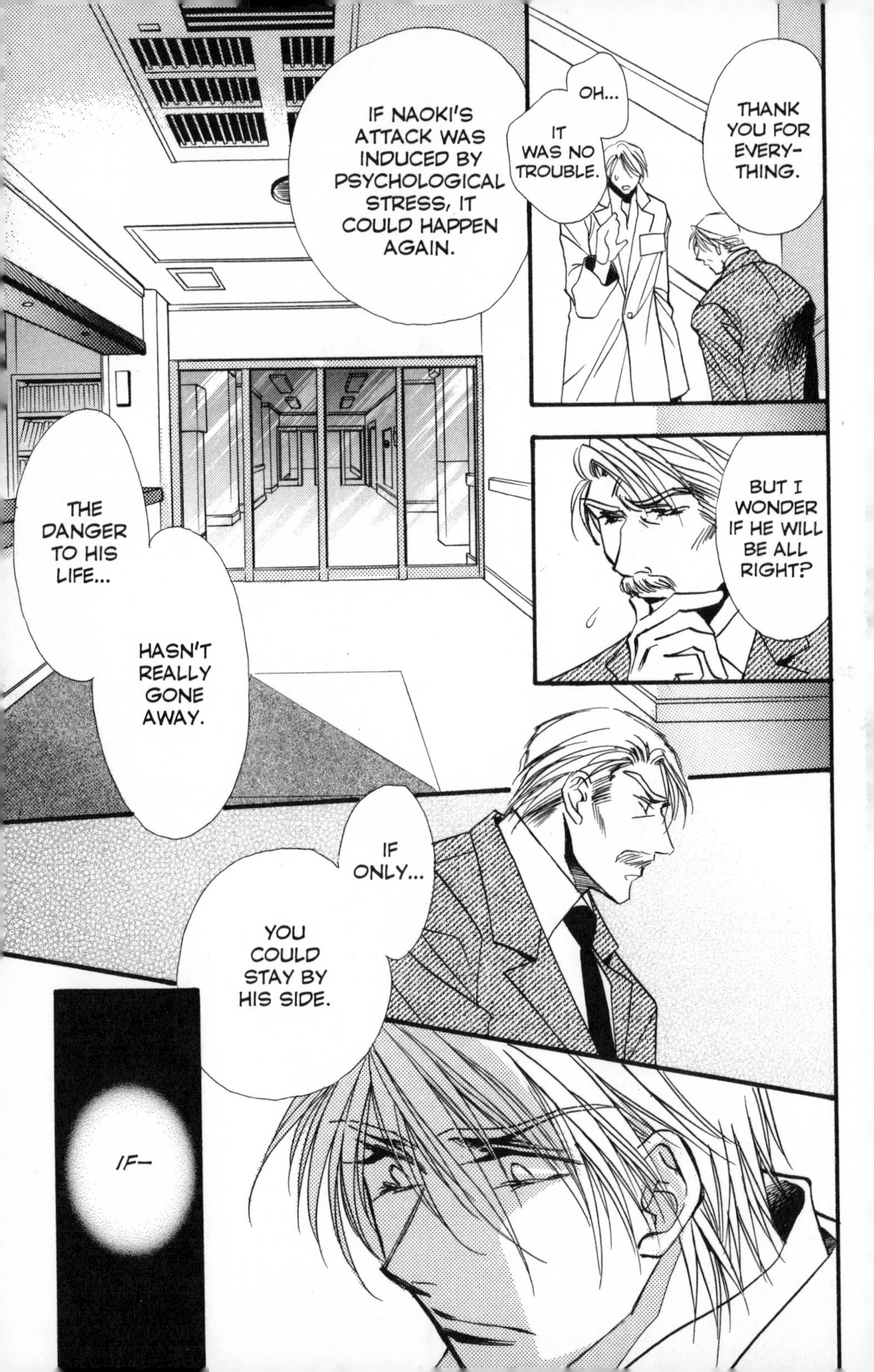
THANK YOU FOR EVERY-THING.
OH...
IT WAS NO TROUBLE.
BUT I WONDER IF HE WILL BE ALL RIGHT?
IF NAOKI'S ATTACK WAS INDUCED BY PSYCHOLOGICAL STRESS, IT COULD HAPPEN AGAIN.
THE DANGER TO HIS LIFE...
HASN'T REALLY GONE AWAY.
IF ONLY...
YOU COULD STAY BY HIS SIDE.
IF—

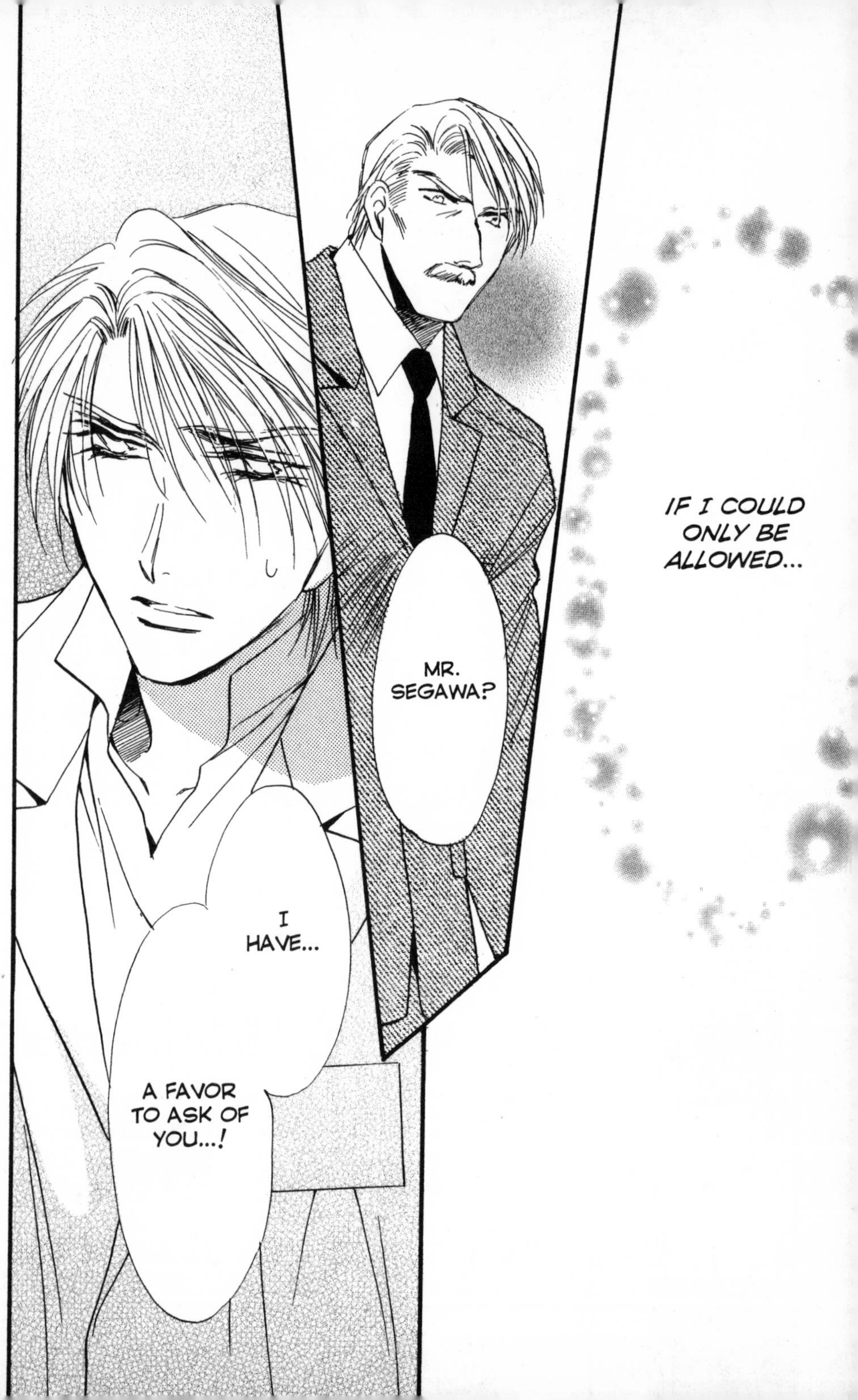
IF I COULD ONLY BE ALLOWED...
MR. SEGAWA?
I HAVE...
A FAVOR TO ASK OF YOU...!

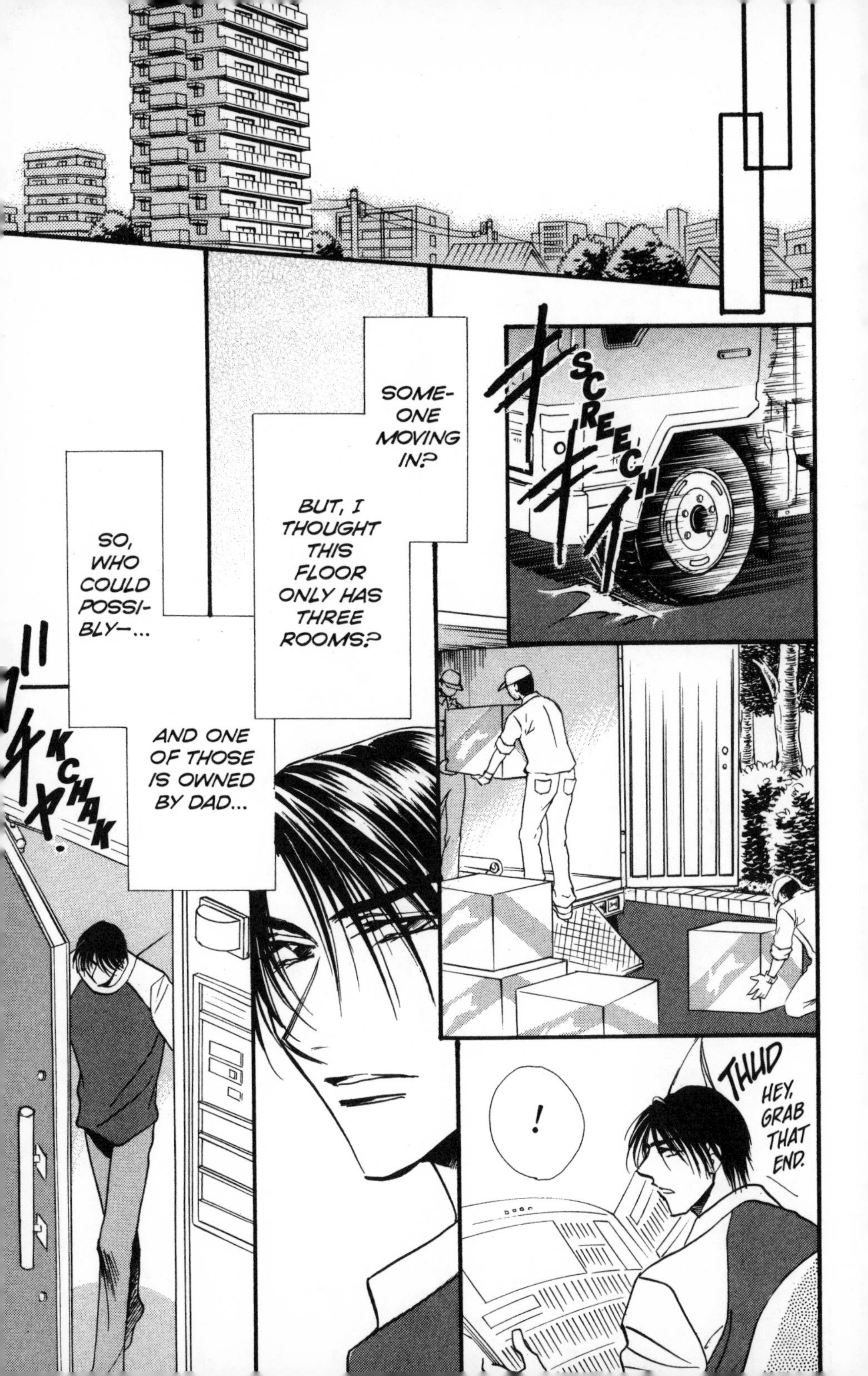
SCREECH
THUD
HEY, GRAB THAT END.
!
SOME-ONE MOVING IN?
BUT, I THOUGHT THIS FLOOR ONLY HAS THREE ROOMS?
SO, WHO COULD POSSIBLY—...
AND ONE OF THOSE IS OWNED BY DAD...
KCHAK

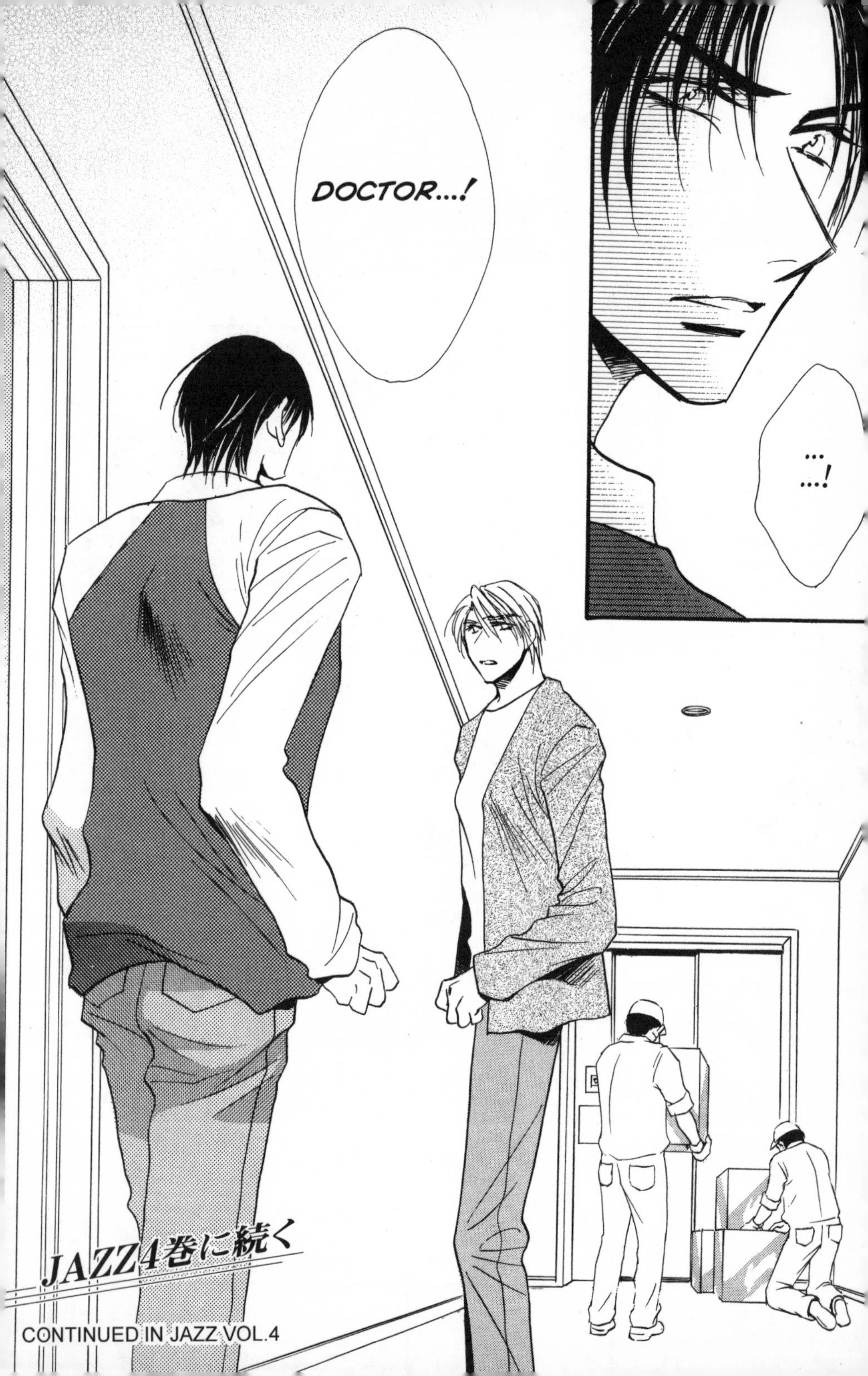
... ...!
DOCTOR...!
JAZZ4巻に続く
CONTINUED IN JAZZ VOL.4

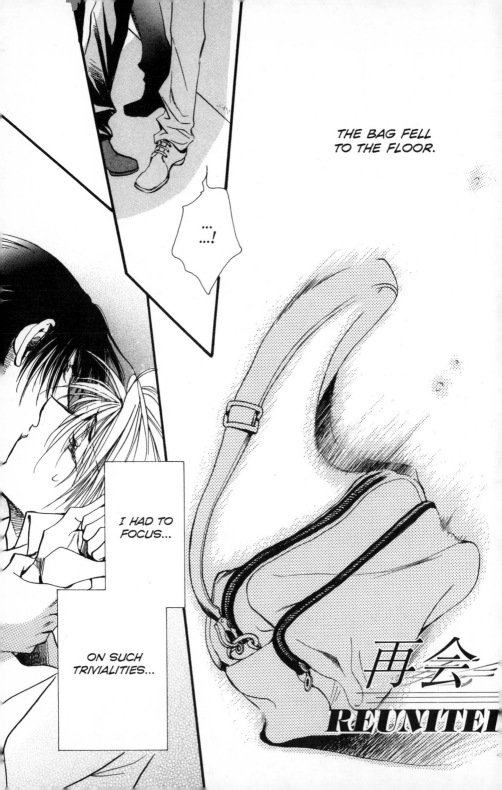

THE BAG FELL
TO THE FLOOR.

...!

I HAD TO
FOCUS...

ON SUCH
TRIVIALITIES...

再会
REUNITED

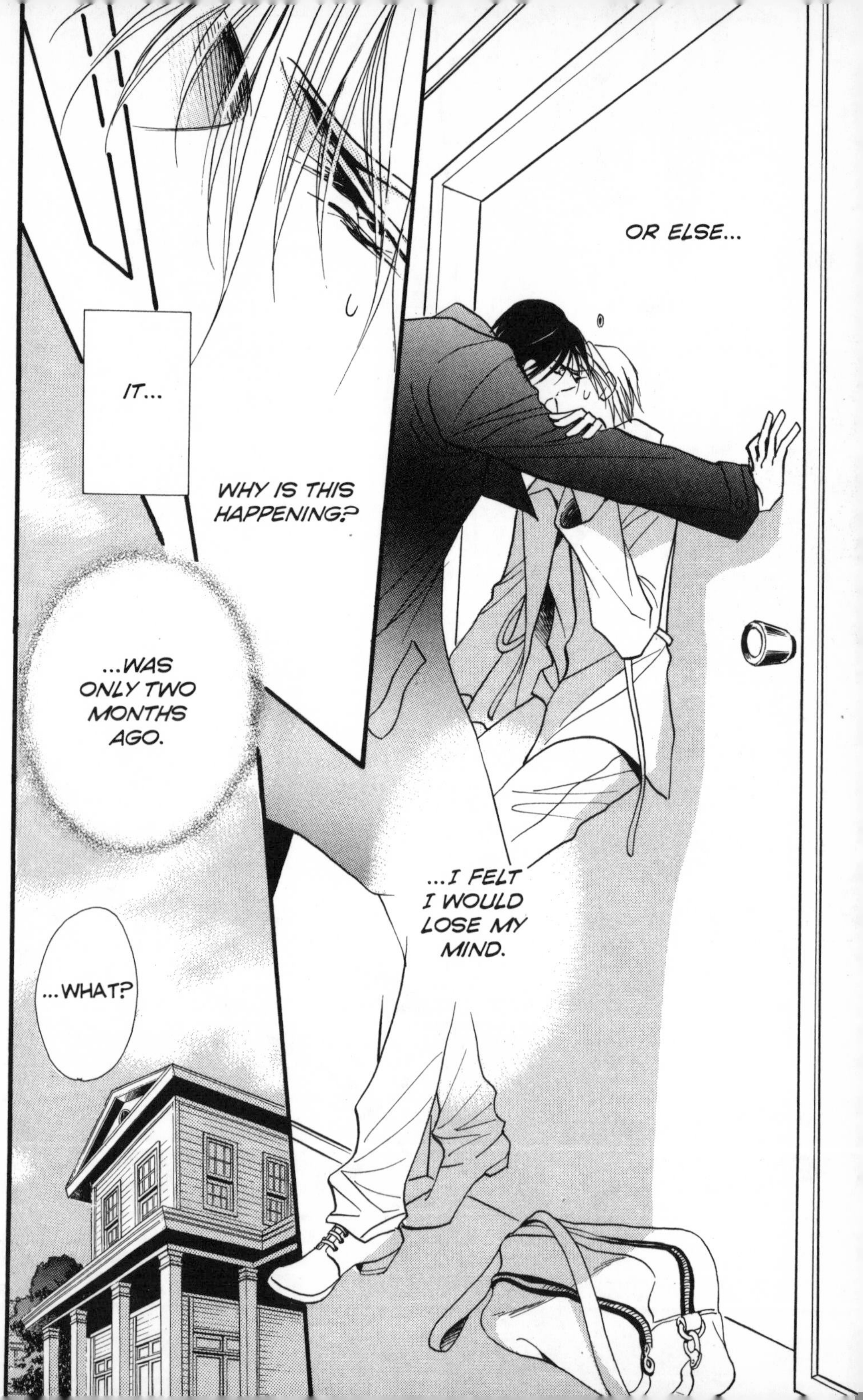
OR ELSE...
...I FELT I WOULD LOSE MY MIND.
WHY IS THIS HAPPENING?
IT...
...WAS ONLY TWO MONTHS AGO.
...WHAT?

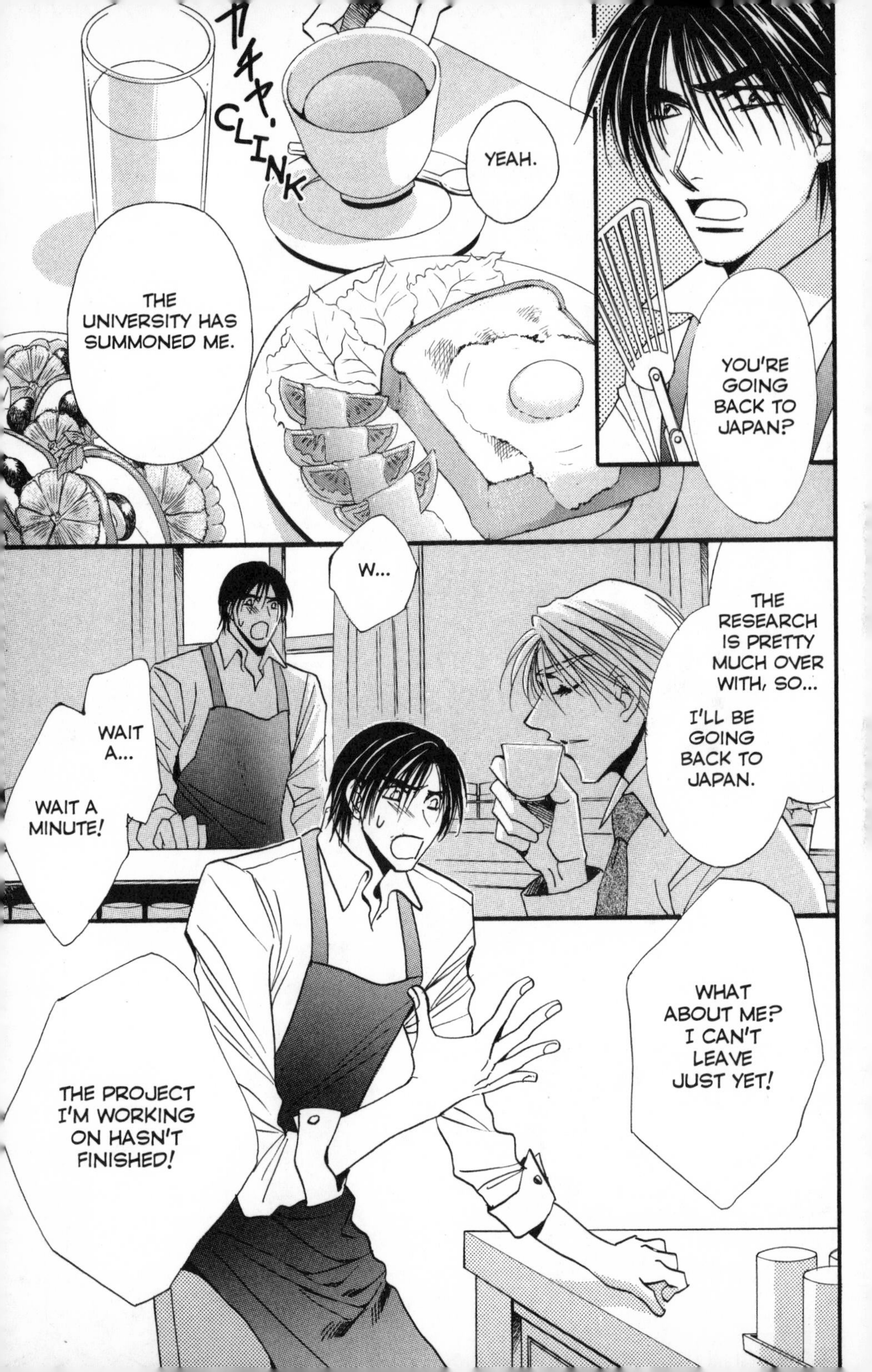
YOU'RE GOING BACK TO JAPAN?
YEAH.
カチャ CLINK
THE UNIVERSITY HAS SUMMONED ME.
THE RESEARCH IS PRETTY MUCH OVER WITH, SO...
I'LL BE GOING BACK TO JAPAN.
W...
WAIT A...
WAIT A MINUTE!
WHAT ABOUT ME? I CAN'T LEAVE JUST YET!
THE PROJECT I'M WORKING ON HASN'T FINISHED!

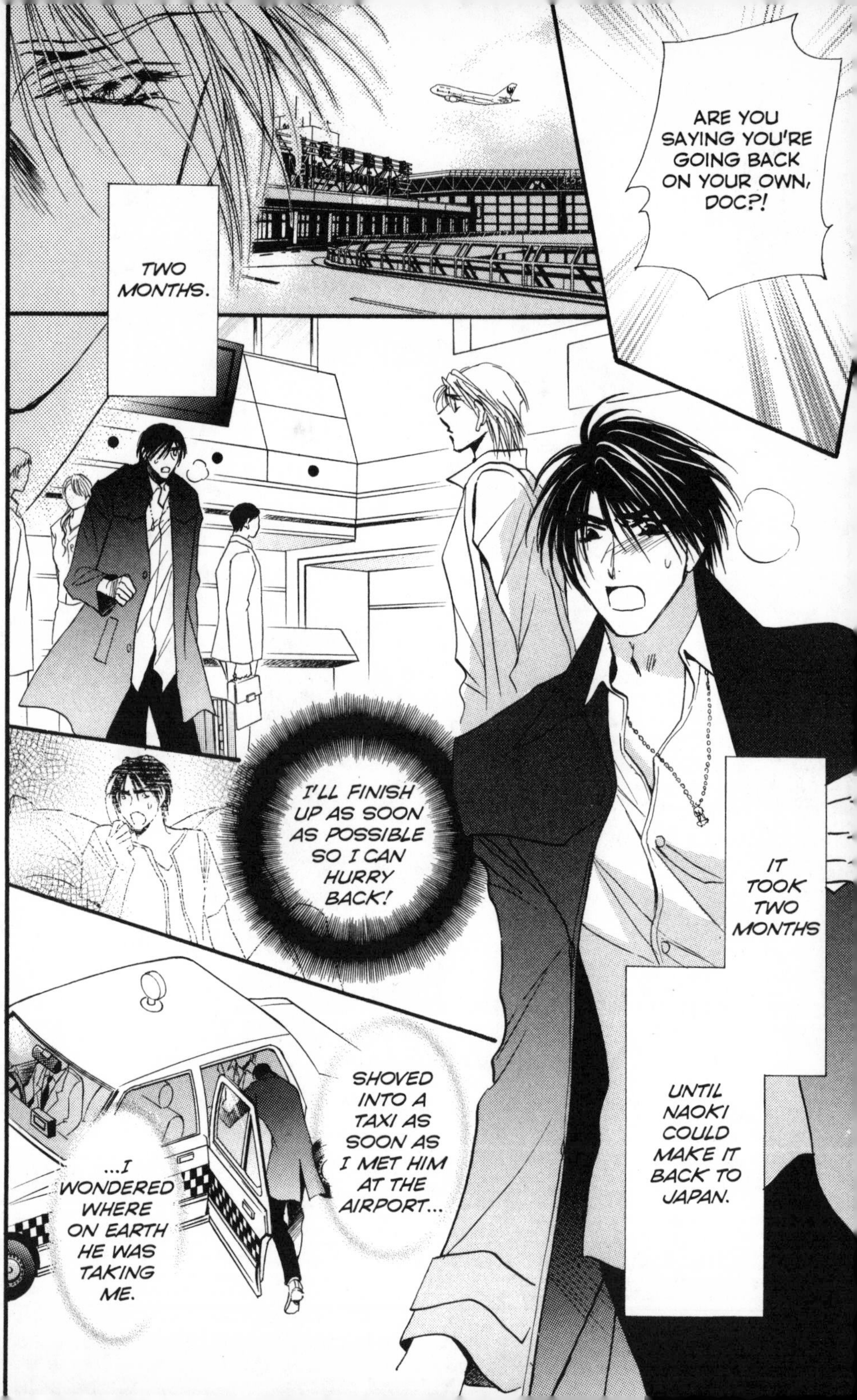
ARE YOU SAYING YOU'RE GOING BACK ON YOUR OWN, DOC?!
TWO MONTHS.
IT TOOK TWO MONTHS
UNTIL NAOKI COULD MAKE IT BACK TO JAPAN.
I'LL FINISH UP AS SOON AS POSSIBLE SO I CAN HURRY BACK!
SHOVED INTO A TAXI AS SOON AS I MET HIM AT THE AIRPORT...
...I WONDERED WHERE ON EARTH HE WAS TAKING ME.

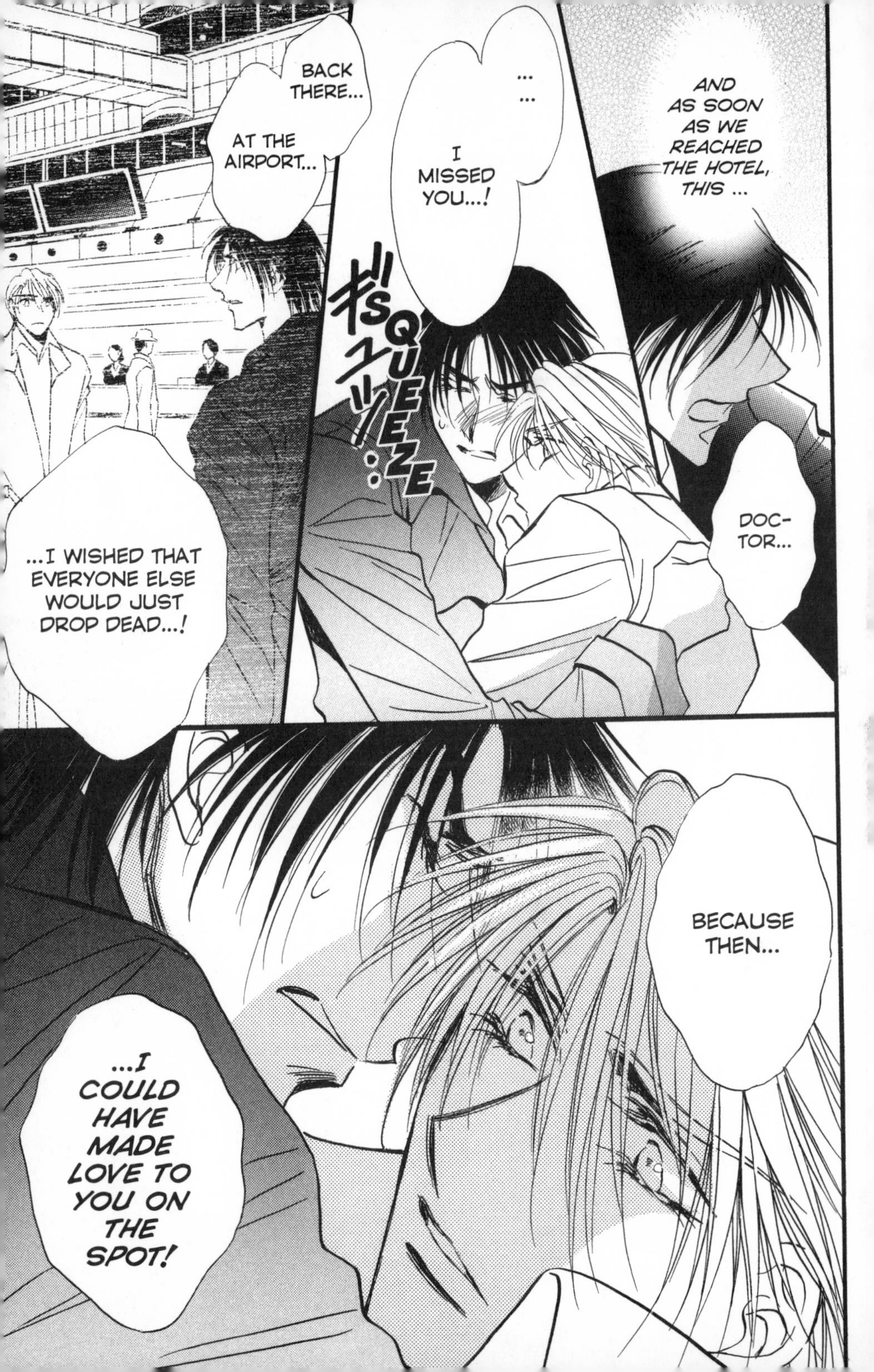
AND AS SOON AS WE REACHED THE HOTEL, THIS ...
DOCTOR...
... ...
I MISSED YOU...!
SQUEEZE
BACK THERE...
AT THE AIRPORT...
...I WISHED THAT EVERYONE ELSE WOULD JUST DROP DEAD...!
BECAUSE THEN...
...I COULD HAVE MADE LOVE TO YOU ON THE SPOT!

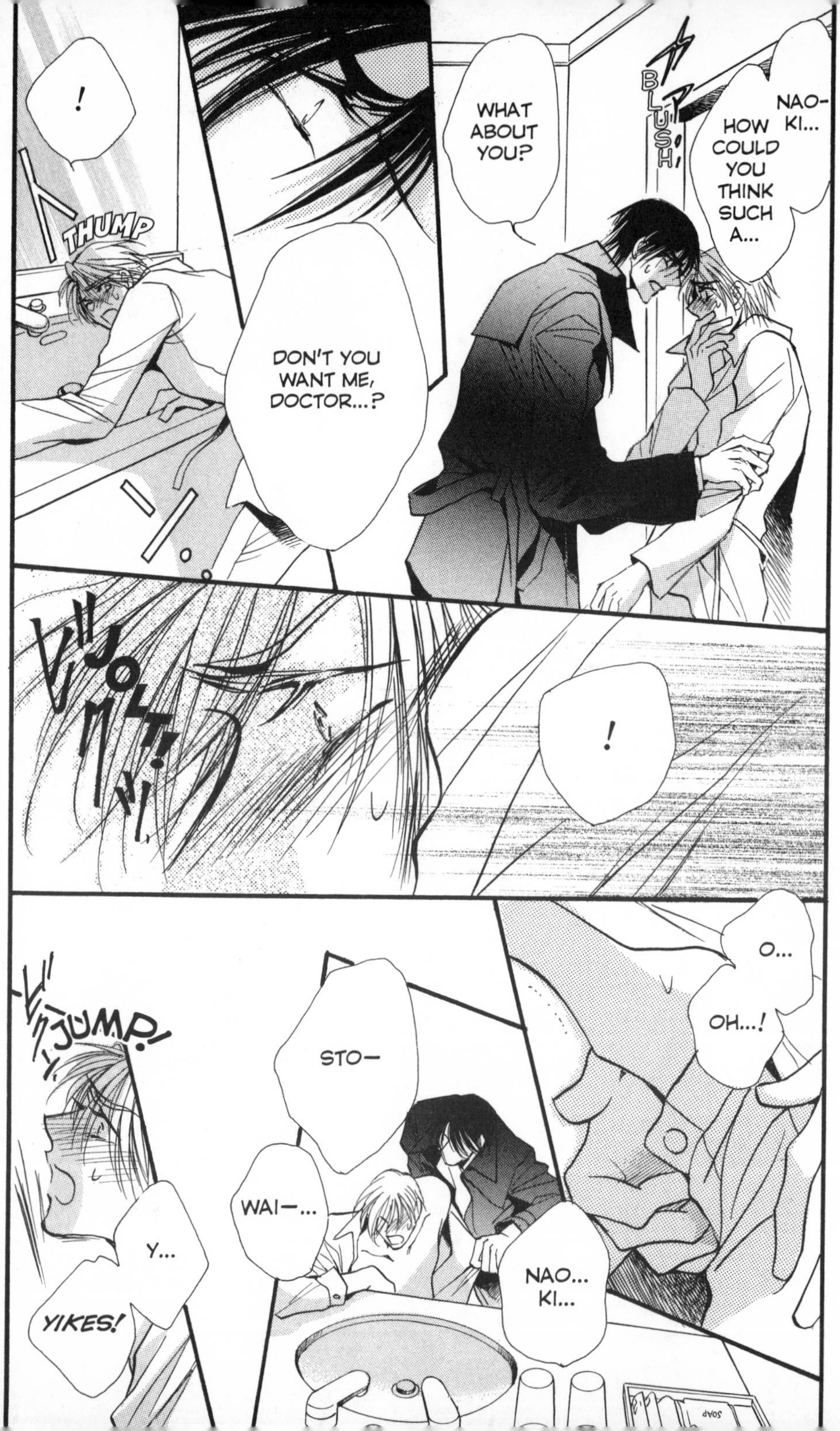
BLUSH
NAO-KI... HOW COULD YOU THINK SUCH A...
WHAT ABOUT YOU?
DON'T YOU WANT ME, DOCTOR...?
!
THUMP
!
JOLT!
O...
OH...!
STO—
WAI—...
NAO... KI...
JUMP!
Y...
YIKES!

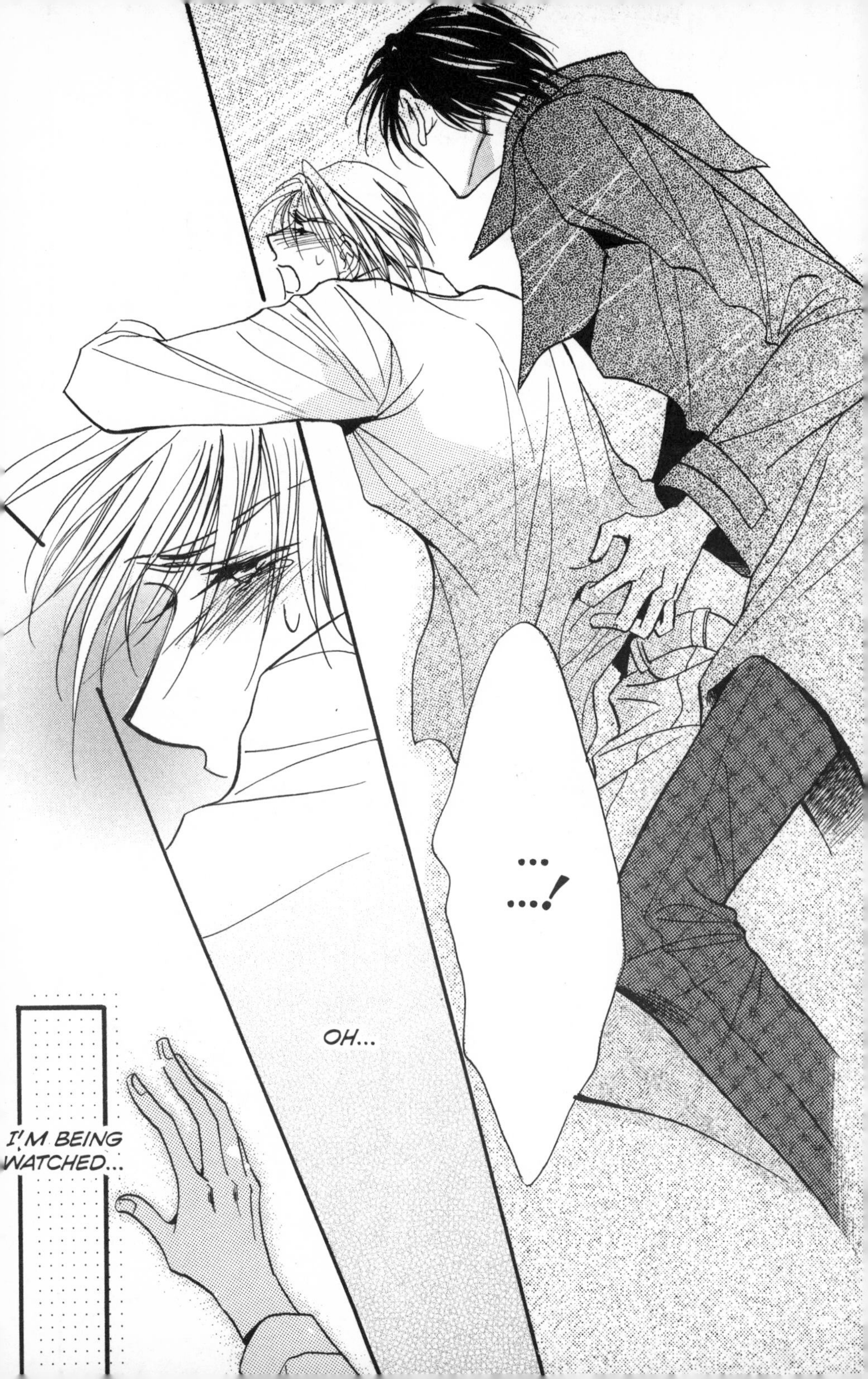
... ...!
OH...
I'M BEING WATCHED...

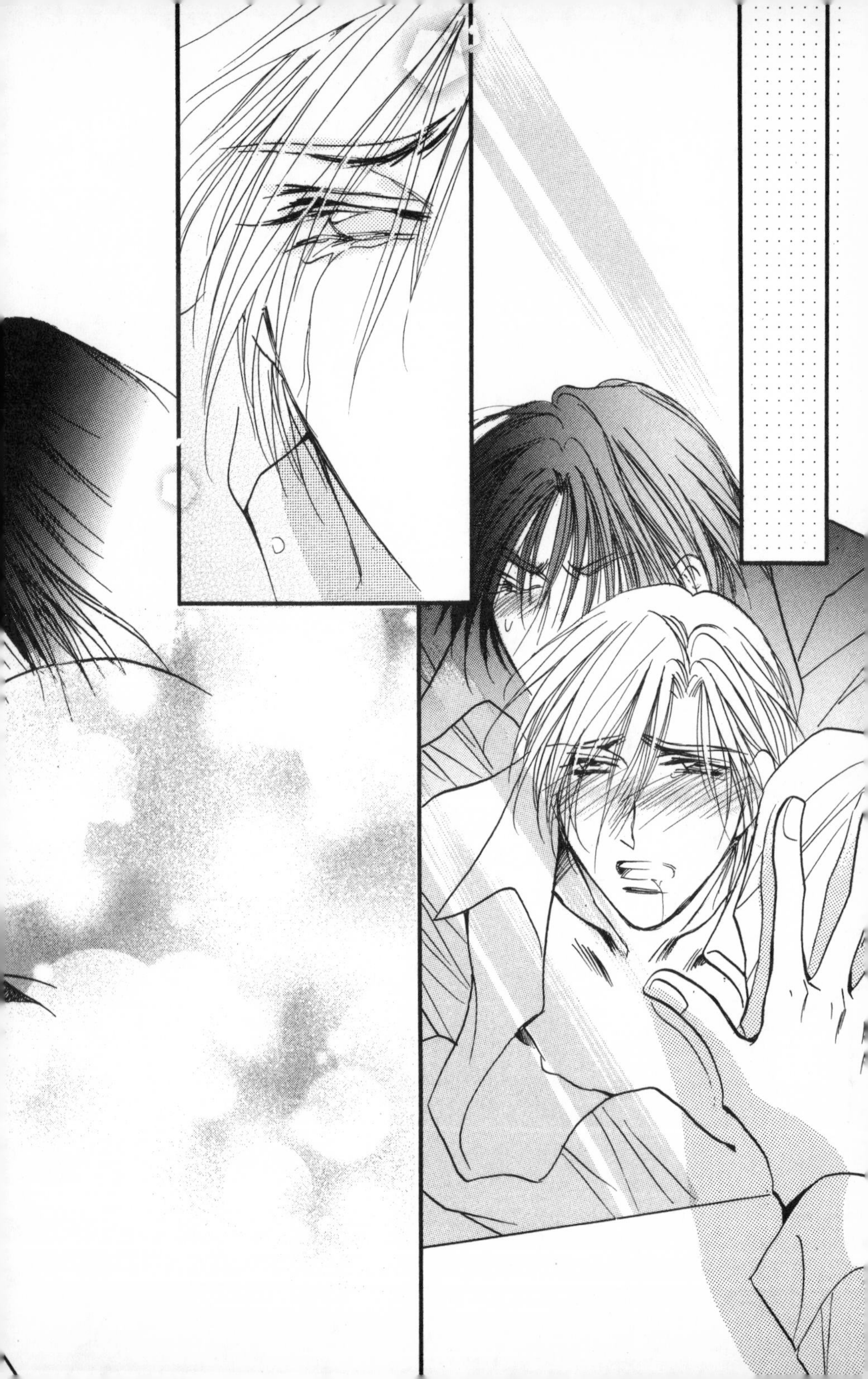

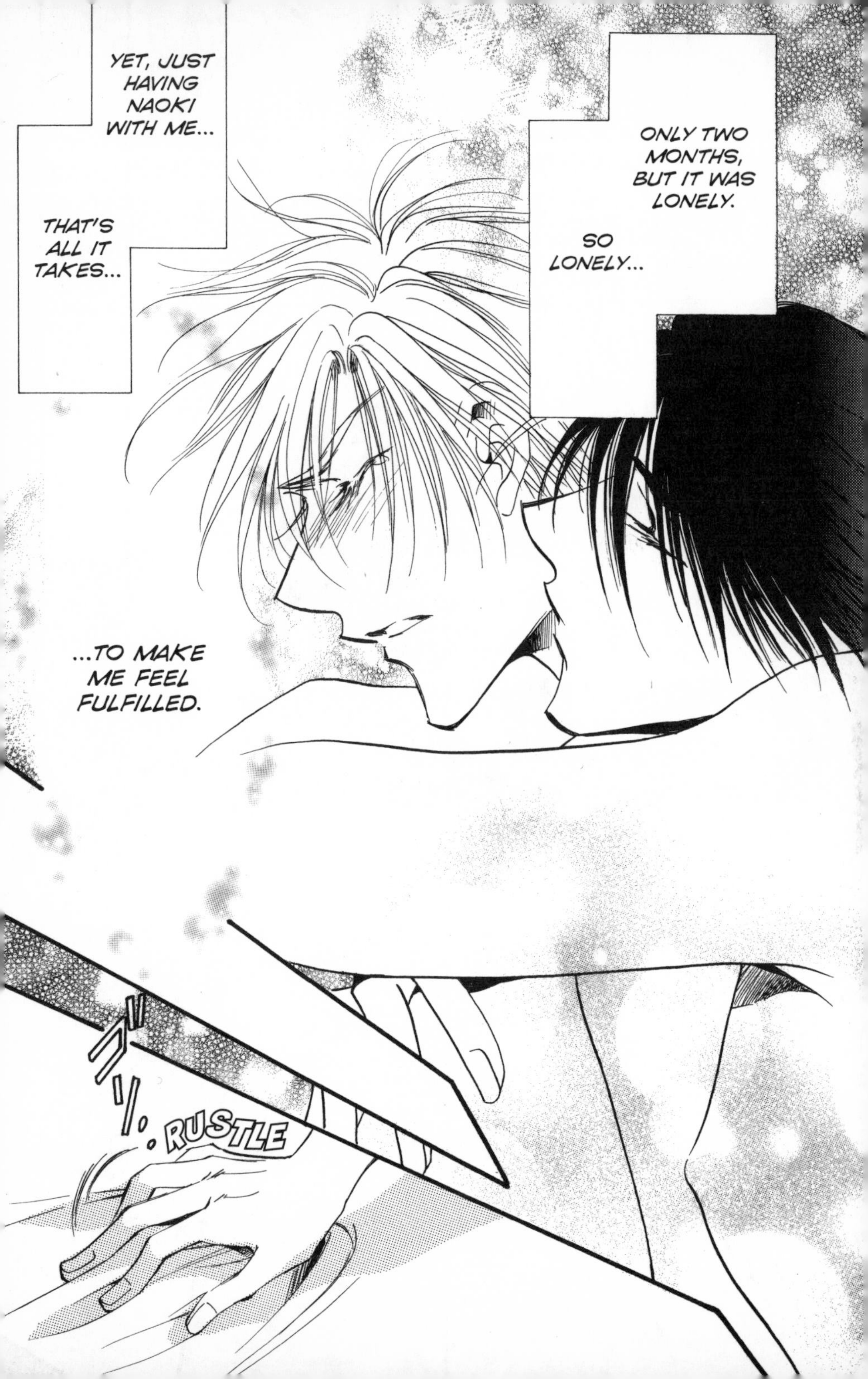
ONLY TWO MONTHS, BUT IT WAS LONELY.
SO LONELY...
YET, JUST HAVING NAOKI WITH ME...
THAT'S ALL IT TAKES...
...TO MAKE ME FEEL FULFILLED.
RUSTLE

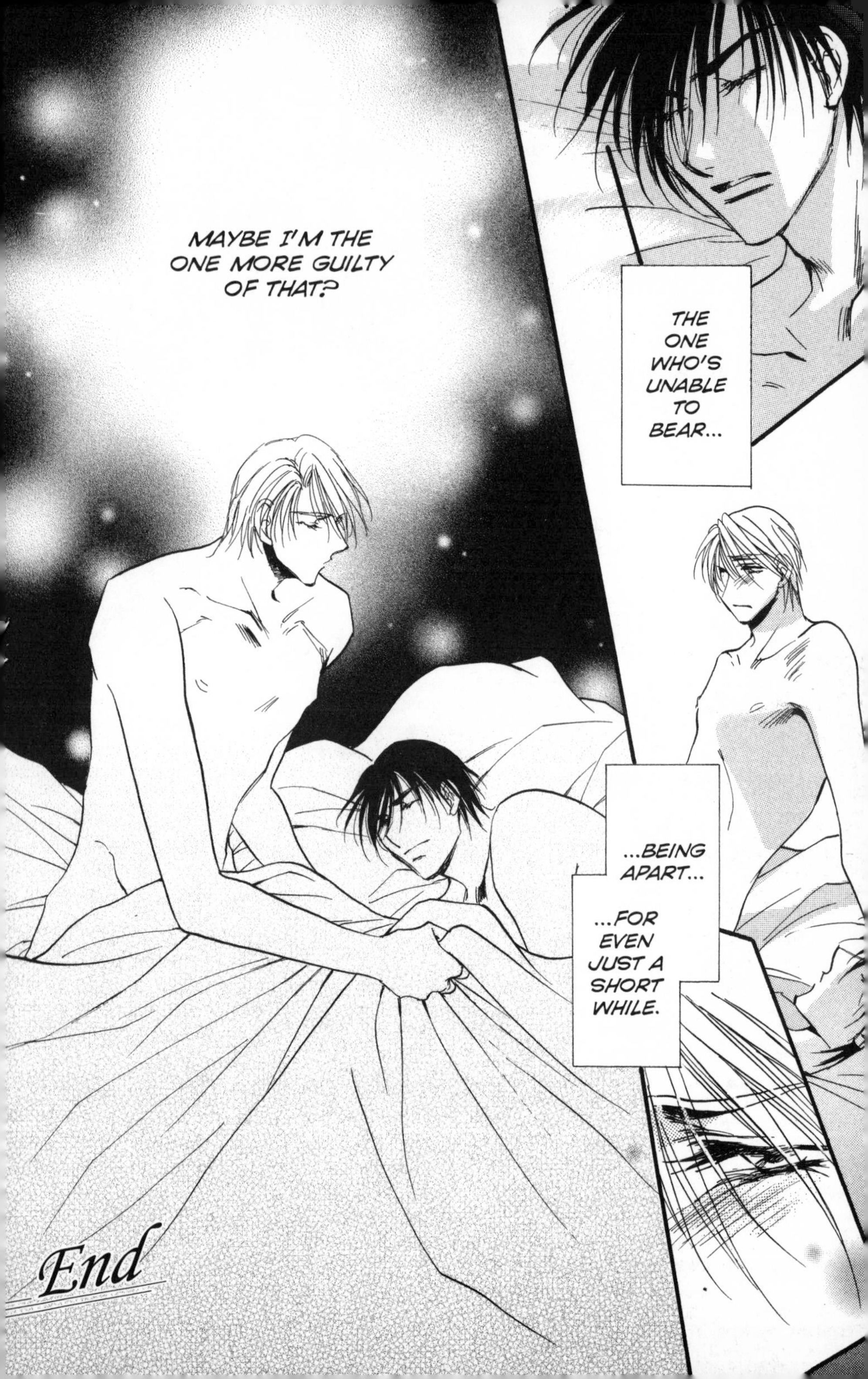
THE ONE WHO'S UNABLE TO BEAR...
...BEING APART...
...FOR EVEN JUST A SHORT WHILE.
MAYBE I'M THE ONE MORE GUILTY OF THAT?
End

CLOSE THE LAST DOOR!

YUGI YAMADA
The Yaoi Legend

Weddings, hangovers, and unexpected bedpartners!

ISBN# 1-56970-883-5 $12.95

june™

junemanga.com

Close the Last Door! - SAIGO NO DOOR WO SHIMERO! © Yugi Yamada 2001.
Originally published in Japan in 2001 by BIBLOS Co., Ltd.

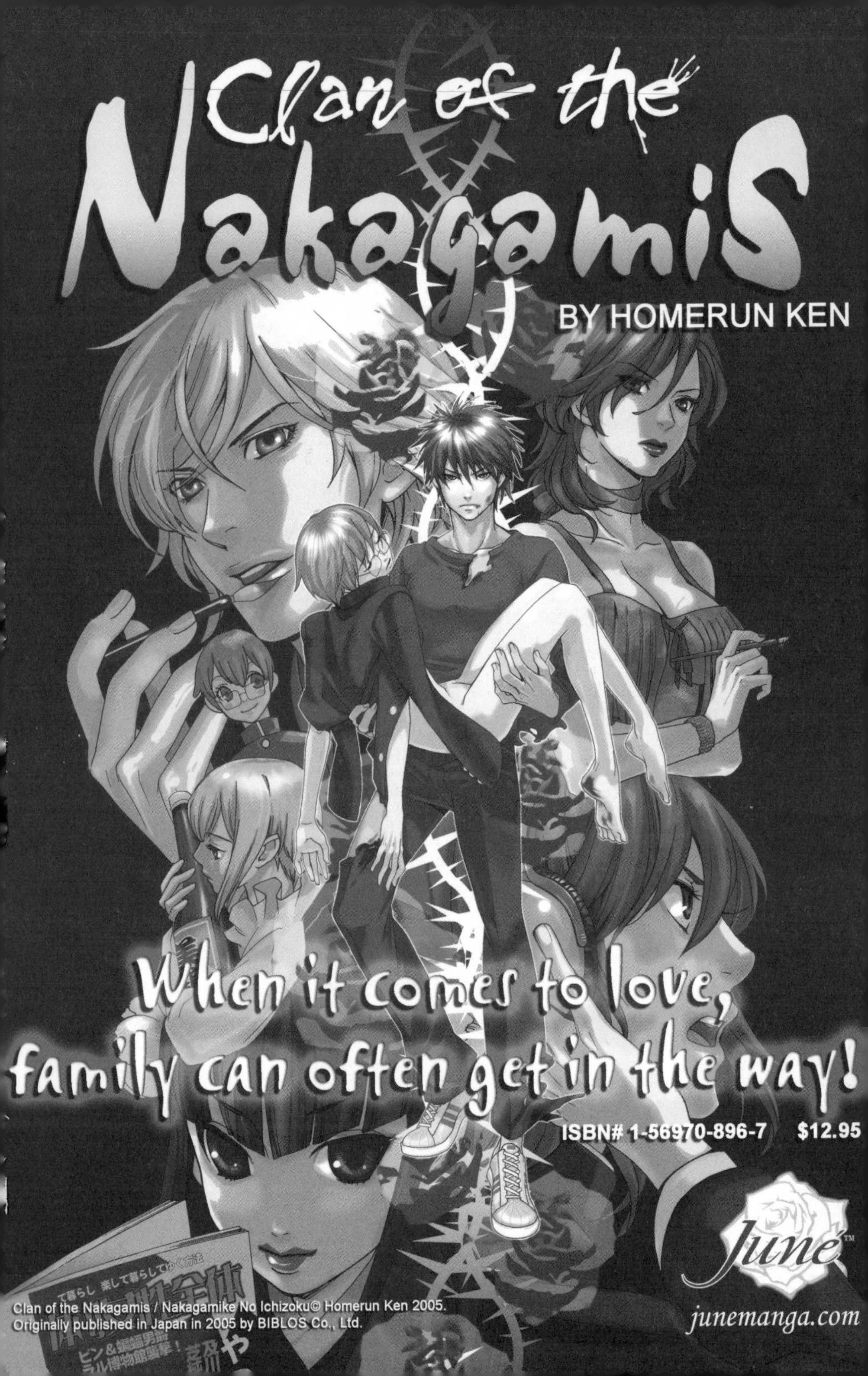
Clan of the Nakagamis
BY HOMERUN KEN
When it comes to love, family can often get in the way!
ISBN# 1-56970-896-7 $12.95
June™
junemanga.com
Clan of the Nakagamis / Nakagamike No Ichizoku© Homerun Ken 2005.
Originally published in Japan in 2005 by BIBLOS Co., Ltd.

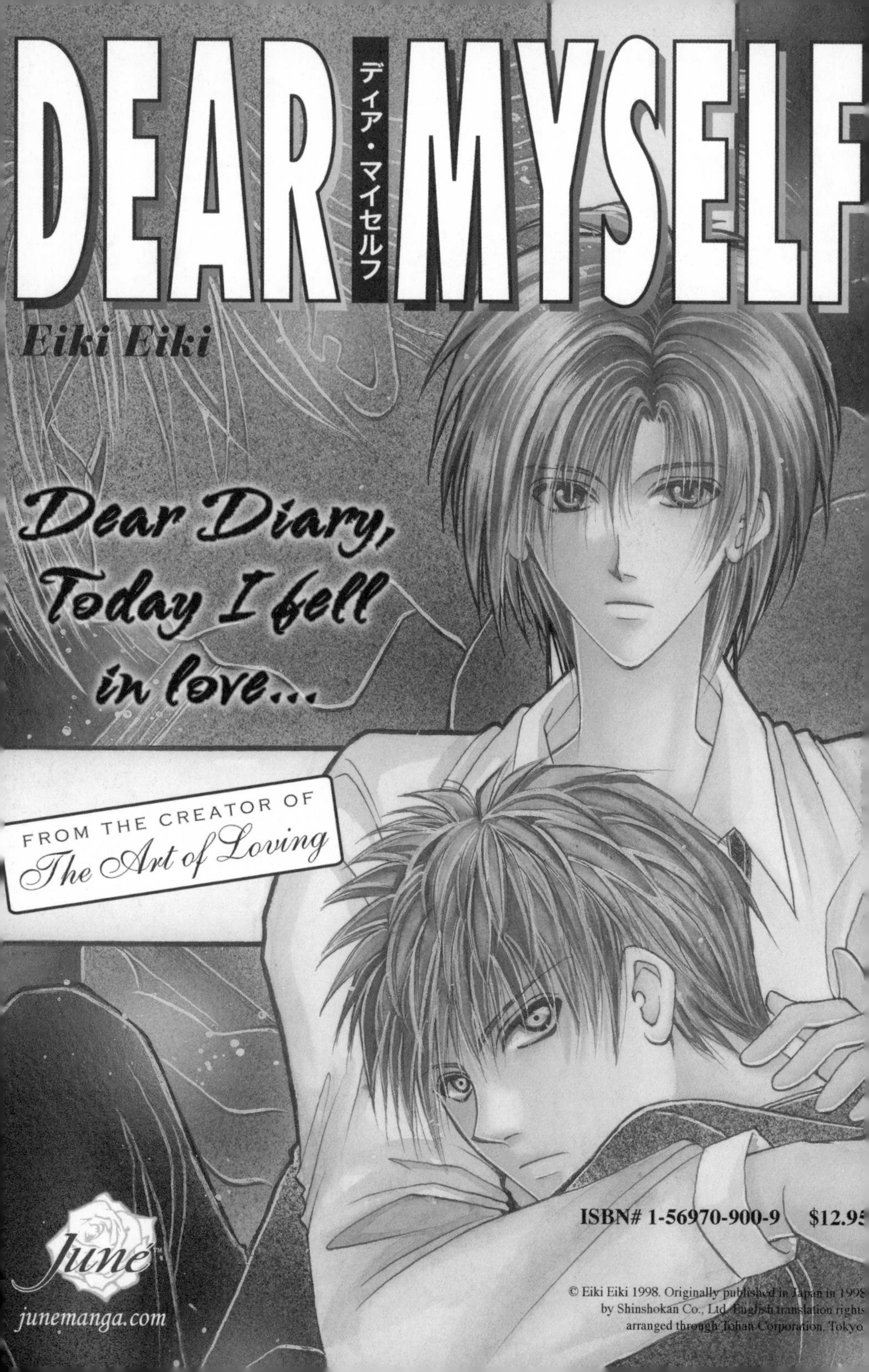
DEAR MYSELF
ディア・マイセルフ
Eiki Eiki
Dear Diary,
Today I fell
in love...
FROM THE CREATOR OF
The Art of Loving
ISBN# 1-56970-900-9 $12.95
June
junemanga.com
© Eiki Eiki 1998. Originally published in Japan in 1998
by Shinshokan Co., Ltd. English translation rights
arranged through Tohan Corporation, Tokyo

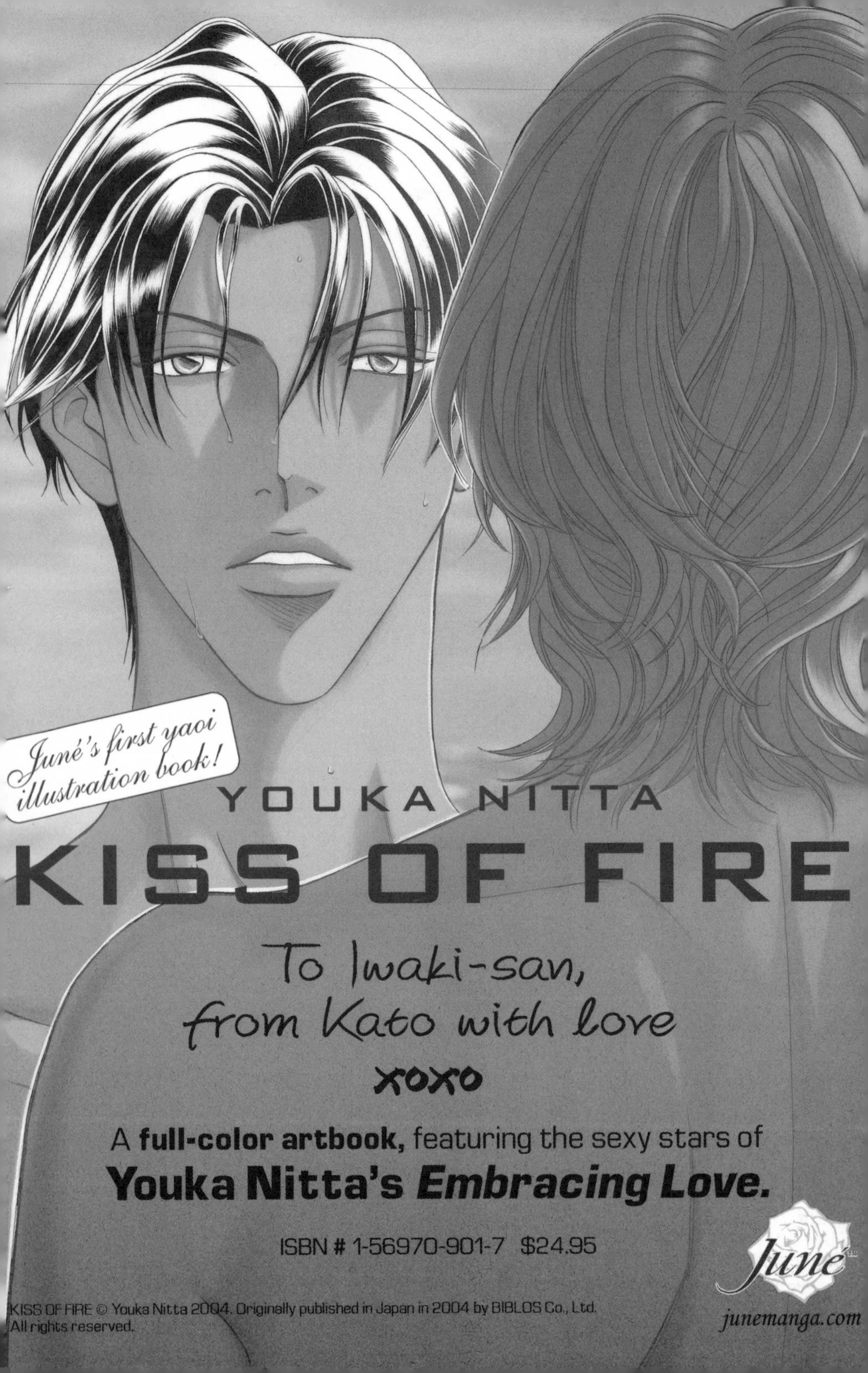
June's first yaoi illustration book!
YOUKA NITTA
KISS OF FIRE
To Iwaki-san, from Kato with love
xoxo
A full-color artbook, featuring the sexy stars of
Youka Nitta's Embracing Love.
ISBN # 1-56970-901-7 $24.95
Juné
junemanga.com
KISS OF FIRE © Youka Nitta 2004. Originally published in Japan in 2004 by BIBLOS Co., Ltd.
All rights reserved.

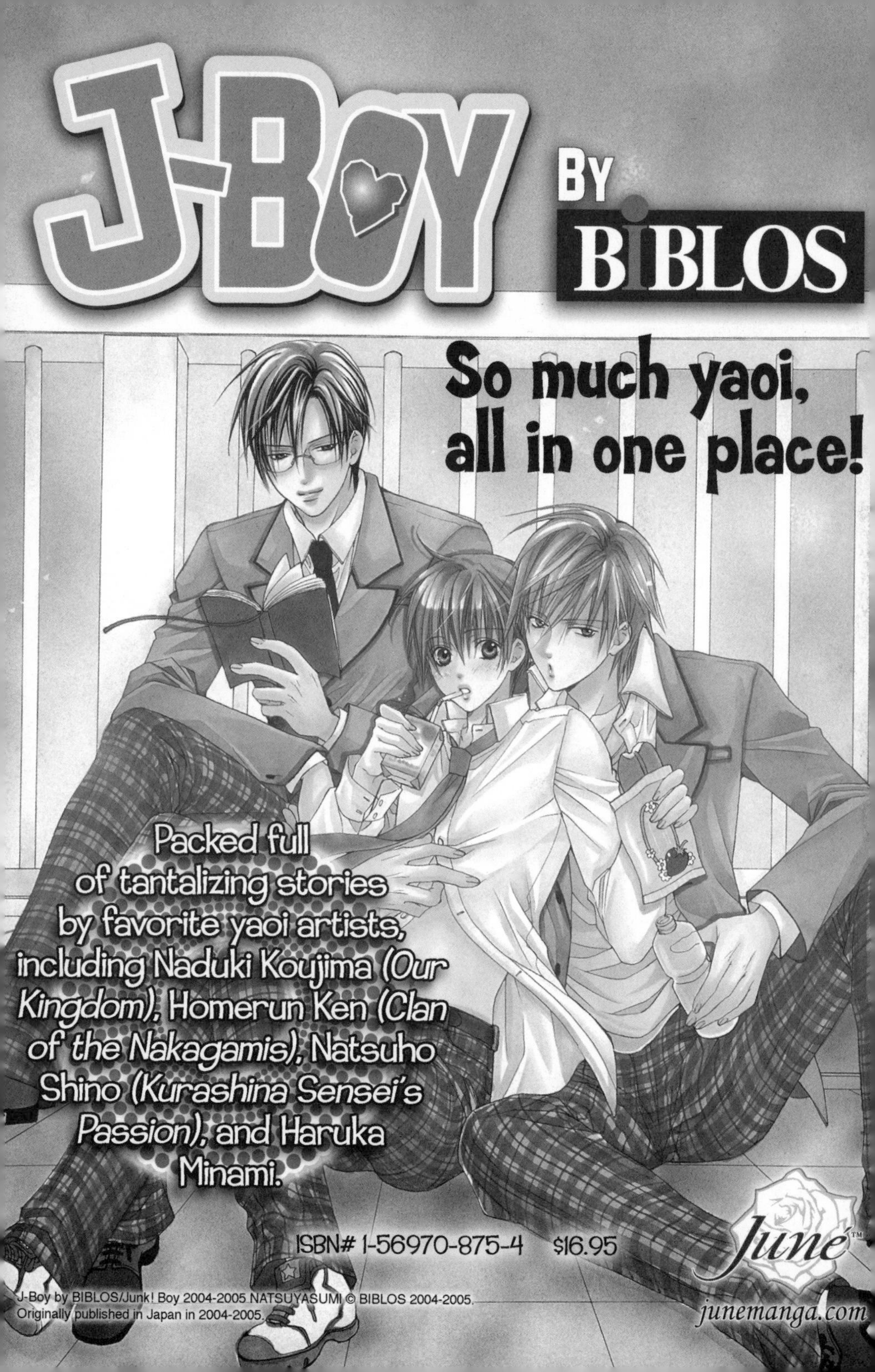
J-BOY
BY BIBLOS
So much yaoi, all in one place!
Packed full of tantalizing stories by favorite yaoi artists, including Naduki Koujima (Our Kingdom), Homerun Ken (Clan of the Nakagamis), Natsuho Shino (Kurashina Sensei's Passion), and Haruka Minami.
ISBN# 1-56970-875-4 $16.95
June™
junemanga.com
J-Boy by BIBLOS/Junk! Boy 2004-2005 NATSUYASUMI © BIBLOS 2004-2005.
Originally published in Japan in 2004-2005.

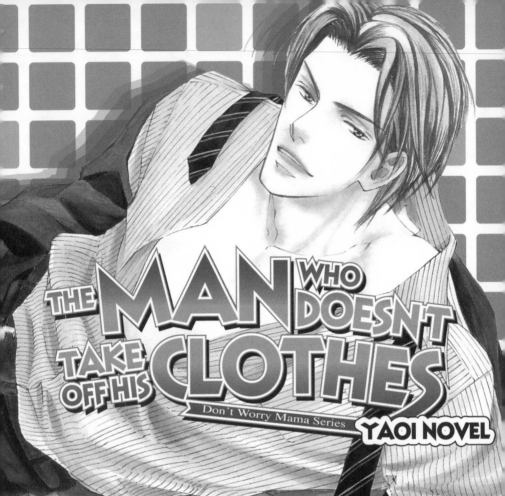

THE MAN WHO DOESN'T TAKE OFF HIS CLOTHES

Don't Worry Mama Series

YAOI NOVEL

Office politics have never been THIS stimulating...

Written by Narise Konohara *(Cold Sleep, Don't Worry Mama)*
Illustrations by Yuki Shimizu *(Love Mode)*

June™

Volume 1	ISBN# 1-56970-877-0	$8.95
Volume 2	ISBN# 1-56970-876-2	$8.95

junemanga.com

The Man Who Doesn't Take Off His Clothes- Nuganai Otoko. © Narise Konohara 2005.
Originally published in Japan in 2005 by BIBLOS Co., Ltd.

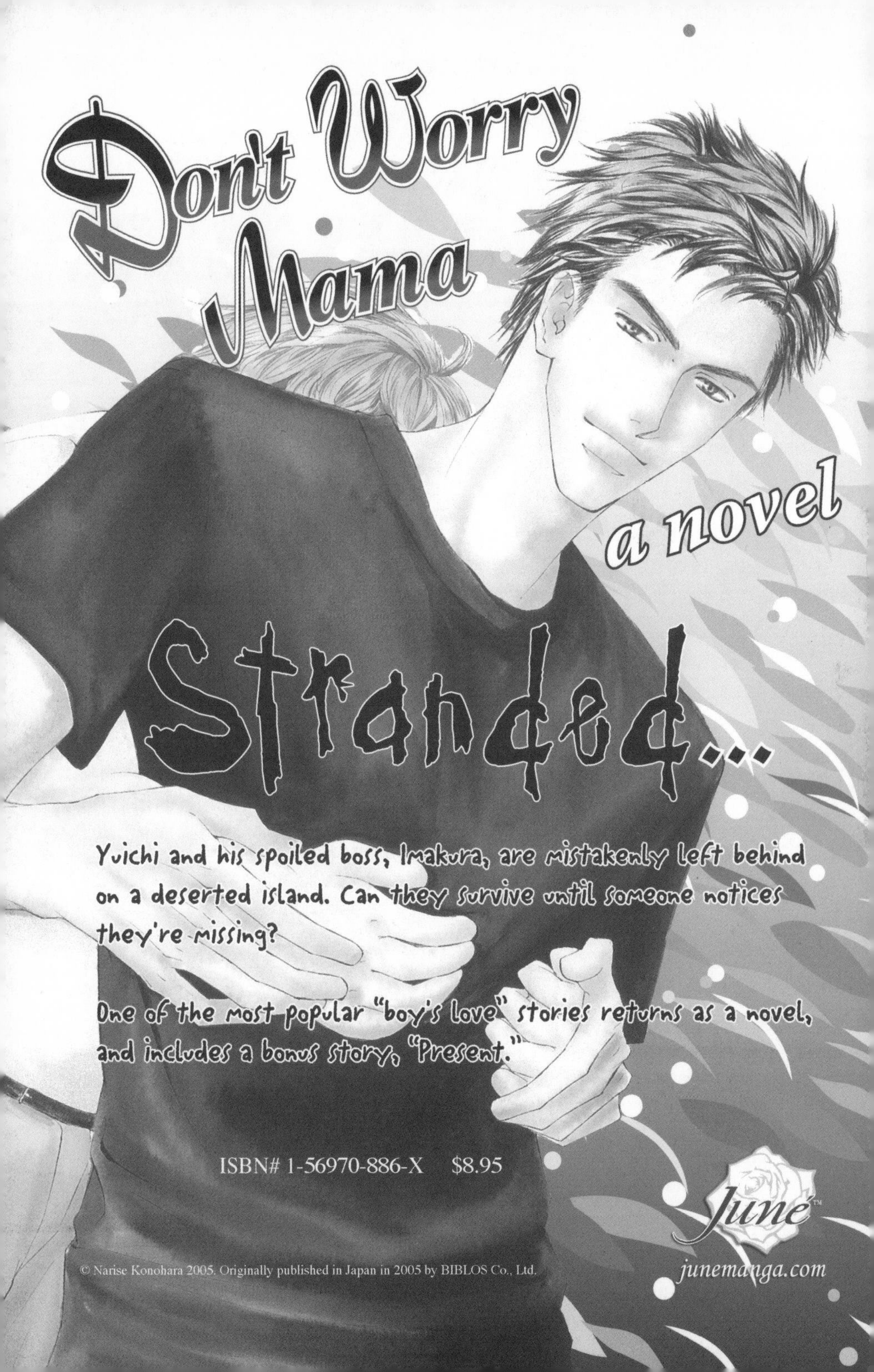
Don't Worry Mama
a novel
Stranded...
Yuichi and his spoiled boss, Imakura, are mistakenly left behind on a deserted island. Can they survive until someone notices they're missing?
One of the most popular "boy's love" stories returns as a novel, and includes a bonus story, "Present."
ISBN# 1-56970-886-X $8.95
June™
© Narise Konohara 2005. Originally published in Japan in 2005 by BIBLOS Co., Ltd.
junemanga.com

Digital Manga Inc. presents...

POP JAPAN CULTURE
Anime and Manga
THE ULTIMATE TOUR!

POP
ポップ
JAPAN
TRAVEL

For reservations or inquiries, please contact:
Pop Japan Travel: (310) 817-8010 Fax: (310) 817-8018
E-mail: travel@popjapantravel.com   Web: www.popjapantravel.com

STOP

This is the back of the book! Start from the other side.

NATIVE MANGA readers read manga from *right to left*.

1
2
1
3
2
3
5
4
4
6
5
8
7
6

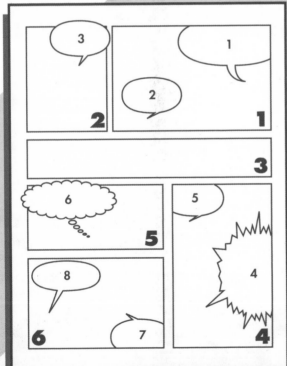

*If you run into our **Native Manga** logo on any of our books... you'll know that this manga is published in it's true original native Japanese right to left reading format, as it was intended. Turn to the other side of the book and start reading from right to left, top to bottom.*

Follow the diagram to see how its done.
Surf's Up!

NATIVE MANGA
READ RIGHT TO LEFT